To Paul
I hope you get a
kick out of some of
these inside stories
All the best!
Joe Hunter
10-11-08

TV ONE-ON-ONE

"Julius Hunter's blend of journalistic excellence and personal warmth made him both a respected and beloved figure in St. Louis. His career has been filled with highlights, and on these pages he shares some of the best. Julius is my friend—but even had I never met him, I would be among his admirers."

—Bob Costas, NBC and HBO Sports

"Most people are unaware of all the hard work that goes on behind the scenes before the news hits the air. Julius Hunter made it look so easy, even though it is not. People not only watched Julius, they trusted him."

—Richard A. Gephardt, Former House Majority Leader

"Julius Hunter has been a trusted mentor to me since I entered the TV news business almost 35 years ago. I call him a 'professor of journalism.' You'll find in this book that he is not only a witty and talented writer—he's a fantastic storyteller. This book will be great entertainment for one and all, and the perfect primer for aspiring broadcast journalists."

—Robin Smith, Anchor/Reporter, KMOV-TV, St. Louis

"Julius Hunter . . . He dresses nice for a large man."

—Cedric the Entertainer

"Julius Hunter has educated those around him with a deep knowledge of news and its impact on society. And I can't think of another newscaster of his caliber who has done prime-time news in his undershorts.

"A long time ago, when the medium was in its infancy, Julius Hunter gave me my first TV interview—which may or may not have been a good idea. Julius was also the first in 1981 to correctly report my newborn son was named Sam.

"As a much-loved news reporter, anchor, and an old friend, Julius Hunter brought wit, wisdom, and first-rate reporting into the homes of St. Louisans for more than three decades. He continues to share his experiences and unique perspective with us in this volume highlighting some of his best interviews."

—Christopher "Kit" Bond, United States Senator

"I was proud to hire Julius in 1974 to give him a key role on the dynamic, world-renowned TV news team that spear-headed a journalistic revolution with Electronic News Gathering that is still being copied."

—Tom Battista, Former VP/GM, KMOX-TV

"Over the years many people have asked me how and why I became a TV broadcaster. When I turned on the television I saw people like Julius Hunter on local television in St. Louis, and the late CBS network correspondent Ed Bradley covering the war in Vietnam, and later the White House. Seeing Hunter and Bradley made becoming a television newscaster seem like a more attainable goal than directing movies because they had already blazed a trail for me."

—Art Holliday, Anchor/Reporter, KSDK-TV

"Julius Hunter is a consummate pro."

—Walter Cronkite, Broadcast news icon

"Ever wonder how journalists pull out the juiciest information from sometimes reluctant newsmakers? Well, get ready to learn a lot, and laugh a lot, as my friend, Julius, clues you in on some of the tricks of the trade used by a master of the trade."

—Anne State, Anchor/Reporter, CBS2 Chicago

"I learned more about journalism in my first two years of working alongside Julius Hunter than I did in four years of college. He's blessed with the two essential elements of a great interviewer: an agile mind and an insatiable curiosity. Combine that with his affable demeanor and you'll see how he gets even the toughest interview to open up and address subjects that would be off-limits in less deft hands. Buy the book and watch a pro in action."

—Eric Thomas, Anchor/Reporter, KGO-TV San Francisco

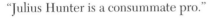

TV ONE-ON-ONE

BY JULIUS HUNTER

GASHOUSE
BOOKS

Library of Congress Control Number: on file

ISBN: 978-0-9800475-2-3

cover design by Bruce Burton

Printed in the United States of America
08 09 10 11 12 5 4 3 2 1

CONTENTS

ACKNOWLEDGMENTS

"If possible, I'd like to have that information YESTERDAY, please!"

That was my favorite mantra during the entire exciting process of putting this book together over the last forty years—this last year in earnest. And I owe sincere thanks to a squadron of my friends, old and new, who were ready, willing, and able to help me out.

Foremost among the talented professionals on whom I've leaned most heavily for incessant help is Joyce Loving, manager of special collections at the St. Louis County Library. You wouldn't believe the information I've relied on Dear Joyce to help me find, confirm, or throw out!

I also want to extend my special thanks to Dan Dillon of KMOV-TV; Laura Geiser of Saint Louis University; Fran DeGregorio, Jim Thebeau, and Charles Brown at the Mercantile Library; Lieutenant D. Sam Dotson of the St. Louis Metropolitan Police Department; Stefane Russell and Jeannette Cooperman of *St. Louis Magazine*; Rachel McCombs in Senator Bond's Office; Greg Conroy, Valerie Toth, and Amanda Bahr-Evola of SIU–Edwardsville; Charlie Hoessle formerly of the Saint Louis Zoo; Jill Barge, Cynthia Holter, and Kim Lovings of the Saint Louis Zoo; Mark Learman of the *St. Louis Post-Dispatch*; Ruth Ann Hager and Jim Bogart of the St. Louis County Library; Jennifer Plaat and Jeff Winget of KSDK-TV; Lucille Grimes, Helen Weiss, Harry Levins, John McGuire, Officer Jeremy Stockman, Steve Schiff, David Clohessy, and Barb Dorris of SNAP and SNAP associates; Mother Mary Regina Pacis and Sister Eva Maria Ackerman of the Sisters of St. Francis of the Martyr St. George; Fr. Greg Lockwood; Tony Huenneke at the St. Louis Archdiocese Communications Office; Nelson Spencer, Jr., of the *Waterways Journal*; Marvin Huggins of the Concordia Historical Institute; and to you, My Friend, if your name should be here, and isn't.

FOREWORD

Julius Hunter is one of the coolest guys I know. An icon in the broadcast and print media, he's the real deal. In a business that can be littered with poseurs and pretenders, Julius has made a career of being a solid professional who always delivers. One St. Louis media critic once put it this way when he looked over the city's airwave landscape: "There's Julius Hunter, and then there's everybody else."

At the height of his illustrious, award-winning career, my friend and mentor was accurately touted by his station as "The Most Trusted Newsman in St. Louis." And an autographed picture that hangs on Julius's wall of fame at home suggests that even the great Walter Cronkite recognizes that Julius is "a consummate pro." But not all the accolades laid on "Jules" have been that glowing. When I worked at a competitor TV station in St. Louis, when Jules beat us—no, killed us—on a big story, my news director called him "that Damn Julius!"

I first met Julius back in 1973. I was a thirteen-year-old in the lobby of the old KSD studios on Olive Street waiting to make an appearance on the *Corky the Clown* children's show. As I waited for my appearance, a dapper guy roared through the lobby followed by two guys with camera equipment who could barely keep up with him. They were headed for a hot story; in this case a really hot one, an abandoned warehouse inferno consuming a square block just north of Downtown St. Louis. Before I could say to myself, "There's that guy on TV," Julius stopped running, walked over to me, and politely introduced himself. That moment is classic Julius. He has always taken the time to encourage and inspire young people to do their best. In fact, his entire three-decade career has been spent bringing young people along on their career goals.

By the time I got to high school, I had decided I wanted to be just like the guy who took a moment to say hello. My aspirations in broadcast journalism were bolstered when I would sit with my beloved grandfather watching Julius reporting from the field and anchoring. I would hear my granddad say things like: "That guy makes it look so easy. . . . He's the best." I grew up watching a top-notch journalist who was at the top of his game, and obviously loving it.

It was well known in St. Louis broadcast news circles that competing stations would go ballistic every time Julius snagged an exclusive interview. How, they would howl, did he get a president to wave at Jetcopter 4? How, they would wonder aloud, did he get "the Gipper" to sit down with him and unwittingly reveal a top White House secret? Did he actually know movie goddess Sophia Loren before he escorted her on his arm into a packed banquet room as stunned diners gasped? How did he end up having lunch with Stan Musial and James Michener together? How did Hunter get crafty conservative curmudgeon Pat Buchanan to commit a gaffe that made headlines? And what movie reprise did "Uncle Miltie" suggest he might make with Jules? This book churns up a fat file of fascinating stories like a Jimmy Hoffa interview that goes on and on and on in more twists and turns than you'd ever expect when you set out to read this account. What did Chuck Berry tell Jules about the Indian girl that got him in all that trouble? What sexy "R-rated" inscription did Bette Midler autograph on the photo she gave Jules?

One of the greatest compliments to his work was to see the respect he was given by his peers. It was not at all unusual to watch competing reporters defer and yield as he commandeered a spot news story or breaking news conference interview. I am sure that scores of aspiring reporters learned a lot by the shining example and standards that Jules set.

Getting the biggest newsmakers in the world to sit down, open up, and bare their souls is not an easy task. I can imagine you've seen and heard some lousy interviews by lousy reporters. But as my grandfather noted, you will see time and again in this book the artful techniques Julius used to make the difficult art of interviewing look easy. You will enjoy seeing how he skillfully skewers some of the guys and gals you see regularly in the news and delivers them to a grill they don't see coming. And you will feel like you are sitting right next to Jules, face-to-face with his subjects, before the interview starts, during the interview, and after the microphone is shut off.

I continue to learn many lessons from my friend and teacher. He delivers his instructive tips and tricks of the trade over dinner and a cocktail. He always offers great insight into some fascinating people and, most of all, there are laughs for days. This book is kind of like having that dinner with Julius. The interviews and the back stories are all here from a man who has spent more than a third of a century covering some of the biggest stories, leaders, and personalities of our time. I guarantee you'll learn a lot, too! So, buckle your seatbelts and get ready for a thrilling ride through the highlights of an incomparably exciting career in journalism. Enjoy!

—Russ Mitchell, CBS News Correspondent

TV ONE-ON-ONE

HE TALKS TOO MUCH!

"Julius is generally a good student . . .
but he talks entirely too much."
—Miss Johnetta Jackson
4th grade teacher, Cole Elementary School

"I am working on getting Julius not to talk so much
when he should be listening or reading quietly.
Hope you can help me with this at home."
—Edgar Burnett
6th grade teacher, Cole Elementary School

Cole School graduation with buddy Gerald Broyles
(left) and first girlfriend Juanita Divers, 1957.

Ha!

So who got the last laugh on this "excessive talking" thing? At the time those gently critical report cards were written, neither teacher, in his or her wildest dreams, divined that the kid who never shut up in class would one day profit from a flaw. He would make a comfortable and highly publicized living doing the very thing he did too much of in grade school. Talking. I am grateful, in hindsight, to these observant teachers' attempts to shut down my motor mouth. If they had allowed me to gab on and on and on without calling this flaw to the attention of my mother and grandmother, I might have suffered a fate that makes verbosity a real art form. I could have become a politician!

The great thing about dear Miss Jackson's and dear Mr. Burnett's diplomatic tolerance of the yackety yack I produced daily is that they each—I'm sure consciously—settled on a policy of extreme patience. I think they figured, "Well, since we can't shut this kid up, maybe we can, at least, get him to talk excessively with good grammar and in some channeled direction."

When I was a grade school kid, Ed Burnett, in particular, graphically demonstrated to my classmates and me that good grammar was essential to a life outside our neighborhood. In fact, all my teachers at Cole Elementary School and at Sumner High School were practitioners of perfect articulation and grammar. I was impressed then, as I am now, with how grammatically proper my female teachers were, but as a fatherless kid, I was particularly taken with how sharply dressed and how consistently articulate the male teachers were in "grammar" school. Messrs. Ed Burnett, John Hartfield, Leonard Evans, and Rufus Young strongly shaped the way I spoke, even when I was speaking out of turn.

These teachers—the "Four Horsemen of my Epoch Ellipsis"—were, as seen through my young eyes, the male role models I held in the highest esteem during my formative years. Let's face it, where else was I to look for a male to stand as a shining example of what I wanted to be like when I grew up? There were not a lot of role models and far fewer pathways to success for my buddies and me. For a couple hundred years in the United States, we black kids could not point to an impressive bank of successful persons known nationally or internationally to emulate. There were role models inside our homes and neighborhoods, of course, but for African Americans a generation before me, their most attainable careers on the highest of levels to which they could aspire were as teachers, preachers, or good jobs at the Post Office.

My classmates and I at Cole School did not have the foggiest notion that people with our skin color could achieve any heights of note. Quite seriously and sadly, our options and worldview were limited to roughly the twelve-block radius around our neighborhood. We could hope to be like our exemplary middle-class teachers who, incidentally, all lived in our neighborhood. Or we might hope to get a good job with the Post Office. Becoming a preacher was not high on our lists, especially for the girls. I was proud to have role models in my family that went into the postal service. My Uncle A. (for Ambrose) was a postal worker in Chicago when I was a boy. And in 1904, my great uncle, George

Byrd, became the first postmaster of the little town of Honey Island my ancestors helped found down in Mississippi right after the Emancipation.

Sure, there were a relatively few black doctors, scientists, lawyers, brokers, engineers, and actors on view in the display case of my youth. But it could be weeks, months, or even years between times that I would see any of these professionals of color up close or in the media. Further, I had absolutely no notion of becoming a *prime time, major market television news reporter and anchorman* one day. When I was a grade school and high school student, there were absolutely no blacks with any dignity on television. Now, you may want to offer up an exception in Jack Benny's manservant, Rochester, or in the black caricatures on *Amos 'n Andy*. But my mother and grandmother would not let my sisters and me watch *Amos 'n Andy*. And the domestic work of Beulah, the housemaid on TV, was too close to the work that my mother labored at every day to be funny.

The St. Louis School Board approved a history book that my peers and I studied at Cole School that painted an extremely limited picture of black achievement—historically and contemporaneously. And, unfortunately, this same myopically produced and purchased partial American history book had a long shelf life. This particular book was used before I got to grade school right up until the time I started teaching grade school. This book, inappropriately enough, was called *This Is America's Story*. Considering the book's contents, the text was scurrilously misnamed. Doesn't the title suggest that the text will provide a comprehensive, all-inclusive look at U.S. history? It wasn't America's full story by any means. There were only five blacks listed as having made any significant contribution to *America's Story* and the story of world development: Booker T. Washington, George Washington Carver, Marian Anderson, Dr. Ralph Bunche, and Jackie Robinson. Sad? Sad.

There seemed to be a conspiracy by somebody somewhere to make sure my chums and I had what I call "tunnelized, parochial vision." And I hope you find this truth shocking: Some of my classmates and I discovered only in recent years at a dinner party at my house that the graphic artists and publishers of our grade school history book had done something absolutely unconscionable: These unscrupulous conspirators had actually shrunk the entire content of Africa down in the graphics to make the "Dark Continent" look significantly smaller than the continent of North America. Imagine. Our school board–issued history book should have been titled *This Is Just a Small, Racist Part of America's Story*. The kids in my neighborhood had no access to the hard, cold fact that down through history black people have had a major role in the societal growth and development of America and many other places on the globe. We didn't have even the slightest clue that a black man was first to produce blood plasma and blood banks. Which of us little black kids would suppose that a black person invented the player piano? Think of how proud we might have been—even subconsciously—every time we dropped a letter in a mail box. The postal mailbox, as we know it today, came from the mind of a black

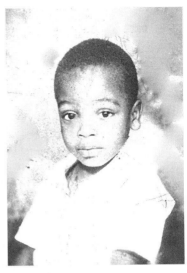

The author at age three.

inventor. We later learned about some of the other essentials of daily life that were inventions of people our color—like the golf tee, the folding chair, the sugar refinement processor, the cellular phone, the lawn sprinkler, the hydraulic shock absorber, the helicopter, the space shuttle retrieval arm, the pacemaker, and the electric stoplight, to name just a miniscule number of accomplishments that came from the inventiveness of African Americans. And to think, a bunch of scalawags robbed us of the knowledge of these inventions and of the fact that the continent of Africa is larger than North America. Oh, before we leave the subject, there's one other black achiever I thought you'd like to know about that probably never made it to any American history book you've studied, no matter your racial heritage. Ever hear of W. B. Purvis? I thought not. Well, Purvis is widely credited with inventing the fountain pen—which I just might use to autograph this book for you. Take the Purvis name with you to enter in the next trivia conversation you're in. His is an invention that is not so trivial, though.

Had I known there were countless other giants on whose shoulders I stood to become a TV newscaster, I might have been writing to you in a book from the standpoint of an astronaut, secretary of state, or a candidate for U.S. president. Or I might be delivering the nightly news to you from the chairs now occupied by Brian Williams, Charlie Gibson, or Katie Couric. But the perspective of a black kid who was born in the ghetto, upstairs over a barber shop located between the 20th Century Bar and the Bird Cage Lounge, was very foggy. In fact, at Cole School, reading from *This Is America's Story*, I didn't have the foggiest notion that I would one day find myself abandoning the grocery store's discarded orange crates we kids played with and find myself climbing into a TV box and spouting the news. It was just not an imaginable option when I was a kid.

And then, to broaden our perspective, consider the outlook of literally millions of little black kids like me who grew up in states like Missouri. Did you know that it was formally against Missouri state law to teach blacks to read until 1870?

I was extremely fortunate not to have to look too far for good role models to teach me the basics of good citizenship and point me toward an upper orbit. Those positive images were all around me in my home, school, and community. Of all the people who provided a vision that cut through the fog of the future for me, I must credit one person in particular who took me on the wildest, most unorthodox, most non-traditional learning journeys ever afforded a little kid. That person was my older brother, Van. He was my father's son, not my mother's, but we never hassled over family fractions that would make him my half brother. (I might suggest that if he was my "half" brother . . . who could or would claim the other half of him as a brother?)

Van, fourteen years my senior, had a master plan for me that only he knew. And he was not inhibited enough to admit that he was making up the game plan for his little brother as he went along. In some circles, Van would have been considered "curious." In other congregations, he might have appeared to be downright "nosey." Van, who was a Junior after my father, was always interested in what was going on in the neighborhood and in the entire world around him. And he was always willing to share his knowledge with anybody who was interested. Not many were. So he put all his efforts in my little basket. I became his little experiment.

He was kind of an odd duck. Van continued to leave his buddies' company to find a newspaper or a magazine to scour. And he liked to study his current events in private. He wanted no distractions. He knew everything any guy his age would or should know about what was going on in St. Louis, as well as in St. Paul or St. Croix or St. Elsewhere. Perhaps it is more accurate to say that from his voracious reading, Van was probably the only person in the old neighborhood who knew—or cared about—where St. Croix was located on the globe.

For some strange reason, this sparsely educated ghetto genius wanted his four-year-old little brother to benefit from his worldly curiosities. He created a personalized and novel version of a "Headstart program" for me that would lead to my job on TV, I'm sure.

Here's how he did it: Recognizing how few books there were at 722-A North Vandeventer (above the barber shop), Van of Vandeventer used the few tools available to us to give me a leg up on educational experiences—especially reading. The Southwestern Bell telephone directory was the one book that was present in almost every home, at least those dwellings with phones. He started out teaching me the basic sounds of the consonants and vowels, and then I graduated to learning the alphabet from Aaron to Zykan—straight from the 1947 edition of the phone book.

This brotherly pre-school teacher had a bit of a problem early on explaining to me that each of the twenty-six members of the alphabet had a "big letter" and a "little letter." Sometimes the little letters mirrored the big letters, but sometimes they differed in shape markedly. Further, Van reminded me later in my life that he taught me a sturdy mnemonic device. He would tell me that because he was the "BIG" brother, his last name began with a big "H." But since I was the "little brother," my last name—which was the same as his—began with a little "h." So in my early pre-school education, we referred to all letters as being either a "Big Brother" letter, or a "Little Brother" letter. Wonder how many early reading teachers ever thought of Van's approach? He called the consonants "con" letters—the letters that went with vowels to "make them sound right" or "make the vowels sound like themselves." Van reminded me, on more than one occasion after I had started my jobs in television news, that when I was learning the vowels, I initially called them *bowels.* A-E-I-O-U. Bowels. Imagine my toddler confusion when I heard my Uncle Walter, the "Master of Too Much Information," incessantly talking about how cod liver oil (he spread his on Wonder Bread) helped him move his vowels.

I learned after many months of at-home training that *"Pf"* sounds like an *"f"* as in *Pfeiffer.* I learned there was a *"soft g,"* as in *George*; and a *"hard g,"* as in *Gray.* I remember, somehow, that I looked to Van's lips for tips on "hard g's" and "soft g's." And I was trained, when help was needed, to watch Van's eyebrows and head feints on whether I was headed down the wrong path in trying to pronounce a word. A flash of a scowl meant that I should instantly try another approach. His program was a *Hooked on Phonics* long before there was actually a *Hooked on Phonics* reading system. When I became a senior TV news anchor, I always insisted that difficult words, like new prescription drug names, be spelled out on the screen for viewers who might not know them. I became a latter-day version of Van. His teaching methods stuck.

And there were many, many concurrent, concentric lessons in Professor Van's tutorial plan. He talked about "names that tell us what people do to make money to buy a loaf of bread or bottle of milk." Like *baker* or *farmer* or *fisher* or *cook*. Or *hunter,* for that matter! It was particularly ingenious for a guy who spent only two years in high school to come up with these unique concepts.

There was no *Yellow Pages* in the old days of my childhood. (Or is it: There *were* no *Yellow Pages* back in the old days of my childhood? I'll opt for the former, based on the English grammar I learned at Cole and Sumner). Anyway, there were neat little woodcuts of automobiles in the old telephone book. Auto body styles didn't change all that much, and the most popular colors were black or gray or tan in the early 1940s. No choices like "Cool Vanilla," or "Light Graystone Royale," or "Deep Lava Red Metallic." The car I drive today is painted a modest "Satin Jade Pearl." Thank goodness I did not have to contend with those fancy names when I was four years old. It was really easy for me to learn the car models pictured in the 1947 telephone book because there were no unique colors to distract from the basic body styles. I knew them all: Buick, Ford, Cadillac, Oldsmobile, Chrysler, Nash, Packard, and Dodge. The Studebaker was introduced in 1947, four years after I was born, which made it the newest entry for my identification in Van's Grand Scheme. The famous Studebaker bullet body style was not introduced until 1950. That was about the same time that my kindly kindergarten teachers, Miss Lauric and Miss Hayes, decided that I was wasting my time and theirs and they concluded that I should skip first grade. Van's pre-school tutorial program began working for me early on.

Ah, how altruistic it would have been if Van had carried on his tutorial as a doctoral thesis somewhere in the interest of advanced linguistics. But, alas, Van had his very own ulterior motive or two. Maybe even three motives. My older brother, with his minimal formal education, was a prophet for profit. He had

Cole Elementary School graduation, January 1957.

figured out that if he taught me to read before I started school he could make a few bucks with me being a profitable curiosity. His masterful plan was to trot me around to grocery stores, barber and beauty shops, taverns, and wherever two or three folks were gathered. And these "marks" would have to be willing to part with a dime or a quarter or both. Yes, there was a bit of con in the conviviality that my big brother displayed on the road to separating the unsuspecting from their money. Wonder if Van ever even heard of P. T. Barnum?

Here's a dramatization of how the ingenious "Van Con" went: Van would mosey up to the mark and start casual conversation— baseball, the weather, a movie he had just seen at the neighborhood Comet or Douglass movie theaters. Once he engaged the fleeceable, and once he got their undivided attention, then the "Grand Grift" could begin.

"See my little brother here?" Van would begin as if he had just noticed I was around. "He can read," Van steered the conversation.

"That little kid? That little snot?" the mark would invariably ask with either sheer disbelief or sheer contempt. Van didn't mind which reaction the "griftee" threw back. "No way that little kid can read," they'd say.

"Oh, yeah he can," Van challenged. "Uh, huh . . . Let's see . . .

I'll bet you a dime he can read . . . if we can just find something to read from," Van escalated the challenge.

My job, all through the set up and the legal vacuum sweeping of the nickel, dime, or quarter from the mark's pocket, was to just act as dumb and as uninterested as I could. I have often imagined in reverie that the dumber I looked, the more money Van would earn off me.

"Here's my dime," Van would offer. "Lemme see yours, Okay . . . uh . . . got something to read around here? How 'bout that . . . uh . . . how 'bout that telephone book over there? Let's use that," my big brother would say as if he had discovered and needed to dust off one of the Dead Sea Scrolls.

If Van was going to lead me, his little organ-grinder monkey, to someplace where there was no telephone book, he would "just happen" to have a telephone book in the shopping bag he "just happened" to have with him. And the real scam was that nobody read a telephone book, so the gauntlet he laid down seemed all the more improbable to the person that was about to lose a nickel, dime . . . or more.

"Okay," Van said in lines he had mastered. "You pick out a name without looking at it on the page I'll just open somewhere. All you have to do is close your eyes and stick out your finger and point. I'll do the rest."

I was always hoping that Van would open the book to somewhere near the *J's* where there were more names that I knew for sure like *Jackson, Jefferson, Jenkins, Johnson,* and *Jones.* Or I hoped that Van would let his own fingers do the walking to the *B's* where there was a treasure trove of surnames. *Ball, Baldwin, Banks, Bannister, Barnes, Bennett, Billings . . .* you get the idea. Those were among the juicier of the consonant options, as I remember. And first names were a breeze. No problem with any of them.

The masterful twist to this little exercise was that while the mark closed his/her eyes and pointed, Van would find a favored page and pick one of the alphabet sections that I had mastered. Van would then put the page at the end of the mark's outstretched index finger. Then he would shout out the all-clear eye-opener: "Okay, open your eyes now. Let's see what you've picked." Actually, it was a page that Van had picked.

If, by any chance, I failed on the first Van-picked page, my conniving, but loveable, brother would say something like,

"Didn't we say the best three out of five?" The mark had either spent too much time concentrating on Van's instructions and forgotten the game rules, they might have had a few too many adult beverages, or they may have also wanted to be compassionate to a cute little

Sumner High School freshmen, 1958.

four year old whom Van would always dress in outfits just short of Little Lord Fauntleroy's attire.

With the mark's eyes now open, Van continued, "Very good, very good. Okay, 'June Bug' (my boyhood nickname that I don't want to hear any of you use after today . . .), let's see what our friend here picked. . . . Go ahead, Junie (a variant on the nickname) . . ."

I'd squint at the name and build up that head of speaking steam that little kids always push out on a first attempt at reading something.

" B-B- rooks . . . B-rooks . . . Brooks . . . Brooks!"

"Go on," Van encouraged. "What's the first name?"

"Dav-id. David. Brooks, David."

"Now turn it around, June Bug. Go on . . . You can do it . . ."

"David Brooks. David Brooks," I'd say in triumph, sometimes clapping my hands in self-congratulatory applause.

"Okay, Lil Brother, what's the name under David Brooks?" Van would then ask.

"There's *three* David Brooks . . ."

"Good. Very good. What's the name under the last David Brooks?" Van asked me, ramping up the veracity of my reading ability.

"Brooks . . . uh . . . Den-nis. Dennis Brooks."

"Okay, okay," the mark usually would say at about this point. This damn little exercise was going on too long for a measly dime. And I had perhaps touched his heart with the reading rendition that appeared to be draining all the concentration and brain matter out of my little skull. "Here's the damn dime. There's some trick here . . ."

"Wanna go again?" Van offered in his most humble, pseudo-sincere and tantalizing tone.

Usually the mark had had enough by this time and would decline to go to the next round of this floating Big Brother/Little Brother Act. But if Van spotted the least inclination of the target to get his/her money back, he would draw the gullible mark into Part II of the Stump a Pre-schooler Game. The next step in the con called for Van's claim that I knew the names of all the automobile models. This was the easiest part of the game for me . . . and the most fun. We didn't care which woodcut the mark pointed to, I could name that car!

After the second dime had been lost, Van would offer the victim the opportunity to take me out onto the street. At curb-side—for fifteen cents—he would have me identify every car that passed by. This was to satisfy the allegations of those who thought that I had just memorized the cars in the book. Van would, if one drove by on busy Vandeventer or Delmar, point out a Studebaker. As mentioned, that make had not made it into the telephone directory yet. I had that car down pat, though. Often in Round 3 or 4, the escalation was another triumph for early childhood education. Or for Yankee ingenuity. Thank goodness that P. T. Barnum was right about the birthrate of suckers.

Our little reading con allowed Van some wonderful opportunities to learn to judge human character. He could tell in a hot second if the mark was a good candidate, whether there was an opportunity to advance the gaming to a second or even third level. Van, in the interest of the safety of both himself and his ward, knew when the targeted person had reached the end of his/her patience, benevolence, or time limit. Van would have fared well as a psychologist, if only he had finished high school. But I began to pick up a lot of cues about human nature by watching Van play the marks he so often and so gently wound around his little finger. My big brother's game was more of an art than a craft. I suppose I picked up a lot of his style, which I employed relentlessly in my subsequent job as a broadcast journalist.

And I should tell you that my older brother, mentor, and shepherd did not expect me to perform my high-wire reading act gratis. For my talent, I was often rewarded with an ice cream cone, a Hershey or Baby Ruth candy bar, a bag of So Good potato chips, or a Royal Crown Cola. The latter was always a bit too strong for my young and tender taste buds, and too much for me to fully consume. Tasted great, but too bad it wasn't less filling.

Van could, if he thought the climate was just right, offer the same little reading trick with any grocery item—particularly with any grocery item we had in our fridge or pantry at home. Like *Crisco* vegetable shortening, *Pevely* brand milk, *Rinso Blue* laundry detergent, *Maxwell House* coffee, or *Wonder Bread,* which "built bodies" a measly eight ways during my childhood. That was before the bread brand started building bodies twelve ways after I was grown up.

And as part of his enrichment program, Van took me on the most exciting field trips right beyond our backyard. He took me to Del-Van's, a shop where we watched men replace cracked auto windshields; he found a factory where wooden furniture was crafted; he sneaked me into St. Alphonsus Rock Catholic Church where we listened in the dark to the organist command a mighty pipe organ. And, while my very good teachers were taking us Cole School kids on field trips to such places that became boring, like the Wonder Bread bakery and the firehouse across the street from the school, Van took me to a fortune-teller's den. For one of the quarters I had earned Van, Swami Verdure would read his fortune and throw in the fortune he read from my tiny hand for free. I don't think he predicted that I would become a TV newscaster

But then, all of a sudden, my world was turned upside down. Van announced to me and the family that he was going to enlist in the Army and go off to someplace called Korea. All I could figure out at the time was that it had to be some place far, far away from 722 N. Vandeventer.

Van Buren Hunter, Jr., was more bored than he was patriotic; more adventurous than violent. Guess he just had to get out of our restrictive neighborhood and away from home. The nineteen year old knew from all his reading that the world had to be bigger than our circumscribed environs. And so, he was off. He didn't believe in big goodbyes. There were no bon voyage parties for him. And it was soon that I realized that a major chunk of my life was gone . . . to Korea.

Right after that day when he marched off to war on September 19, 1950, I began practicing some of the teachings that Van had passed on to me; practices that would be invaluable to a broadcast news reporter. He encouraged me to become a voracious reader. He taught me not only to read from standard book fare, but he also wanted me to read everything that had printing on it: a soup can, a box of cereal, a carton of eggs from the kitchen, the names of shops and stores on their front windows, every traffic sign, every billboard. And there was other less tangible reading matter he taught me. He instructed me by his examples on how to read faces. And Van even taught me to read the handwriting on the wall. I didn't need a graduate degree to begin figuring out as a young kid when to hold 'em, when to fold 'em, when to walk away, and when to run from any kind of situation that arose in the old neighborhood.

My older brother passed on to me even more tools to use years later in the broadcast trade without even knowing he had developed a lesson plan. He taught me to always ask who, what, where, when, why, and how.

When Van set out to learn something new, he didn't mind putting anybody on the spot to find out what he needed to know. When I was a teenager working as a sexton (fancy word for a church janitor) at my little Lutheran church, I remember "Van, the Grand Inquisitor" putting my pastor on the spot. Van had returned from Korea a broken and damaged vet, and sadly enough wasn't doing much with his life and all those brains. He popped by the church one Saturday where I was in the middle of my chores to earn a little extra pocket change. I turned off the vacuum sweeper and took a break to talk a bit to the mentor who had spent so much time with me. Van wasn't much for church and religion, but he was glad that I had become, at age sixteen, the organist and choirmaster of the tiny church. In my later life, I wondered if Van had related his slipping me into St. Alphonsus Rock Church to listen to the organ music with my eventually playing the organ at Holy Sacraments. The two experiences just had to be related, don't you think? I introduced my agnostic-at-best brother to my minister whom I was almost certain he had met before. After a few cautious pleasantries between the two, Van began a classic interrogation.

Van: "Pastor, who runs this place?"

Name **Hunter, Julius**

Adviser *A.S. Harris*　　　　　　　Group_____

School year 19 **60** 19 **61**　Sept.-Jan. ☒　Jan.-June ☐

PUBLIC HIGH SCHOOLS
SAINT LOUIS　　MISSOURI

PUPIL'S REPORT CARD

SUBJECTS	PERIOD 1 ACHIEVEMENT	PERIOD 1 CITIZENSHIP	PERIOD 2 ACHIEVEMENT	PERIOD 2 CITIZENSHIP	TERM GRADE ACHIEVEMENT	TERM GRADE CITIZENSHIP
T.V. Comp	B	2	F 3		C	3
Psychology	C	1	B	1	C	1
French	4 D	1	C	1	B	1
Chem	2 C	1	F 2		C	2
Choir			A	1	A	1

EXPLANATION OF MARKS

ACHIEVEMENT:

A circled mark indicates that the pupil has the ability to do better work with reasonable effort.

Key to Grading System

A—Excellent　　90% to 100%
B—Good　　　　80% to 89%
C—Medium　　 70% to 79%
D—Poor　　　　65% to 69% (barely passing)
F—Not passing　Below 65%

CITIZENSHIP:

Citizenship includes industry, responsibility and co-operation.

1—Above average
2—Average
3—Below average

Pastor: "You mean the church?"

Van: "Yeah . . . I mean . . . Yes, sir. The church?"

Pastor: "Well, son, our Lord and Savior Jesus Christ is the head of the Church."

(Van obviously couldn't see the capital "C.")

Van: "Who takes care of the church . . . like keeping it fixed up?"

Pastor: "That, my boy, is the job of our Deacons."

Van: "Deacons, huh? Well, who's in charge of taking care of the money and big stuff like that?

Pastor: "In our church, that's handled by our Board of Elders."

Van: "Do you go out and visit the sick people and stuff . . ."

Pastor: "No, young friend, visits to the sick are made by our 'Sunshine Club.' And they do a wonderful job of it."

Van: "Well, can I ask you one more question, Rev?"

Pastor: "Yes. You seem to have a lot of questions . . ."

Van: "Well, if all those people do all those things . . . what the hell do you do around here, sir?"

The pastor had been "VANdalized!"

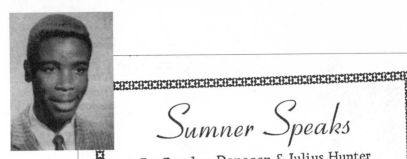

Sumner Speaks

By Carolyn Donegan & Julius Hunter

Sumner's halls are mute and stilled
The school is not with students filled.
Our summer vacation has now begun
And we've started on our summer fun!
And now some comments we'd like to make
To those concerned with this summer break.
To graduates: All the luck in life
May your lives be good and free of strife.
And as the years pass swiftly by
May you ne'er forget your Sumner High!
To teachers: Enjoy your well-earned rest
We wish you, too, the very best.
And on your aspirin we want you to stock
To come back to your aspirin' flock.
To parents: It seems that you're just stuck
With us, so all we can say is, "Lotsa luck".
Just take our presence at home in stride,
And let tranquilizers by your guide!
Oh, maybe this pause won't be so long
And soon we'll be singing "September Song".
Until next time we'll sincerely miss you,
Aloha, till the next Prom issue!

cBride Memos

cDonough & Tom Wojciechowski

nonth out, first month of relaxation,
f work, first month with no home-
onth of summer school. After our
ut of school, most of us are probably
these things. For some of us two
and back to school, and for others

PROM
EXCLUSIVELY FOR THE YOUTH
OF GREATER ST. LOUIS!

JULY 1960 10c
Mail Subscriptions
(12 Months) $1.00

MARY INSTITUTE
MAY FETE

PHOTOS · MUSIC · SPORTS · FASHIONS

One television interview I did in my first year of television news reporting was almost a carbon copy of Van's interview with my pastor when I was just a kid. And the technique was sprung on none other than the powerful president of the two-million-member Lutheran Church, Missouri Synod.

The Rev. Dr. Jacob Preus had been elected as head of our worldwide group of Martin Luther's descendant flock in 1969. His mission was to bring the Church's Concordia Seminary in St. Louis in line and away from its suspected liberal theological leanings and teachings. The big Lutheran group of which I was a member since early childhood baptism, split with a group that protested the firing of Concordia's president, the Rev. John Tietjen. The ousted seminary president became a good friend of mine through my next-door neighbor, who was also a Lutheran minister. My neighbor shared theological beliefs with Tietjen. Their interpretations of church doctrine and liturgy were, indeed, more liberal or moderate than those of the Church hierarchy. I think it must have been the spirit of Van that whispered in my ear that I need not recuse myself for the interview with Dr. Preus even though my theological leanings favored the breakaway group that became known as Seminex—the Seminary in Exile. As I sat down facing Preus in his downtown office, I steered smoothly through the obligatory cordialities and pleasantries. I think my interviewee was genuinely surprised to learn that I had grown up in an LCMS church. I then, with catlike stealth, asked Dr. Preus about his authority in asserting the strict tenets of the LCMS's ultra-conservative doctrine.

"Dr. Preus," I approached. "I would imagine that you would say that Jesus Christ is the head of your Church. Would that be a correct assumption?"

"Why, yes, Julius. I think that is a very accurate statement. Jesus, as Lord, is the Head of the Lutheran Church, Missouri Synod. Yes."

Reel him in now, the spirit of Van urged me.

I continued, "How can you be sure, with Jesus as the head of your Church, that Jesus would sanction what some call your hardliner stance on how the Bible should be interpreted?"

Dr. Preus—a small man—did not appear, in person, to be as menacing as his detractors painted him. In answer to my pointed query, Dr. Preus spouted a mini-reproduction of the many, many sermons I had been forced to sit through during my years as pa-

Junior Prom with sweetheart Phyllis Parks, 1960.

rishioner, Sunday School teacher, janitor, organist, and choirmaster of a church whose teachings were seldom made applicable to a tiny all-black congregation. But as he sat across his executive desk from me, I stood ready to spring my Van-inspired set-up question.

"So, Dr. Preus," it might seem that you are imposing your interpretations as president of the LCMS that might lead some to ask, 'Just who is the head of the Lutheran Church Missouri Synod?'"

"Well, Julius. There is no question that Jesus Christ is the head of our Church . . . and there should be no persons or factions that doubt that He is the Alpha and Omega in our Church. And there is no doubt that the Bible is the divine word of God that should not be taken figuratively or loosely as some in our Church are espousing."

"Well, sir," I responded, with Van's spirit prodding the direction of my probe, "if Jesus is the true head of your Church, what's your role?"

Dr. Preus gave what was almost a little chuckle to the way my entrapment had been framed, and then he launched into the nature of his administrative role in the LCMS as compared to Christ's role in the administration of his Church. There is no doubt about the comprehension level of this very bright church administrator. His quasi-chuckle that followed my pointed question might well have been produced by his instant recall of my credentials. He may have even had some latent respect for the way that this kid who grew up in what I called in some subsequent lectures a "CCC," a "Colored Colony Church" of the LCMS, had caused him to wriggle internally, but certainly not externally. The spirit of my big brother Van would, no doubt, give me a grade of at least a "B" on the way I handled the parrying.

But there is no way that Dr. Preus would have been able to divine—even with help from the Divine—that the seed for that armor-piercing question I had launched from my reportorial quiver had been fashioned by that "master fletcher," Van Buren Hunter, Jr.

I wish that Van could have sat across the executive desk from Dr. Preus. It would have been a true match between *exegetical theology* and *street smarts*. Where would you put your money?

I haven't said much about what happened to my brother/mentor. Well, as you know, he marched off to war in the Korean Conflict before he finished high school. He saw actual combat on that soil so far away from Vandeventer and Delmar. As a consequence of the killer cold in Korea, Van suffered frostbite and eventually lost some of his toes. He returned to 722 N. Vandeventer a war hero to his family and friends. There were no medals, but the sheer fact that he returned

alive made him a larger-than-life homeboy to all of us who had never been any farther than Chicago to the North and Mississippi to the South. None of us had been anywhere much beyond the environs of St. Louis.

The war veteran had some fascinating stories to tell about Korea, and that in itself was an extension of Van's education of his younger brother. I sat with widened eyes and perked up ears as Van, always the enchanting raconteur, detailed how he was transported to Korea. He told how he took a train from Union Station in downtown St. Louis with other black recruits out to California. Then he told me one-on-one that he got eight weeks training at a boot camp and was shipped out to someplace in Japan. He said the trip overseas took about ten days. He lost track of time, he said, because he got so seasick. He said going into dock in what they told him was Japan, the waters were so choppy that guys were throwing up all over the place, especially those landlubber soldiers who had never before stepped outside the confines of their hometown concrete jungles.

And when he elected to expand his audience beyond his entranced kid brother, he told whatever fascinated audience he could how cold it had been in Korea in the winter of 1951. My brother told those of us who had complained about St. Louis's cold winter of 1951 that in the trenches in Korea, it was sometimes so cold that he and his new buddies had to hold their canteens on a stick over hot coals to thaw out their drinking water. Plus, the war-battered vet remembered that all he ate was frozen food in the K-Ration cans—barely palatable gunk that was supposed to be warmed up before eating. An occasional hot cup of coffee was a treat, he said. And he said that some of his fellow soldiers were going crazy because of the cold, and because their weapons would freeze up and they had no way of protecting themselves from the enemy. Van did not hide the fact that he was scared nearly to death every single night that he tried to go to sleep in the sub-zero temperatures, afraid of freezing to death in his sleep, and with "a whole bunch of crazy Chinamen shooting at us." He said he never did understand what we did to the Chinese "'cause we was in Korea."

Van was not exaggerating the cold. I checked on his stories after I got into college—as he would want me to do—and found that the winter of 1951 was the coldest winter in North Korea in that country's recorded weather history. There were reports in some regions of temperatures plunging to as low as forty-five degrees below zero! I also learned from filling in some of the gaps in Van's stories that even though Harry Truman had ordered the military to end racial segregation in 1948, Van, in the 24th Infantry, was still in an all-black, poorly trained and equipped unit two years after the executive order. And it was sadly obvious to me on investigation that my big brother was assigned to what the Army at that time called a "Class II" unit. That translates to "canon fodder."

JULIUS HUNTER
Choir, President
Human Rel...

SAMI IE

When Van was discharged on disability, he was paid a lot of money. Too much money; an overpayment. Before a year was out, Van had spent all his disability payment. The Army discovered the error. Van was told that he would have to pay back every cent of the overpayment, despite the fact that gangrene had developed back here at home and he had to lose four toes—one on his right foot, and three on his left. He spared none of the grotesque details on me. That gave me a human anatomy and medical course.

Realizing that he had no marketable skills above menial labor, the war-ravaged vet figured that he would have to work the rest of his life to pay off the overpayment. So he decided to drop out—drop out of society, and basically drop out of life. He became a hopeless wino. He was often homeless and sometimes got the best care of a stretch when he had to be confined to Veterans Hospital. That's where the toes were amputated, and then a foot, and then his leg below the knee, and more.

Van disappeared for a very long time. And then he resurfaced in St. Louis and gave the distinct impression he was looking over his shoulder all the time. He was afraid he would get nabbed by the very government that had left him maimed for life. He announced that he was changing his name to "Van X" to discard his slave surname and duck "The Man." The combination of alcohol and complications from diabetes made him often delirious and paranoid.

As the wretched figure hobbled around through the old neighborhood on one leg and crutches, he was a pitiful sight. And there was not much I could do for him; not much he would allow me to do for him. Pride maybe. But I would find him every chance I could for a meet-up in my always-new car. He wanted to chat about current events, and he wanted me to know that he watched me on TV whenever he could find a TV set. I would always give him every cent I had on me during our visits. He would never tell me where he was laying his head. He'd just give various intersections of streets near 722-A North Vandeventer when he would call me for a hookup. For years before each winter, I would take him a big box of warm clothes, often and ironically from an Army Surplus store. And I would take him a huge box of non-perishable food. I got the distinct idea, though, that with each spring thaw, Van would hock items like the heavy coats and sweaters I brought him in order to buy more cheap wine. As we sat in my car on the corner of Delmar and Boyle or Newstead and Olive, prostitutes working the so-called Stroll would often peck on the window of our car and be scared away by the anger in Van's scraggly, weather-beaten face. He would always yell epithets at them through the window glass. They would sometimes curse him back. He didn't approve of their profession.

Why didn't I take him in? He would never have that in the first place. He bragged and laughed about how something would come over him inside that compelled him to steal a few little things from anybody who had a nice home and looked like they were living more comfortably than he was. Nothing really big or valuable, though. And a lot of our relatives who tried to help him can attest to the fact that, indeed, every time he paid a visit, he'd pinch a little souvenir to help him remember his visit. Besides, with his physical disability, rapidly declining health, and the presence in my life of a wife and two small children, Van would not have been a good boarder.

On several occasions, with obvious spite and delight, an old woman who owned a small grocery store in the old neighborhood would telephone either of my workplaces, Channel 5 or Channel 4. She would cackle in her shrewish voice that she had called the police on my "thieving brother" again. And she seemed to love to tell me that she had had him locked up for shoplifting. With his being disabled by crutches and on one leg, Van, the storekeeper, and the police knew full well that his chances of outrunning the storekeeper or the law were slim to none. But she'd begin each phone call to me in the newsroom with some nasty remark like: "Well, Mr. Big Time Television Man, I just had your brother arrested again for stealing from my store. He stole such and such." And she'd repeat the charges over and over again till a broadcast deadline would force me to hang up on her. One time, after hearing her tirade, I mailed her a check for a hundred dollars "to cover any upcoming items my brother might need from your limited, overpriced, stale stock in the coming months." Both Van and I had worked in that very store as delivery boys at different eras. And this same woman had violated child labor laws by making us work twelve-hour delivery days, while giving us no lunch, and on paydays tallying up and deducting for each snack we picked up to sustain ourselves on those long days.

After each arrest, I felt it my brotherly duty to go to the Lucas Avenue Police Station and spring Van. And each liberation would call for a sit-in-the-car celebration featuring cheap wine in paper cups. And he'd always have to have a newspaper. My brother never missed an opportunity to play pundit. He would want to comment, between sips, on everything going on in the world at the time. He would critique my on-the-air delivery of stories; tell me what I should have and shouldn't have said about this or that story; and comment on something I said that made him laugh. I didn't need Mr. Nielsen when I could get an insightful rating from Van.

On the hot and steamy night of July 12, 1973, I was routed out of bed around 2:00 a.m. by a call from the Channel 5 newsroom to get out to the Military Records Center in Overland. Little did I know at the time of the callout that this story was not only for Van to talk about, but the event also gave him a big and continuous sigh of relief. Between 16 and 18 million records were destroyed in the conflagration when the entire sixth floor was wiped out by fire. Records dating from 1912 to 1960 were toast. "Guess they can't get me now," said my fugitive brother. He told me I did "good" with my all-day coverage for both Channel 5 and its sister station KSD-Radio.

The Army vet who had been honorably discharged and overpaid on his disability payout eventually began to have trouble keeping his balance when he hobbled around on one leg through the old neighborhood. He had all the bearing of a pitiable fugitive whose only crime had been to overspend an overpayment for losing his toes to frostbite while serving his country. Large and consistent quantities of cheap wine—combined with overdoses of prescription painkillers and chain cigarette smoking—began to seriously chip away at Van's most valuable assets, his brain, his creativity, his mobility, and his adventurous nature. By late 1992, he began to bombard the Channel 4 newsroom with outrageous telephone calls at all hours of the day, every day of the week, even when I had a day off. His irrationally placed calls reminded me of what I have always questioned about the staple slogan of the United Negro College Fund: "A mind is a terrible thing to waste." I've always wanted to change that statement of fact to what it really means as clearly illustrated by the ravaged shell that was now my brother: *"It is a terrible thing to waste a mind!"* Van would be the first to opine that our minds are not "terrible things."

Then, one evening in the summer of 1992, just before the six o'clock newscast, Van phoned. "I need to see you. I need to see you. I need to see you," he pleaded. He wanted to tell me that he was in Veterans Hospital where surgeons had just whittled away yet another slice of his rotting leg, getting closer and closer to his hip. It is ironic that the architecturally grotesque VA Hospital at which Van received occasional carvings was one block east of 722 N. Vandeventer, where my schooling with Van had begun before I went off to get a formal education. The hospital had replaced bucolic Vandeventer Place where Van and I rode our bikes in a fountain basin that was big enough for us to bank our bikes on the sides. Now grand old Vandeventer Place was flattened; demolished. And Van was heading for demolition.

I agreed to come by to see him between the six and ten o'clock newscasts one night. I had expected to find a bedridden brother who was rotting away. *Au contraire.* The one-legged and spirited adventurer was in a wheelchair waiting for me right inside the front door of the hospital lobby. I wonder if it is possible to pace in a wheelchair. I leaned over and gave him a hug. And then Van, ever the teacher, made his wheelchair appear to be motorized as he gave me a whirlwind tour of the entire first floor. You would have sworn he was the hospital administrator. He told me where every department on the first floor was, and he introduced me to a brigade of mangled and shattered veterans of war. He made sure that each knew that this TV guy they saw on the news all the time was his brother. I sat in his ward one time as Van queried a doctor—obviously not for the first time—about the diagnosis and the prognosis. In my mind, I tried to precede Van's line of questioning and tried to outguess him on where he was going next. But I soon had to remember that he was the teacher emeritus, and I still was a student.

Van passed away at the VA Hospital on November 13, 1992, shortly after my visit to the hospital. It was a loss to society; to family and community. It was a particular loss to me. I was happy that he was able to see the product of his teachings any night when he could find a TV. I know he was proud. And I was proud of him, too, but extremely sorry about how he began his descent into Hell. His torturous decline began in Korea, seven thousand miles away. He made me find out the distance one time following one of his impromptu geography lessons.

Look at all Van taught me, with the exception of the artful crime of shoplifting. When I am often asked how I got from there to here, this is the story that comes out—usually in far less detail. And how did the hand of Providence play into my life's good fortune? Well, I have absolutely no problem with believing that that Providential hand does exist. And I believe that it appeared in the form of the least of these . . . my brother.

From the positive influences of their mother, Barbara, the richness and juiciness of the environment in which they sprouted their wings, and surely from some of the interests and curiosities Van sparked in me, my daughters each became Harvard honors graduates. And maybe at least one of my grandchildren might want to be a television news anchorperson, if TV news is still around. Two of those grandchildren, then aged seven and four, refused to go to bed before they heard Barack Obama's historic victory speech as the presumptive Democratic presidential nominee. And during the heat of the Campaign '08 Democratic Primary season, the four year old—from his own little political mind—suggested to my daughter and son-in-law that "all those people who want to live in the White House should be put in a really, really, really, really dark room. And the one who doesn't get scared should get to live in the White House." Van, whom they never met, would be proud of that analysis.

One of my grandkids, at age seven, can read this book right now from cover to cover if we allowed her to. But then, after reading about how Grandpa Jules had to push, pull, plot, plan, promise, prowl, proselytize, plead, pucker, punch, pander, preen, and produce to get the interviews in this book, the four grandchildren just might choose some other profession. Or at least, another book.

There's no question that I had extraordinary basic preparation to be a broadcast newsman from my variegated informal education under the tutelage of my enterprising older brother, and my formal from my exemplary teachers. Is it odd that I never had a single journalism or mass communications course anywhere—high school or college? So it was a bold step to set out into the world of journalism with none of that book-learning to buoy me up. Any success I've had in the news business comes from on-the-job training with the planks of a good, solid, general, really, really liberal arts life experience under my feet. You might call this book, chock full of scores of exciting interviews and encounters, my doctoral thesis.

BASIC TRAINING

My career in television news got off to a rocky start. My first teaching assignment right out of Harris Teachers College (now Harris-Stowe State University) in 1965 was at Hamilton Elementary School in St. Louis City. My first class was made up of forty-four post-pubescent students packed into a self-contained classroom. One girl in my class was pregnant. I was with these kids from the start of each school day until the final bell rang at 3:15. Some of those youngsters in my first class were already sixteen and seventeen years old. I was just twenty-one. I learned a simple life-guiding rule at Hamilton: "LAW AND ORDER MUST PREVAIL BEFORE LEARNING CAN BEGIN." The law was almost just for self-defense.

After three years of vigorously trying to help shape young minds and fresh aspirations, as Van had done with me, I decided to try a new adventure. So I applied for and landed a job as an advertising copywriter at Foote, Cone & Belding in Chicago. At FCB, the third-largest ad agency in the world at the time, I was privileged to work with a very creative group that wrote some of the prime print and TV ads I'm sure you saw back then. We pressed all our creative juices—between goblets of fermented pressed wine and martinis—to crank out ads for Dial Soap & Deodorant, Kleenex/Kotex, Kraft Italian Macaroni Dinners, Raid House & Garden Spray, and PF Flyer tennis shoes . . . long before anybody ever heard of Nike. FCB afforded great preparation for a TV reporter job.

I could not take more than a year of the high cost of Chicago living—the fast pace and days of wine and roses. So I came back home to St. Louis for rehab and a quieter life. I looked into and accepted a dual position in the Washington University Student Affairs Department. I was in charge of a program that promoted student voluntarism. And I was, get this, housemaster of a dormitory of 140-some freshmen girls. It is in this post that I learned another adage for life: "HELL HATH NO FURY LIKE A WOMEN'S DORM!"

Student voluntarism in 1968 had a short shelf life in which students were interested in helping others outside the university while they polished their courses of study. And then the Vietnam War blew up in all our faces. Add the traditional academic stresses—newfound boyfriends and girlfriends, mid-term and final exams, new puppies, spring break, summer break, and Christmas holiday break—and you have a potent formula for putting dampers on altruistic pursuits.

But the other part of my job at the university as a dorm master kept me quite busy—and exasperated. Besides, I got married just after taking the Wash. U. post and elected not to live in the suite at Umrath Hall provided to the housemaster. The uniqueness of a male—a black male at that—holding the job of governor of an all-female dormitory might have seemed all the more strange if my soon-to-be good friends, Ed Rollins and John Duvall, had not been simultaneously appointed to similar positions in neighboring all-girls residence halls. The Three Musketeers found it incumbent quite often to repair to Krueger's Bar down the street from the university to commiserate and compare notes. In a memorable meeting of the Council of Masters one night—I think there were twelve of us masters—Ed, John, and I once proposed eliminating the master's position altogether. We were just kidding, of course, since we found ourselves, like the other masters, taxed by the pressing issues we had to monitor 24/7/365. My attention was always challenged by such matters as unauthorized overnight stays by male visitors, illegal alcohol consumption, drug abuse, roommate conflicts, uncomfortable seasonal dorm temperature fluctuations, unauthorized pets, flunkouts, homesickness, and a general and sometimes specific resistance to authority. And sometimes it seemed that any and all of these issues might come up in just the first hour of any given workday on the university's South Forty.

While I was engaged in my harrying day-to-day concerns with student affairs—and the affairs some students and staff members were having—I got an interesting request from what was then KSD-TV, Channel 5. The station was producing an hour-long documentary and wanted to send a film crew to the campus to follow me around for part of my workday. The subject of the documentary was something like "What It's Like to Be Black in 1969," or some such nonsense as that. But I was adventuresome. I had learned from my big brother, Van, many years earlier, to seek out new experiences. So I okayed the Channel 5 visit to my little "kampus kingdom."

Sure enough, a film crew showed up and tagged along as I

The author was invited back on three different occasions to give the Sumner High commencement address.

went about my daily duties as director of the volunteer program and my professional chores as warden of the all-girls dorm. And then a producer/reporter did a one-on-one interview with me in my office. I was viscerally turned off by the line of questioning and the anticipated shallowness of such a project as this. I thought I could have asked more salient questions than the producer asked me. But I had a real hang-up about the subject matter. How could a TV program adequately convey what it was like to be black in America in a scant hour? It had taken me twenty-five years at the time to get even close to an answer to that burning question.

Channel 5 had lined up about a dozen African Americans—even though we weren't being called by that racial title at the time. I think we were "Afro-Americans" then. We had just come out of being called Negroes. And we were still being called a variant on that latter racial title in too many sectors of our nation. The local citizens of color Channel 5 selected were employed in a broad spectrum of occupations and professional pursuits.

I guessed—even before I sat down for the interview—that I would approach the question with subtle derision. When asked what the toughest part of being black was, I responded that the most difficult thing about being black was the constant bombardment by Caucasians at social functions as they lined up to plead with me to show them the latest "Negro" dances. The rest of my responses were equally disingenuous. When asked what I thought my greatest achievement in life was, I responded: "Getting so far away from Mississippi." (Home of my slave ancestors.) When the crew left, I just knew there would be no way that they would use my comments in their documentary. But they did.

In fact, during the editing process before the program aired, producer Paul Campbell was hard at the tough job of making all the comments of all of us exemplary Negroes fit into the allotted hour block of time. As he was cutting and pasting, Channel 5's program director at the time, the inimitable Keith Gunther, passed through the editing room to check on how things were going with the editing. "Pinky" Gunther, as he was called, took note of my smart-alecky answers. I'm sure my unorthodox responses at least added a wink, a chuckle, and a tongue-in-cheek atmosphere to all the serious attempts by my fellow participants to answer the unanswerable, sometimes absurd, question of the day.

After his perusal of my attitude, style, and articulation, it was sheer wonder that Gunther phoned me at Wash. U. He actually asked me if I was interested in becoming a television news reporter. What he did not tell me was that there were pickets out in front of the station at 1111 Olive Street—perhaps at the very time of his phone call to me. The demonstrators were demanding that the station hire its first black anchor or reporter. The pressure from black activists might have been the impetus for what was to be the aforementioned documentary on the quickie course in black being. I have no doubt that the station was trying to assuage the picketers' demands. The station had hired a black woman, Diane White, as its "weathergirl" many years before my chat with Gunther. But the black community was not bemused.

Gunther seemed to be taken aback a bit when I told him that I was not at all interested in leaving the secure blanket of Washington University for the unworn trench coat of a TV news reporter. Even though the housemaster job was stressful and taxing on a new marriage and an old quest for perfection, I was making the respectable salary of $17,500 ($5,000 more than I made at the agency in Chicago and $12,000 more than I made on my first full-time teaching gig); I lived within walking distance of the university; I had a comfortable suite in the dorm; I could set my own hours; and I didn't have much direct supervision. What more could I want?

And then Mr. Gunther let fly a statement that would surprise nobody who knew "Pinky." He had the nerve, the audacity, and the temerity . . . the balls to say to me to my astonishment: "Well, I should think you should at least get your ass down here and see what I'm offering."

Channel 4's Front Four: (from left) Tim Van Galder, sports; the author; co-anchor Steve Schiff; weathercaster Ollie Raymand, 1977.

I could not believe my ears. A white guy talking that way to a black guy he didn't even know! But this highly unorthodox approach piqued my interest, and before I knew it, I was sitting in Gunther's office at Channel 5. One of the first things he said to me was: "If you come to work here, we gotta change your name right away. Joolyus, Joolyus," he said in a mocking way. "Joolyus makes you sound like some sort of Jewish Negro."

That was just about it. I didn't have to take this abuse from a guy I didn't know from Adam before I stepped into his lair. I would rather take the pressures of shepherding the 140 freshman women at Wash. U., I thought. When I started to get up, Gunther said, "Sit your ass down and let's talk money. If I hire you, what kinda salary do you want?"

I asked him to be more specific about the job I was applying for, and he explained what a TV news reporter was expected to do at Channel 5 in 1969. That job description alone seemed like a far more interesting story to tell in a TV documentary than the subject of the stuff they were about to put on the air about the essence and experience of being black.

I had played the salary game before and was hesitant to name a specific pay amount. I think Gunther picked up on my hesitancy right away. "Let's see," he calculated, "you're making $17,500 at Washington U., and you have absolutely no experience as a TV news reporter. So I should think you would be satisfied with making a little less than you're making now, so you can get some TV experience under your belt."

"You're crazy, Mr. Gunther," I managed to get spine enough to say. "You gotta remember that I'm not interested in the job in the first place. So I'm not about to take some job I've never done before and make LESS money," I said firmly.

"Well, give me a figure. Give me a number. Give me something to work with," the program director demanded.

"Can't do it," I told him. "If I wanted the job, and if I took the job, I'd have to at least talk it over with my wife first. I can't make the decision on the job or on a salary today . . . just like that," I snapped my fingers. I was sure that I was arguing from a position of weakness.

"Well, go home to your little wifey," Gunther said in a mocking tone. "Talk it over with her, but you better get back to me right away. You know there are other guys we can hire," Keith threatened.

I left Gunther's office with a rush of thoughts—almost too much to think of on the way home to discuss this unexpected offer with Barbara.

A couple of days later, just before Christmas 1969, I phoned Gunther and asked to see him. He granted another interview. In the interim, I rehearsed aloud stating the salary I wanted over and over. The day of reckoning came too soon. Within seconds of sitting down in his office, I spilled out: "I want the job, and I want $25,000!"

"Twenty-five thousand dollars!" he said mockingly. You expect me to pay you—a nobody with no experience—$25,000? GET OUT OF MY OFFICE!" he yelled, raising his voice for the first time and raising his finger pointing to his door. "GET OUT!"

That seemed pretty final to me, and I fled his office right away. As my relatives might have said back in Mississippi, "I felt low enough to crawl under a snake with a high hat on." Oh, well . . . it would be back to the bucolic (though internally tumultuous) grounds of the university. I told Barbara that I was out as a candidate, but she expressed her comforting comment that I would not have liked the reporter job anyway.

Nearly two weeks and the Christmas holidays passed. It was a long, long two weeks. In fact, they were two weeks that seemed like two months. I watched a lot of television news over the holidays. And then, two days before the last day of 1969, Gunther phoned me at my campus office.

"Get down here. This is Gunther. Get here in an hour." And then this brass-balled stranger hung up the phone. I didn't even get a chance to say a word. I raced home and put on a suit and tie and roared down to the station. I guess I wanted that job

The photography staff poses with the author after a St. Louis Magazine *cover shoot, July 1982.*

after all. I was determined that I would not accept a pay cut, but maybe "Pinky" and I could work something out.

I took a little more than an hour to get there, but not by much. When I entered Gunther's office, I was mildly shocked to learn that he was out to lunch. He kept me waiting, and stewing, and fidgeting for more than an hour.

Finally, he blew into his office. "Joolyus," he said mockingly as he brushed by me. His receptionist, Mary, said, "You can go on in."

When I sat down in front of him, Keith, while tapping a pencil on his desk, said emphatically: "I'll give you twenty-two five ($22,500), and not a penny more. Take it or leave it. And if you're not going to take it . . . get out of my office so you don't waste any more of my time!"

I took it. He stood up and gave me a smile of triumph. He probably had much more than the $25,000 that he could have offered me. We shook hands, and he said, "I think you'll be 'Mark,' 'Mark Hunter.' Be here next Monday."

And that was it . . . my glorious, glamorous, historic hiring as Channel 5's first black reporter.

I thought for a while after this unceremonious start to a new career that after I showed up for work the station might just bury me somewhere. Or maybe, I thought, they might stick me up front at a highly visible desk and expect me try to look important. I'll bet, I speculated, they'll want the protesters on the street to be able to see me, so I guessed I'd be a front-of-the-newsroom kinda guy. Some of my old high school buddies and some of my college frat brothers had been hired to keep their new companies out of trouble with the feds, and with the Civil Rights Movement. Their job titles were sometimes ambiguous and sometime bigger than their paychecks. I was determined not to allow that to happen to me. And it didn't.

The news director, Austin Bridgeman, never seemed to know quite what to do with me initially. But then he hit on the idea of having me tag along on assignments with veteran anchorman/reporter Chris Condon and his crews for a couple of weeks. Keeping up with Chris was a challenging first test. The guy worked tirelessly. Twelve-hour days including field reporting and anchoring the evening newscasts were a normal and regular schedule. He took on the task of training the new, inexperienced recruit admirably. Condon was a great teacher. I think he would agree that I was a quick study. I've always thought, and still believe, that it isn't all that hard to be a good reporter. And, as controversial as my stance is, I don't think many, if any, journalism schools can prepare a hopeful better than actual experience on the beat. On the new job, I really just asked the questions I thought Van would ask. And that was my guiding light for the more than three decades that followed my traipsing around with Chris Condon.

Then came my first assignment without Chris. I had imagined that the station would have sent me on some stupid little local story on my very first assignment. So imagine my shock when I learned that I was going to be dispatched to a biggie at Ft. Leonard Wood. With me was a three-man crew and a ton of equipment. We would fly to the story site in a borrowed old twin-engine Beechcraft owned by the *Post-Dispatch*. The story? There was a meningitis epidemic at the Army base!

As the old aircraft strained to get off the ground with all that weight, I thought to myself, "Well, they can always say they tried to initiate a Minority Hiring Program, but it never got off the

ground." Or perhaps there was some sinister plan to have me contract meningitis and that would get rid of me. But I did the story and returned safely as the prelude to a very long career of delivering glad and sad tidings in town, across the nation, and around the world. I think Van would be proud.

After nearly five exciting years as a reporter and eventually a weekend anchor, I was wooed by Channel 4 General Manager Tom Battista. He made me an offer I could not refuse, and I jumped to Channel 4. "Pinky" Gunther scoffed that I wouldn't last a year at Channel 4. I was there twenty-eight years.

ON THE COURT WITH ARTHUR ASHE

Don't believe everything you've read about the incomparable tennis phenom Arthur Ashe. Although he was, indeed, born in Richmond, Virginia, just three months before I was born in St. Louis, Arthur did *not* graduate from a segregated high school in Richmond. He graduated from a segregated high school in St. Louis, and I know that for sure because he was my classmate and archrival. We did not do battle on the tennis court; we once did battle on the Sumner High School auditorium stage.

Just when I thought I was BMOC, Arthur Ashe rode into town on a white horse with a tennis racket in his holster. And just like a metaphorically mixed pied piper, Arthur, or "Spider" as we began to call him, soon led the attention and the girls away from guys, including me, who once held sway.

Arthur had fled the segregated South on the advice of his Lynchburg-based mentor and coach, Dr. Walter "Whirlwind" Johnson, who felt Arthur's sky would otherwise have a low ceiling. Dr. Johnson arranged for the rangy kid with inimitable potential to move to St. Louis in his senior year. In St. Louis, still very segregated just like Richmond, Arthur would live with and get coaching from the legendary Richard Hudlin. The municipal tennis courts in St. Louis's Forest Park are named after Hudlin, whose home was the pad from which Arthur's superstar rocket was launched.

When Arthur rode into town, some of us guys thought that basketball, football, and baseball were the only manly sports. What was this "tennis" thing? What a "sissy" game, we thought collectively. But then we noticed how much hard-driving practice the new kid put into his game under the tutelage of Mr. Hudlin. He worked at least as hard as the junior varsity guys in training.

Before we tough guys knew it, Spider had unwittingly snagged a lot of our girlfriends in his web. Some of the girls were beginning to buy tennis rackets! Mary Dixon became the first girl to try tennis at Sumner with Arthur as her idol.

In 1960, I was senior class president of the oldest high school for blacks west of the Mississippi; president of the A Capella Choir and one of its student piano/organ accompanists and

Tennis Team

Mr. R. H. Hudlin, Coach

Eliza McClure, Victor Kirkpatric, Romond Turner, Arthur Ashe, Mary Dixon, Manager; Mr. Hudlin, Coach; Carl Bibbs, Captain; Thomas Spearman, John Pena, Jimmie Colbert, Willie Johnson, (not shown).

student conductors; president of the Spanish Club; and the president of, and often leading actor in, the Carter G. Woodson Dramatic Club. I once played the lead character in Moliere's *The Miser*. Still, I lost out to Arthur, who courted one of my crushes, Sheila Grimes, and stole the attention of another cutie, Helen Wade, voted as the girl with "Most Personality" by our senior classmates. I was Mr. Congeniality, so to speak.

As my popularity began to slip, I stooped to some actions of which I am not particularly proud. I once openly made fun in class when Arthur was giving an oral report. My derision sprang from the way this Southern import pronounced *hospital*. I piped in just loud enough for the students around me to hear: "That's *hospital*, Spider, not *horsepital*! There's no horse in hospital." It got a few giggles but accomplished nothing longterm. For the entire time he was at Sumner, Arthur's Southern twang shone, along with his blazing tennis racket and shy nature. The skinny kid had charisma!

Maybe, I thought at one point, Arthur would fall for Mary Dixon, since she obviously had fallen head-over-heels for him and had started to learn tennis. Mary once had a bunch of us kids over for dinner at her house on Windsor Place, down the street from

36

where I lived. I whispered to the person sitting next to me to look at how crudely Arthur held his knife and fork. Out of bounds, Julius!

The underhanded attempts to compete with Arthur had less effect than a performance, rendered in a dignified manner and setting, that restored my rusting crown to luster. The school history department decided to hold a mock presidential election debate to mirror the real one between Richard Nixon and Jack Kennedy. Guess who was chosen by lot to portray whom? Meet Arthur Richard Milhous Nixon Ashe versus Julius John Fitzgerald Kennedy Hunter. And our wives were, Pat Sheila Grimes Nixon and Karen Jackie Kennedy Thomas, who came complete with a pillbox hat. With these two gorgeous women, this was truly a mixed doubles match if I ever saw one.

Arthur studied up on the Nixon platform when he wasn't sweating it out on the tennis courts, and I perused Kennedy's positions when I was not rehearsing for *The Miser*. On the day of the big debate, Arthur and Sheila strode onto the stage in their Nixonian style; Karen and I took the stage in our best Kennedy impression. Since I was sure that Arthur's drawl would make Nixon sound like a Son of the South, I decided to sound like I was born and reared in Massachusetts.

Let the debate begin! Arthur shot volleys and I returned them. I fired my killer serve and Arthur smashed back. The penchant for the "win at all costs" approach, which later permeated my TV news career, reared its head for one of the first times.

After a grueling match, the game was over and the balloting began. The sponsors of the program and all the kids voting should have known that there was no way "Richard Nixon" was going to pull off a victory against "JFK" in an all-black high school in 1960. Even the student odds makers couldn't get extra lunch money off this contest. "Kennedy" won in a landslide!

Sumner Holds Mock Election

Sumner High School held a mock election on October 20, 1960. It was conducted by the Social Studies Department and many students participated in it.

Speeches by those representing the candidates and the members of their parties helped the students to choose the man they felt was capable of becoming our next president.

Miss Ida Goodwin was the mistress of ceremonies. Those representing the two main candidates on the Democratic ticket were Julius Hunter as Senator John F. Kennedy and Arthur Ashe as Senator Lyndon B. Johnson. The campaign for this party was conducted by the A Cappella Choir and managed by Harvey Vaughn.

The students portraying the two main candidates on the Republican ticket were Ronald Glenn as Vice-President Richard Nixon and Samuel Hutchinson as Senator Henry Cabot Lodge, who is also the United States delegate to the United Nations. This campaign was sponsored by the Student Council and managed by Samuel Hawkins.

Other participants were Mary Dixon, Sheila Grimes, Leoner Shelton, and Karen Thomas as the candidates' wives.

Following the demonstrations by the audience and platform guests, each student returned to his homeroom where ballots were issued. Kennedy was the winner of the election and the choice of Sumnerites for the next President of the United States.

And that is how I once beat the great Arthur Ashe in the only way I could—not at his game but at mine.

I learned that Arthur still kept in close touch with Sheila as his career roared toward the skies. I took Helen Wade to the Senior Class Lunch, eventually lost touch with her, and, just ten years after the Great Sumner Debate of 1960, got a job in television news.

Arthur became the first African American to win the U.S. Championship at Forest Hills, and among his many, many other accomplishments on the courts, he became the first black to make it to the finals of the South African Open in apartheid-tarnished Johannesburg. And by the time he rode back into town in 1973, he had become a formidable international voice for racial equality and justice for all. When I found out he was coming to town, I invited him to come to Channel 5 to be my guest for a sit-down interview. Arthur was too much of a gentleman to hold a grudge against me for my immature high school antics, not to mention the thumping JFK and I had given him. I read somewhere that Arthur once said: "I think Republicans tend to keep the ball in play, Democrats go for broke." Wonder if our mock rumble influenced that view.

On the set, we reminisced about the good-old carefree days, when he had brought an excitement about tennis to Sumner, where some of us skeptics thought it would never catch on. When I asked him during the interview how he got his initial interest in tennis, he gave two reasons: 1) his father worked for the Richmond city recreation department and maintained the largest playground—including tennis courts—for blacks, and 2) tennis was just something to do when he was a kid. We talked about some of his concerns about humanity and how each of us has a responsibility to make the world better for all people. He certainly did his part.

How wildly odd it seemed to me that here we were again—high school rivals with one of us much more secure that his charm and skill would win out. Here we were back on that stage at Sumner High. This time the roles were obviously reversed; I give the match to Arthur . . . hands down!

Ethics (or Lack Thereof) in TV News

The news media, in general, and television news, in particular, is often demeaned by sensitive viewers as having little taste and no ethics. It is still true after decades of criticism that the abiding watchword in TV newsrooms is: "If it bleeds, it leads," meaning that the goriest, most sensational stories on a given day get the number one slot on a newscast. And, the most sensational stories of the day are used to "tease" the viewer and create an appetite for tuning in later. You will hear ten-second teases throughout the day that say things like:

"Popular local restaurant burns to the ground! Details at ten."

"A recall of a major toothpaste brand. Don't brush your teeth till you check out what brand it is tonight at ten."

"Four students shot at a local high school. We'll take you to the hospital, and the morgue, following tonight's Country Music Awards."

Over the years, whenever I was chastised by a viewer who was sickened by these ratings-driven teases, I've responded that the news stations are serving up nothing more than that which viewers want. I have seen it happen all too often that motorists and passengers stalled on the highway by a massive traffic accident will get out of their car and walk a quarter mile to get up close to the mangled carnage. In fact, another truism in the news service is that if a station wants to perk up the ears and focus the eyes on a particular story, make a statement like this: "Coming up after this commercial break, some footage you may find hard to watch, especially if you are an animal lover . . ." or "When we come right back, a story filled with language you may find objectionable."

We are known to pander to the lowest common denominator in the race for highest ratings. But TV news operations are not always whores. I can sight many examples of the media exercising restraint, good taste, and mature judgment. As senior anchor, I squawked so much about Channel 4 showing fires in

abandoned buildings just because the flames were spectacular that we virtually stopped showing valueless video of these blazes. But, if the fire was started by homeless people trying to keep warm in that abandoned building; if the fire represented the latest in a string of arson incidents; or if the fire in the vacant building came dangerously close to an occupied structure, then the fire was fair game in my book. If there were extenuating circumstances or a message that came as a warning to viewers, then my news philosophy was to broadcast the story.

We must always be on our guard if we want to claim high standards to avoid airing a story just for its salacious sensationalism.

I remember a story that really put the ethical standards of local stations to the test. A gunman who appeared to be both drunk and deranged took hostages at a local bar. He eventually released all the hostages but remained holed up in the bar. After many hours of refusing to come out, the gunman conveyed to police that he would come out if all the TV stations on the scene would come up to the entrance so that he could be assured that police would not harm him as he surrendered. The police chief at the time, Gene Camp, mulled over the request and then gave his approval. I was on the scene and didn't think much of the permission given to move right up to the door with my photographer. When our cameras were all neatly assembled in front of the bar, the gunman came into plain view and began to ramble off a slurred spewing of gibberish. He put the gun to his head several times and threatened to blow his brains out. He threatened, and threatened, and then he did it. In plain sight of all of us with cameras rolling, the poor guy pulled the trigger and sprayed his brains all over the place as he fell to the floor. Right on camera.

We had not yet entered the era of live camera shots, which meant that the stations had to process their film. And if ten minutes worth of film was shot, it took ten minutes to roll through "the soup." If thirty-one minutes of film was shot—you got it—we had to wait thirty-one minutes for processing before the film could be put on the air. If it was really a hot story, the freshly processed film would be put on the air raw and unedited.

So, as the news director, you know that your photographer has close-up video of a drunk man putting a pistol to his head and blasting a fatal hole in his head with blood spraying everywhere. Okay, news director, do you:

a. Race the film to the processor and throw it on the air unedited?

b. Check the edited film to see if you can air it right up to the gun blast?

c. Wait until you are sure the man's family has been notified and air the entire episode?

d. Scrap the entire filmed incident, refuse to air it, and destroy the film?

Should the time of day the video would be aired make a difference in your executive decision? If you decide to use the gory video, would it fly as tastefully at noon, five, six, and/or on your late newscast?

This is a very typical situation a news director, executive producer, reporter, and general manager must respond to on a regular basis. Have you decided yet what you would do? You have, perhaps, already taken more time pondering this situation than the professionals have at their disposal.

Here's what happened: Only one local station showed the actual suicide—in living color. I was proud of our station for not showing it.

Here is another question for you as a viewer. Should a reporter get important information for you using deceit and any other means necessary to get the story?

There were many instances in which I resorted to outright trickery to get newsy information from an unwitting interviewee. In November 1970, just after Senator Ted Kennedy had returned from attending the funeral of Charles de Gaulle, he spoke in St. Louis to an East Coast university's local alumni group. The word had been put out that the senator would do absolutely no interviews. But being the cub reporter at Channel 5 at the time, I was dispatched to get a certain story at any cost.

The tabloids were exploding with the allegations that Senator Kennedy had had a dalliance during the period of mourning in Paris with a certain "Italian princess."

My crew and I arrived at the downtown hotel where Senator Kennedy was the keynote banquet speaker. Sure enough, there were more gatekeepers and security blockades than one could imagine. Dejected, I sat in the hallway trying to figure out what I could do, since, in those days, when a reporter was sent out on a story, a certain time block was left open and the reporter had better fill that time with something.

Before I came up with a plan, in strode a new friend, Senator Tom Eagleton. He asked why I was sitting in the hallway, and I told him that I was barred. The senator, using an epithet, said he'd get me in. And sure enough, telling all the security forces that I was with him, he marched me right up to Ted Kennedy and introduced me as his friend who wanted to ask just a couple of questions.

"What do you want to ask me?" Kennedy wanted to know in that unmistakable Massachusetts brogue that made "ask" sound like "ahsk."

"Nothing in particular," I lied. "Maybe something about the problems with the Alaska Pipeline and gas prices . . . maybe reflections on the de Gaulle funeral."

"Ah, yes, I'll answer a question of two," Kennedy said. "But I won't comment on that ridiculous tabloid story coming out of Paris . . ."

I agreed to avoid that story, ordered the camera and lights turned on, and then rambled on about a couple of insignificant items—including Kennedy's presidential aspirations. And then:

"Senator, I know you don't want to talk about that rumor mill story from Paris. May I ask why not?"

Kennedy, realizing that he was on camera, said: "I don't want to dignify that trash with any comments. I'm not going to help those baseless stories about my private life. Thank you."

Kennedy was not at all pleased. It was an ambush, for sure.

And without a handshake or any other farewell greeting, the senator turned on his heels and began pressing the flesh of his adoring fans.

That night on the late newscast, a beaming anchor and mentor Chris Condon, introduced me as: "Julius Hunter, the only reporter in the world to get a comment from Senator Ted Kennedy on rumors swirling . . ."

Ethics? Maybe not.

DIRTY TRICKS FOR THE QUICKER FIX

dirty tricks: (1963) underhanded stratagems for obtaining secret information about sabotaging an enemy or for discrediting an opponent (as in politics)

—Merriam-Webster Dictionary

dirty tricks: unethical behavior especially acts undertaken to destroy the credibility or reputation of an opponent

—American Heritage Dictionary

The world's greatest journalism schools have no coursework in a tool that every good journalist, print or broadcast, will use at one time or another to one degree or another. I have yet to find the j-school professor who will admit that a little larceny creeps in when pursuing some challenging goals. To put it plainly, the reporter who is too ethical to employ an occasional "dirty trick" will not see "award-winning" attached to his or her name. I'm not talking about tricks that are flat out illegal. I'm referring to those near-pranks that are employed to give an enterprising and creative reporter or news operation the scoop, the exclusive, the leg-up on a key story the competition does not have.

Two of the biggest scoops of my career have involved abductions—with yours truly choosing the role of abductor and two notable citizens as the abductees. And both incidents—as with many escapades—are steeped in politics.

To appreciate the symbiotic relationship between TV and politics, you'll note that the Merriam-Webster citation points to a specific year in which the term "dirty tricks" was coined. You'll also find the name of one H. R. Haldeman. In case you've forgotten who he was, or never knew or might not care, Haldeman, paired with John Ehrlichmen, made up one half of President Nixon's Frick and Frack of Dirty Tricks. Actually, it was a Nixon operative, Donald Segretti, who made dirty tricks an art form. Segretti was a master of the unsigned pamphlets strewn around to damage an opponent. Candidate Jones prints a lot of nasty, perhaps racially charged, dirt about himself and blames

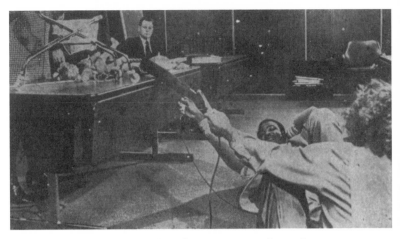

It sometimes takes a twisted angle to get a straight angle on a story.

it on Candidate Smith so that Candidate Jones can gain sympathy from fair-minded people. Then there are the so-called "push polls" where phone bank operators call voters and say something like, "We know for a fact that Senator So-and-so admits that he smoked pot and snorted coke in college. Do you think that fact makes him unworthy to be president?" Another dirty trick is for the supporters of Candidate C to jam the phone banks of Candidate D so that no calls can come in or go out of the opponent's headquarters on Election Day. Segretti actually spent some time in the slammer—four months of a six-month sentence—to serve as an example that dirty-trick crimes do not pay.

In reality, they often do. Tricks were employed in American politics as early as the 1790s, when presidential candidate Thomas Jefferson hired an unscrupulous journalist to write a lot of untruths about rival candidate Alexander Hamilton.

Merriam-Webster specifies that politics is the mother of the invention called "dirty tricks." In television news particularly, getting more scoops generally translates into higher ratings, which translate into more revenue for a station.

One of the few post-Watergate dirty tricksters to serve actual slammer time and pay a hefty fine for his misdeeds is Allen Raymond. He once ran a company called GOP Marketplace, which on the surface provided telemarketing services. As the name implies, the actual premise of the company was to get out the vote for Republican candidates at the national, state, and local levels of government. On the morning of November 5, 2002, Raymond's firm, hired by New Hampshire Republicans, jammed Democrat-based

Getting the scoop at any cost.

election efforts by clogging up the Dem's phone bank with more than eight hundred computer-generated phone calls in a ninety-minute time frame.

In February 2005, for his and his company's sins, a federal judge in New Hampshire fined Raymond $15,600 and gave him five months behind bars to ponder the error of his ways. But Raymond is likely to recoup the fine he paid, and more, with his bestselling tell-all book called *How to Rig an Election*.

Raymond apologized to the judge on his way to the pokey and said, "Your Honor, I did a bad thing." A bad thing, indeed. But there are still news of blatant dirty tricks in every election . . . most recently in the 2008 presidential race. A group that claims to comprise military veterans began spreading the word in January 2008 that GOP presidential candidate John McCain gave away vital strategic information to his Vietnamese captors when he was being tortured for five and a half years in a concentration camp. During McCain's 2000 bid for the White House, some of his detractors spread a rumor that he had fathered a black baby. In actuality, McCain and his wife had adopted a child from Bangladesh.

There was also push-poll mudslinging in the run-up to Election Day 2008. Senator and candidate Barack Obama was a Muslim and had taken the oath of office for his Senate seat on a copy of the Koran and not on a Bible. Neither is true.

I can tell you after serving on the inside for more than thirty years that there are plenty of print and broadcast journalists who might consider push-polling and distributing leaflets with flat-out lies a mere prank. They'd tell you that everybody is doing it, so it must be a fair game. If no one was killed or maimed, I was, during my tenure as a TV news anchorman and reporter, a staunch supporter of a dollop or a wallop of chicanery every now and again. Several cases come to mind without much dredging.

It was a day when all the local print and broadcast media were staked out near the Jefferson County courtroom waiting for the prime suspect, recently captured for a heinous double murder and now appearing for arraignment. We would be allowed to shoot pictures through the courtroom window, but we could not enter the courtroom. I walked down to the pay phone at the end of the hall and made a call that yielded a hot tip. A well-placed source on the other end of the phone told me that sheriff's deputies would bring the suspect through a back entrance of the courthouse. My source was sure that the ETA was going to be about five minutes. I whispered something quickly—a mock message—in the ear of each member of my news crew seated, alongside all the other print and broadcast reps, outside the courtroom.

Suddenly, the Channel 5 team—my three guys and me—leaped out of our seats, ran down the courtroom steps, jumped into our news wagon, and roared away, burning rubber. The news crews from all the stations raced out and followed us in hot pursuit. But our driver, photographer Dick Deakin, careened around a corner and swung around into an alley. He then rumbled back to the courthouse, losing our pursuers. We had doubled back just in time to hop out and shoot the shackled suspect getting out of the sheriff's car and being escorted, with a deputy on each arm, into the courthouse through the back door. It was the classic "perp walk" that the paparazzi and the arresting cops just love. Sometimes, even the perp seems to relish the exposure. I'm almost ashamed to admit that, yes, I did ask the stupid "cub reporter questions," thrusting the shotgun mike towards the alleged bad guy: "Did you do it? Did you kill those two people? Was it a drug deal gone bad?" Of course, the prisoner didn't answer a single one of these questions. Why should he convict himself on the way to his arraignment?

With exclusive "Eyewitness News" footage in the can, my crew and I walked around to the front of the courthouse where our colleagues were just getting back. The buzz on why and where they had been diverted and bamboozled began to circulate quickly. As a Vesuvius began to brew, I decided to go around back and wait in the news wagon.

In a different instance, when I was covering a story for Channel 4 in 1990 on the levee in the shadow of the Arch as part of a series about firefighter training, we were shooting rookie firefighters being trained in the use of aerated foam for extinguishing chemical fires. While talking foam, my crew and I were among the scores of people who watched a humongous oil barge slam into an Eads Bridge abutment. I immediately got on the two-way to the newsroom and said cryptically in my best code:

"Hunter to newsroom! Hunter to newsroom! Got an exclusive! Will be our lead at five o'clock! Do not try to contact me for the next 15 minutes. Do you copy, newsroom?"

" Copy, Hunter. Copy. Where are you?"

"Cannot say. Trust me. Over and out."

The crew and I, as if we did this every day, hopped in the news wagon and raced to an area south on the levee where a tugboat was docked. I quickly found the captain of the *Mary Burke* and told him what had just happened. I asked him—no, begged him—if he would take us out to the leaking barge less than a thousand feet north of us. He agreed, and off we bobbled toward the leaking barge. The pilot remarked that he hadn't ever seen the Mighty Mississippi so, so mighty! The waves were worthy of surfers' delight. But I became very uncomfortable aboard the good ship *Mary Burke*. And after just a few minutes of the rough ride, I was glad I had skipped breakfast and hadn't had lunch yet.

The oil spill was sadly spectacular. There were hundreds of gallons of oil spewing into the river from the ruptured barge. Bobby Baur, a veteran photographer, got some great up-close shots, but enough already. We were getting slammed around the deck till it was beginning to hurt. The seaworthiness of the *Mary Burke* was really being put to the test. I took command of the craft and gave the good captain the order to take us back to dock. I could take no more. But the good news was that we were going to have some incredibly graphic and exclusive footage to show our viewers what a nasty oil spill looks like.

When we got back to the dock, I thanked the captain, thanked God, and, just for good measure, thanked my lucky stars that we landlubbers had made it back from a roaring, churning, angry river. I gave the *Mary Burke* a "thank-you" pat, and we headed back towards the news truck.

Had I known what would happen to the *Mary Burke* just a few weeks later, I would have dropped to my knees and kissed the levee cobblestones.

Imagine my surprise when I saw a Channel 2 crew shooting away from the shore. How did they find out about this so fast?

When I got close enough to ask reporter Gene Randall, he winked and whispered, "'Cause, we monitor your radio and knew that you were on the riverfront doing your firefighter foam story. When you radioed to your newsroom with alarm in your voice, we decided to high-tail it down here."

Well, I'll be damned, I thought. My station monitored all the police and fire emergency radios on both sides of the Mississippi, but we never had stooped low enough to monitor the messages of our news competitors at Channels 2, 5, 11, and 30.

There went my big exclusive on the oil barge rupture, but we got those SOBs back that day. After a little huddle in the Channel 4 newsroom, we conspired to completely re-code our radio transmissions. First, we would refer to north as east, east as south, south as west, and west as north for the rest of the day. And every now and again one of our reporters would come up with something like this:

"Jackson to newsroom! Jackson to newsroom! Do you copy, newsroom?"

"Roger that, Jackson Crew. We copy. What's up?"

"We have got one helluva fire out here! Apartment complex! Fully engulfed. I . . . I . . . I think there are people trapped."

"What's your 10–20, Jackson Crew? Over."

"We're in the Central West End. Eichelberger. Near Warson Road. Forty-four hundred or forty-three hundred."

"Can you give me a cross street, Jackson Crew?"

"Yeah! Yeah! Cross street is St. Louis Avenue. St. Louis Avenue!"

"Roger that, Jackson Crew. Eichelberger and St. Louis Avenue. I'm sending two more crews and I'm putting the chopper up. Over."

"Over and out newsroom. We'll report back in a few minutes. This fire is unbelievable. Never seen anything like it."

Well, I have to confide in you that a) there was no fire at all, b) Eichelberger is nowhere near the Central West End, c) Warson Road is not in the city—it's in the suburbs, d) St. Louis Avenue is nowhere near Eichelberger. St. Louis Avenue is in North St. Louis; Eichelberger is in South St. Louis, and it is absolutely impossible for the twain to ever meet . . . except in street-scrambling from a major earthquake.

We chuckled with glee as we learned from a couple of monitoring posts that our opponents were scrambling all over town trying to find stories that just didn't exist.

By the way, remember the tugboat my photographer and I went out on to shoot the oil spill? Well, it sank in the Mighty Mississippi in waters far less turgid than what we'd witnessed.

Two of the crewmen aboard the *Mary Burke* were lost when the towboat sank in fifty feet of waters just a few weeks after Bobby Baur and I steamed out to get close-ups of the oil spill. Four other men aboard the towboat were rescued. The Coast Guard Search and Rescue Unit determined that the exceptionally swift Mississippi, coupled with the high water, contributed to the accident. The *Mary Burke*, according to a Coast Guard spokesman, had gotten caught sideways in the high raging current, and water roared in through the engine room and flipped the boat over and under. The accident might have been avoided if the towboat had only been hooked to a barge, the Coast Guard spokesman said. The boat that took us out to the oil spill was located underwater about 420 feet off the levee where we had encountered Channel 2's crew. I learned a lot about Mississippi River service boats after the *Mary Burke* was lifted and put back into service. Nelson Spencer, Sr., publisher of the *Waterways Journal,* taught me that the vessel that had taken my photographer and me on the harrowing ride out to the oil spill site is really not a "tugboat nor a towboat." Nelson schooled me on the fact that the craft, because of the shape of its bow, is more properly called simply a "harbor boat," a "switch boat," or a "fleet boat." Jim "Goat" Patterson, who runs the harbor off downtown St. Louis, let me know something else that most assuredly would have kept me from going out on the raging river that summer day in 1990. He helped create a little knot in my stomach by telling me that the *Mary Burke* sank, not once, but twice in swollen, fast-moving currents. And "Goat" informed me that you'll find that boat this very day operating under a new name after its two horrific baptisms. Her new moniker, he told me, is the *Jackie Sue.* And this master of the river trade confirmed for me something I've always known: We should never underestimate, not even for one second, the power of the Mighty Mississippi.

Back to the necessity of journalistic dirty tricks. Some of the mildly larcenous antics that have come out of my little black bag included two abductions pulled off in 1972 while at Channel 5. The first involved the kidnapping of East St. Louis's first black mayor. James L. Williams, Sr., was a soft-spoken, low-key guy with no visible ambition. Yet he did have aspirations for his disintegrated city. If you got Williams talking even softly, you learned that he wanted to be the David to conquer the town's gargantuan crises.

In fact, there was an actual Goliath against whom Williams faced a formidable uphill battle to become the mayor in 1972. That giant of the Old Machine was none other than Charles Merritts, an ambition black man who desired to be the first African American mayor of East St. Louis. Merritts' past and present associations at the time were shady at best. When he ran for mayor, he owned a taxicab company, a nightclub, a construction company, and a number of liquor stores. Some sources swore that Merritts was pulling in as much as one hundred grand a year, but that number may be low. Merritts, who became head of the East St. Louis School Board, was eventually nabbed for taking kickbacks and for shoving a pistol into the chest of a school supplier in the attempt to net $30,000. What's more, Merritts was busted for trying to hire an undercover FBI agent to snuff out a rival school board member, Clyde Jordan, an unfettered critic of Merritts' school administration.

Williams' campaign to become mayor seemed downright dangerous and foolhardy to political observers. However, by a very narrow margin, the meek underdog won! Within minutes of the Election Board declaring Williams the victor, I grabbed the arm of the startled winner and almost threw him into our news wagon. Away we went! We moved so fast in snatching Williams, the competitor stations weren't able to react quickly enough to stop me. As we roared west over the Eads Bridge, I told His New Honor that I wanted to give him a good "first interview" as East St. Louis's newly elected leader. I was afraid that if I didn't get him first and exclusively, those other animals in the print and broadcast media would eat him alive in a crude, rude way. No question about it, Mayor Elect Williams seemed as if he had been hit with a stun gun.

I radioed ahead and told our assignment editor to hold a spot at the top of the upcoming Noon News for an exclusive with the new mayor. We had about twenty minutes until air time, so I told the mayor to relax in my office and that we would get him a cup of coffee. He asked for tea instead. No problem. If he had asked for a Scotch and soda, I would have found some way to keep him contented, comfortable, and out of sight of my rival reporters. At noon, Dick Ford and Lee Shepherd, the regular hosts of the Noon News on Channel 5, introduced the proud reporter who had pulled off a coup. I conducted the chat from the interview set to the right of the anchor desk. Yeah, I tossed softball questions. I felt a bit sorry for a guy who was about to take a thankless and near-impossible job. His beloved city, which ironically had been named by *Life* magazine in 1960 as the "All-American City," was crumbling with a bleak prognosis. After about four minutes of interview, a long time for a TV interview, I thanked the mayor, and Lee and Dick thanked both of us.

I was told by a newsroom staffer, as Williams and I unclipped our mikes, that there were a couple of TV news crews outside our station along with a couple of newspaper reporters. They were gritting their teeth, cursing the day I was born, and doubting aloud that my parents were ever married. Knowing their anxieties, I moved slowly as I took the mayor back into my office, where I ordered up another cup of tea and asked how I might help him, short of becoming his press secretary. Sadly, he asked me if I knew where he might buy some inexpensive suits, since the one he was wearing was the only one he had. I said I could get him a card to join the Government Employees Mart, where discount clothing was sold. I knew he would not be able to purchase suits at Famous-Barr, where I bought mine.

I thanked Williams and escorted him to a back door at the station where a news wagon drove us slowly across the river to East St. Louis. He did not appear on the other stations until their five o'clock newscasts. Pity. All's fair in love . . . and news coverage.

In that same year, 1972, I committed another celebrated abduction. Just as soon as we got the wire service bulletin that Democratic presidential aspirant George McGovern had just named St. Louisan Tom Eagleton his vice presidential running mate, we got a big tip. Senator Eagleton's older brother, Dr. Mark Eagleton, was on the golf course at Bellerive Country Club, an exclusive golf sprawl in suburban St. Louis. In a flash, my crew and I raced out as we often did into the general direction of a story with absolutely no confirmation that our targeted subject was, indeed, at the terminus of our destination.

Sure enough, upon reaching Bellerive we learned that Dr. Eagleton was out on the links. We didn't bother to ask permission if we could trot out and find him. In fact, we gave a little spending money to a keeper of the caddy shack to borrow a golf cart, and off we went again, headlong without specific directions. Somehow we found Dr. Eagleton, and with all of the camera-rolling splash of the Publishers Clearing House million-dollar check bearers, we informed Dr. Eagleton of the high honor just given to the senator from Missouri. We captured pure elation and even a tear or two from the good doctor who whooped with joy upon receiving the news we broke to him.

Then with all of the skills of a newsman who had pulled this kind of trick before, I convinced Dr. Eagleton to drop his game, drop his partner, and hop in the cart with my crew and me. In retrospect, I think Dr. Eagleton was in such shock he would have boarded a spaceship at that moment. We raced back to the station while I gave Eagleton every unconfirmed, unverified assurance I could think of that we would provide the fastest opportunity to getting him hooked up by phone with his brother in Washington, D.C.

"Hunter to Desk. Hunter to Desk," I radioed ahead to the station's assignment desk.

"Go ahead, Hunter," a voice crackled back.

"I have the package. Repeat. I have the package. Please effort a hardline hookup with Little Brother and the package. Over," I instructed in my best code to avoid any of the competition getting a tip-off on what would be a major scoop.

"What's your E.T.A., Hunter? Your E.T.A.?" the desk responded asking about my estimated time of arrival at the station.

"Make it twenty to twenty-five, desk. Clear a spot on the early with brotherly hookup. Over," I ordered.

"That's a roger, Hunter. Roger that. Efforting that hookup now," the desk assured me. Over and out."

"10–4, desk," I blurted with excitement that the desk was working on an historic telephone hookup.

Just in case Dr. Eagleton was not following that amateur, but official-sounding code, I explained it to him as we exceeded the speed limit eastbound on Interstate 70 headed for downtown and the station.

When we roared into the newsroom, several staffers cheered and applauded Dr. Eagleton. Some of the old-timers rushed up and congratulated the good doctor who was drenched in perspiration from, no doubt, his harrowing ride down the highway. One would have thought our guest had just been picked as McGovern's running mate.

I spirited the doctor away from the staff crowd and all the

questions they were asking him and took him into the little office I shared with sportscasters Jay Randolph and Ron Jacober. Dr. Eagleton requested a glass of water, and I got that ordered up. We had almost forty-five minutes to kill before the five o'clock newscast. But within half that time we were informed that phone contact with Senator Eagleton had been made.

After a stop by the men's room to pat off some of the glistening perspiration and other things done in a restroom, I proudly led Dr. Eagleton into the studio where star anchor Chris Condon was waiting for him on the anchor set. With a couple of seconds to go before airtime, the doctor asked if he could speak to his brother before he went on the air. The answer was a polite but firm no from Chris and the stage manager. The idea was to get the fresh, unrehearsed first reaction from the two brothers.

After the musical news opening that was composed and played nightly to stir a sense of urgency—even if nothing urgent was going on—Chris set up the big news and then told our audience that we had the senator's brother in the studio as the camera shot widened out. And Chris quickly congratulated the doctor and told him Senator Eagleton was on the other end of the line.

What great television! A thrilling, chilling moment. And let the other stations eat their hearts out. I didn't get any on-air credit for the abduction, but I got a sufficient number of "atta-boys" from station management that I knew would be a feather in my next raise. In a quick huddle outside the studio door while the two brothers were engaged in lively on-air chat, news director Austin Bridgeman, assignment editor Warren Kiesewetter, and I decided to try to hold on to the doctor through at least the top of the six o'clock newscast so we could plaster the big EXCLUSIVE key over a replay of the first conversation between the two brothers after McGovern's announcement. It became my job to devise a stalling scheme . . . a craft for which I became a quick study.

At the end of the on-air interview, I collected Dr. Eagleton and purposely took him the long way around and back to my little office.

I made a telephone available to him to make any calls he might want to make from the station to family and friends. I was relieved when he took me up on my offer.

Without eavesdropping entirely on the doctor's conversations, I could tell that he was using the quiet of my office and the phone availability to contact and whoop it up with close family members and friends to his joyous heart's content.

And then a bit of "the con" that is partially learned, but also partially genetic, I think . . . I whispered to the doctor to be sure to tell the people he phoned to watch at six because we would be running a videotape of the entire first post-announcement conversation between the two brothers.

"Will we be on again at six?" the doctor asked with a bit of incredulity?

I assured him that not only would he be on at six, he would be welcome to wait in the control room to watch the replay before we headed back out to the country club. That seemed to please the good doctor, and I was thrilled to hear him include the replay message at six to the next several people he phoned. The gentle larceny of the tactic here, if you have not already divined, was to keep the doctor tied up at our station and away from any possibility of going live at the top of any of the competitors' six o'clock newscasts. All I would have to do was keep Dr. Eagleton at the Channel 5 studio till just five minutes after six, and I would spoil any opportunity the competition would have for an interview.

And the strategy was very obviously bearing fruit. The news director, with a snicker and grin, pulled me outside my office to say that the competition was waiting on the sidewalk out front in an angry line demanding that we free Dr. Eagleton! He said there were not only TV crews out front, there were even radio and newspaper people demanding the liberation of Mark Eagleton.

It was good to know there was a howling mob outside the station's front door on Olive Street, because we would be exiting out the back door and into a covered garage before we rolled out onto the street headed slowly, slowly back west to Bellerive.

Glued to the monitors in the control room, Dr. Eagleton watched the interview footage with glee. And then I told him we would take him back out west. I wondered quite often in the days and weeks after the kidnapping of the senator's brother that there was a big difference in the speed we got him down to the station and the speed—or lack thereof—with which we took him back. My big brother, Van, at whose feet I had learned the art of the con, would, I was sure, be proud of me.

It was ironic to me that this was the second time I had seen a big protest demonstration outside the Channel 5 studios. The first was just before I accepted the job at Channel 5.

A PEARL OF WISDOM

When I was a cub reporter, I was dispatched from the Channel 5 newsroom to interview the inimitable Pearl Bailey in the sweltering summer of 1971. I was so green that my head could have been used on a traffic light. I had been on the job as a TV news reporter for less than a year! "Pearlie Mae," as her closest friends called her, was in St. Louis to take on the spirited title role of Dolly Levi in *Hello Dolly!* at the outdoor Muny Opera in Forest Park.

Ms. Bailey was no stranger to me at all, and I was excited about interviewing her . . . even on the short notice I was given. I had only about half an hour—during the drive from downtown to Forest Park—to think up some clever questions. But that is the typical amount of prep time for a reporter doing interviews. Sometimes it was better, though, *not* to get too much notice, because it is possible for a reporter to worry him or herself silly rehearsing a line of questioning over and over again. For example, when I got several weeks' notice that I was going to conduct a secret, exclusive, one-on-one interview with incumbent President Ronald Reagan, I must confess my stomach was in knots for weeks. But when I got the one-minute notice that I would be talking on-air to President Jimmy Carter in a shore-to-ship phone call while he sailed the *Delta Queen,* I hopped into action, fueled strictly by adrenaline, and didn't collapse until the historic interview was done.

When I was a young boy, I had seen Pearl Bailey's act several times live at Kiel Auditorium. She would come into town with her husband, drummer Louie Bellson, and the two of them would play the big "Y" (for YMCA) Circus. The "Y" Circus was the biggest annual event in my old neighborhood. There were some good and novel acts that performed at the show, which was produced by popular Antioch Baptist Church preacher James Cook. And there were some real "dogs" that wouldn't have lasted ten seconds in the *American Idol* competition. The "Y" Circus brought with it a festive atmosphere to the old neighborhood as handbills and big, colorful posters plastered everywhere announced the show dates.

Below: Pearl Bailey in St. Louis Woman, *1940s. Courtesy the Library of Congress.*

Right: In 1971, Pearl Bailey performed at the Muny in Hello, Dolly!, *where she gave the author his very first celebrity interview.*

The show was easy for my whole family to attend. Tickets were set at modest family-friendly prices, and we could jump on the old Hodiamont Streetcar twelve hops and a skip from our front door on Vandeventer. And everyone in the neighborhood gathered at the streetcar stops all along the Hodiamont line. It was fiesta time in the 'hood!

Other than Pearlie Mae's comedic antics, one of the most interesting acts I remember was the acrobatic dancing skills of a fabulous entertainer named "Peg Leg" Bates. And, you got it, his tap-dancing, whirling, jumping, leg-splitting stage act was all done on one real leg and one wooden leg. Ah, how he took to the air with the greatest of ease, but I always wondered, as just about everyone else did, if it was painful to land on that stump leg. Peg Leg always left the audience spellbound and always on their feet at the spectacular finish to his act.

Pearl Bailey was always a riot of sultry song and crazy comedy. In fact, even when I was a kid, her act reminded me of my mother, aunts, and other female relatives when they came home from their jobs as domestics. Pearlie Mae's act always included her complaints on stage that her feet hurt. Her shtick was that she was always just flat out tired, Honey. In fact, that fatigued foot syndrome was the name of one of her hit songs, "Tired." She'd complain about her general weariness, to roars of laughter from the audience. When she established her condition through comedy, something everybody in the audience had heard from at least one relative at home, Pearlie Mae would kick off her shoes and look for a place to plop down. The genius of Pearlie Mae's comedy act was that while she was effecting a credible impression of the simple-minded, uneducated, lazy cleaning lady, there was not a soul in her audience who didn't think that an exceptionally bright and clever artist was hidden underneath the hilarious subterfuge.

When my film crew and I arrived just outside the Muny Opera amphitheater on that sweltering late-June day, it was the first time in my life that I would interview a big star I recognized from my childhood. Ms. Bailey, who would have to endure the St. Louis heat on stage for an entire week, approached me with her Muny Opera escort just outside the historic amphitheater. She was dressed in a cool-looking, backless, flowery summer dress. Her golden brown shoulders glistened under the spaghetti straps attached to the halter. I was really "buttoned down" that day, as I was wont to be in the earliest days of my career. A suit, long-sleeve dress shirt, necktie, and shoes that were as shined as allowed to a properly dressed reporter in those yester years. My dapper grade school teachers, Messrs. Burnett, Evans, Young, and Hartfield were surely proud of my attire as they watched me on the nightly newscasts. Proper dress in my cub reporter days was not like it is today with TV news reporters, male and female. Jeans have become the foundational attire for whatever a reporter—or anchor at the formal anchor desk—wears these days. Presentable dress is only done from the waist up. I remember on that blistering hot day when I met the legendary Lady Bailey, I wore a blue plaid jacket. How do I remember the jacket? Well, before I could even introduce myself, Pearlie let out with a: "Oooh, ooh wee! Look at this young man, Honey. Now, who in the world do we have here?"

I fumbled badly. "I . . . I . . . I'm Julius Hunter . . . Channel 5 Eyewitness News, ma'am."

"Is that your whole name, Honey Chile?" she asked while obviously having fun with me like a cat with a cotton ball on a string. "I mean, that 'Eyewitness News' part. Is that stuck on your name?"

"No, no, ma'am. I'm just Julius Hunter," I answered as if I was being excoriated, which I was.

"So, you've already changed your name with that 'Eyewitness News' thang on the end of it to 'Just Julius Hunter?'" she mocked.

I was totally flustered and would have been red-faced, I'm sure, if my skin were not about the same hue as Ms. Bailey's. But I have to say here, she had the most beautiful, smooth, unblemished copper skin I had ever seen before and rarely since. But I digress. Again.

"Well, what can I do for you, Mr. Just Julius Hunter?" She obviously knew why I was there. But she was obviously messin' with me. I'm sure, in retrospect, Pearlie Mae was just trying to put some starch in the collar of the perspiration-soaked shirt worn by an obviously inexperienced reporter. Her Muny Opera escort looked slightly amused; slightly embarrassed.

"I'm here to interview you . . ."

"About what, Honey?" She was really pressing me and having fun right up to her smiling, twinkling eyes, which became more squinty when she smiled.

"Uh, uh . . . about your career . . . and, uh . . . how you like working here at the . . ."

"Honey Julius, do you plan to interview me in this hot weather with that damn jacket on? Take it off, take it off, take it off, Chile!" she said as she made a back-flipping motion with one hand. She used a big, white hankie to dab the gathering perspiration on her forehead with the other hand. "I'll wait, Honey."

Pearl got the author to loosen up.

I wrestled with the jacket to get it off in a hurry. If my jacket was all that stood between me and an interview with this queen of comedy, I'd get rid of the sucker! I handed my jacket to one of the guys in my crew.

"Now, don't you feel better, Honey?" Ms. Bailey asked. "Dontcha? Tell me true . . ."

"Yes, ma'am. A lot better," I agreed. I was fully unaware that I was addressing her with the ultimate in respect as "ma'am," just like I did with my teacher, my mother, my aunts, and my grandma.

"Okay," she said. "Now, let's get that tie off, too. I ain't talkin' to you till you get comfortable." She folded her arms to wait.

So, off came the tie in a flash. And then a modicum or two of starch appeared in my wilted collar: "You're going to let me keep my shirt on, aren't you, ma'am?" I asked in mock timidity in the humidity.

Miss Pearl let out a hearty, throaty, sandpaper laugh, and her unexpected amusement infected all of us standing there.

Pearl Bailey had a lot going on in 1971, the year she made

me perform an impromptu striptease on the Muny grounds in Forest Park. In addition to her starring in *Hello Dolly!* in 1971, she started hosting her very own short-lived TV variety show on ABC that year. And 1971 was the year in which her autobiography, *Talking to Myself,* hit the bookshelves. My conversation with her—after she broke the ice we desperately needed on the blazing hot summer day—was a breeze. A cool breeze.

I can say, in all honesty and candor, that Pearl Bailey was the first in my career to teach me to relax; not to take myself too seriously; and to incorporate humor, when appropriate, in every interview. Those are qualities about which I've received compliments for more than thirty years after that indelibly wonderful interview nearly forty years ago.

And here is testimony to the comfort level she inspired in my anchor delivery for three decades: In the summer in particular, as my career and comfort level took off, I finally came around. I took a lesson I learned from stories about the inimitable network anchor David Brinkley, who reportedly riled his more sedate co-anchor, Chet Huntley, by kicking off his shoes before each newscast. That feels really comfortable, my friends, especially relaxing when you are rattling off distressing news of death, destruction, and disaster. And during the summer months, well into my career track, I very often wore shorts under natty top-half attire. I got compliments from all over about how well-dressed I was, but I would never ever accept any awards for "Best Dressed Anything."

Thank you, Pearl Bailey, for teaching me to cool it, and never take myself too seriously.

THAT'S MR. CHILD
TO YOU

During my first year out of the chute as a reporter, I encountered many trials and tribulations, all of them unexpected. But I never thought for a moment that my personal safety would have been put on the line by the husband of a world-famous chef.

Yes, that's right. If not killed, I might have been summarily thrown on my butt by a guy more than twice my age. By my math, which has always been suspect, in 1970, my opponent was sixty-eight years old; I was just twenty-seven.

Here's how it happened: Channel 5 had dispatched me, as one of my first assignments, to interview famed chef of French cuisine, Julia Child. How exciting! I love to cook, and I used to watch Chef Child on KETC, the PBS television station in St. Louis, fairly regularly.

When my crew and I arrived at the old Famous-Barr department store in suburban Clayton, I had cooked up plenty of questions for the illustrious interviewee. And I was fully prepared, in the "Eyewitness News" tradition, to don an apron and have Chef Child give my viewers and me a few kitchen tips for our newscasts later that day.

As my crew and I entered the auditorium at the department store, I was shocked to be physically restrained by an elderly, distinguished-looking gentleman. "May I help you, young man?" the senior sentry asked rudely as he blocked our admission.

Taken aback, I said: "I'm Julius Hunter, Channel 5 Eyewitness News. I'm here to interview Julia Child."

This guy was totally ignoring the fact that there were three grown crewmen with me lugging a ton of equipment necessary in those days to film an interview. The self-appointed guard demanded: "Show me some I.D."

"I.D.?" I asked incredulously. As I looked around, one of my colleagues from another station was already interviewing Ms. Child, and others were setting up. I would bet my last dollar that none of them had been challenged in such a brusque manner. My immediate conclusion was that I was being stopped because of my skin color. All of my colleagues on the other side of this one-man barricade were Caucasian.

"Yes, I will need to see some I.D.!" the older gentleman insisted as he put his hand on my chest to restrain me.

Well, I must say that the physical contact caused me to lunge toward him defensively, and we found ourselves nose to nose. And his nose was considerably more pronounced than mine. In fact, after later learning that he was Julia Child's husband then of twenty-four years, the whole scenario seemed patently absurd and regrettable.

As we found ourselves almost leaning on and pushing each other, the lovable Helen Weiss, the May Company director of special events, did her best boxing referee impersonation. Helen literally physically separated us.

"Gentlemen, gentlemen . . ." Helen intervened to pour cold water on the hot fire that had erupted.

"This man will not show me any identification," the red-faced Paul Child gave as an excuse for his intervention.

"I'm not showing this son of a bitch any I.D.," I yelled in very uncharacteristic determination . . . and profanity. "He pushed me! He touched me! He put his hand on me!" I shouted.

"Settle down, Julius. Settle down," Helen advised. She must have realized that my temperature was hotter than my adversary's. She then turned to my opponent. "Mr. Child, he's alright. This is Julius Hunter. He's from Channel 5, and he's on the list of reporters we invited to come out today. Julius, this is Paul Child, Julia Child's husband."

This would have been a perfect opportunity for us to apologize, shake hands, and move on. But the scowl that remained on this man's face left no room for me to offer anything conciliatory. He made no concession; I made none. And we simply turned and put some distance between ourselves.

"Come on, guys," I said to my crew. "The 'bouncer's' going to let us through," I said in provocation, causing Mr. Julia Child to make a start toward me again. My guys and I proceeded up to the front of the auditorium where they began to set up and we began to wait for our turn for an interview with the great culinary genius. I kept looking to the back of the auditorium, and I didn't see Mr. Julia Child challenge anybody else who came into the room. My initial conclusion that Paul Child didn't like blacks was reinforced. Or maybe he was just suspicious of a black guy in a commanding position. Or maybe his wife was preparing food and hadn't fed him his lunch yet.

The altercation did nothing to make the interview as warm and as friendly as it might have been. I think Julia was totally unaware of what had gone on at the entrance to the auditorium, but I wasn't as loose and glib as I might have been without that near-pugilistic incident.

Chef Child burbled, gurgled, and bubbled a promotion of her then new book, *Mastering the Art of French Cooking, Volume Two,* in her incomparable style of speaking. The new volume had just come out of the oven, so to speak. She had written the book with her close friend and associate, Simone Beck, and Child had decided to write a second edition of their French cookbook with Americans in mind. Volume One of the book had come out in 1961, she told me.

I must say that I was overwhelmed by Julia's height, and quite frankly I was distracted by it. I'm six feet tall; she must have been at least a couple of inches taller than I am. I may be wrong, but her answers to my questions sounded a bit soaked in the cooking sherry that was on the console. But I could be wrong.

After the interview was over, my crew and I made our exit, intentionally blowing by the still-angry old man, Child. I know. Childish on my part.

The next day, I went to an encyclopedia and several other reference books—there was, of course, no Internet in 1970—and I discovered that Paul Child had had quite a distinguished career with the U.S. State Department. He was ten years older than his wife, and he had traveled the world. Paul Child was also an artist and poet of some note.

My sour opinion of the man was confirmed when I read a copy of a letter that he wrote to his brother soon after he met his future wife, Julia. Paul stated that she was a "sloppy thinker" who was "unable to sustain ideas for long." He bragged that "she also washes my shirts! Quite a dame!" Chauvinistic, elitist snob!

And then I read something about the cranky old guy that produced a little knot in the pit of my stomach and a little lump in my throat. In fact, HE could have easily put a knot in the pit of my stomach and a lump on my throat! Paul Child, approaching seventy years of age I learned, was a master of the martial arts! At the time I had my confrontation with him he had held a black belt for a long time in judo! If provoked any further, or if dear Helen Weiss had not stepped in to referee, the tiny Child might have flung me into the next county!

I could see the headline that would have appeared the day after I encountered Julia's hubby:

ZOO STORIES

Some of the wildest assignments in my cub reporter days were nothing short of animalistic! The best of them included a giraffe drop, a cobra cop, and a big cat/little cat bumper crop. And all of these stories in my earliest days in broadcast news happened in the feature-friendly confines of the zoo. Whose zoo? The world-class Saint Louis Zoo.

I determined quite early in my formative years at the NBC station in St. Louis—then KSD-TV and KSD Radio—that I wanted to be a feature reporter covering more mirth than murder; more good times than bad slimes; more humorous than hazardous news. And what better place to hang out than the Zoo?

The first Zoo story I want to share with you concerns a mother giraffe named Reggie. She was ready to drop a calf while I was a cub in August of 1970. I was on the scene to film a play-by-play Eyewitness News account with highlighted bits and pieces to be played back later in the day's newscasts. None of the following kibbles and bits would constitute Peabody Award entries. They were presented back then just to give our viewers a break from the traditional "downers of the day." And nothing gets an audience's attention and its oohing and ahhing to a higher level of appreciation than stories about children and animals.

This Zoo report on a hot and steamy August day in St. Louis was "eyewitness" news in its most literal form. Charlie Hoessle, who was general curator at the Zoo, provided me with excellent background material for the upcoming birth. Reggie (actually Reggie II, after her mother), Charlie taught me, was a *reticulated* giraffe. Guess I could have said that Hoessle *articulated* that the giraffe was *reticulated,* but I didn't for some reason. Charlie would occasionally lay a little genus/species stuff on me to give my viewers the erroneous notion that I knew what I was talking about. I could pepper my reports with enlightened descriptions like "the Giraffa camelopardalis's period of gestation will come to termination with sensation today." Just give the pronouncement a slight British accent and you can sound like naturalist/zoologist Sir David Attenborough. Try it with your friends next time you're describing an animal delivery! Or a human delivery.

They'll be impressed, I'm sure.

And, of course, if you're going to effectively give details of an animal birth, you've got to lay on that *sotto voce*. You know, the same voice used by announcers during televised golf tournaments.

Charlie then told me news that would make the animal lovers in my audience a little nervous. It was very common for a giraffe to drop a young 'un right smack dab in the middle of the outdoor paddock in plain view of any spectators. That, said Charlie, is for two reasons: 1) the delivering mother finds it more comfortable to walk around a lot to facilitate the emergence of the baby, and 2) the newborn would enter the world with a thud after being dropped about five feet to the ground, according to Charlie "to get the newborn's breathing started; the mucous jarred, and the heart rate going. A splat does that." Hmmm. Jarred mucous. I'll pass on lunch, thank you.

Courtesy Saint Louis Zoo

I milked the giraffe birthing for every cornball pun I could think of. I mentioned that Reggie wasn't taking this birth "lion" down. I noted that it would be a "stretch" to say that the delivery was going to be easy. I recorded that the elephants had brought their trunks for the smaller animals to stand on to get a better view. And I was a bit critical of Jeep, the father-to-be. He was not around for the birth. Does that make him a "deadbeat dad" even before he became a dad? But I cushioned the Jeep jab by noting how squeamish many new human dads can be.

With camera and play-by-play rolling, I calculated and articulated "the blessed event" without a hitch. And all kidding aside, I was astounded by how quickly the newborn—nameless at birth—was up and walking around. Within fifteen minutes! And, no doubt, she was surprised to find so many of us in the delivery room. The newborn's quick pop-up to a standing position was just one of nature's protective elements to discourage a hungry lion from getting too excited about a creature that laid around on the ground for a few hours. (I had, tongue in cheek, suggested that the newborn rose to its feet so quickly because it found its mother and all us gawkers on our feet.)

> *Giant, gawking great giraffe*
> *Why fear the gentle gerbil?*
> *Just glimpse the rodent's photograph*
> *And you will feel just terbil.*
>> —*Julius K. Hunter*
>> Absurd Alphabedtime Stories
>> *1976*

On another memorable reporting assignment at the Zoo, I was actually allowed to sit in a cage with some newborn tiger cubs crawling all over me—cubs on a cub reporter; five of them, in fact—shortly after they were born on July 9, 1972. At that time, Charlie Hoessle was the curator of reptiles, and he set up the interview. So why would the curator of reptiles be in a position to introduce me to tiger cubs? "Well, in those days we acknowledged that the reptile keepers generally had a lot less work to do than some of the other Zoo staffers," Charlie told me. "So, those of us reptile keepers would try to help out some of our colleagues in some of the busier areas. We'd often babysit big cat cubs for days at a time in the reptile area. In fact, a few times some of us would even take newborn cubs home with us to bottle-feed and take care of them till they required less care and surveillance." And in a recent phone conversation, Hoessle remembered me as a skinny young reporter who was more than a little nervous with the cubs walking all over Charlie and me. I mimicked the memorable faces that Johnny Carson put on when he was presented with flapping, hissing, growling, spitting, panting, and generally unmanageable guest zoo animals.

"Should I be scared?" I asked Charlie, with camera rolling.

"No," Charlie assured me. "These little guys are gentle and not dangerous at this point. And if you were around them later in their lives, you would not want to show fear. Predatory animals sense fear and often challenge it. Look at the paws of these little guys and you can tell how big they're going to be."

"Well, I plan to end this interview before their bodies catch up with their feet," I said, getting a chuckle out of Charlie and my film crew.

The Saint Louis Zoo often had bumper crops of big cat cubs.

The specter of a tiger maiming was most recently raised when a tiger somehow got loose at the San Francisco Zoo on the day after Christmas in 2007. The big cat killed one person and injured two others. And the audience at a Las Vegas Siegfried and Roy show was stunned on October 3, 2003, when Roy Horn, half the team, was dragged offstage like a rag doll by a seven-year-old white tiger. Those headlines might have made me a less-willing "eyewitness news" reporter back then had they happened around the time that I semi-bravely climbed into that cage with Charlie.

"Looks like they like you," Charlie said assuredly back in that 1972 in-cage interview. "If they *really* like you, they will wet on you."

Feeling a warm, wet spot on my left knee covered by the pant

69

leg of my new tan suit, I said: "Well, this little fella right here must *really* like me. Really, really, REALLY like me."

More laughter all around.

"And, Charlie . . ."

"Yeah?"

"You're sure they won't bite me?"

"Right."

"How do you know they don't prefer dark meat?"

Raucous laughter to close the interview.

And Charlie, who for twenty years served as director at the Saint Louis Zoo, a position once held by the internationally acclaimed zoologist Marlin Perkins, told me in a recent conversation that no reporter would ever be allowed inside a cage with cats of any size or age these days because of the potential danger and the liability. Thanks, that makes me feel really good.

On the subject of reptiles, I happened to be around when one of the most sensational Saint Louis Zoo stories of all times was unfolding. It was, what I called in my feature report, "The Case of the Vanishing Viper." The African spitting cobra flat out disappeared from its cage on August 18, 1970. But the media and the general public were not informed about the mysterious disappearance until weeks after the fact. In a recent conversation I had with him, Charlie admits that Zoo officials may have made a mistake in holding on to the information on the vanishing act for so long. I remember that there was a lot of flack fired from the *Globe-Democrat* and *Post-Dispatch* editorial pages at the Zoo's management. "We didn't want to set up a panic," Hoessle explained to me. "We were relatively sure the snake wouldn't make any daytime appearances and was hiding somewhere in a crawlspace, crack, or crevice," Charlie told me again recently. This was a restatement of exactly what he had told me during an on-camera interview at the Zoo nearly forty years ago.

"But we were well aware of what could have happened if

some visiting grandmother with her grandkids came face to face with the snake," Charlie continued. "It could have been a nasty situation if the snake had bitten either of them or sprayed them with blinding spit."

In my little feature bit with Charlie, in which I suggested we were "Sleuths of the Slither," we each took a flashlight and, mostly for the camera, went on a Great White Hunter—and I suppose a Great Black Hunter—mock search for a reptile I was secretly hoping and praying we wouldn't find. "Let's hope we come up 'snake eyes,' eh, Charlie?" I had to throw in the overly occasional trademark Hunter cornball of the era. I was really hoping to become a fine feature reporter. "Maybe we could name the snake, Bill Bailey," I suggested. "Then we could sing that song 'Won't you come home, Bill Bailey?'" (Boy, was I desperately bad back then!) Charlie, who was being a good sport on camera mainly to keep the community from going berserk, told me during our "hunt" that the Zoo had been getting calls from all over town. There were "sightings" here and "sightings" there that proved to be unbelievably bogus. Some of the suggestions were from honestly caring would-be helpers; other tips were from folks who had perhaps been smoking some of the "snake in the grass" grass.

"We went running off to North St. Louis on a tip that the cobra was lurking in a resident's basement behind a furnace," Charlie remembered. "We checked, and the sighting turned out to be an old fan belt. Another 'sighting' in the little park across the highway from the Zoo on Oakland turned out to be a decaying banana peel. And we got more advice by letters and phone calls than you can believe from citizens suggesting how we might lure the snake back. There were several suggestions that we find a charming female snake to offer mating opportunities to the missing snake. And we got our fair share of people suggesting that we play loud snake charmer's music over the Zoo loudspeakers," the now-retired Charlie Hoessle remembers. I could tell during a recent conversation all these years later that Charlie was not quite ready yet to have a hearty ha-ha about the cobra story.

As humorously as we played this "exclusive" Eyewitness News interview back then, this was no laughing matter for Charlie and the overwrought, hand-wringing Zoo crew during those dark days of 1970. They patrolled the grounds day and night for twenty-four-hour stretches. They baited traps with mice. They

Absurd ALPHABEDTIME Stories

by Julius K. Hunter

dusted areas with flour to see if they could detect any slither marks.

The snake turned up all on its own on October 6, after a seven-week absence and was snared with a grappling stick. "It was the most tense period in my whole career," Charlie admits. Wonder how it was for the cobra?

> *Some say snakes seem sorta sad,*
> *But in the chats with snakes I've had*
> *I've found them glad to slink and slide the way they do.*
> *So some slow snakes don't show sharp smiles?*
> *They're merrier than crocodiles!*
>   —*Julius K. Hunter*
>   Absurd Alphabedtime Stories
>   *1976*

BETTE MIDLER AND THE FLAMINGO KID

It is not often that a rank amateur rates a two-and-a-half-minute interview on your nightly newscast. After all, the Evening News is not *American Idol*. So the newsmakers you see are likely to have been around a while and have already made their mark in politics, entertainment, sports, or one of the other arts. That is why it was a particular kick to interview a then little-known Bette Midler back in 1973. Bette and I had been in the public eye just about the same amount of time. She released her first album, *The Divine Miss M*, in 1972. I had started out as a TV news reporter just two years earlier.

It was a campy first meeting, and it was the direct result of my having done a lot of narration work for the St. Louis Symphony Orchestra. If I did *Peter and the Wolf* and a *Young Person's Guide to the Orchestra* once, I did each about three dozen times before tens of thousands of kiddies at Powell Hall. In the early 1970s, the symphony was a co-sponsor of the wildly popular Mississippi River Festival (MRF) held just outside of St. Louis at the Edwardsville, Illinois, campus of Southern Illinois University. The spot was found to be perfect as the orchestra was looking for a pastoral venue for outdoor concerts. SIU-E offered up a 260-acre outdoor space with a naturally sloping amphitheater. A stage, a large circus tent, an acoustical band shell, and a state-of-the-art audio system were set up on the site. Then somebody got the bright idea that the site should be used for more than classical concerts. Much more. And so the idea was hatched to hold regular symphony performances as well as pop, jazz, rock, blues, folk, country, ragtime, vocal, theater, and dance concerts on the site. The entertainers and fans that eventually flocked to the spot made the SIU-E plot legendary. I attended several concerts with friends sprawled on a blanket. There were folding chairs up front for a good fee, but sitting on the grass was a less expensive proposition. There was even an evolutionary step up here from sneaking kids into drive-in theaters in the trunk of the car to people learning how to slip into the largely unfenced Mississippi River Festival grounds without a ticket. And sometimes, depending on the

Courtesy SIU–Edwardsville Archives

size of the crowd, some fences were broken down.

A normal-size traffic-snarling crowd was about four thousand, but the crowd that turned out for a concert by The Who was estimated at thirty thousand. Janis Joplin opened the place with a bang—and a lot of straight Southern Comfort—on July 1, 1969. Ironically, Bette Midler would portray Janis in the movie, *The Rose*, ten years after Janis played the MRF, and six years after Bette walked on the MRF stage for the first time.

So Bette Midler's agent, Aaron Russo, was no slouch in booking her into the MRF in the summer of 1973. (We'll get back to Russo in a moment.) Bette put on a wild, raucous, and memorable concert at the MRF on August 28, 1973, as part of her thirty-six-city tour. One reviewer said of the three-hour set that Bette "was all over the stage like a crazy woman." And he said that one of her antics was like "cakewalking at triple speed as if she were strobe lit from the inside." The *Alton Telegraph* called the show an "outrageous . . . bizarre, but entertaining concert."

The Divine Miss M's act was preceded by a few major acts, including Kenny Rogers and the First Edition on August 24, followed by Chicago, and then Pat Boone kicked around with his blue suede shoes two days before Bette's gig. What a heck of a swing from Rogers, to Chicago, to Boone, to Midler, to Crosby (minus Stills) and Nash to close the 1973 MRF season. Creative booking, eh? Early in the summer season, there was a lot of guitar strumming on the MRF stage at a time when there were nearly as many folk singers as there were folks. Joan Baez, Bob Dylan, Arlo Guthrie, Judy Collins, John Denver, Joni Mitchell, Jim Croce, Harry Chapin, and tons and strums more were all there. But then, too, eventually, were the Grateful Dead, Ike and Tina Turner, REO Speedwagon, the Fifth Dimension, the Beach Boys, the Pointer Sisters, and dozens more.

Courtesy SIU–Edwardsville Archives

With the exception of playing small clubs, stage productions, and even bath houses, Bette Midler was far from a household name on August 27, 1973. That's the memorable date on which I sat next to Bette on a rumpled sofa in a cramped, dinky little motel room. This was far from the big time. In fact, we were in a place on the outskirts of Edwardsville in Mitchell, Illinois, of all places—thousands of miles from New York, Detroit, Las Vegas, and L.A. In many respects, Mitchell is much farther than thousands of miles from the lights of the big city. Mitchell was a town where you would expect to find the Philadelphia Cream Cheese on the gourmet shelf, but that's where I found this newcomer, Bette Midler.

Her handlers—perhaps at the direction of the strong-willed, Rasputin-like manager/lover, Aaron Russo—were very guarded and restrictive about their ward. They hovered and recorded every word of my interview with Bette in their hawk-like vigil,

Mississippi River Festival Background

The Mississippi River Festival became too big for its bridges. And fences. And toilet facilities. The crowds that started out to number around 4,000 swelled to as many as 30,000, packing Woodstock-style onto the 260 acres of once-bucolic property. But more problems were concomitant with the sardine packing. Fistfights fueled by alcohol and heavy drugs broke out all over the place all the time; the billows of marijuana that wafted over the pastureland gave new meaning to secondary high. To combat the blatant use of heavy drugs during the MRF concerts, a special unit called ACID RESCUE was formed. Members of this unit, with their white arm bands, would roam the concert grounds and cart away any spectators who had passed out or were acting erratically and take them to a special "tent of immunity," I'd call it. That way they would not have to come into contact with police. At least a couple of fatalities were reported from drug overdoses. There were widespread thefts and pickpocketing reported. And the roads and bridges around the concert site became frustrating car-strangled spanners as patrons tried to get onto the grounds or tried to flee them at the end of an evening. While all of these destructive concerns were taking place, the state of Illinois reduced its subsidies to the university. The university/host finally turned the Mississippi River Festival over to an outside management firm. That arrangement lasted about three years before the management company finally threw in the towel—onto which some underage drunk patron probably barfed.

The Allman Brothers closed out the MRF with a final show on June 22, 1980. Today, nearly forty years since its debut, there is very little visible to demonstrate that the festival was ever on the site. Trees, brush, and wild grass now cover an area that once rocked and rolled like few other outdoor venues have.

but they seemed to back off from their tightness a bit when it became obvious to them that I was the darling of the Symphony Society and had been quid pro quoed into the only one-on-one interview her handlers had allowed.

The mercurial chanteuse was like a little unkempt knot of a gnome: red, untouched-by-a-stylist hair; a prominent schnoz, freckles, and very pale skin. She couldn't be a hair over five feet tall. And she was in a rather cheesy-looking terry cloth robe. Some men might describe it as a "birth control robe," because one look at it and no intimacy is encouraged. Of her wardrobe she wore on stage the next night, the *Alton Telegraph* observed, "She comes on stage looking like a truck driver in drag . . ." But I found something honest-looking and non-intimidating about Bette's appearance. Sort of like the next-door neighbor you might have had to wake up after midnight to give you the spare key to your house she keeps for you to replace the one that you've just lost. I felt comfortable talking with her right away.

She sounded like a young, sultry, nasally Sophie Tucker. Almost everything she said sounded sexy, even though she didn't look so sexy at the time. Ms. Midler told me about being born in Hawaii and never feeling that she was one of the pretty girls, because at her school with all the Polynesian and Asian kids, she was the only "colorless" girl in her class. She told me that being Jewish didn't get her any extra points with her classmates. Then she taught me a new word. She said, "I was the only *haole* in the class. That's Hawaiian for 'the only white girl in the class.' hah-OH-lee," she instructed me.

I jumped in with "Better a HAOLE than an Ass HAOLE!"

We laughed uproariously at my blue ad lib. A handler scowled and feigned a gag, but most of the stuff that came out of Bette's mouth was blue or double entendre, at best. It was the same kind of stuff Bette batted back and forth for more than a half-dozen appearances with Johnny Carson on his late night show. A lot of her chat with me, as later with Carson, had references to gay or lesbian stuff. From her, it seemed more natural than offensive. She would never have offended the share of her audience that held her in the highest esteem. I sensed that the Divine Miss M soon felt as comfortable with me as I felt with her.

Bette proceeded to lay more effacement on herself. She wanted me to know that when she was younger she thought of herself as an ugly little Jewish girl who had a lot of problems adjusting.

"Adjusting to what?" I asked.

"Life in general," she responded.

I asked her if it was true that she actually got her start singing in a New York bathhouse, and she told me that she did, indeed, and had made as much as fifty dollars a night singing. Her debut was made at a bathhouse called the Continental. I asked her if she was expecting to make a little more than fifty bucks at the MRF concert the next night. She chuckled as she called up her thickest New York accent to say, "I sointly hope so." We both laughed.

She offered up that singing in one of the world's most celebrated bathhouses had gotten her a large following of gay guys. "But," she quickly chimed in, "so does Streisand. And I think that puts me in good company, dontcha think?" She gave me a wink.

I didn't know it at the time, but the Continental Baths was set up in the basement of New York City's old Ansonia Hotel in the 1960s. The spa can serve up to one thousand gay men at any time 24/7/365. Patrons can avail themselves of all sorts of dalliances in the cabaret, disco dance club, giant swimming pool where splashing in the nude is expected and no big deal, a mammoth Turkish bath, saunas. And the "cover" charge to get in to uncover was a mere eleven to fifteen dollars when Bette started singing there.

The entertainment in the Continental's cabaret was first class for a place homophobes considered low class. In addition to Bette—with Barry Manilow playing the piano as her accompanist—the patrons heard the likes of Cab Calloway, the Manhattan Transfer, Melba Moore, John Davidson, and even Metropolitan Opera diva Eleanor Steber. In fact, when Bette was belting out old standards at the Continental, she told me that she used to complain that trying to sing over the very loud water cascade really pissed her off. The waterfall didn't seem to bother Manilow, though, who always accompanied Bette wearing only a white bath towel in the exact style and positioning his audience wore.

And why was her backup group called the Harlettes? I asked her. "Does that have anything to do with Harlem?" I asked, giving her a nice, big, fat set-up line.

"Of course not, dahling. They're called the Harlettes because they're whoores, dahling. Whoores!" she said a second time for emphasis, with the Bronx pronunciation of what might be "whores" in Edwardsville or St. Louis. "They're trashy ladies just like me, and I love 'em dahling. Just like me! Trashy."

When I asked her if being a big-time singer was her ambition when she was a young girl, she responded, "No, sweetie, I always wanted to be the Sanitation Commissioner in New York City. Get it? I'm trashy. Trash. Sanitation Commissioner."

That was Bette's "funny" response to the question of what she wanted to be when she grew up. But those in the know say that Bette had repeatedly demanded of her one-time manager/lover, Aaron Russo, the fulfillment of her "serious" dream: that he make her a LEGEND. Maybe that demand, if it is true, was the spark for, and the underlying but ultimately unjustifiable reason for the reported domestic violence that ensued between Bette and Aaron.

I began to wonder if a large part of Bette's day and night was spent trying to overcompensate and cover the fact that she had a rather pesky, recurring inferiority complex. She had an incredible voice, but she was short and not a raving beauty. How real was her own self-effacement? I wondered then and have pondered the question since.

But then, my Channel 4 co-anchor of nearly ten years, Steve Schiff, told me why Bette might have had some self-esteem problems. Aaron and Steve and a bunch of other guys were best buddies. "In fact," Steve told me, "the movie *The Flamingo Kid*, starring Matt Dillon, was written about our gang by another of the guys 'Turk' [Russo] and I grew up with."

"You kiddin' me?" I asked.

"No, no," Steve assured me. "Turk and me and my buddies hung out with Neal . . . Neal Marshall. And Neal sold his screenplay about our gang of buddies to Garry Marshall, the producer. But in the movie we were all sixteen year olds. Me, Turk, Jeff Robinson, Jerry Portnoy, Al Zimmerman, Billy Schecter, and a few other guys."

"You never told me that," I said in genuine astonishment.

"You never asked me," Steve said.

"I gotta admit that I didn't see the movie. I will now," I promised. "But is it true to life? Which kid in the movie are you?"

"Well, I'm the kid ironically named 'Steve,'" Steve told me. "In the movie, I'm having a thing with a rich babe and spending a lot of time with her in the family mansion. The girl's father is played

A "Flamingo Kid" and the author.

by Richard Crenna in the flick. The girl's moneybags dad, played by Crenna," Schiff continued, "spends a lot of time at the El Patio Beach Club playing high stakes gin. And every time he got *gin* he'd lay his cards down and say, 'Sweet Ginger Brown!' That was the name of the screenplay before Producer Garry Marshall changed it to *The Flamingo Kid.*"

"I never knew," I said, as if I knew the story lines of trivia about ANY movies. "Go on," I coaxed. "What were some of the parts of the real-life story of you and Turk and the gang that couldn't be put in the movie?"

"What's the statute of limitation on . . ." Steve chuckled. "The movie obviously was toned down to protect the guilty."

"Fascinating," I said, hoping to draw out more.

Steve continued, "We parked cars at the El Patio Beach Club because that was the only way we poor guys could get into the club to check out beautiful babes, drink a few gin and tonics, and maybe get a few phone numbers."

Steve continued, "In the movie, 'Steve' gets caught in the back seat with a chick."

"Was that Steve, or 'Steve' in the back seat with the girl?" I asked, to give Steve wiggle room he didn't need.

"Well, let's just say I should have known from living that scene in real life what was in store for me for the rest of my life with ladies."

"I get your drift, my Brother," I acknowledged. "But let's go back to Turk. I wanna talk about Turk, Bette's manager and lover. Aaron. First off, how in hell did he get the name, 'Turk?' Was he Turkish?"

"I don't think so," Steve opined. "We called him Turk 'cause he looked like one . . . a Turk, we thought. Dark. Swarthy. Could look really menacing sometimes. But I believe his parents were Sephardic Jews and came from somewhere in Morocco."

MATT DILLON ● RICHARD CRENNA ● JESSICA WALTER

"Well, if his parents came from Morocco, why didn't you guys call him 'Rocco?'" I suggested just to be corny. "'Rocco from Morocco.' Wouldn't that have worked better?"

"I guess we weren't as smart then as you are now," Steve suggested like a guy who put up with my corn on-air for ten years.

"But Russo?" I asked. "Isn't that Italian?"

"It all beats me, Jules," Steve offered to get off the hook to explain how Turk was a Sephardic Jew from Morocco with an Italian last name.

It actually beat me, too.

Changing the subject just a bit, I asked, "So how and when did Turk hook up with Bette?"

"I'm not exactly sure when they got together. But eventually our gang of guys knew Turk was dilly dallying around with Bette. That's how he got his interest in show biz. Just before he met Bette, he was part owner/bouncer at a place in New York called the Electric Circus, kind of a hot spot for a while. I think that's probably how he met her. I think she might have been a singer there."

This was getting juicy. "What was their relationship like?" I asked.

"Well, it was hot, spicy, and rocky, I'd have to say," Steve told me.

"How was that?" I continued my line of questioning.

"Well, Turk used to slap her around from time to time. One time, my Dad and I met up with Turk and Bette in New Orleans. Nice girl. I liked her. But I think their relationship was strange and kinda sick, if you ask me."

"Strange? . . . and sick? . . ." I asked in my best reportorial extraction technique. Few words in the question. Keywords only.

"I gotta tell ya man, Turk was no midget; he was built like a bull. He proclaimed himself Arm-Wrestling Champion of the World. And I remember, one time he took down former heavyweight wrestling champion, Bruno Sanmartino, on the arm-wrestling table in a bar. And I don't think it was any kind of fixed deal. In fact, when word would spread around that Turk was going to take on somebody in arm wrestling—oftentimes at Falcaro's Bowling Alley—when the betting began, you were a fool not to put your whole paycheck on my man, the Turk."

"So when he gave Bette a whack . . . she would really know that she had been hit," I projected.

"Yeah," Steve went on. "He'd give her a rap across the kisser with an open hand. Stan [Steve's dad] and I saw that in New Orleans one time. But that was one minute, and then the next minute, they'd be all lovey-dovey as if nothing had happened. And then I knew she'd look a little bruised sometimes, but soon she'd be sporting some new jewelry or other bauble or bangle, and she'd be all cuddled up with Turk, and they'd look like two lovebirds. Strange?"

"Strange," I agreed. "And sad . . ."

The tempestuous, off-again-on-again relationship lasted for seven hellaceous years for both Turk and Bette. Russo became a filmmaker with Eddie Murphy's *Trading Places* to his credits. And he was always fired up as a Libertarian Party activist. Tragically, Turk contracted bladder cancer and died on August 24, 2007, at age sixty-four—the same age Steve and I were at the time of his passing. Bette has, to my knowledge, never admitted in any interviews that she and Aaron had actually broken up. When asked about their torn relationship, she would only say: "I have excused my manager." Is that double entendre?

Back in the messy motel room with Bette, I concluded the interview and asked her if she would do a favor for one of my associates. Scott St. James, who was a deejay on KSD Radio when

I worked for KSD-TV and KSD Radio in my cub reporter days, was in the vanguard of everything coming down the pike in the music world. Scott went wild when I told him I was going to be interviewing Bette Midler. He asked me if I could please get her to call into his radio show on the night I did the chat. When I gingerly asked her, she graciously declined the invitation to phone Scott. The handler, with ever so slight a head feint, had telegraphed a response in the negative. "No . . . no, I really don't want to do that," she said. "But tell your friend I love him anyway." The handler shifted the gears in her head and nodded approval of the disapproval.

I liked the chanteuse's honesty. But would she autograph a picture for me? My friends from the symphony who had driven me over to Edwardsville had gotten one of their promotional photos for me. That might have been the second big autograph I had dared ask for in my budding career. My first autograph, I think, was from Pearl Bailey.

And what would the classy/raunchy Divine Miss M write in large cursive script on the picture she autographed for me? Well, what she wrote gave all of us in the room a hearty laugh. But I realized instantly when I first read it that I would have to be careful where and to whom I showed it. Bette Midler scribbled:

"To Julius . . . the best lay in St. Louis!"

And that's all she wrote. Thankfully.

We gave each other a parting hug. Only.

"Good night, Bette, and thanks."

" Thank you, Julius."

"Break a leg tomorrow night."

"Thanks."

SIX DEGREES OF JIMMY HOFFA

On Christmas Day 1971, I had been given an exceptional holiday gift by Channel 5 assignment editor Warren Kiesewetter. Almost by default, since in descending pecking order anchor/reporters Chris Condon, Bob Chase, Dick Ford, and John Auble had chosen to be with their families on Christmas Day, "Kiesey," the "affable walrus," handed the then new kid on the reporting block the assignment to interview Teamsters boss Jimmy Hoffa. The internationally known labor leader had just been handed a controversial pardon by President Richard Nixon after Hoffa had served almost five years of his thirteen-year original sentence in the Lewisburg, Pennsylvania, federal penitentiary. The conviction was for jury tampering and hanky-panky with Teamster pension money. Nice Christmas present from the White House.

The spirit of Christmas was abundantly apparent at the home of Barbara Crancer, Jimmy Hoffa's daughter, who is now a retired St. Louis County associate circuit judge. When my crew and I pulled up in front of the split-level suburban home in Glendale on Christmas morning 1971, the weather was unseasonably warm. The colorful Christmas lights blinked and twinkled, and a big, fat plastic Santa Claus was posted as a sentry outside the Crancers' front door. Barbara Crancer graciously greeted us at the door. She said, almost in a whisper, that her mother, who was still recovering from a heart attack and all the excitement of seeing her husband again, was resting inside. So, we could not do an interview. But my baleful eyes, displaying almost exaggerated disappointment and, no doubt, the spirit of the Christmas season, got me a quick reprieve. My crew with its heavy gear—camera, tripod, bright portable lights, sound box, and wiring—spelled "intrusion" with a capital "I." I offered to go around to the backyard and do a quick outdoor interview with her newly released father without all the men and clutter. Also, we wouldn't create such a spectacle for the neighbors. I could understand why Mrs. Crancer did not want us trampling through her house and disturbing her ailing mother, so an interview out back under the sunny sky would be, as we called outdoor interviews, "down and dirty," even if there was no "dirt" involved.

Jimmy Hoffa and his family celebrate a special Christmas, 1971.

Mrs. Crancer bought my plan, and I told her that I would tap lightly on the back door when we were all set up, at which time she could send or bring her father out for a short interview. When I tapped, Hoffa soon came through the back door. The great and legendary labor boss emerged, squinting a bit in the bright sunlight. He was holding onto the hand of his beloved grand-daughter, and young Barbara Jo was beaming and holding on to his hand for dear life and for the joy of life. I was rather surprised at how small Hoffa seemed. I stand at six feet even, and he was at least a head shorter than me. And he was pale and gray like a mushroom that has not seen the light of day for nearly five years.

After I introduced myself, Hoffa wanted to know what I was going to ask him. I stumbled and said: "Well, of course, first of all I want to find out how it feels to be back with your family."

Dumb question. Dumb, dumb question! But a reporter sometimes has to start from a dumb position like this to get an interview started.

His answer was as you might expect it to be. What else would he have said? "I hate being here with my family. I'd rather be back in prison."

And what is it like on the inside? Another question bordering on stupidity. But he let me know he thought the Lewisburg Penitentiary was the pits, a horrible place to pack in prisoners. And, in fact, he told me that he hoped to spend some of his new time trying to clean up the entire U.S. prison system.

And what did he get for Christmas from his family? "New clothes!" was the first response out of his mouth. Although the *Post-Dispatch* and *Globe-Democrat* plastered their holiday coverage of this historic prison release with Hoffa wearing a newly purchased suit, shirt, and tie on that leisurely Saturday morning, he was outfitted in a nice new windbreaker, plaid shirt, and khaki pants. The new togs had been purchased at a men's store in the nearby Warson Village Shopping Center. When he entered prison, he gave all his clothes to a halfway house. And, as if to further prove that it is, indeed, more blessed to give than to receive, Hoffa described to me the pony he was going to give to his granddaughter for Christmas. Barbara Jo was fidgeting with delight and holiday expectations as any child would when Santa was in the form of a grandfather who entered prison when she was a toddler. She never let go of her grandpa's hand. Or was it that he never released her little hand?

"She's getting a new quarter horse. Black Gold is its name," the proud grandpa cum Santa told me, as if he was extra proud that he had executed the horse acquisition while he was still behind bars. One can only imagine all the Teamster business Hoffa carried on while still behind bars.

Judge Crancer, Hoffa's daughter, told me recently that "the horse was so gentle, you could a put a baby on it. When Barbara Jo was nine years old, we gave her riding lessons. The trainer said: 'This is gonna be a tough job, training a two year old and a nine year old at the same time.'"

Black Gold lived to a ripe old age for a horse: twenty years after Barbara Jo first saddled up.

Long after that Christmas Day interview—too late to affix it as an addendum to my television report that night—I learned that Black Gold was a gift to Hoffa from a fellow inmate at Lewisburg Federal Prison. And what a colorful character this gift-giver turned out to be. He was none other than Donald L. Plotnick, a podiatrist with an interesting sideline. Dr. Plotnick headed straight to jail without passing "Go" after pleading guilty to the illegal sale of guns, ammunition, and explosives. U.S. Treasury agents raided a garage that the foot doctor had rented as storage for his munitions. According to the Associated Press (AP), the T-Men uncovered a huge stash of munitions and explosives. The illegal cache included seven quarter-pound cylinders, five half-pound blocks of TNT, and more than 50,000 rounds of ammunition, most of it of a military type. The AP reported that "undercover agents of the U.S. Treasury Department said they purchased two automatic carbines from Plotnick before raiding his home and office and arresting him on July 31, 1970." The podiatrist claimed that he was just holding all the heavy hardware as a favor to a seventeen-year Air Force veteran stationed at Lockbourne Air Force Base. When investigators tried to reach the Air Force sergeant in question, the base information officer reported that the sergeant was in the AFB hospital "for observation." Plotnick also reportedly claimed that all the guns, ammo, and dynamite seized belonged to his wife and children! A judge and jury bought neither story, and Dr. Plotnick was sentenced to two years in the penitentiary. That's where the foot physician met Jimmy Hoffa. Plotnick was paroled in 1972, soon after Hoffa's release, having served eleven months of his original two-year sentence.

Ten years later, Dr. Plotnick was again busted and convicted for what the UPI reported as "setting a man on fire April 29 [1982], to extort money for a drug debt." On this charge, Dr. Plotnick was freed on bond after putting up his airplane, his yacht, and his farm outside Columbus.

Hoffa and Dr. Plotnick teamed up after the time they spent together in the joint to found a prison reform group called the National Association for Justice, headquartered in Washington, D.C. Their stated aim was to improve everything from the physical grounds, to lighting, to creature comforts, to food, to recreation, to providing inmates with skill training to better enable them to find jobs outside prison walls once they were sprung.

"I stuffed a lot of mattresses and I read a lot," Hoffa had told me. I decided on the spot to pick up on the mattress bit and decided later that day in my on-air report not to get cute and

Jimmy Hoffa gives twenty, while former cell-mate Dr. Donald Plotnick (far left) looks on.

even intimate that mattresses could be stuffed with a lot of things—bodies and loot. But I did ask: "So, Mr. Hoffa, what kind of things did you read at Lewisburg?" (I couldn't bring myself to say the words "in prison.")

He told me he read a lot of books. No fiction. Books on economics. Too bad I had been a reporter for only a year, or there could have been some great follow-up questions on the fact that Hoffa was reading about economics. At the very time that I was speaking with Hoffa, the United States was feeling the pinches of high oil prices, a worldwide recession, hikes in the foreign exchange value of the dollar, and export competition was narrowing. It might have been interesting to have learned the take on America's economic outlook of this non-card-carrying economist who carried the Teamsters top business card.

Would he be taking over the reins of the Teamsters Union again? His response to this question was soft. He told me that he needed to still examine the terms of his pardon, and on the advice of his attorney, Morris Shenker, he thought it best not to comment on his future union plans.

Ooooh . . . attorney Morris Shenker. Jimmy Hoffa's trusted legal counsel. Shenker was considered by many to be the sharpest mob attorney next to the legendary Meyer Lansky. In fact, former *Post-Dispatch* reporter Ronald J. Lawrence once wrote of Hoffa's attorney:

> *Most law enforcement officers were unable to comprehend the complexity of the man and his operations. Shenker . . . was a mover and shaker and a financial genius of the caliber of (Meyer) Lansky. It was Shenker who tapped the Teamsters Union's Central States Pension Fund to finance much of the mob's penetration of Las Vegas casinos and other ventures.*

Shenker was a clever cookie. In fact, on several occasions after the historic Christmas Eve Release of 1971, I had the occasion, as a more seasoned reporter, to quiz the elusive and oft-suspected Shenker on allegations of his mob connections. I began to realize after only a couple of "ambush interviews" that the more trouble Shenker was in, the thicker and more unintelligible the Russian-born immigrant's accent became, and the thicker his eyeglasses seemed to get. But then again, I must acknowledge that on a couple of occasions I had lunch at Culpepper's restaurant on Saturday afternoons at the invitation of Mayor Al Cervantes to join him and his attorney, Morris Shenker, and other friends for food, drink, and chat. Cervantes was a very sallow color at those lunches, dying of cancer. And, ironically, at Cervantes' funeral at the Cathedral Basilica in 1983, I found myself sitting in a pew directly behind Mr. and Mrs. Morris Shenker and giving them shared greetings in our mourning of our friend. Shenker followed Cervantes six years later and gave an account of his alleged mob connections to St. Peter.

Back at the Crancer household, I could read on the face of Hoffa's congenial daughter, Barbara, that it was high time to wrap up the exclusive little backyard interview that was imposing on the family's treasured reunion time. I thanked Mr. Hoffa and Mrs. Crancer and Barbara Jo, and my crew and I headed back downtown to edit the piece that ran a little over one and a half minutes on our evening newscast that Saturday Christmas night.

Jimmy Hoffa flat out disappeared on a Bloomfield Hills, Michigan, restaurant parking lot around 2:30 in the afternoon on July 30, 1975. His disappearance occurred about four and a half years after we stood in his daughter and son-in-law's yard to chat at Christmas during one of the happiest days in his life. He was declared legally dead in 1982, even though his body has never been found.

The mystery that surrounds his vanishing gives increased meaning to Jimmy Hoffa's middle name: Riddle.

He remains one of the most enigmatic characters I have interviewed in my thirty-three years on the hunt for interesting subjects. Quite honestly, I wish I had been better prepared; I wish I had not been so new at the business of interviewing; I wish I had had more relaxed time to talk to Hoffa; and I wish I knew where the hell he is.

Just two months before Jimmy Hoffa's release from Lewisburg and that joyous Hoffa family reunion, a story was unfolding on the streets of St. Louis that would make any crime/thriller movie produced by Hollywood look like a Disney film for kiddies by comparison. This true-life spine-tingling episode has only a tangential, indirect relation to Jimmy Hoffa. Get this:

On October 21, 1971, two bandits held up the Cass Federal Savings and Loan and got away with more than ten thousand dollars in loot. It wasn't exactly a clean getaway. The robbers' would-be getaway car raced through the streets of North St. Louis. Just like in the movies, they abandoned the original auto and set it on fire. This car would be a key piece of evidence in another story that spun off the robbery. Remember this car. They then got into the car owned by one of the bandits. And that's when shots were fired at the pursuing officers. Officers fired back. But the pursued car veered out of control and crashed into a gas station, narrowly missing the gasoline pumps, which would have been ugly. The crash was the end of the road for one robbery suspect, forty-six-year-old Paul Lockhart of Leslie, Missouri. Lockhart threw up his hands and surrendered, and all the stolen money was recovered.

So one bandit was in custody, but his partner, thirty-six-year-old James Leroy Cochran, was a long, long way from giving himself up. After engaging police in a ten-minute shootout at the gas station, Cochran managed to slip into nearby Northwest High School. I was dispatched to that scene, which was one of the first big action stories I covered as a cub reporter. Once inside, Cochran, who had been wounded in that gun battle, grabbed football coach, Don LePlante, and held him hostage with a gun pointed at the coach's head. I had never seen so many red police cruiser lights flashing at one scene before.

Using the coach as a hostage, Cochran got into a nearby family's home, and after two hours, he made the man of the house drive him into Illinois where he made the hostage buy a re-supply of ammunition. Cochran then abandoned his captive and drove the man's car to Kansas City. Somehow, Cochran then turned up in Booneville, Missouri, where he took a female hostage. In the hostage's car, Cochran drove her back to St. Louis, where the unwitting lady was released. Two more shootouts followed, one of them at Calvary Cemetery, where I was sent by Channel 5's assignment editor.

The surrealistic night scene featured a then 121-year-old cemetery surrounded by flashing red lights, more than 100 cops with their weapons drawn, canine units with their barking police dogs, and more than one crew from every news operation—print and broadcast—in the metro area. A crowd of neighbors and curious spectators who had heard about the big event on television that night camped out on lawns and formed a concentric ring around the whole scene. There was even money on whether Cochran would sneak away or whether nervous police officers would blow him away with their riot guns.

Paul Lockhart

Overhead, a helicopter, borrowed from the St. Louis County Police Department, swept its bright light over and around every shrub, bush, and tree clump in the nearly five-hundred-acre Calvary Cemetery. The only thing missing from this spectacular scene was vendors peddling refreshments and souvenirs. Each reporting team was hoping that there would be a grand finale to the scene within camera sight of their encampment.

Police Chief Gene Camp, who was always on the scene of every major crime sight and catastrophe, looked tired and appeared almost embarrassed by Cochran's elusiveness. More than that, Chief Camp told me on camera: "I can't believe this. This guy has held up a bank, tried to shoot some of my officers, taken a lot of hostages, kidnapped people and taken their cars, and people think he's a 'good guy.' He's got to be getting a lot of help in getting away all these times."

I remember the consensus of our "man-on-the-street" interviews (which included women, of course) ranged from: "He ain't hurt nobody, has he?" to "The bank got their money back. What's the big deal?"

There was no doubt that Cochran had become a colorful folk hero. And he knew it. He often asked his hostages if they had been following his exploits in the media. Some of the cops I spoke to off the record speculated that Cochran was getting food, clothing, and shelter from some of his kinfolk and buddies in his old Baden neighborhood near the cemetery. There were even reports of Cochran casually having a drink at a local tavern while he was on the lam. This guy knew the environs in and

James Leroy Cochran

around the historic graveyard like the back of his hand. In fact, when he was a teenager he was busted by cops several times—beginning when he was in grade school—for breaking into the crypts at the very cemetery where he was holed up and perhaps wounded by police. Cochran's widowed mother, with whom he had been living, still resided in the old neighborhood. She pleaded with her errant son through the media to give himself up so he wouldn't get hurt or killed.

I ran into my old friend, Florissant Police Captain Bob Lowery, at the cemetery search scene. He was also head of the area's Major Case Squad. (Lowery later became Florissant police chief and then that community's mayor.) "What's going on? Got anything to tell me?" I asked Lowery.

"Well, Julius, I think it's best for me to pull my guys (the Major Case Squad) out of the park and take up some positions farther out around the periphery. It might be getting a little too dangerous with everybody on edge."

"What do you know about this guy, Cochran?" I asked Lowery.

"He's a small-time hoodlum who thinks he's Jesse James. Loves publicity."

"You think he's really dangerous?" I asked in one of those questions that might have been dumb, in an effort to illicit information.

"Ask the cops he's been shooting at," Lowery said succinctly.

That's what Lowery told me *on* camera. He nudged me out of earshot of my crew and the spectators who had gathered around our bright lights. Off camera, he told me that FBI Director J. Edgar Hoover was mad as hell over the spectacle that Cochran was creating. According to Lowery, Hoover had issued the old "dead or alive" order. He thought the taciturn fugitive was embarrassing the bureau.

Cochran was, without a doubt, increasing in popularity as time marched on, since no one other than him had been injured, and he was, through his folksy charm, able to work the Stockholm Syndrome in record time. None of his recently held hostages could muster up a bad word about their captor. In fact, he would take only minimal amounts of money from his more than twenty hostages because, as he assured them, he did not believe in taking money from working-class people. He was variously described by his captives—in their words—as polite, courteous, likeable, humorous, good-looking, handsome. Police described him as armed, dangerous, and a publicity hound. Cochran boasted to a number of his hostages that he was toting two pistols and a rifle and had told them that he had "100 bullets—99 for cops and one for himself."

Sometime during the late night or early next morning, Cochran commandeered a thirty-year-old suburban St. Louis man and his car as the man was heading to an appointment with his chiropractor near Calvary. The free-wheeling escape artist then forced this unwitting guy to drive him all the way out to Gallup, New Mexico, and then back to St. Louis again, where he forced two couples to drive him to Kentucky. That's where an understandably exhausted and wounded Cochran surrendered at a Lexington motel without incident. Police had traced him by calls he had made to a girlfriend in St. Louis. He had asked that the girlfriend come to Lexington to accompany him after the arrest so that police wouldn't kill him. And the vain ex-con asked for clean clothes so he would look nice at his arraignment. Right after he surrendered, Cochran told law officers he had planned to marry his girlfriend, Mrs. Judy Wright, the day before Thanksgiving that year, but he told them he guessed he had blown it.

For his crime and benign but crazy ten-day, ten-state adventure that covered an estimated 3,500 miles, Cochran was convicted and sentenced to twenty-five years in prison to ponder the error of his ways. When he filed an appeal, my old friend, Norm London, who had defended Peter Busch in the shooting death of his friend, represented Cochran. Part of Cochran's appeal hinged on the fact that at least two prior prison terms had made Cochran nuts.

Norm wanted to call an expert witness to testify as to Cochran's screwed up mental state. But the Eighth Circuit Court of Appeals, meeting in St. Louis, barred testimony from the avowed expert witness who had alleged, in preparation for a new book he was writing, that the court should know about the destructive nature of life inside a maximum security slammer. The witness had firsthand experience that federal prison life "could create mental problems which could lead to one not knowing right from wrong and being able to act within the reasonable law."

The appeals court found that the witness didn't know beans about the prisons where Cochran had served before the Cass Bank conviction. What's more, the court found that the so-called expert witness, Dr. Donald L. Plotnick, had never even so much as met Cochran in person.

In 1977, another convicted bank robber and self-confessed hit man murderer escaped from a Massachusetts prison and hid out on the Blacklick farm outside Columbus owned by, yes, you guessed it, Dr. Don Plotnick. The two had met at the Lewisburg Penitentiary where Hoffa had already served time.

There is more to this bizarre story. There are several connections to the St. Louis police force, and there seemed to be purpose behind Cochran's seemingly random travels. First, the original car used in the bank robbery was registered to the estranged wife of a St. Louis police officer. She had mysteriously disappeared the day before the bank robbery. Also, the pistol that Cochran used in the Cass Bank robbery had been given to him by a St. Louis police officer. This same pistol was used to kill the cop's wife, who had once dated Cochran. Her body was later found near a little Missouri town an hour's drive from St. Louis. That town was Leslie, Missouri—one of Cochran's stops while on the lam. And Leslie was the hometown of Cochran's accomplice in the failed bank robbery, Paul Lockhart.

I'm with you. I wouldn't believe the spiral to this story either. But all these points are true.

Mrs. Marilyn Oliver vanished, along with her car, the day before the Cass Bank robbery. She had been living apart from her husband, patrolman William Oliver, for about five months at the time. Mrs. Oliver's sister, and some of the missing woman's co-workers at the Continental Baking Company, became alarmed when they saw and heard the name James Leroy Cochran in the sensational news stories splashed on radio, TV, and the local newspapers. Marilyn had mentioned Cochran to them. In fact, she told her closest friends and associates that she had dated Cochran after she and her husband had split. But she didn't like him and tried to give him the shake, she told them. But he continued to stalk her, Marilyn complained.

Police began to fear the worst when the first family Cochran held captive after releasing his hostage at Northwest High School told them they overhead Cochran tell somebody in a phone conversation that he had "killed a woman . . . shot her five times."

Marilyn Oliver

Marilyn's mother reported that she had not heard from her daughter all day on Tuesday, normally a day off. But that wasn't unusual. When Marilyn didn't show up for work on Wednesday, October 20, 1971, a lot of suspicions were raised about her whereabouts. Wednesday was payday. Officer William Oliver was reportedly one of the people who phoned Marilyn's mother to report that she was nowhere to be found. Odd, if it was true that the husband from whom Marilyn was separated called to say he was worried about where she was. Read on.

When relatives checked Marilyn's suburban apartment, their discovery sounded an alarm. Her two precious poodles were left alone. She never left them alone.

The relatives phoned Florissant police.

Captain Lowery told me at the missing woman's home: "There's no way she would have left those two dogs . . . and left her apartment in the messed up shape it was in when we got there. No doubt, something was wrong."

Fast forward to Thursday, October 28, 1971. A farmer walking on his property just outside Leslie, Missouri, reported to authorities that he had discovered a badly decomposed body of a female under some burlap sacks on the porch of an abandoned farmhouse used to store feed. The dead woman's sister and

James Leroy Cochran

brother-in-law identified the body as that of twenty-one-year-old Marilyn Oliver. The jewelry on the corpse was the dead giveaway. She had been shot four, five, or six times—depending on the report, and the slugs were later connected with the nickel-plated .38 Cochran used in the bank robbery. The murder scene was just two miles from a farm owned by Lockhart's parents. Lockhart was in the pokey on the bank robbery charges.

There were those conflicting stories that Marilyn had been shot four, five, or six times. I went with the count of my friend and neighbor, Medical Examiner George Gantner. He put the number of bullets at six. And I would go with George any day of the week. He and I had developed an early friendship, and for years after this story he would often gave me background info, a discreet tip, or a wave-off if he thought I was headed off in the wrong direction in an investigation. And, even in those pre-CSI days, Dr. Gantner told me in an interview that he had no doubt that Marilyn was shot inside the farmhouse and was finished off after she made it out to the porch.

Cochran was initially charged with the murder, but that charge was eventually dropped by the Franklin County, Missouri, prosecutor. There was not enough evidence, even though some witnesses reported seeing Cochran in and around Leslie with a woman that was the spitting image of Marilyn Oliver. Cochran denied killing Marilyn. Captain Lowery assigned two crack detectives to the case, Sergeant J. D. Noser of his department and Ron Moser, an investigator for the Franklin County prosecutor's office. They were not so sure that Cochran was smart enough to carry out the robbery attempt and the murder without help. Besides, they noted, the slugs pulled out of Marilyn Oliver's body were Swedish hollow points, used almost exclusively by police officers. Marilyn's estranged husband was a police officer. Marilyn's husband, patrolman William Oliver, was a drinking buddy of James Leroy Cochran and Paul Lockhart, and they all hung out together in a small potatoes hoodlum gang. After splitting with Marilyn, Oliver was dating the sister of another one of the band of losers.

James Leroy Cochran

So, hold the phone. Get ready for yet another unexpected twist and turn. Cochran was charged with the murder of Marilyn Oliver, but the charge was dropped, even though he had boasted and confessed to the killing to a number of his hostages during that crazy flight of more than three thousand miles. A grand jury indicted William Oliver on July 10, 1972, for the murder of Marilyn Oliver. After that indictment, Oliver quit the city police force after six years in uniform to "take another (unspecified) job."

Now let's pause here to look at something quite remarkable, if not unusual, about this story: James Leroy Cochran, at the time of his arrest in Kentucky, was dating Marilyn Oliver, the estranged wife of his buddy, Bill Oliver. While dating, and apparently harassing, Marilyn, Cochran was betrothed to Mrs. Judy Wright. Mrs. Wright was the sister-in-law of Mrs. Sandra Little. Oliver was dating Mrs. Little, who was arrested

William Oliver

for carrying a concealed pistol in her handbag when accompanying Oliver to a grand jury hearing investigating him for murder in his wife's shooting death. And while all this was going on, Mrs. Little's husband was ensconced in a state penitentiary on convictions of rape and sodomy. Need a runback on all this?

To take you on still more of this journey into the bizarre, four years after the death of his estranged wife, William Oliver—not Cochran—was found guilty in the second-degree murder and sentenced to twenty-five years in prison. Oliver got a get-out-of-jail card for a fifty-thousand-dollar bond and appealed the verdict. He got a second trial on a technicality when the Missouri Appeals Court found that the judge in the first trial had given the jury improper instructions. Then on Halloween night in 1975, Oliver was found guilty a second time and sentenced to a twenty-year prison term—considering time already served. Oliver's appeal went all the way up to the Missouri Supreme Court. The state's highest court upheld the last conviction.

The prosecution had argued in both murder trials that Oliver set up Cochran and tried to frame him. Prosecutors from the Cochran case produced the pistol that the then twenty-nine-year-old Oliver had given to Cochran. It was the same pistol used to murder Marilyn Oliver. And Oliver had loaned Cochran the getaway car used to flee the Cass Bank robbery scene. Police were not on the scene of the Cass Bank robbery just by happenstance in time to foil it, by the way. Somebody had tipped them off. Who do you think the tipster was?

While serving his time for the Cass Bank robbery, Paul Lockart was stabbed to death with a shiv by a fellow inmate serving time for murder.

Dr. Plotnick, who had given Jimmy Hoffa's granddaughter a Christmas horse and had served time in prison with Hoffa for illegal arms dealing, helped Hoffa form a prison reform organization and was later returned to prison for trying to recover a drug debt by dousing a man with gasoline and setting him on fire.

At the time this book went to press, James Leroy Cochran was seventy-two years old and living in a comfortable suburban St. Louis neighborhood. Bill Oliver, the ex-cop convicted of killing his wife, was, the last time we checked, released on probation in the spring of 1987. His probationary period was up in October of 1992.

So, there you have it. A long and winding saga that begins with the prison release of a charismatic titan of a labor leader. His simple Christmas gift of a two-year-old quarter horse to his then nine-year-old granddaughter might have been the end of that segment of this book. But when we gave just a passing glance at the identity of the original owner of the horse, we opened up an incredible can of plethora. I want to emphasize emphatically that the start of this story has absolutely nothing directly to do with its conclusion. Not one of the principals in the opening pages bears responsibility for the outcomes of the major players at the end of the story. But all the elements in the *alpha* of the story are still somehow inextricably bound to the *omega* factors. Is this that enigmatic *six degrees of separation* phenomenon? It just might be.

Playmate of the Month, July 1983

All hell breaks loose on the narrow Colombian jungle road through the mountains. A local bus, jam-packed with natives and all their bundles and baskets and farm animals, speeds recklessly and slams into a disabled jeep parked on the side of the road. Upon impact, the driverless jeep is upended and loses its precious cargo of bamboo-caged tropical birds. The squawking exotic birds are quickly the target of fowl play as the natives snatch up and claim the prized booty. The shaken-up passengers are lucky to be alive . . . including the gringo woman, Joan Wilder, who learns far too late that she has gotten on the wrong bus for Cartagena, her intended destination. In fact, it may have been Joan herself who is responsible for the crash. Just before the smashup, Joan had distracted the driver with her questions about the bus's destination.

Jack Colton, the current owner of the smashed jeep and former owner of the exotic birds, is suddenly and for some reason engaged in a gun battle with the sinister-looking guy who had met Joan before they boarded, and who could not keep his beady eyes off her on the overloaded, ill-fated bus. When the smoke clears, Jack is not a happy camper as he approaches his crippled jeep only to learn he has lost the fowl cargo that could have made him a small fortune.

Our hero tries to salvage anything of value he can from the wreckage. He pulls out and tosses away a can of Pepsi and a *Playboy* magazine. It does our hearts good to know that Ruth has survived the crash.

No, Ruth is not a survivor lady friend he had left in the jeep. Ruth was the "Playboy of the Month" featured ever so fleetingly on the cover of the July 1983 issue of the magazine Jack pulled from the bashed jeep. (Ah, it's lonely in the rainforest on moonlit nights.) And this is the same Ruth—Ruth Guerri—that was the delightful and pulchritudinous subject of an interview I did in the Channel 4 newsroom when the magazine paid tribute to the attributes of the St. Louis beauty that month and year.

Jack was actually actor Michael Douglas; the mousy Joan was

played by Kathleen Turner. The movie was the 1984 action/
adventure *Romancing the Stone*. You can go straight to Ruth's
still-frame movie debut at about 27:56 into *Romancing the
Stone* when you punch up the movie on your DVD player.

Ruth Guerri's name created quite a buzz when her voluptuous
Playboy photo appeared on newsstands around the globe, and
when *St. Louis Post-Dispatch* columnist and premier privacy
poacher, Jerry Berger, blasted the news in a June 1983 column.
In this column, Berger had ceremoniously announced that a
twenty-four-year-old local beauty had been named *Playboy*
magazine Playmate of the Month for July 1983. To hundreds of
thousands of curious teenage boys and full-grown men, too, ever
since *Playboy* first published in December 1953, "Playmate of
the Month" has meant "Classy Nude Three-Page Color Foldout
of the Month."

Ruth might not have considered it at the time, but the
playmate honor was heralded in every corner of the city and
nation and world . . . except in homes and regions and spots
on the world map where prudes or prunes hold forth. *Playboy*
magazine is the centerpiece of now-ancient *Playboy* magazine
founder Hugh Hefner's vast worldwide empire. There should
be honor and glory in the fact that only a dozen heavenly
bodies each year are chosen to bare it all in the monthly artistic
abandonment of apparel.

One of the joys of working in a television newsroom is the fact that no two days are ever exactly alike. On one day in late June 1983, the element of surprise delivered a real treat. I'll tell you more on that in a minute.

In fact, with total disregard for the clock, one day can sometimes quite easily turn into a second day before a TV news staffer knows it. Nobody on the news staff knows the vagaries of employment better than TV weathercasters, who so often come in for work on a given day and find themselves held over for a second day by popular demand. Let there be impending death, doom, and devastation from wind, water, or fire, and it's, "Hello, honey, I'm going to have to stay over until this tornado blows through; the rain and flooding subside; or firefighters get a handle on these brushfires. Love you, too."

A good TV newsroom staffer is never afforded the luxury of being surprised. Or perhaps more accurately, it is a piss poor TV newsroom staffer who will *admit* to being surprised. So often, the newsroom staff does not have a clue when a legitimate candidate for president is going to show up for an unscheduled interview, like when then Georgia Governor Jimmy Carter did one day on the presidential campaign trail. The newsroom assignment desk can never be prepared for a gunman's rampage inside the council chambers of a local suburban community killing five before he is cut down. That actually happened in normally quiet Kirkwood, Missouri, in February 2008. Nor is there any way a TV newsroom can get geared up for news of major indictments in town naming respected business leaders. That's happened quite a few times in towns all over the world from Israel to Russia to Japan to Washington, D.C., recently. But that's the challenge! No two days are duplicated.

A very pleasant surprise was thrown my way when I got a call from station General Manager Allan Cohen one day in late June 1983. He wanted me to come up to his office to meet a special guest who was visiting the station. It was standard but unwritten protocol for any guest who could be recognized on more than a couple hundred thousand TV screens to be taken to the office of the GM for a special, official "howdy-do." This is much like the signs that appear in the front hallway of every school in the nation: *All Guests Must Report to the Principal's Office.* At a television station, that proclamation would apply whether that guest happened to be the likes of crazy man Richard Simmons, CBS Anchor Dan Rather, visiting star of stage and screen

Debbie Reynolds, or Dave Letterman.

As the senior anchor/reporter and oldest native St. Louisan on the on-air staff, I was frequently summoned to the GM's office or the news director's lair to bring greetings from the station, the town, and myself. In fact, if the mayor of St. Louis was ever too busy to receive a visiting dignitary, he could have left a box of ceremonial keys to the city with me. I might have emptied that box of keys more often than the mayor's office.

There were only two visiting celebrities I flat out refused to come out of my office to greet. In both cases I holed up in my office and refused to answer the knocks at my door. I didn't care to meet O. J. Simpson's lead attorney, Johnny Cochran, for my own personal reasons I could not discuss on or off the air with anybody. And at the time that David Letterman was on a nationwide tour of stations to encourage general managers and program directors to put his show up against Leno, I was not a Letterman fan. The few times I had watched the show on its tape-delayed basis on Channel 4, I thought Dave's brand of humor poked too much fun of just plain, down-home, common folks. The Letterman program, I thought, was too often not laughing "with" a subject but laughing "at" their physical appearance, their mental defects, or their genuine efforts at making a humble honest living. So, Johnny and Dave saved me from giving out two more "keys."

Well, anyway, since I had not created any controversies of late (like a couple of accidental open-mike comments I had made), I assumed that my subpoena to appear in the GM's was issued cordially. Lord knows some of my trips up to the second-floor corner office featured an official reprimand from the Man upstairs regarding something I had said, should have said, didn't say, or was perceived to have said on one of my newscasts.

"Jules," Allan said with a big smile upon my entrance in his office, "I'd like for you to meet Ruth . . . Ruth Guerri. She's the *Playboy* magazine Playmate of the Month.

"Pleased to meet you, Ruth," I ogled. "Playmate of the Month? Which month?"

"For July," the twenty-four year old offered perkily.

I was careful to hide the fact that I had never subscribed to nor owned a *Playboy* magazine—even though I had lived near the infamous Playboy Mansion in Chicago for a while. And I

was, at the time I met Ruth, living very near the site of the once-popular Playboy Club on Lindell Boulevard. I had visited the club only a couple of times, but I had never contracted *ocular bunnyitis*, as some of my best buddies had. However, I didn't want to appear to be the Senior Nerd at Channel 4. Cross my heart, the few times I had opened a *Playboy* magazine, I had gone straight for the joke section. Even though I had been raised Missouri Synod Lutheran, I attached no puritanical labeling on Playboy Bunnies nor their organ . . . er . . . their magazine. Even on the couple of occasions on which a bunny or two had perched on the arm of my overstuffed chair at the old Playboy Club during the late 1960s—very near my birthplace on Vandeventer—I never got all hot and bothered over their comeliness.

The lovely Ruth Guerri was at Channel 4 on our first encounter to tape a half-hour show on the announcement that she would be the Playboy Centerfold for the upcoming month. After the half-hour taping, Ruth and her Playboy handlers had agreed to stay on for a live interview on our five o'clock news that day. I'd be doing that interview. Just as I had done in live on-set chats with the likes of Oprah Winfrey, Julio Iglesias, Gregory Peck, Carol Channing, Milton Berle, and Richard Simmons, among other luminaries. I loved doing the live interviews. The segments hardly ever ran longer than three minutes, so a lot had to packed into that limited time. For the glib celebrities, the three minutes would zip by too quickly. For some of the duds, three minutes live could seem like an eternity.

When Allan announced that he had an important meeting coming up in his office, I asked Ruth and her publicist if they would like to walk down the hall to join me for a cup of coffee. It was a courtesy, since I am not and never have been a coffee drinker. It was during that block-long walk that I realized that Allan, in his infinite wisdom that I occasionally challenged, might just have wanted me to use some time with Ruth to determine in a pre-interview what would be tasteful and what would be risqué during the actual live interview. In my frequent Sunday night KMOX Radio interviews with sex therapist and feminist Shere Hite in the 1980s, I had learned that my program, the station's license, and I often hinged on a quick change of subject, or a quicker pitch to a commercial break. While interviewing Shere on live talk radio, the sky was only the suggested limit on what she would dare say. The woman was absolutely without filter. A quick pitch to a commercial break once followed Ms. Hite opining, "There is no reason in the world, Julius, that a woman should not have four, five, or six orgasms in a single session."

Hunter: "Ourguesttonightistheauthorofthe'HiteReport,'Sher eHitehereonKMOX,TheVoiceofSt.Louis.We'reback'AtYourSe rvice'rightafterthis," I said, running all the words together and getting to that commercial as rapidly as I could spit them out.

The genteel Ruth Guerri would certainly not intentionally spike our interview with eyebrow-raising comments as Ms. Hite often did, but the Playboy nature of my interview with her would inevitably touch on sexual content. After talking to her in the coffee lounge, I was certain that she and I could keep our viewers' eyebrows at their normal configurations.

Yes, indeed, I was charmed by Ruth right away, not just by the prospect of how well I might eventually get to know her when I opened a *Playboy* magazine the next month. In person, I found her to be quiet, charming, alluring, articulate, and intelligent. And she wasn't hard to look at either. There, I said it. At age twenty-four, she was able to hold her own in the gambit game with an old-timer like me. In fact, she had a subtle sense of levity that she revealed sometimes only with the alluring twinkle in her eyes.

But let's face it . . . I was not going to try to hit Ruth with any arrows of the sharpness of those I fired at the likes of Michael Dukakis on Election Eve; a local girl and her mother who had pulled a scam on the girl's need for a donor kidney; or the interview with a chieftain of the White Socialist Workers' Party. In each of these live interviews, the station switchboard lit up, and the mailbag got stuffed with comments from viewers who thought I had been too tough on the interviewee.

Over a couple of cups of coffee—for her—in the Channel 4 coffee room, with the publicist listening in, I learned that Ruth had not made her grand entrance into the Playboy Empire in a golden carriage drawn by white horses. Quite to the contrary. On a summer 1981 modeling job and agent-hunting venture with two male friends in Chicago, Ruth tired out and wanted to call it a day. Besides, she told me, she had a bad case of poison ivy she got while fishing at a lake in Moberly, Missouri. She said she had big red, itchy blotches and patches on her face and the rest of her body. But her friends were relentless and dragged her into the Playboy agency anyway. Ah, sweet fortune! As the three friends were on an elevator heading to the lobby and out to the beach, Ruth was spotted by, of all people, Playboy's senior photographer, Pompeo Posar. For him, it was centerfold love at first sight, despite the poison ivy. Lana Turner's storied discovery at a soda fountain counter was pale in light of Ruth being spotted as a future supermodel on an elevator. It takes far longer to sip a milk shake than it takes to go down a few floors on an elevator.

The Trieste-born photographer wasted no time in making Ruth an offer she couldn't refuse. How would she like to take a "Playmate Test" for Hugh Hefner? To give legitimacy to an offer that might sound like a rant from a scurrilous old lecher, Posar offered Ruth the opportunity to turn around in the lobby and go right back up to the Playboy office with Ruth—splotches and all—to meet his editor and shoot a few Polaroids.

Ruth was skeptical at first, she told me, and not particularly dazzled by the seemingly incredible offer, but her two guy-buddies urged her to turn around and go back up with Pompeo, meet the editor, and take a few candid shots.

During my one-on-one with Ruth before the cameras, she told me she had been modeling since she was seventeen, so she was not at all camera-shy. She had done layouts for Famous-Barr, Dillard's, Venture, and Baker's Shoes, among many other commercial clients. "Oh, heck," Ruth thought. "This is weird, but why not give it a whirl?"

Ruth certainly didn't know it at the time of that chance

encounter on the elevator, but Pompeo Posar was no slouch, no con artist, no flim-flam film flinger. During his distinguished career, he produced sixty-five *Playboy* centerfolds and forty *Playboy* covers from the early 1960s until his death at the age of eighty-three in 2004. An active website called "Life in Legacy" says of Posar: "He had an uncanny ability for finding a model and convincing her to take her clothes off."

Posar told Ruth, in one of his many phone calls that began to border on harassment, that the great Hugh Hefner himself had seen the Polaroids and wanted to meet her. Ruth told Posar that she needed time to consider his offer, and she wanted to talk the deal over with her mother and father, and her family and friends. "I'm just not impulsive," she told me.

This was no easy decision for Ruth Guerri. Would baring it all for *Playboy* ruin her modeling career or propel it?

Finally, Ruth took the plunge. She decided to do the centerfold. And her life, thereafter, would never be the same.

As the father of two girls myself, I wondered aloud in my question to her during our live interview how her parents—her father in particular—had taken the news. And that turned out to be a juicy little story in itself. She had told her mother, and there was no problem. But she hadn't had a chance to tell her first-generation Italian father about her upcoming exposure. Oh, boy. Papa learned the news before his youngest child and only daughter had had a chance to tell him first in person. He had gotten the news in a column written by the "King of Off the Record and Background Broken Promises," Jerry Berger. Papa Guerri, Ruth told my audience and me, was more hurt than angry.

Then my television audience and I learned in the brief interview that the actual photo shoot for the magazine had taken months. It took the *Playboy* photographers six months to shoot the "pictorials," the pictures of the hometown girl in her native habitat in St. Louis, and posing in custom studio sets built in L.A. and Chicago. It took a full five days to shoot the one celebrated centerfold. Ruth told us the photographer had used the old boxy 8 × 10 Polaroid camera, and she said the shoot was particularly grueling in that she was not even allowed to move a muscle or an eyebrow when the photos were being shot. She said one of the sets on which she posed nude—a bathroom— had to be completely scrapped and a new set built because every time the editor looked at the proofs she claimed she saw

flaws in it that nobody else could see.

Overall, we had a good interview, but darn it, I didn't have a chance to follow up on how the editor could find a flaw. But the director had barked in my earpiece, "Wrap. Outta time." I didn't know it at the time, but it would take me twenty-five years to get clarity on that one.

As fate would have it, when I starred in my first television and radio commercials in January 2008, as a pitchman for a windows replacement company, I was given a list of makeup artists available to take on the commercial shoot. I couldn't believe my eyes when one name jumped right off the page. *Ruth Guerri (Ebinger)* was now working part-time as a makeup artist for the local Talent Plus Agency. I wanted Ruth! Let me rephrase that. I wanted Ruth to do my makeup. She got the job through the agency, and I spoke with her to let her know she was the chosen one. She told me by phone that she would love to do the shoot and agreed that it would be nice to get together again after all these years.

I suggested that she come by my house early on the day of the shoot to have a cup of coffee or two (that she would have to make herself, since I still don't drink coffee) and catch up on our lives.

Ruth arrived at my house toting her professional makeup kit on the shoot date almost an hour earlier than the video crew was scheduled to arrive so we could chat a bit. Ruth, looking as gorgeous as she did in our first meeting, made a pot of coffee, and she and I picked up the interview right where we had left off twenty-five years earlier.

One of the first questions I asked Ruth was about the *Playboy* editor who was so persnickety about the point of destroying a bathroom set and having a completely new one constructed.

"Well," Ruth confided. "To tell you the truth, those of us who saw the proofs couldn't see a thing wrong with any of them. But she was the boss on a photo shoot."

"Was it just that she had a keener eye?" I asked.

"She claimed to have," Ruth said.

"And they tore down a whole set because the editor didn't like those proofs? It wasn't YOU that she didn't like, was it?" I asked.

"No, she didn't indicate that I was the problem. But, yes, they tore down the whole bathroom set—the whole thing," Ruth answered. "And ripping down the one set and building another cost us a lot of time. And, I'm sure, money."

"And what caused the other delays . . . the delays that cost you six months of your life?" I wanted to know.

"Well, weather was a factor. I gotta give it to the photographic crew and that editor. The weather had to be absolutely perfect for what they wanted, or they wouldn't shoot. They wanted perfection, and you can see that each *Playboy* photo, in whatever issue you look, there is portrait quality."

"What other delays were there?" this enquiring mind wanted to know.

"Well, there was the time that I fell off a horse during a shoot, got the wind knocked out of me, and came to with *Playboy* photographer Steve Wayda standing over me. He was gently slapping my face to get me back to consciousness. And then, since he was new to *Playboy* at the time and trying to make a name for himself, he insisted that I get right back on that horse so we could continue the shoot in the right light. I did."

I later learned that the hard-driving, prolific *Playboy* star photographer, who took up his profession only after his grandfather died and left Wayda his cameras, once said, perhaps tongue in cheek, about his craft: "When you don't know what you are doing, fake it. If in doubt, add more lights. Everyone is always impressed with more lights. It looks like you know what you're doing."

And what about the thrills a guy could get from photographing so many gorgeous models like Ruth Guerri wearing nothing at all? Wayda, whom Pamela Anderson calls "The Bomb," said: "In the beginning you are like a kid in a candy store . . . but too much sugar can cause headaches later on. What you could once do, you can probably only do once now."

Ruth continued, "And there was one time we were shooting a sequence in a hot air balloon, and the balloon got blown off course and crashed on a downtown street. We crashed! I got some bumps and bruises out of that one."

"Who would ever have thought that a Playmate of the Month should require hazardous duty pay?" I sympathized.

"Exactly," Ruth agreed. She went on, "And there was one time we had to hold off for weeks to re-shoot some pictures. The reason was my hair."

"Your hair?" I asked.

"My hair. After the first round of shots I thought we were finished with that sequence. So I had my hair cut. But then I learned that they wanted a do-over. So we had to wait for my hair to grow back."

"Incredible," I said. Then changing the subject, I asked the question that was lurking just below the surface of every enquiring mind: "Was there any *quid pro quo* expected from you by Pompeo, Hugh, or any other Playboy topper, male or female?" (*Quid pro quo* in this case is Latin for "casting couch.")

"Absolutely not!" Ruth insisted emphatically. "I became like a daughter to Pompeo and his wife, Melita, and I was a frequent dinner guest in their Lake Shore Drive penthouse up in Chicago. And I didn't even meet Hugh Hefner till well after the magazine shots were taken."

"But you did spend some time at the famous/infamous mansion out in L.A., didn't you?" I continued my query.

"Well, it probably wouldn't shock anybody to learn that the Playboy bunch was a 'party hearty' group. After I appeared in that July '83, I had a lot of modeling gigs and appearances to make out in L.A., so it was convenient for Playboy and for me to live in the mansion. But after a couple of days and nights there, I decided that lifestyle was not my cup of tea . . ."

"Cup of coffee," I corrected as a kind of joke.

"Tea or coffee, I just didn't feel comfortable living around a certain old guy running around all day and night in his pajamas. I couldn't live in the mansion. There was too much twenty-four-hour activity going on there."

"Like what?" I probed.

Well, I don't want to say. I don't want to get sued or anything. But I saw too many girls throw their lives away in that place trying to move up the modeling and acting ladder. A lot of lives are destroyed there."

"So, how did you handle the housing thing?" I asked.

"I was able to live out back of the mansion in a guest house," Ruth told me at my kitchen table.

"Was everybody in the Playboy organization okay with that?"

"Not really. I got lots of little hints that I needed to be 'more sociable.' So I would spend some time hanging out in the game room at the mansion, on the tennis courts, swimming in the outdoor pool, and swimming into the grotto where there was a sauna. But I generally stayed away from the big, noisy parties."

"Lotta booze? Drugs? Sex?" I asked.

"I don't want to bite the hand that fed me," Ruth demurred. "I'll leave details of what goes on in the mansion to others."

I wanted to hurry and seize upon the opportunity to get more information in the time I had remaining with Dear Ruth before the production crew arrived. "Was Hugh Hefner as much of a lecher . . . as much of a 'dirty old man' . . . as some people say he is?" I asked.

"You said that. I didn't," Ruth dodged my question deftly. But her real response was obvious. At least to me.

Ruth Guerri today

"Okay, tell me now. No 'dodge-ball,'" I asked looking her straight in the eyes, "Surely a grown old man like that doesn't run around in the mansion all day in his pajamas and slippers."

"Well, every time I saw him in the mansion, he was in pajamas and a smoking jacket or robe and house slippers. I saw him leave the mansion just one time in a suit and tie. He was going out to do some television show."

"Did you see him a lot?"

"Probably not as much as he would like," Ruth remembered.

"What does that mean?" I asked trying to draw out more juicy tidbits.

In response to that direct question, Ruth changed the subject completely. "I liked his daughter, Christie," Ruth volunteered. "She was really sweet every time I met up with her at a reception or any show at which we were introducing a new line of apparel. She was good for Playboy; had some good ideas for expansion." (Christie Hefner was named Playboy CEO and chairwoman in 1988, five years after Ruth was named Playmate of the Month.)

"Well, the mansion . . . sometimes I'd get dressed up and go over. Sometimes I wouldn't. But sometimes after I got there—depending on who the hotshot guest was—I just didn't feel like mixing and being all that friendly. I'm a really shy and quiet person, and I value the quiet life. I had a real hard time feeling like a piece of meat; a 'thing' that they owned."

"You go, Girl," I thought to myself. Good for you on behalf of my daughters . . . and daughters everywhere!

Ruth told me over her third cup of coffee at my kitchen table that in addition to her work as a makeup artist, she now dabbles in antiques—buying and selling. She and her husband, Tom, have two beautiful daughters, seventeen and eleven. The family lives in a spacious log cabin outside St. Louis that Ruth and Tom built by hand with the help of friends and neighbors. Ruth is extremely proud of her extended family that includes three horses, three dogs, two cats, two rabbits, and she and her family are currently building special quarters to house a peacock that will be joining the menagerie soon. Gardening and cooking are among her favorite pastimes. And she says she is interested in interior design.

I can truly say that the years have been extremely good to Ruth. She is as youthful, gorgeous, trim, intelligent, and witty as she was when I first met her twenty-five years earlier. But I must say that with all the high points in her exciting life, Ruth is going to have to record one failure. Despite the specific orders I gave for the TV commercial I shot, Ruth's cosmetic makeover completely failed to make me look twenty years younger and fifty pounds slimmer!

Goldwater, Silver Lining, and Julie's a Jewel

My September 13, 1972, attempt to interview Julie Nixon Eisenhower about the then new Watergate buzz turned out to be a major disaster. Times three! Nobody Republican and nobody even remotely connected to the Nixon Administration wanted to talk to the media about the events that would lead to the resignation of the thirty-seventh president of these United States. I should know. I had an incredible encounter with Julie Nixon Eisenhower that taught me a lesson in tenacity, but this experience had a precedent with a tough, Republican lion of the U.S. Senate.

The very crusty, no-nonsense Senator Barry Goldwater had given me the blow-off on Watergate before a luncheon speech he gave at the old Jefferson Hotel right after the news of the break-in broke. I had approached the senator while he was still eating the rubber chicken hotel grub at the luncheon before he spoke. And I acknowledge that interrupting the old guy's lunch was discourteous on my part. But I saw an opening, or so I thought. As I approached the Arizonan rather timidly with mike in hand and crew in tow, he growled, "What do YOU want?"

That was one heckuva way to scare a cub reporter into repentance.

I stammered, "Senator, I . . . I just wanted to ask you a couple of quick . . . uh . . . questions . . ."

"About what?" he curmudgeoned. "Can't you see that I'm eating?"

"Well, sir," I continued with the timid look and tone of voice that would have sent an instant signal to a tiger in the jungle to attack a smaller animal. Zookeeper Charlie Hoessle had taught me that. "Just a couple of questions about the news of the day."

I was actually fibbing about my mission. I wanted to ask him only about Watergate, but I had planned to lead him down the garden path with a couple of throwaways, saving the "kill question" for my third query or so. I tried to look as green and pitiful as I could, although coming face-to-face with Goldwater made me immediately realize that this warrior had spent little time traversing the garden path.

"If there is one minute . . . after I eat—and before this program gets started . . . and I'm only going to give you one minute—I'll talk to you," the senator offered in as much generosity as he might ever muster.

"Okay, sir . . . okay. We'll just wait over there," I said jubilantly, pointing to an area just off the dais.

"Yessssss!" I thought. I had him in my sight, but not in my snare.

All senators, and politicians in general, ultimately want to be on television, I think. Television is free advertising and a visual notice to their constituents that they are on the job, unless of course, they are embroiled in a major scandal. Senator Goldwater finished his lunch, wiped his face and hands with his napkin, threw the napkin down on his plate, stood up looking in my direction, and started to step down the dais stairs. Was I nervous as the old lion approached me? I hoped it didn't show, but I was cowering a bit, to be honest with you. And now here he and I were face-to-face, one-on-one. Our bright light lit us up in the corner of the banquet room. Conscious of the minute I had been granted, I made my throwaway questions brief, and then asked: "So, senator, what can you tell me about this Watergate incident?"

Goldwater flushed and unleashed a blast of phraseology that he might well have coined. It was a retort that began to blossom over and over in the following weeks and months from the mouths of every prominent Republican.

"I don't know why you press guys always try to make a mountain out of a molehill," he replied menacingly. "THIS WATERGATE BUSINESS IS NOTHING BUT A SECOND-RATE BURGLARY blown completely out of proportion."

Yesss! I had a response. I thanked the senator who turned away from me disapprovingly and mounted the steps back up to his dais seat.

Back to Julie Nixon Eisenhower. She was in St. Louis for the first-ever St. Louis Golf Classic, a pro-amateur tournament held to benefit Children's Hospital. This event featured Bob Hope and golfing great Lee Trevino. The big tourney was held at Norwood Hills Country Club. After a plaintive plea, the head of the Secret Service contingent gave me the okay to approach the president's daughter, who was surrounded by an adoring crowd and a bunch of ever-vigilant hawks in the Secret Service. The decision to allow

Bob Hope did his best to keep Julie Nixon Eisenhower from talking to the author about (the then new) Watergate scandal.

me to approach Princess Julie was helped along by a whispered recommendation from a local Secret Service agent who either told the top guy that I was too inexperienced to put out some bad behavior, or I was on some Secret Service log as having avoided spouting any anti-Nixon sympathies in my nightly reports. I quickly introduced myself to Mrs. Eisenhower and found her to be an instantly smiling, charming, and accommodating surrogate for her father's re-election campaign. She seemed so friendly, in fact, that I didn't even waste the powder puff questions on her. I went straight for the key point of my being there: "Mrs. Eisenhower, what can you tell me about this Watergate affair?"

She began the ascent into a gracious response. She told me she didn't think this Watergate thing was a major news story. And as she smiled convincingly and told me that her father's re-election in November was of far more importance than . . .

Suddenly, I got an interruption that could only mean something bad. I braced. Henry Eisenkramer, a part-time photographer who did a lot of vacation relief work, was tapping me frantically on my shoulder. I turned to see what no reporter or photographer wanted to see in those last gasp days of using film before videotape became vogue. The 16 mm camera was literally belching out a curly-cuing spill of celluloid onto the golf course. Oh, no! I turned with my heart thumping to Julie and, not finding words to explain what was going on, I just pointed helplessly to the debacle unfolding before our eyes. But my precious time for an interview had expired, and the Secret Service moved Julie along the field and through a big crowd of spectators. I was enraged! But I was more embarrassed than angry.

Henry popped another roll of film onto the camera and tried gathering up the spent film as I cursed the very idea of vacation relief workers. The film would be of absolutely no use to anybody, so I can reason that Henry might have just not wanted to be reminded of the accident. With a great deal of maneuvering through the crowd, we miraculously caught up with Julie again, and with the approval of the unusually understanding Secret Service chief, I dared approach the charming first daughter for a second time.

"Would you mind? Please? You . . . you saw what happened back there with our film. May I just ask you the one question again about Watergate?" I begged furtively.

Seemingly on cue, Bob Hope appeared from nowhere behind Julie. The comedian was a frequent golfing buddy of President Nixon and the chief executive's golf-loving daughter, Julie.

"Come, on, Honey," Hope said in a commanding tone I had never heard from him in any of his comedic roles. "You don't want to talk about that. Come on." He looked directly at me and said sternly, as if I hadn't gotten his message or his mission, "She's not talking about that stuff!" And he manhandled her away from me. She looked at me hopelessly, and I could have sworn that she appeared almost apologetic. The whole episode looked like a little girl being dragged away by her daddy. But there was some consolation for the perspiration-soaked Henry and me. We got Hope's hauling Julie away on film!

I remained 0 for 2 in regards to obtaining a usable quote from Mrs. Eisenhower, but it is three strikes before one is out. Henry and I raced to the dirty white, unmarked station wagon that was the mode of transportation of choice for news crews of that era, and we sped toward the next destination on the Eisenhower–Hope itinerary: The Marriott Motor Hotel out west

IKE IN ST. LOUIS

When Julie Nixon Eisenhower's father was in St. Louis to address a Knights of Columbus convention in 1970, I had been a TV news reporter for only a few months. The president made a quick visit to the grassy area just west of the Gateway Arch, and quite unexpectedly, he got out of the car to press the flesh with the crowd. My photographer handed me a "shotgun" mike to get in closer to pick up some natural sound. A shotgun mike looks like . . . like . . . a shotgun. Just as I got the mike to about my waist level, BAM!!! I got hit simultaneously left and right by two Secret Service men and knocked to the ground completely winded. Sprawled on the ground and trying to figure out where I was, a Secret Service agent looked down on me and warned: "Sir, I wouldn't use that kind of microphone again in a situation like this!" The visit to the site in the shadow of the Arch was relatively brief. As the presidential limo and motorcade were leaving the area at Third and Memorial Drive, where my future station Channel 4 is located, an invigorated Nixon shocked everybody by jumping out of the limo again. This time he jumped onto the trunk of the big black presidential limo and began that famous two-armed, four-fingered Nixon victory wave. An ever-ready Secret Service agent quickly grabbed Mr. Nixon by both ankles. Exciting! But, if any sound of the event was to be had, it would have to come by way of another crewmember. As I continued to catch my breath, to me, a picture ALONE was worth a thousand minutes of sound!

a short distance off Interstate 70. Bob and Julie and Lee and their entourage were headed out to a twenty-five-dollar-a-plate chicken salad luncheon for Republican women.

Our exit from the country club grounds to get out on the highway was blocked for a while as the celebrity motorcade headed the short distance to Highway 70, but once we were allowed to proceed, I coaxed a reluctant Henry to catch up with—and PASS—the motorcade. The instant I gave the order, I realized what a foolhardy and dangerous instruction it was. The Secret Service could have mistaken us for assassins trying to do harm to their special passenger, and they might have fired a bazooka or rocket launcher or something atomic in their arsenal to blow us to smithereens. Our gambit would never have been allowed to move out like that these days. There is a zero-tolerance policy for such maneuvers like ours, in place since 9/11.

"Smile!" I ordered Henry, as I waved and grinned to beat the band. "Smile and wave friendly like. Smile." We passed the flatbed truck carrying the traveling media, who waved and smiled back at us—some of them with puzzled looks on their faces. And then we pulled alongside and then ahead of the motorcade. We must have appeared to be fugitives from a loony bin. We didn't look like terrorists, I'm sure. For the rest of my long career, I never knew a news crew to be allowed that kind of leeway by the Secret Service.

We roared onto the hotel parking lot and in the truest of paparazzi styles, we abandoned our car, slamming the doors in flight as we raced to the hotel entrance. We got into position just seconds before the motorcade pulled onto the lot and up to the hotel's front door. A large crowd erupted into cheers and chants of pro-Nixon re-election slogans. As Julie alighted and approached, she seemed to recognize me emerging from the crowd as the hapless, clumsy, bumbling young reporter that I must have appeared to be.

"Julie! Julie!" I called out. By now, I thought we knew each other well enough for me to be on a first name basis with her. And I'll be darned if she didn't take a couple of steps in my direction. "Watergate! Watergate!" I called out.

And just as she was about to open her mouth to shout a response to me . . . No! No! No! Oh, no-oooooo! (You can use the echo chamber effect here.)

Just then, as I thought this third time might be the charm, all twenty-five members of the Ladue High School Marching Band struck up a blast of near-deafening music. The young musicians completely drowned out Julie, me, and any other sounds within a quarter mile of where the welcoming band was positioned. Julie was then quickly ushered into the hotel where we could hear the women cheering. We weren't allowed into the private luncheon. Curses! Curses! Foiled again! For the third straight time within an hour that day. But, at least, we got the band blare on film. And we had pictures of the Bob Hope intervention.

Totally dejected, I headed back to the station with . . . with . . .

not much. But I decided to make a silk purse out of a sow's ear and to drink the lemonade I had made from the lemons I had been thrown that day. After the film came out of the "soup," and after some serious editing, the story I put together was ready for air. We went on the air that evening at six with a lead-in from senior anchorman Chris Condon. With a glint in his eye with me sitting right next to him at the anchor desk, the silver-haired news icon proudly introduced the story of "Julius Hunter's courageous attempts to interview a presidential daughter."

And with a lead-in to the story that telegraphed to my audience that what was to follow would not be the breaking of a Watergate-type story, I opened: "If at first you don't succeed, try, try, etcetera." We ran a few seconds of overexposed film to replicate the film that the camera had burped out during my first attempt at the interview. Then we showed a clip of Bob Hope dragging Julie away during my second try. And then my light little feature showed the Ladue High band drowning out my third attempt to get a word with Julie on Watergate.

I closed the piece on-camera with a compliment to Julie Nixon Eisenhower for being so kind as to acquiesce three times in an attempt to be charming and gracious and answer my burning question. I was sincere in my salute to her kindness.

And then Chris, who was never above throwing a young cub a challenging question on the set or in the field, asked me in front of tens of thousands of viewers: "So, Julius, does this mean you're going to vote for her dad in November?"

I wasn't willing to declare any political affiliations in front of God and everybody. I declared: "Well, Chris . . . I'd vote for Julie any day."

Pat Buchanan Is Color-Blind

I was surprised to discover that former presidential candidate and perennial political pundit Pat Buchanan has quite a sense of humor. In fact, at three different Washington, D.C., cocktail and dinner parties where I rubbed shoulders and traded humor with Pat, I found that he has the most raucous laugh and unbridled jocularity imaginable.

The three parties were thrown by or for my good buddy, ubiquitous Republican strategist Ed Rollins. Two soirees were Christmas parties at Ed's home, and the third was a fiftieth birthday party thrown for Ed at Union Station in D.C. At the second Christmas party, which took place in 1992, I re-introduced myself to Pat, with a particular mission to show him exactly what my face looks like.

During the hundreds of interviews I've conducted via telephone and satellite, I have learned that these non-face-to-face interviews are both convenient and handicapping. The news operation and the anchor/reporter can quickly throw a still photo of the interviewee up on your TV screen—often with a locater to tell you the geographical point from which the interviewee is talking. The problem with these types of interviews, however, is that you and your viewers can clearly see the person being interviewed, but the interviewee on the other side of the camera cannot see his or her interrogator.

This handicap proved to be very embarrassing to Pat Buchanan. Pat, as you know, not only occupies the farthest right of the Republican Party but also always has, according to his tone, the right answer. During the 1992 presidential campaign, Buchanan was a fierce warrior in the first of his three runs for president. He was an "also ran" in both 1996 and 2007. Buchanan inflamed liberals, moderates, and even some staunch Republicans by his flame-thrower rhetoric, particularly on the subject of multiculturalism and immigration.

That renowned one-on-one interview I had with Buchanan in 1992 was not my first encounter with him. In 1970, I was a cub reporter with less than a full year of experience wielding the microphone, and Pat was a thirty-two-year-old post-wunderkind speechwriter. He teamed up with William Safire to put words in the mouth of President Nixon and Vice President Spiro T. Agnew. At age twenty-three, Pat had become the *St. Louis Globe-Democrat*'s youngest editorial staff member. I remember one time when Pat stood shoulder to shoulder with his boss, Agnew, for an impromptu news conference on the Lambert Field tarmac. I learned later from a Safire interview that Buchanan once handed a highly flammable anti-press speech he wrote for Agnew to Nixon for the chief executive's approval. Nixon looked the speech over and, according to Safire, said, "This really rips the scab off, doesn't it?" Yet Nixon, who often referred to the press as "the enemy," gave the go-ahead for Agnew to use that same Buchanan-penned speech to spew some venom to attack the media.

The 1970 airport interview to which I was sent by the assignment editor was truly like leading a lamb to slaughter. I wasn't prepared to face both Agnew and Buchanan at the same time, but I dared to ask this flammable question of Agnew: "Mr. Vice President, I understand that after your recent period of being muzzled by the White House, there are reports that President Nixon is going to unleash you on the media again. Is that true?"

Agnew looked at Buchanan then back at me and snarled: "Where did those reports come from?"

I stammered. I stuttered. I was embarrassed. I rifled through my notes. "Uh . . . uh?"

"Where did you get the reports you're referring to?" the veep repeated raising his volume a bit. I remember that Pat Buchanan was beaming through tight lips as if to say: "Way to go, Boss. Don't let this black sonafabitch get away with that unverifiable crap!" It was almost as if Buchanan was transmitting words to Agnew by osmosis. The young writer was standing so close to Agnew.

Finally, after what seemed like a long, long period of time of my standing on ground that not one of my colleague news reporters would dare tread, I was on my own. Finally, in what was probably no more than two or three seconds, I came up with a response.

"The report comes from the Associated Press, sir."

"Report?" asked the vice president. "How many reports are there from AP?"

Before I could answer, and as Buchanan looked on with proud encouragement, Agnew asked: "Who do you know at the Associated Press? Name one person you know at the Associated Press. If you can't, let's go to another question."

And the duo did. They went on to another question. I dropped into an instant oblivion of absolute embarrassment on that tarmac. There might as well have been a tarmac trapdoor through which I plunged to the depths of nothingness.

On the way back to the station that day, I didn't have a single response from the veep that I could call my own. I knew I'd have to use a response on-air from some other reporter's question. And I knew something else for sure, even with my minimal experience. I could never let that embarrassing exchange between Agnew and Cubnew get on the air. It was a lesson I will never forget. From that day forward, I never again used a generality as the basis of a question. I checked and rechecked my sources before I quoted a source. Even if that source bears the first name "Unnamed" or "Highly Placed" or "Informed," I always tried to get corroboration before going on air with a shaky premise. What is that old adage? *It is better to do a job half slow, than to do a job half fast!*

I was never allowed to make any declarations of my personal political feelings on the air or at any public forums. But that was hard to do. I remember the almost annual meetings in which Channel 4 brought in its legal counsel to advise the reportorial and editorial staff on their responsibilities to ethics and the law. I remember how often I cringed when I heard Pat dodge in and out of his stints as a pundit and then as a candidate to rail against allowing immigrants into the country, especially émigrés of color. Buchanan simply explained that Haitian immigrants, for example, should not be allowed to pour into the United States because they just would not, according to Buchanan, assimilate into Massachusetts culture as well as immigrants from European shores. He always pointed with pride to his own forebears from Scotland and Ireland who came over the ocean and blended into American culture perfectly in the late 1700s. The only way I would give Pat an A+ on that controversial racially tinged stance would be for his having the balls to make that controversial declaration in the first place.

Buchanan had even alleged in one of his books that Hitler wasn't really any kind of a threat to the United States when he was doing his thing leading up to World War II, and Pat suggests that the United States should have minded its own business. His theories resonated with more Americans than one might think. Buchanan got 37 percent of the New Hampshire vote in 1992; 22 percent of the popular vote in 1996.

Needless to say, I was thrilled with the prospect of going *mano-a-mano* with Pat on my six o'clock newscast on February 7, 1992. The station set up one of those one-way satellite interviews with Pat from one of his stops on the campaign trail. Candidates will often do back-to-back interviews with news anchors/reporters in a whirlwind flurry. The advantage to the candidate is that he or she can maximize precious exposure while minimizing the cost of getting around in person to five or six cities. The stations—most often in conglomerate ownership—split the cost of the "bird" (satellite) time. So, Pat could sit pat and talk to ten or twelve stations inside a couple of hours. Saves a ton of dough on jet fuel, too.

The only instruction the anchor gets for one of these interviews is to be told the total number of minutes available for the satellite window. And that is in hard time. If, for example, the interviewee is assigned twelve minutes, that means twelve minutes . . . not a second more; not a second less. A station can opt to take less time, but never more. Time is kept by a stage manager signaling the anchor, and often the director in the control room will give a countdown in the anchor's ear.

These satellite interviews are often set up at the last minute, with little time to prepare. Once seated and "laced up," the only audio signal the anchor gets is the director in the master control room in whatever city saying: "Stand by St. Louis. Coming to you in thirty seconds. Fifteen. Stand by. Go, St. Louis!" Sometimes, if the anchor is the first in a string of interviews or the only interviewer, time for a little off-air warm-up conversation is allowed. I personally preferred to avoid warm-up chit-chat like the plague. The most information I preferred to give by way of warm-up amounted to disclosing only my name, rank, and serial number to the person on the other end of the interview. "Hi, senator, this is Julius Hunter from Channel 4 in St. Louis. Thanks for talking with us today." That's enough. Some of the effervescence of an interview can be lost if those involved get too chummy. And I NEVER like to get to a point at which the interviewee asks: "What are you going to ask me?"

I don't ever like to declare upfront. I want a natural, unrehearsed response from the subjects that I put in the hot seat. In fact, when CBS owned KMOV where I worked, it was strictly forbidden to tell an interviewee a question in advance unless viewers were notified that the interview had been rehearsed.

Back to my historic 1992 interview with Pat. Did you think I had forgotten? Well, the interview with Buchanan was live and had to hit at a precise time—like 6:06:30. So the producer had to time out all the material that preceded the Buchanan interview. We could have gone to the live interview with Pat at 6:06:48, but we then would have screwed ourselves out of eighteen seconds of our allotted "bird" time. And our end time had to be precise, or the satellite video would be cut off— maybe in his or my mid-sentence.

After reading all my news stories before the Buchanan interview, I was given the go signal. I would assume that my producer had given Pat my name, rank, and serial number seconds before he appeared on the screen. I wasted no time and immediately hit Pat with my best stuff. I would have loved to have grilled him for a full half hour, but having a subject for a shorter time forces certain disciplines on the interviewer. There is no time for courtesies or fluff. Let's get on with it!

I was once criticized roundly about town when I did a satellite interview with presidential candidate Michael Dukakis on Election Night minutes before the polls in Missouri closed. Some of the brickbats I received by phone, mail, and comment on the street alleged that I had been too harsh on Dukakis— especially about his silly *Snoopy* look in that military tank. Criticism also surfaced after an interview with then Archbishop Justin Rigali. I was accused by some critics of being curt, interruptive, and rude to each of these gentlemen. I was sure that I was not being such a tough character with Pat, but I was on a mission guided by a strict clock.

Pat handles all questions deftly. He is a master of the sound bite. Nice and short and pregnant with leads for follow-up questions. But he did throw in his standard talking points like any good politician. Some of the things he said I had certainly heard before in his interviews. And I had taken mental notes of what Pat and all the other contenders spewed on the national newscasts and

Sunday talk shows. And I figured that if I recognized it when he would swing into one of his stump speech ho-hums, some of my audience might recognize the same old thing from Pat.

Near the end of my allotted satellite time, as determined by the stage manager giving me a countdown, I pulled Pat into one of his positions that bothered me as an African American. It was the Buchanan thesis that Haitian boat people should be turned back at American shores because with their black skin they would not mix well with the whites in the Massachusetts neighborhood. That's the same neighborhood where Pat grew up in a middle-class family.

I had an ace-in-the-hole question, which was subsequently reported in St. Louis's *Riverfront Times:*

Hunter: Pat, I've got only about thirty seconds left, so let me put this question to you succinctly. Pat, are you a racist?

Pat: Well, Julius, I think that blacks deserve the same rights as you and I have. Blah-blah-blah-blah, ya-da-ya-da-ya-da.

The director in the control room opened the mike key to give me a "Wrap!" and I could hear the control room crew in hysterics. The stage manager nearly fell onto the floor laughing.

Without missing a beat, I said with Pat and I on a split screen: "Thank you, GOP Presidential Candidate Pat Buchanan. We can see you just fine. But you obviously can't see us. We'll be back with more news after this."

The *Riverfront Times* reported that I had a "twinkle in (my) eye" and observed that "it was a nice little moment of reality in a medium filled with fakery."

The shrewd and sharp Pat Buchanan had assumed or thought that I was Caucasian—like he is.

At Ed Rollins's Christmas party later that year after Buchanan was knocked out of the presidential race, I met a host of luminaries. I rubbed shoulders with the likes of Sam Donaldson; fuddy-duddy talk show caricature John McLaughlin; Andrea Mitchell and her now hubby, Alan Greenspan; Chris Matthews; Vernon Jordan; and a host of other politicos. When I found out that Pat was there, I couldn't wait to go up to him and introduce myself. I said: "Pat, I'm Julius Hunter, and I'm an anchor at the

CBS station in St. Louis. You performed a miracle on me when I interviewed you by satellite back in February."

Pat, with drink in hand, looked at me quizzically waiting for the rest of this strange introduction. "I did what?"

"You performed a miracle on me," I continued to tease.

"How's that?" Pat asked, looking fully prepared to make a mad dash to another corner of Ed's rathskeller to get away from what might have appeared to him to be a Grade-A Large weirdo.

"Well, after nearly fifty years as a black guy," I said, "you made me a white guy in ten seconds!"

When I told him the story in full detail and told him my remarks to cap the interview, Pat broke out into a whole-body eruption of laughter. He squints his eyes when he laughs, but I do think I saw tears in those eyes as we laughed and shared the story with others around us. Sam Donaldson, then of ABC, strolled over to find out what was so darn funny. And when we told them the story he joined in the guffawing.

If only I had had the presence of mind while we were chortling to say: "Well, Pat, looks like we Haitians can blend in pretty good with folks like you after all."

Since that 1992 encounter—on the air, and at Ed Rollins's Yuletide Party—Pat's stances have turned to more of a moderate position. He has distanced himself on-air from the most conservative of the GOP pack. He has decried the so-called wing of the Republican Party that hoodwinked voters in 1996. I might share with him the opinion that *compassionate conservatism* as practiced by the Bush II Administration is oxymoronic. In fact, Buchanan has written a book called *Where the Right Went Wrong: How Neoconservatives Subverted the Reagan Revolution*.

The mood at the Rollins Christmas party was too festive to bring up to Pat my first personal encounter with him on that airport tarmac in 1970. Next time I see him I will conjure up the memories of him and the vice president who was run out of town on a rail after he sliced and diced me. And I don't know how strange this is: even though Pat and I will never share any political views, after my latter-day encounters with him, he might just be the kind of guy I'd enjoy having a beer or two with. After all, he and Spiro T. Agnew, of all people, had taught me a valuable lesson. And who knows, maybe in that now famous 1992 satellite interview with Pat, I might have taught Pat a thing or two.

A SWORD FOR PEACE

One of the most impressive, intelligent, and visionary persons I have met is Oscar Arias Sánchez, the president of Costa Rica. By the end of 2010, he will have served a second unsuccessive four-year term as that Central American nation's CEO. He was elected to his first four-year term in 1986.

We met on Thursday, April 7, 2005, when he was the keynote speaker at Saint Louis University at the Fifth Annual Atlas Week program—designed to highlight and celebrate the university's position in and service to a growing global community. And what better role model than Dr. Arias Sánchez. He is the 1987 Nobel Prize winner for his valiant, tireless work to bring a lasting peace to Central America. He emits no fire, no eloquence when one meets him for the first time. But he exhibited sheer genius when he convinced his country and nine other neighboring countries to beat their swords into plowshares and study war no more. The document that has sustained peace in a major region of Central America is called the "Esquipulas II Accords."

Ironically, the man who convinced ten Central American nations to essentially do away with their military manpower and hardware was presented with SLU's highest honor. Arias Sánchez received the coveted "Sword of Ignatius Loyola." This unique award is a full-size, authentically heavy, golden replica in the Spanish Toledo style. Since a sword represents battle and war, maybe SLU can come up with an alternative award specifically for those honorees who have worked to eradicate battle and war. How about a *"Dove* of Ignatius Loyola?" I'm sure the bird symbolizing peace could be linked with the Holy Spirit.

At a time when the efficacy of standardized testing in our schools is being vigorously challenged in the United States, President Arias Sánchez is being heralded for restoring standardized academic testing at the end of primary and secondary school experiences in Costa Rica.

Sword of Loyola recipients are asked to give a speech in return for their honor. Arias Sánchez's words during his address to the SLU audience were quiet but exceptionally powerful and inspirational. At the cocktail reception that followed the

Costa Rican President Oscar Arias Sánchez is presented the mayoral proclamation by the author.

outstanding speech, I was asked by SLU President Lawrence Biondi, as SLU vice president for community relations, to present our special guest with a welcome and an official proclamation from the mayor's office. My Spanish teachers in grade school, high school, and college would be pleased that I spoke part of my greeting and presentation in Spanish. *"Que buenas dias, Senor presidente. Bienvenido a San Luis y el campo de La Universitas de San Luis. Tenemos allegrios que Usted tenia el tiempo de honor nosotros con su presencia."*

His soft voice was almost inaudible when he graciously thanked me for my greeting in his native tongue and accepted the mayor's proclamation. He had spoken very softly when he was holding forth at the microphone. And it was very difficult to hear Senor Arias Sánchez over the din of the cocktail reception that followed. Although the words and actions of the Costa Rican man of peace are strong—even forceful—his eyes are soft and weak. As he talks to you, his sleepy eyes are cast almost downward, but I'd bet he is seeing far, far beyond those who chat him up into depths we might not be able to grasp.

During the reception, as in his speech, Arias Sánchez continued his sharp criticism of the Bush Administration's handling, or lack of handling, of international policies. He repeated to a small clump of us his simple, yet complicated thesis that if the major military powers of the world would do away with their weapons of mass destruction, not only would there be more peace all over the globe, but there would also be more money freed up to feed the hungry all over the world.

I peeled him away from the crowd for a moment to chat further over my Manhattan and his glass of red wine in the restored nineteenth-century SLU library. I asked Dr. Arias Sánchez for an amplification. Did I understand him correctly during the speech he had just given that he didn't have much faith in former Deputy Defense Secretary Paul Wolfowitz? Was he concerned that Wolfowitz was not capable of carrying out the promise he had made to the world just three weeks before our chat in the Pere Marquette Gallery? Wolfowitz was nominated by President Bush on April 7, 2005, to head the World Bank. Wolfowitz, considered by many to be a neocon warmonger, had promised to "help the poorest of the world to lift themselves out of poverty." Did the Costa Rican leader think that Defense Secretary Donald Rumsfeld's former deputy was capable of carrying out his ambitious promise? I had to crane to hear his response. "How," the former Boston University student asked quietly over the reception noise, "can we expect a man who was one of the main architects of the War in Iraq—the man who has almost single-handedly pushed your president to destroy a major part of the world—to now be expected to be the top agent for helping the places in the world that need the most economic attention?" And before I could even hazard an opinion, I cupped my ear to hear the illustrious world statesman respond to his own rhetorical question. "Well, I suppose we can only hope and pray that the Devil himself has the ability to change his ways," Arias Sánchez said softly enough that his last sentence sounded almost like a prayer.

The world's neediest nations did not have to wait for Wolfowitz to travel along the Road to Damascus. He was forced to resign his World Bank leadership on June 30, 2007, just two years after I spoke with the remarkable Arias Sánchez. The downfall of Wolfowitz had nothing to do with a failure to use the World Bank's money to stem international poverty. He got routed for the self-serving crime of giving his girlfriend, former

World Bank staffer Shaha Riza, a $50,000 a year, tax-free salary hike. Wolfowitz got the ax just two years after Arias Sánchez offered up a glimmer of hope for Paul Wolfowitz's salvation and the plight of the world's poorest people.

I guess receiving SLU's highest honor means that he who lives to get a sword can still be a peacemaker.

AND THEN WE LEARNED:

Arias Sánchez was elected to a fierce constitutional battle to take a second term as president of Costa Rica. He was sworn in on May 8, 2006. I learned in May of 2008 why he spoke so softly during his SLU speech and subsequent conversation with me. Doctors in Philadelphia found that he had a nonmalignant cyst on his vocal cords. He was ordered not to speak for a month.

❉   ❉   ❉

Shaha Riza, the girlfriend of Paul Wolfowitz, was put on "external leave" from her job as senior communications officer for the Middle East and North Africa after the scandal broke. Ironically, she was absorbed as head of the Foundation for the Future, a semi-independent organization to promote democracy in the Middle East and North Africa.

❉   ❉   ❉

The disgraced Paul Wolfowitz is still traveling the world when he is not pondering the error of his ways at his home in Chevy Chase, Maryland. On a visit to a Turkish mosque in late January of 2007, photographers took a picture of him with holes in his socks. The Turkish Hosiery Manufacturer's Association sent him a dozen pairs of socks.

ROLLINS AND REAGAN

I almost dropped my teeth and fell over the back of my chair when I heard on one Friday afternoon right before Christmas 2007 that the new chief strategist and national campaign chairman for former Arkansas Governor Mike Huckabee's White House run was none other than my old buddy, maverick Republican campaign adviser Ed Rollins. "Where in hell will this guy show up next?" I asked myself almost out loud.

I could tell just from what I heard and read about the Huckabee/Rollins alliance that Ed was having a ball. He not only enjoyed the challenge of putting the ultimate underdog in the White House, but for those of us who know him, we recognize that our friend, Ed Rollins, never met a headline with his name in it that he didn't like.

I phoned Ed right away and got his earliest observations about running the Huckabee campaign for the White House. "It's the only campaign I've ever been in where there's no donuts and no booze, so it's going to be a real struggle for me." But, on the other hand, Ed was widely quoted when he first hopped aboard the Huckabee bandwagon: "It makes the governor proud to see me as a prime example of what he does not want to be. He can point to me and say, after shedding the hundred pounds he lost, 'Never again will I look like that fat old man over there.'"

Could this be the same Ed Rollins with whom a motley crew of Washington University staffers and I played macho poker while chomping on disgusting cigars during the late 1960s? Does this new Head Huckabee Huckster bear any resemblance to the Ed Rollins who used to get hammered with me and the guys after slamming back too many ultimately destructive "stingers" with beer chasers at a popular bar just off campus? (It didn't take long for the guys and gals in our Washington U. bunch to realize that "stingers" should be banned from public consumption because of their destructive side effects.)

What a ride Ed has had. He worked mightily on the campaign to get Ronald Reagan into California's governor's mansion. And then Ed was a key component during the Gipper's two terms in the White House. If eventual historians try to construct a profile

Ed Rollins and the author relax on the Eastern Shore.

of Ed, then they have their work cut out for them. I know for a fact that Ed, descendent of a blue-collar family, had early associations with and respect for the Kennedys. But before I knew it, Ed was a GOP big shot. (For my money, I have always associated him with the "Mercenary Party.")

After leaving the White House at the end of the second Reagan White House term, Ed was a much-sought-after political whiz kid. I remember when Pat Robertson wanted Ed to run his presidential campaign. To persuade Ed to take the job, the peculiar televangelist brought Ed from Washington to his sprawling Virginia farm. Ed said he felt a little uncomfortable with Robertson because, Ed told me, he didn't believe in a damn thing that Robertson espoused. In fact, Ed had, has, and will always have a lot of gay friends; my pal of forty years seriously doubts that prayer can turn away hurricanes; he contributes more to bar bills than to collection plates; Rollins has had a better-than-average personal appreciation of the so-called fairer sex than the men in the Robertson flock might admit to; and he would ultimately trust the pronouncements of his Pope over those of a Baptist preacher who has been known to go off the deep end more often than Obama's former pastor, Jeremiah Wright.

When the press waited with full or unbridled curiosity for Ed's return from the Robertson Farm, the fun-loving Republican political analyst was bombarded with questions from his chums in the media. Would he take the bold step to run the Robertson presidential campaign? What response had he given Robertson?

Ed's detailing of his decision was Rollinsian candor at its best: "I told Pat that if he could heal my hernia through prayer, I would run his campaign." Needless to say, Ed never heard from Pat Robertson again.

But the famous foot-in-the-mouth Rollins pose became legendary in the Reagan White House. I list but a few of the Rollins transgressions:

1. Once, when the Reagan White House sent Ed to change maverick Vermont Senator James Jefford's planned vote against more B-1 Bombers, Rollins was asked by a student in a closed university audience what techniques he had used to influence Jefford's vote. Ed was quoted far and wide as having said: "Well, we beat him up around the head and ears pretty good."

2. When George H. W. Bush sought out Ed to head up his plan to succeed Ronald Reagan, Ed put out the word that he didn't want to work for a "loser." And Ed elaborated that he didn't mean a "loser in terms of the popular vote." Ed got no more invitations to White House dinners, but the major fallout from this forthright, if crudely put observation was the status of Sherrie Rollins's job. She was fired almost immediately from her White House position right after Ed opened his big mouth.

3. When Ed ran Christine Todd Whitman's successful gubernatorial contest in New Jersey, he sullied the victory by boasting that he and the Whitman campaign had paid off black preachers around the state to have their flocks sit on their hands on Election Day. Ed later said that was just a joke to gig his archrival, James Carville, but the Baptist preacher boast produced an investigation by the U.S. attorney general, the FBI, a New Jersey State probe, a Democratic Party inquisition, and a $500 million lawsuit brought by Al Sharpton and Jesse Jackson. Some big names like Bill and Bob Bennett, Bob Beckel, Barbara Walters, Chris Matthews, and Senator John Warner bucked the trend of abandoning Rollins and stepped up to stand with Ed. But a lot of the pundits, personalities, and talk show hosts who had hounded Ed for many years to be on their shows for no pay and had fed on Ed's sizzling comments dropped away as if Ed had leprosy. Ed writes on page 296 of his autobiography, *Bare Knuckles and Back Rooms:* "One of the first (friends) to call was Julius Hunter, my old pal from the Barricades of Washington University. 'This is all horseshit,' the first black anchor on St. Louis television reassured me. He offered to get on a plane that night to help, and he called every couple of days to hold my hand."

Ed came through all the pounding of this last indiscretion without prosecution. In fact, the tenacious former boxer came out virtually unscathed, except for whatever was done to his head, his heart, and his assessment of some of the media people he had once called friends.

Ed's roundtrip voyage on the River Styx did little to provide a filter for my old buddy's mouth. In the heat of the 2008 GOP primaries, he reportedly swore that he "would like to knock Mitt Romney's teeth out." Romney deflected the threat with a light-hearted: "Just don't touch the hair."

I couldn't resist asking my friend, the veteran political operative who is connected with Washington politics like few others, for a flash round of assessment of a few of the big names out there in the political arena. He was game. So was I:

Hunter: *Mitt Romney*

Rollins: *Central casting; pollster's dream; borrows and steals ideas from competitors right from under their noses and tries to make them his. Plastic. Unimaginative. What's that old joke about Xerox Copiers? They never did anything original! That's Romney. And then there is that religion of his that I guess I and millions of other voters have just not figured out yet.*

Hunter: *Fred Thompson*

Rollins: *Laziest candidate to come down the pike. His wife wanted to be First Lady far more than he wanted to be First Dude. Didn't hit the deck till ten every morning. Did one, maybe two events a day. And then, those occasional campaign outings would last ten or fifteen minutes apiece. Sometimes. Shame he lost his day job on* Law & Order. *Hope he put a good chunk of change away for retirement. Or I hope his lovely wife, like so many other big-time candidates' wives, has a lot of old family money.*

Hunter: *Hillary*

Rollins: *Tough lady! Incredibly tenacious candidate. If she doesn't get her party's nomination, she might just keep on campaigning for the next four years or more while the elected president is in the White House without ever even taking a day off. But, you know . . . I wouldn't personally like to see Bill banging around the White House without anything official to do for four years. Talk about a recipe for hanky-panky. But Hillary could actually be a damn good president, I think. At least she'd give it her best shot.*

Hunter: *Barack*

Rollins: *He sure speaks pretty. But I don't know whether he has the balls to kick enough tails and move enough mountains. Just giving good speeches won't do a damn thing for what this country needs right now after seven years of this disastrous Bush Administration. And we can try to sugar coat it, and it's sad, but race is still going to be the most important factor in this election. There are some whites who would not vote for a black man just outta hate handed down to them by their great-great granddaddies. And to be perfectly honest, there's a lot of racial hate coming from the other side, too.*

Hunter: *McCain*

Rollins: *Well, all I can say is that you know how you and I feel when we haul our aging butts outta bed in the morning these days. Just think what a seventy-one-year-old vet who was bruised and battered and mistreated in a Vietnamese concentration compound for more than five years must be feeling like when the alarm clock goes off. He's gotta see and feel some scars and hurts you and me never ever see—physically and emotionally. He's publicly admitted he doesn't know anything about the economy. Bad mistake. Never should have admitted that out front . . . up front. We would have found out how dumb*

he is about the economy sooner or later anyway. He's the worst speech-giver I have ever heard. The TelePrompTer is still one of his worst enemies. And I think he has a natural, inborn tendency to wanna make war and not love. Plus, I've known John for a long time, and those undercurrent rumors about him having a hot temper are absolutely true. In fact, they may be understated. And his campaign folks are going to have to work overtime to keep that hot temper from coming out.

Hunter: *And what about "W?"*

Rollins: *Well, polls don't lie all that much. He is the worst president we've had since Nixon and Carter. Historians could well end up calling him the absolute worst president this nation has ever had—a disaster-and-a-half. His main fault is that he just wouldn't listen to a lot of people who are smarter than he is. And there are a lot of those out there. Most people are smarter than "Junior Bush." And he's failed to recognize for almost eight years now that a lot of his top people have been pulling wool over his eyes that's 40 percent cotton. He didn't have enough people on his staff who would be bold enough to say: "Mr. President, that's the most stupid idea I've ever heard." He's surrounded himself by people whose heads are so far up his ass—or up their own asses—that they wouldn't recognize the light of day if it hit them in the face.*

Atta boy, Ed. Tone down that rhetoric. Love the kinder, gentler you.

But back to what is probably not—when I think about it—Ed's last hurrah: Huckabee. So, why did he choose to go with a Baptist preacher for the 2007–08 presidential election?

"I love the guy. He and I bonded instantly, and I saw a lot of potential in him right away," Ed said of the Arkansas phenom with rare, but obviously genuine tenderness in his tone.

"But you're so different," I challenged. "Like he's a fitness nut; lost 140 pounds . . . the equivalent of a whole person. You and I are on "Jared's Diet" alright enough, but only if we can eat three or four Subway sandwiches at a sitting. And he's a big-time Baptist born-again evangelist, and you, you're more like a "born every now and again Catholic."

"Yes, all that's true," Ed quickly admitted. "But, Julius, and don't think I'm losing it . . ."

"Too late," I interrupted.

"No, no. Hear me out. And I know you're going to think this sounds corny. I was sitting in a Catholic church at Mass just before Christmas. And some thoughts of my dear father—you knew him, and he knew you well, and you two loved each other—I was thinking of him on the anniversary of his passing away. I asked myself what he would want me to do next in my life. He cared a lot about what I was doing. Didn't always understand what I was doing. Didn't always agree with me. I really didn't want to get mixed up with another presidential campaign. But I thought: my Dad might have wanted me to do this. Just one last time. And after some deep thought and a few visions, I left that church and put in a call to Huckabee right away. He wasn't in, but he called me right back in just a few minutes and I signed on and he welcomed me aboard. All within fifteen minutes."

"What was it exactly that turned you on about this guy?"

"Well, I was impressed by his humor, the core of his belief system, his statements about his faith, his incredible ability to communicate. He may have been even better at communicating than my old boss, President Reagan. And that's saying something! And he could spout what he was trying to say in perfect sound bites. The Bush people dicked over everybody with the bullcrap term "compassionate conservative." The Bush Gang completely sucked the air right out of the term and its meaning. But Huckabee, this was the real deal.

And I liked the fact that I had come into a small campaign. Not a lot of people tripping over each other. Not a lot of money. Chip Saltzman, who had worked for Bill Frist, was the head honcho when I came on. He is a sharp cookie. We didn't clash ever. And it was unbelievable and very impressive to me when I joined up that Huckabee was really in charge of his own campaign. He made the final decision on everything. He knew where every penny was coming from and what we would spend every penny on. And even if he is so talented and we were working so hard on a shoestring, Huckabee still took time out to lay out all the messages he wanted to put out there. *And* he is the only candidate I've worked for who wrote all his own speeches! Sometimes he didn't even write anything down. I became the governor's traveling companion and made every whistlestop with him. He always welcomed my advice, even if he didn't use it or if he modified it and put it in his own folksy style. I've never been in so many Baptist churches in my life!

"Had you *ever* been in a Baptist church before?" I had to laugh.

"No," he confessed and we both had a chuckle.

"And, how, my Brother, did you mask your tendency to want a Scotch every now and again on the campaign trail with an avowed teetotaler?" I wondered aloud.

"Well, Julius, you know a thirsty cowboy can always find a cactus plant or a saloon on the dusty trail," Ed confessed. "The governor allowed me to catch a drink or two with his twenty-five-year-old daughter, Sarah. But he made me promise to keep an eye on her and have her in by curfew," Ed chuckled.

In our recent conversations on his foray into Huckabeeland, the two old soldiers dredged up some memories of our colorful yesteryears. One of our fondest memories began with a phone call from him in mid-June 1982.

"Mr. Hunter? This is Mr. Rollins. How the hell are ya?"

"Hey, Ed. How the hell are you? You still running the country?"

"You still running St. Louis?" Ed asked with a laugh.

The early morning phone call to my home came when Ed was President Reagan's trusted domestic advisor and political maverick. Ed and I became instant friends in 1969 when he came to St. Louis to teach a Washington University course in urban studies. Ed and I were also two fish out of water in our positions as housemasters in two neighboring all-female dorms. We've often wondered aloud: "What in the world was the university thinking in giving us those appointments?"

I had just gotten married two months before Ed and I met, and he was a dashing, athletically fit Chico State grad with a fancy for boxing. Ed became an idol of a lot of the off-limits female students, and there were several of the female staff members on campus that took a fancy to this fireplug of a guy with the rippling muscles. But there were perhaps as many ladies who were in love with Ed's massive St. Bernard, Sampson, as those who took a shine to Ed. Although Ed had acquired tolerable social graces, Sampson was a free spirit with total disregard for the standard rules of acceptable etiquette. One of Sampson's favorite violations was to rumble willy-nilly through any campus cafeteria door he could find open, and rather than humble himself by begging for food, Big Sample would just hop up on a bench or chair and begin slurping at a plate that was already occupied with someone else's breakfast, lunch, or dinner. So many students and staff found the act amusing that the darling dog never learned that he was doing anything wrong. He thought all the laughing and cheering and commotion meant that he was doing something that was totally acceptable.

Ed had cut his political teeth in the California State Assembly and in the successful Reagan gubernatorial campaign in California. He was a natural for the eventual role he held as President Reagan's chief political advisor. Reagan recognized what a scrappy political operative Ed was, and although Ed probably swung as many shady deals as Carl Rove is accused of pulling off, the media spotlight didn't shine so brightly on the White House during the Reagan years as it did during the era of the Second Bush.

"I need a favor, buddy," Ed continued during that phone call in late May 1982.

"Anything at all," I responded.

"The president is coming to your town on July 22, and he's got a couple hours to kill."

I interrupted right away: "You may want to rephrase that, buddy. We don't want to use the word 'kill' in the same sentence as 'president.'"

"Yeah, yeah, you're right," Ed allowed as he charged back into the purpose of his call. "We need to fill a couple of hours on the president's schedule that day. Can you think of a really good photo op for us for that day? I mean something that would make the chief look good?"

"Hmmm," I mused. "I'm going to have to think on that for a bit. Let me get right back at you."

"Okay, but we need to set up something on the calendar right away. And I would appreciate it if you would keep it under your hat. We would get swamped if the (GOP) party folks in your town knew we had a little time on our hands."

"Got it. I'll get right back at you."

Ed could be certain that my telling him I would get back to him in "a bit" would be the same thing as my telling him, "I'll get back to you within the hour. Or less." It's well understood that news people and those in positions similar to Ed's work on a totally different time schedule than people in other jobs. "In a bit" to an archivist, librarian, artist, auto mechanic, or an astronaut on the way to Mars might mean in a day, a week, a month, or in a couple of years. But broadcast newsrooms and White House offices want things to happen "yesterday."

I thought with my heightened metabolic rate in effect: *Where might I put the president of the United States in a photo op?* With St. Louis not having had a Republican mayor in my lifetime, I remember being asked by representatives of the Ford, Reagan, Bush I, and Bush II administrations from time to time if the Democratic mayor should be in the tarmac welcoming party when their man came to town. So Republican Reagan should not be placed into any photo op scene that would embarrass him, the White House, or the city for that matter. Hmmm. Hmmm. And, of course, I was thinking of my favorite bird when thinking of where I'd suggest the president spend those two hours he had to fill.

My favorite bird? The crow. As in *Quid Pro Crow.* What would my service to the White House, and thus to my country, be worth for me? Certainly an exclusive interview should be part of the deal.

I thought and thought and thought as I got dressed to go to work. Eureka! I got it! How about having President Reagan visit the highly novel and successful Mathews-Dickey Boys' & Girls' Club. At the time, this learning, recreational, and athletic facility was bursting at the seams as an after-school, weekend, and summer center for more than 2,000 youngsters . . . almost all of them black and from the inner city. In 1982, the club claimed to have served more than 30,000 youths in its twenty-two years of operation. It was founded by two tireless soldiers in the ongoing war against juvenile delinquency. Martin Mathews and Hubert "Dickey" Ballentine literally founded what was at first just a boys' club under a shade tree with about thirty young guys.

The president, Ed, and the White House press corps would love this story, particularly because this booming oasis for kids was set up and maintained strictly by private corporate and individual contributions. The president was always calling on the private sector to get involved in ventures like the Mathews-Dickey Club to keep the federal government out of this kind of business. And three St. Louis companies, in particular, had answered the call. Anheuser-Busch, Emerson Electric, and Monsanto were the primary donors in the creation of the youth club.

I phoned Ed back at the White House within forty minutes. That was a long "bit" for me, but I was sure that this would be a good idea. And Ed agreed. He would get back to me, and I knew it would be in our kind of "bit." Sure enough, Ed called me once I got to the newsroom later that afternoon and said the idea had been floated up the flagpole and everybody involved in setting the president's agenda had saluted. Ed wanted to know if a White House advance team that included the Secret Service could take a look at the Mathews-Dickey physical plant up close and in person.

On the day of the inspection, there were eleven people in the president's advance party, with me making an even dozen as the host. Remembering that Anheuser-Busch was a big-time sponsor and promoter of Mathews-Dickey, and remembering that A-B had a little luxury bus on which I had traveled for some event, I phoned my good friend, Wayman Smith. Wayman was an A-B executive vice president who had ingratiated himself to the brewery by being the point person to decimate the Jesse Jackson–launched boycott against the brewery.

I asked Wayman if he could arrange for me to borrow the bus for some visiting dignitaries from Washington. I preserved the secrecy of the visit by avoiding the specifics of who exactly were the bus riders or where they were going. I did assure my pal that his boss, August Busch, III, would love the reason for the bus loan and that the outcome would be a feather in A-B's cap . . . or cup. No problem. The bus was mine for four hours on the appointed date.

I called Ed right back, and he gave me the name of the White House staffer who would be working with me on the inspection tour.

On the day of the visit to the boys' club, the A-B bus rolled up on Memorial Drive outside the station right on time. Newsroom and building staffers wondered aloud why the bus was there, but only the general manager, news director, and I knew. And we weren't talking. The eleven guests had stayed overnight in the Adams-Mark Hotel just across the street from the station. I think. I never quite saw how and when they arrived, but by the time I got out to the bus five minutes before blastoff, they were already aboard. Like magic. After a quick round of introductions, we were off for the twenty-minute ride northwest. Although there were, as always, a variety of A-B's products offered by our genial driver, none was accepted. These guys were on a mission! From the White House, no less!

I had phoned Martin Mathews a couple of days before the visit to make sure he would be there. I had told him the most unlikely cover story I have ever concocted. I told him I was bringing some businessmen from Kansas City to take a look-see. They were, I told him, interested in setting up a club in K.C. modeled after his youth center. When we rolled up, he was there with his typical, big, warm welcome. My guests looked as much like K.C. businessmen as I looked like a Disney character at the North Pole. Mr. Mathews—I've never been able to call him Martin out of respect—looked warily at the "K.C." bunch. They fanned out instantly as if each had a grid assignment. Some headed for the cellar; some headed for the roof; some checked out all the entrances and exits; some headed for the periphery of the lot. Exactly the way Kansas City businessmen would inspect a property, right?

I don't think Mr. Mathews was fooled for one second. He began to gently ask questions of any of the inspectors who came near him. "Where in Kansas City you gonna put your place?" The responses were as vague as many White House press conferences. "Did you get your financing already, or do you have to do that?" Same brand of response. But when he was asked the question, the club creator was very specific. "How many kids do you have coming in here?"

"We got more than two thousand youngsters here on sixty-five teams. And we got uniforms of one sort of another for almost all of them."

"That's amazing," a member of the White House advance team offered.

"How many kids you think you can serve in K.C.?" a wise old bird that was Martin Mathews asked.

"Oh, we're not sure yet," a White House staffer said. "We gotta get that financing you were asking about earlier."

Right . . . Mr. Mathews grew more and more suspicious of the real purpose of the visit. You could just see it in his eyes. But he was cool. As always.

After about half an hour of combing the facility with a fine-tooth comb, the guests began to board the bus again after thanking their host and giving him a good hearty handshake. He might have noticed, as I did, that each of his guests had been warm and friendly, but not one of them—not a single one of them—had given him a name or a business card. That's unusual.

I was last to thank Mr. Mathews, and in an attempt to give him a coded message so that he would not eventually call me a complete liar, I said: "You may be seeing some of these gentlemen again soon. And you just might meet their boss, too." I gave him a wink. And I think he had all but figured it out.

In our next conversation, Ed told me the advance team LOVED the Mathews-Dickey site, and they were setting the date as July 22. The White House would take it from here in dealing with the boys' club, but we all would be asked to play it low and keep the presidential visit quiet.

And now on the subject of the "Crow." Remember *Quid Pro Crow*? What would my reward be for the idea and front-running? Ed said he would see what he could do. It would all come down, he said, to whether James Baker, President Reagan's powerful and media-unfriendly chief of staff would okay an exclusive interview.

Ed was confident that it could happen. Quite honestly, I was not so sure. But I was confident that Ed would do all he could to make it happen. If the proper approval was done at the top, I would then have my third exclusive interview with an incumbent U.S. president with Messrs. Ford and Carter having the honor of talking to me before this.

My interview with the president was approved, apparently, by James Baker. A pleasant surprise. The condition was that we did not publicize the exclusive interview in advance. Nothing like: "Coming up next Tuesday at ten . . . Julius Hunter's exclusive one-on-one interview with President Reagan." That would produce howls of protest from the local media and even the traveling press corps. After all, many of the network reporters and reporters for the nation's most respected newspapers would never get an exclusive sitdown with the nation's chief executive.

In the interest of full disclosure, I must make a little confession here. Although respectable news operations never pay for interviews, I didn't think there was an ethics violation in getting station general manager, Allan Cohen, to approve the purchase of a bottle of Dom Perignon to thank Ed for his lobbying efforts on our behalf. I sent money to a friend in D.C. to get the bottle of the expensive bubbly into Ed's hands. Quite honestly, the bottle sent to my old drinking buddy was also to keep the issue of the interview in Ed's mind so it would not be forgotten in the daily hustle and bustle of the White House scheduling.

The only way to keep a secret in a television newsroom is for there to be a limited number of identifiable people allowed access to certain information. Newsrooms leak like sieves. News crews are notorious for spreading gossip and information to their peers at the other stations they come in contact with every day on the scenes of stories. The loose lips are often innocent traits, but in other cases, the news crewpersons are pissed off with the station for this or that and spread secrets maliciously. The same is true with reporters, producers, writers, and other newsroom staffers. There are always a few watering holes around town where newsfolk hang out. Loose lips sometimes have alcohol flowing through them.

So, the secret of the upcoming news exclusive was a tightly held secret between the general manager, news director, and me. We were able to ride right up to the eve of the interview without the news leaking out, but we had not counted on the fact that a president's daily schedule is released the evening before a certain day. When the White House press office released the news the evening before the president's St. Louis visit, it caused a conflagration from Channel 4's competition! There were not only charges that the White House was unfair, biased, prejudiced, slanted, and any other negative charge that could be hurled, but also we got wind that Senator Jennings Randolph, father of Channel 5's sports director, Jay Randolph, made a special trip to the White House to lay out an argument on how unfair giving an exclusive to me would be.

I must admit that as the heat was turned up on July 21, 1982, I began to sweat bullets. Might the competition sway the White House decision to deliver the president to me? Might some news operation discover that the exclusive was a payback for setting the president up at the Mathews-Dickey Boys' Club? I phoned Ed at the White House to find out if my interview was threatened. His answer didn't give me much confidence.

"It's still on the schedule, pal." That's all he would say. He was obviously busy at the time, too. That didn't help. His assistant, Michelle, had been advised to always put my calls through. I didn't call often at all. But I never had trouble getting through to the guy with whom I had slammed down many a "stinger" at Krueger's Bar and many a Gatorade and vodka after vigorous handball games when we worked together at Washington U. a dozen years earlier.

I didn't sleep a wink the night before the scheduled Reagan interview.

When I finally hit the deck around nine in the morning of Thursday, July 22, 1982, my wife, Barbara, handed me a note from our daughter, Jennifer, who was twelve years old at the time. Before she and her sister, Julia, were carpooled to school, Jen scribbled this note:

> *Dear Dad,*
> *Good luck with your interview with*
> *President Reagan today.*
> *Ask intelligent questions.*
> *Don't embarrass me.*
> > *Love,*
> > *Jen*

I had to smile through my tension.

When I got to the Channel 4 newsroom, I discovered that the

place was under siege. The phone lines were jammed, and the phones were ringing off the hook. I remember quite clearly one beleaguered staffer cradling a phone and covering the mouthpiece to say to me: "You and your damned president interviews!"

The calls were coming in from broadcast and print outfits all over the nation. They were demanding to find out exactly where the interview would take place. Some wanted to speak directly to me; others wanted to give me questions to ask; still others were demanding to be allowed to sit in on the interview. The frustrating thing for me was that there was no specific instruction to give to the staffers to handle all the different questions and comments. And the volume of calls was beginning to interfere with the production of the noon, five, and six o'clock newscasts.

I had begun to put together a list of questions I wanted to ask the president. I thought I would first tackle broad international issues, then I would go to specific domestic issues, including the assessments of the Reagan Administration by the more vocal groups who showed up most often on our daily newscasts. The president had faced sharp criticism in particular from environmentalists, the poor, blacks, educators, and organized labor.

The verdict on John Hinckley, Jr., the man who had come close to snuffing out the president's life, had just come in almost a month to the day before my big interview. I had to make sure I had the facts about the timeline:

March 30, 1981	Reagan shot by Hinckley
April 11, 1981	Reagan released from the hospital
June 21, 1982	Hinckley verdict comes in
July 22, 1982	My interview with Reagan

My wife, Barbara, was, as always, a savvy consultant for reviewing my questions and for suggesting others. I also relied on a few colleagues to suggest some questions once the news had broken the evening before the interview. Soliciting advice and question ideas is a tricky business. The best consultants are those opposed to the interviewee's policies, and suggestions are often discarded and never credited.

Seated at my desk in the heart of the newsroom frenzy, I quickly reckoned that the best way for me to approach the big

President Reagan speaks at Mathews-Dickey Boys' & Girls' Club.

interview in the coolest and calmest manner possible was to sequester in my private office on the other side of a hallway from the newsroom. I tried to avoid feeling cowardly—unwilling to help out in the epicenter of the chaos for which I was responsible.

There in the relative quiet, broken only by the perpetual buzzing of the phone lines, I totally ignored several knocks on my door. Had there been a legitimate emergency—like the cancellation of the interview or a modification of the sit down time—a newsroom tactical team would have kicked in my locked door, I assumed.

I began to organize my selected questions in my mind, closing my eyes to recite them aloud. Hearing what the president and my viewers would hear. Weeding out phrasing that sounded confusing or lightweight. I had also come to realize that the order of the questions on my list was inconsequential. A respondent rarely answers your list of questions in the exact order in which you have listed them. When you hear a rookie reporter stumbling around, it is often because after question one is answered, the interviewee will answer questions three and six. And it is important to both look the subject in the eye and hear what is being said for a reasonable, logical, and obvious follow-up.

A reporter should also avoid taking copious notes during an interview. Furious scribbling makes an interviewee nervous and cautious to the point of your getting stilted responses. And taking notes with the intensity of a court reporter also prevents the reporter from hearing what his/her interviewee is saying. Among the most embarrassing responses a reporter can hear from an interviewee is: "Well, as I just said a minute ago . . ."

So, I would be loaded for bear. Or loaded for Gipper. For certain, I could not let my daughter, Jennifer, down. She had, after all, ordered her father to ask "intelligent" questions.

My instructions had been clear and concise from the White

House communications office: "Report to the Marriott Hotel lobby exactly one hour before the interview." I was given no floor to report to, and I am sure that was by security design. "Bring no electronic equipment, like a tape recorder, with me. Just a note pad and pencil (no pens)."

The interview would last exactly twenty minutes. It would be cut shorter upon the first embarrassing question I put to the president. When I was asked what I might want to talk about, I hid proudly behind the CBS policy for its owned and operated stations: I could not reveal any of my questions in advance unless the interview was declared as "REHEARSED."

We had selected two veteran photographers to videotape the interview, Tom Martin and Charlie Bohn. The two were also instructed to wear a coat and tie. The station had absolutely no authority to order working photographers—members of the International Brotherhood of Electrical Workers Union to dress in any certain style. Tom and Charlie could have easily declined to dress up for this job, but they would have just as easily been replaced by two photographers who would have eagerly worn tuxedos if ordered to do so.

An interview of this level of importance required two cameras: one for the president and one trained on me for my questions and reactions. The other reason for the two cameras was a no-brainer. The second camera was there in case the first camera had a malfunction. I don't think the most powerful man in the Western World could be asked to hang around while the crew ran back to the station or out to the truck to get replacement parts. The potential breakdown factor also necessitated that the crew lug extra equipment to the scene: extra light filaments; extra power batteries, should the hotel power blow; extra filters; extra electric cords and cable; extra lapel mikes for the anchor/reporter. News crews are not allowed to bring extra microphones for a president. That's a special military/security assignment.

Every president's microphone is carried to each presidential interview by a member of the Navy Signal Corps. Yes, there is a Navy officer assigned to travel around with the president to each point he travels outside the White House. That officer carries a little case with him, and just before an interview, that officer removes the presidential clip microphone and affixes it gingerly and professionally to the chief executive's lapel. It doesn't take much imagination to conjure up images of a terrorist's microphone sneaked into a news crew's equipment exploding and taking out the nation's leader. Our news crews all knew not to even begin to approach a president.

And the Navy Signal Corps technician isn't the only specialty job that comes into play when there is an interview with the president outside the White House. Wherever the president appears, no matter where he dines or speaks, his hosts are never, ever allowed to pour a glass of water for him! The president's official drinking water carrier is a Navy man assigned to that specific job. Should anyone ever say to him: "You couldn't even carry the president's water," he can beg to differ with his critic.

The U.S. Navy, the same guys and gals who run the White House Mess (dining room), are the same ones who go around from city to city, port to port, toting a little letter case/box in which there are several bottles and cans of sparkling and distilled water and a few cans of the president's favorite soft drink. Also in the portable potables case are several glasses. I also thought I saw some paper cups on one of my five presidential interviews, but I cannot swear to that. As wars rage and conflicts fulminate, if I had to do military service, I would prefer earning a distinguished service medal or commendation for carrying a president's microphone or his drinking water.

I have always, quite frankly, been curious to note that the official water carriers and just about everybody who works in the White House Mess (where I have eaten several times with Ed Rollins) appears to be Filipino. But I was never bold enough to make a vocalized generalization about the crew or the water carrier like President Bush awkwardly did on June 25, 2008, in a photo op with Gloria Macapagal-Arroyo, the president of the Philippines. Incredibly, he said verbatim:

First I want to tell you how proud I am to be the president of a nation that—in which there's a lot of Philippine-Americans. They love America, and they love their heritage. And I am reminded of the great talent of the—of our Philippine-Americans when I eat dinner in the White House. (Laughter) Our chef is a Philippine-American.

An awkward moment at the White House for sure. Some day I may be able to say: "Some of my best friends are presidents."

With the Reagan interview set for five that evening, I had decided I would head for the slow one-block walk to the Marriott Hotel at 3:45 p.m. I had every intention of arriving with not one bead of sweat on my body. It was, after all, July in St. Louis. And there was absolutely nothing unusually cool about that day. Shortly before 3:45, there was a pounding on my door that was unmistakably that of News Director Fred Burrows. His voice confirmed the source of the banging: "Jules! You in there? Time to go, Babe. Time to go! Jules!"

Fred was a hard-nosed, chain-smoking, highly excitable, energetic newsperson's newsman. He knew news like few other news directors because he had literally risen from the bottom rung in the newsroom. Right out of high school, Fred had taken a job as a copy boy and stage manager—both entry-level jobs below the entry level. Fred knew all his troops like a scoutmaster; he knew every local politician, Catholic priest and bishop, city official, newsmaker, and bartender in downtown St. Louis and beyond. During his eleven-year reign, from 1975 to 1986, Fred had been with me on every major story and interview I had covered. It was obvious to one and all that Freddie would rather be out there helping to nail down the big story than being nailed down to his desk.

The White House had granted him special dispensation to accompany the two Channel 4 photographers to the Marriott interview room because Fred knew somebody or other in the White House communications office. Burrows had helped me set up the exclusive interview with Gerald Ford just seven years earlier, and the shore-to-ship exclusive interview with President Jimmy Carter four years after that. So Fred had smelled the catnip and experienced the glory of two one-on-one presidential interviews with me before this July 1982 exclusive. And now, we were going for the trifecta!

As I took a deep breath, I gathered up my questions in a manila folder and headed out to the much-coveted interview. In the station lobby, I was set upon by the president of the local equivalent of the chamber of commerce. He had a beautifully framed color photo of the Gateway Arch enshrouded in a spectacular barrage of fireworks from the display related to the Independence Day festivities a little more than two weeks before. It was more of an entreaty than a request that I present the photo to the president. I shrugged and accepted the gift I was sure would be pitched into that vast cellar of gifts and keys to various cities presented to a president. When I arrived at the Marriott I learned that the

White House had taken over an entire tower of the hotel. As I entered the hotel, I took a quick glance at a familiar sight: a huge otherwise non-descript RV parked on the sidewalk outside the hotel.

Ed Rollins had confided in me that this huge vehicle was the command post for security for the president wherever he went. In fact, he told me, there were several of the vehicles that hop scotched all over the country. They had license plates for every state. This was NOT the Secret Service, he told me. This was an elite unit—all dressed in black, wearing black baseball caps with the bibs turned backward—armed with what I would call in my ignorance about weaponry, Uzis.

I had seen these guys at previous presidential events, and they were ninja-like in their mysteriousness. They manned the doors at the hotel, the front desk, and even the elevators. They were humorless, non-conversational, direct and to the point, laconic, professional, basically unfriendly SOBs. Just the kind of guys I would like to see guard my president.

Ed told me that the RV contained enough firepower to take on a small country and enough electronic equipment to communicate with any place on this earth . . . or beyond. Once, when I was visiting Ed while he was serving in the White House, there had been some news reports of intruders sighted outside the vice president's residence. Ed told me that this special "Unit in Black" would be the ones to scour the area and patrol while an investigation was ongoing.

Two of these unsmiling men greeted me as I arrived in the hotel lobby. Without ceremony and within the splitting of a second, one of them snatched the photo of the fireworks at the Arch from me and began shaking it and holding it up to the light while examining it closely. I got it. The same bunch of people who would put an explosive in the president's lapel microphone are the same people who would plant a bomb in a picture of the Arch on Independence Day.

I was instructed, in as few words as is necessary, to accompany the two American ninjas to the elevator. Two armed ninjas were on the elevator. Although I offered a greeting to them: "Hi, guys. How are you? Hot enough for you?" Nothing.

Using all of my reportorial and investigative skills, I noted that we were soon at the twenty-third floor. As I stepped off with my two escorts, I looked to my left down the hallway and saw a scary, nightmarish vision. Two Doberman Pinschers the size of Clydesdales were galloping in slow motion towards me. I cannot tell a lie. I was intimidated. Scared out of my mind. I froze.

One of the ninjas said in an ever-so-brief order: "Don't move and they will not harm you."

And then, as one of the highlights of my journalistic career, I scored a victory. I managed to get one of my somber escorts to flash a semblance of a smile. "How do you know they don't prefer dark meat?" I asked with a bit of wavering in my voice.

The dogs executed their perusal promptly and efficiently. They pointedly examined every pocket, crease, and crevice in and on my body. My ninja guide did not have to tell me twice that I was not to make any sudden motion. With their job done and nothing threatening found, the two giant beasts turned and galloped back down the hallway. I have no idea where they went and who was waiting for their return. Very mysterious. But very effective and impressive.

After passing the dog test, I was ordered back onto the elevator. It soon became clear to me that my original destination on the elevator had been to a security clearing area one floor below the president and his top staff. The elevator door opened on the twenty-fourth floor, where Ed was there to greet me.

We exchanged a handshake and hug and went to his room, which was noticeably neater and cleaner than any room I had ever seen Ed have before . . . especially at Wash. U. But, he had only been in town a few hours.

After about a half hour of reminiscences, a Secret Service agent moved into Ed's room and loudly snapped his fingers. Just once. But the snap was like a crackling of thunder and lighting. "This is it," Ed said. "We gotta go." Ed put on his jacket and I straightened mine.

As we stepped out into the hallway, there before me was a once-in-a-lifetime scene. Approaching me with an aide practically whispering in his ear was "Dutch," "The Great Communicator," "The Gipper," "The Teflon President." Which one of them would I be interviewing?

Although I know we were surrounded by a battalion of security, there appeared to be only four of us in that hallway, the Reagan aide, Ed Rollins, President Reagan, and me.

From more than six feet away, the president began to extend

his right hand to me. I extended my hand and he gave me a good, warm, firm handshake.

"Julius, how are you. Pleased to meet you," the president offered in a greeting that was both disarming and warming. How did he know my name? Well, of course, the aide was whispering the name and a brief bio on me.

"I'm just fine, Mr. President. And I hope you are well. Welcome to St. Louis," I responded.

"Well, I'm glad to be here," the president volunteered. "Met a lot of nice people today here in your fair city."

We were ushered into the interview room. It was a regular old hotel room, and rather small, too. There were Fred, Tom, and Charlie nattily dressed like I seldom saw them. There was only one visible Secret Service agent in the room and one outside. I'm sure there were more lurking somewhere, but I was comforted to know that if I could not see all of the president's security detail, the bad guys would not be able to see them either. There were also two people from the White House communications office, and let's not forget the two Navy men. One officer was ready to clip on the president's microphone, and the little guy with the drinking water arrived on cue.

That was a lot of people for the surprisingly small hotel room selected for the interview, but there were only two chairs and no other furnishings. The bed had been taken out. The closet doors had been taken off. Even the toilet and wash basin in the bathroom had been taken out and the plumbing capped. There was not a single place to hide anything that could be hazardous to the president's health and safety.

My crew had positioned the president's back to the wall, rather close to the unappealing wallpaper. In a moment of insanity about security, I asked aloud why my guys had not chosen the nice drapery framing the curtained window as a background for the interview. Without even answering me, the Secret Service agent, the two White House communications staffers, and even Fred gave me a look that required no response to my question about positioning. Would anybody in their right mind think that the president's back should be put in front of a curtained, draped window? I let the request drop just as soon as my senses returned to me.

As the lighting was being set, the two White House communications people were actually peering through the camera lens to check how the president and his lighting would look on camera. And as the Navy Signal Corpsman was adjusting the president's mike, I thought to share a little personal matter with the president. I reached inside my shirt pocket and pulled out my daughter's note and handed it to the president.

"Mr. President, these are my instructions from my twelve-year-old daughter, Jennifer."

Mr. Reagan took the note, read it, and gave a little chuckle. He then asked for a piece of paper and a pen and using my manila folder with my questions inside as

backing, the president of the United States took the time to pen this note back to Jennifer *before* the interview got underway:

> *Dear Jennifer,*
> *You can be very proud of your father.*
> *He did a very fine job with his questions.*
> *—Ronald Reagan*

I was floored by the gentle kindness of a man whose election had made Iran release the hostages they had held for 444 days, the man who had faced down the nuclear threat without firing a shot, and the U.S. leader who dared tell Mikhail Gorbachev just five years after he talked to me to tear down the Berlin Wall.

This larger than-life-figure had taken a moment of his valuable time to pen a note to my pre-teen daughter.

I thanked the president, and this is how the interview went:

Hunter: *Mr. President, welcome to St. Louis.*

The President: *Thank you. It's good to be here.*

Hunter: *And thank you for allowing us this opportunity to talk.*

Tell me about your time out at the boys' club. I understand you had a great time.

The President: *Well, yes, I did. And it was a most inspiring thing. From the history of that place, those two men that had a dream and literally, as they've said, took it out from under a shade tree and into a store front and now into that magnificent building. And all those thousands of young people who were there, sixty-five baseball teams, it just shows what someone with a dream and with determination to make it come true can do.*

ASSASSINATION ATTEMPT

Hunter: *On another subject, you were noticeably silent following the Hinckley verdict. Yet, for someone who was so personally involved in that shooting incident, you must have had some feelings about what that jury's verdict, what effect it will have on your safety and security and on the safety and security of future presidents. Would you share those feelings with us?*

The President: *Well, I'd rather not comment. I haven't commented on that particular verdict. I would, however, touch on the subject that has been brought up by that, because that goes back before this trial, this whole question of insanity as a defense. And the attorney general has recommended and the Justice Department is studying the idea of making insanity—in other words, it's guilty or innocent, but then insanity introduced at the time of sentencing as a mitigating factor.*

I think that justice is not done under the present system. And I know this has been studied by the American Bar Association, many legal groups, for a long time. And they have come to the decision that the technical experts in front of a jury on both sides, giving conflicting opinions with regard to this, it doesn't really belong in the trial.

Hunter: *Does it mean to you that a president is open game for anyone who can prove that he or she is insane?*

The President: *Well, you don't have to limit it to a president. This defense is being used more and more in murder trials. And we've seen, I think, something long before this trial that led to the study of this question, with the incidence of people found innocent by reason of insanity put in a mental hospital and turned loose, you might say, virtually by the members of the same profession that had gone into court and proved they were insane, then a few months later telling them they were cured. And we've had the double tragedy if they go right out in the street and commit the same crime over again.*

SPECIAL INTEREST AND MINORITY GROUPS

Hunter: *If the polls are to be believed, you are not a popular president among such groups as environmentalists, the poor, the black, educators, organized labor. What are your feelings on a president's responsibility to try to meet the needs and demands of groups which feel they are alienated from the White House?*

The President: *Well, I think the biggest problem is one of communications. And maybe the media has something to do with that, because I think if representatives of those groups that*

THE WHITE HOUSE

WASHINGTON

April 6, 1983

Dear

Nancy and I were very pleased to receive the copy of your *Sagebrush* which Ed Re—— I am particularly pleased that your —— have been designated to finance the ———— proceeds from the sale to this beautiful section of the entry gates to this beautiful section of St. Louis. The fact that this project is being funded wholly through the private enterprise system at its best. We congratulate you on your fine publication and wish you and your colleagues great success in your worthy endeavor.

I recall with much pleasure our interview last September during my visit to St. Louis. It was good to hear from you, and I want to take this opportunity to reaffirm my deep appreciation for your staunch support.

Nancy joins me in sending you our very best wishes.

Sincerely,

Ronald Reagan

you've just mentioned and others who are listed in the polls as not favoring me—if they understood my views and understood what it is we're actually trying to do.

Environmentalists, for example. I'd never heard the word, but as governor of California, one of the first things I did was correct a problem, and before I left as governor, the environmental movement was underway nationwide—and from the federal level under an administration that was not necessarily supportive of me. People came to California and said that we were out ahead of the Nation. We took the federal government to court in order to have automobile standards in the State of California with regard to the smog problem.

Hunter: *So, are you saying that you are perhaps misunderstood by some of these groups that feel alienated?*

The President: *Yes, you mentioned—what were some of the other groups?*

Hunter: *The poor, blacks—*

The President. *All right, well—*

Hunter:—*organized labor.*

The President: *Blacks—just having been to that wonderful boys' club this afternoon, let me touch on that one—and misunderstanding.*

I was raised in a household in which there was no tolerance whatsoever for prejudice or bigotry. And I grew up that way. And as a sports announcer in radio, broadcasting major league baseball, how many young people today remember that when I was broadcasting baseball, no blacks were allowed in organized baseball. There were no Willie Mayses for me to talk about or Hank Aarons—anyone of that kind. And there were a number of

us in the sports field then who editorialized and used the pulpit that had been given to us by virtue of our job, to campaign
against that. And finally, the dam was broken. And baseball is
better for it and the nation is better for it.

But then when I became governor—I was the thirty-third
governor of California—I found out that the civil service tests
were rigged to prevent blacks from getting any but the lowest
possible jobs in State government. I changed that. More than
that, up and above civil service, I appointed to policy-making
and executive positions more blacks than all the previous thirty-
two governors of California before me put together. Now, we're
doing the same thing at the federal level. And I could go on
from there.

But let me also point that when you say the poor, I know that
there's been a misconstruing of many of the things that we're
trying to do in getting control of this uncontrollable budget—the
spending that has brought the country into this recession and
caused the trillion-dollar debt.

Much of the misinformation about what we're trying to do
comes from the bureaucracies who feel threatened because they
have a nice living administering those programs. But as to the
people, let's take one—you mentioned educators—the educators
and the charge that we are somehow taking away the possibility of help for needy students to go to college. What we're
really doing—we found that much of the aid, the low-interest
loans and the grants, were going to students whose families had
incomes that suggested the families could do more to help send
their children to college. We have redirected this help down to a
financial level that makes sure that those people who are close to
the poverty line can have the help they need for their sons and
daughters to go to college.

And probably the greatest thing that we've done for the poor
is the reduction in the rate of inflation which was roughly 12
1/2 percent when we started—for two years, double-digit inflation. We have more than cut that in half. We've reduced that way
down to where for the last few months it's probably only a fourth
of that amount.

THE NATION'S ECONOMY

Hunter: *What are your predictions about where the inflation rate will be and where the economy will be three months from now, six months from now?*

The President: *Well, I think there is an improvement. I think we've bottomed out. But let me tell you what that inflation rate already has done for those who are poor, who have to spend every penny for the necessities of life, and therefore as the prices go up, they can buy less and less of the necessities. Families at the poverty level today, with the cuts that we've already made in the inflation rate, have several hundred dollars more in purchasing power than they had a year ago under the previous high inflation rate.*

Hunter: *Now what are your projections?*

The President: *My projections are that the signs are kind of mixed when you bottom out in a recession. But in these last few days, the Federal Reserve, cutting the discount rate for the banks—the prime rate being set by the banks at a lower rate. The interest rate was 21 1/2 percent when I started a year and a half ago. For the first time in several months we are showing an increase, small though it may be, in the gross national product.*

Now, I'm not going to jump up and down and say that, well, you know, there's going to be a boom just around the corner. It won't get cured that way. The previous seven recessions have seen the government using what I call a quick fix—artificially stimulating the economy, pouring printing press money into the marketplace. And, yes, temporarily there is an easing of the situation. But look back at those recessions, and you'll find that about two or three years later, we would have another recession, deeper and worse than the one before. This one is the deepest and the worst of those since World War II.

Now, what we're embarked on is a plan to restore the economy, to restore industry—not a quick fix—to get back to where we're on an even keel without government deficit spending, without the government having to go into the market and use up the capital that belong to the people. We have given the tax cuts to the people with the third installment yet to come next year to provide incentive for them. And for the first time, again, in a long period of time, real earnings—not inflation earnings of phony dollars—real earnings are increasing at a rate of 4 percent. That's the highest it's been in years.

Soviet Gas Pipeline

Hunter: *On the international scene, were you surprised, this morning when France announced that it was going to go ahead and give U.S.–developed technology to the Russians for the development of that Russian pipeline? And have you and your foreign policy advisers determined some sort of way to dissuade France from taking that action?*

The President: *Well, what really they are doing is going forward with contracts that were already signed. I have talked with President Mitterrand about his situation. He said when he came there he found the contracts already agreed to and signed by the previous administration, and they feel legally bound by those.*

What I have asked our Commerce Department to do is do a study and come back to me with a report on what our situation is, because where it involves us—with our sanctions that we've imposed against the Soviet Union—where it involves us is what is our legal position with regard to subsidiary companies in France and in the other European countries owned by American firms, and whether they are legally bound, possibly, by contracts that were made before.

Hunter: *What are your options that are available to dissuade France?*

The President: *Well, we tried our best in the meetings over there. I think they knew what we were going to do, because we'd announced what we were going to do way last December. They, as I say, had gone forward with the contracts. We have been investigating, with some of the European countries, the possibilities of energy sources closer, and that would not have the two problems which we are very concerned about with our European allies—number one, making themselves dependent on the Soviet Union, and putting themselves in a position to be blackmailed by the Soviet Union if they decide to shut off the gas. There are sources in the North Sea, in Norway, in the Netherlands. We would be happy to help them with the development of those.*

The other one is, they would be cash customers. The Soviet Union has poured so much money into its great military might, that we're now trying to get reduced, that they're up against the wall. They don't have cash for those purposes the way they did. This would give them 10 or 12 billion dollars a year in cold, hard cash for doing this. And these are the things that we tried to point out.

Our allies, on the other hand, pointed out to us that they had already gone forward to the point that they did not feel they could retreat from that—although they did join us in shutting off or reducing credit, so that we, at least, aren't helping finance a potential adversary.

1984 PRESIDENTIAL CAMPAIGN

Hunter: *One final question, Mr. President. Washington is buzzing with some stories that your top aides are telling your Cabinet members not to look for any jobs soon, because Ronald Reagan has decided to run again for reelection. Have you decided that you want a second term?*

The President: *No. No, and that isn't a decision that should be made now. But what had happened was I suddenly found out that some people were spreading the word around that I had decided I wouldn't. And I just thought that since that's a decision yet to be made—and I think the people help you make that decision as the time goes on—that for the purposes of my own staff and my own cabinet and all, they'd better know that no decision had been made. And so, I used the phrase, in telling them that, that—or publicly I told them to stop reading the "Help Wanted" ads.*

Hunter: *So the door is still open?*

The President: *Yes.*

Hunter: *Thank you very much, Mr. President.*

The President: *Well, thank you. I appreciate the opportunity.*

ANSWER THE PAGER, STUPID!

It is not often that reporters—even good and competent journalists—like to publicly admit to making monumental, glaring errors. In fact, every time I was forced to make an on-air correction, I tried to make the goof appear merely a simple human or electronic error. I would preface a correction in a cool-as-a-cucumber manner like this:

> *"Let's take another look at that budget story I told you about in our last news segment. I believe I said the Board of Aldermen has approved a $3 million bill to replace fire hydrants. Let's make that $4 million . . . $4 million for those new hydrants.*
>
> *Sorry about the slip of the tongue. Now, in other news . . ."*

And while I would appear to take the correction in a pleasant, I'm-only-human kind of way, inside I would seethe and glare at the careless writer who had given me wrong information to read on the air. I had inestimable faith in scripts I wrote myself, but I hated to be handed a piece of copy while I was on the air—copy that I had not proofread myself.

Sometimes on-air I would candidly lay the blame for an error in the general direction of the actual source of the mistake with a finger-pointed line like:

> *"Sorry, I seem to have been given some incorrect information that I mistakenly passed on to you. Let's make that amount allotted by the Board of Aldermen for new fire hydrants $4 million instead of $3 million. 4 instead of 3. Okay? Okay.*

But when it was absolutely appropriate and honorable, I would lay the blame on myself:

> *"I have got to apologize for an incorrect figure I gave you about the price tag of new fire hydrants for the city. I completely*

goofed . . . my fault . . . in saying aldermen had voted $3 million for the new fire hydrants. Please get out your erasers and rub out the $3 million I erroneously told you about. And replace the 3 with a 4. It's $4 million for new fireplugs. My error.

I've made a mental note over the years of the really big on-air screw-ups I've made. While making my list, I hoped that nobody in the viewing audience was keeping tally to present me with a cardboard plaque specifically detailing all my on-air errors as a retirement gift. I have secretly feared that a professional gaffe-keeper would show up at my retirement party and when introduced to my colleagues would say: "Ladies and gentlemen, as we wish our friend, Julius Hunter, all the best at the end of his distinguished thirty-three-year broadcast career, and as we listen to his impressive list of accomplishments, I am here to give you some other news. What I have here, dear friends, is the list and specifics of each and every time he screwed up on the air. All engraved on this suitable-for-framing cardboard plaque. These are Julius's *on-air* goofs. A full report on the number of times he made a glaring mistake OFF the air can be yours in this beautiful leather-bound edition for the amazing price of two payments of only $19.99 each."

At the very top of the list of my most monumental screw-ups would be, without a doubt, the time I blew the opportunity to scoop the journalistic world during my one-on-one exclusive interview with incumbent president, George Herbert Walker Bush. The date was October 30, 1992. I had had some heralded scoops with sitting presidents on my resume. Among the most notable of the presidential scoops was the time I was the only broadcast newsperson in town to score an exclusive half-hour interview with then President Gerald Ford. That date was September 12, 1975. And I was first on air anywhere around the country to call out the fact that President Ford was visibly wearing a bullet-proof vest after a recent assassination attempt.

I was the only journalist to interview Jimmy Carter from shore to ship live via microwave when the thirty-ninth president took a leisurely cruise down the Mississippi. Critics floated stories that President Carter's cruise was an attempt to get away from the tempests in Washington and the conditions that led to the hostages being taken in Iran three months after the river cruise.

On July 22, 1982, I scored international points for gently coaxing the Great Communicator, Ronald Reagan, to unwittingly and quite prematurely divulge that the chief of his council of economic advisers, St. Louisan Murray Wiedenbaum, was jumping ship. Why would Murray leave the White House if the economy was in as good of shape as the Reagan Administration made it out to be? Reagan's accidental leak of that story in casual, off-the-cuff

*To Julius Hunter
With best wishes,* G. Bush

chit-chat, with me standing right by his side, led every national network newscast the next night. Dan Rather led off the CBS Evening News with: "There's a leak at the White House. And that leak is none other than the president himself." The *Washington Post* banner headline the next day was "Reagan: 'I goofed.'"

Your clever reporter just may be the only reporter in the nation to get the Leader of the Western World, Bill Clinton, to personally deliver a handwritten note from me to an old friend, Nancy Hernreich. She, not Betty Curry, ran the Oval Office at the time of certain Clinton/Lewinski indiscretions. The book has more on this exclusive story in the section devoted to my interview on April 18, 1984, with President Clinton. I actually used the nation's chief executive as a personal courier!

There's a good chance that I was the only reporter in St. Louis who had had two knee-to-knee interviews with George Herbert Walker Bush. The first one-on-one interview on November 13, 1991, was with the "Jovial, Friendly George"; the second was with the "Crabby, Short-Tempered George." When his brother, Bucky Bush, introduced me to President Bush on that first encounter, the president was in a good mood. My old friend, Bucky, whose daughter had gone to school with my daughter at John Burroughs School, piped up with, "George, I want you to meet a friend of mine, Julius Hunter. He's got two daughters at Harvard." "What?" George the First shot back in a flash, "they couldn't get into Yale?" It was a great comeback. The three of us chuckled, and if I were awarding points for a quick comeback on a scale of 1 to 10, I'd have to give

Mr. Bush a strong 9 on that rapid response.

My second meeting with G. H. W. Bush was a strange, dark day. Oh, there was plenty of bright sunshine outside on that crisp Friday, October 30, 1992. But it was an extremely gloomy day inside the room where I was to face George the First a second time. This day loomed precariously near the November 1992 presidential election. The White House hierarchy seemed drawn, fatigued, and depressed, and they were snapping at each other and everyone else like hungry tigers. Unlike our first meeting a year earlier, it appeared that few preparations had been made for the sit-down. In all the other presidential interviews I had done, the interview room had been set up meticulously. But on this day at the end of October, we were stuck this time in an unremarkable hotel room and nobody fussed over the president's comfort or the lack of security. That was very odd when compared to the interviews with every incumbent president since Ford. Before the president arrived in the interview room, my photographer and I became stagehands as we frantically scrambled to find a set and backdrop that looked presidential. We found and set up the biggest chair in the room for the president to sit in, and we dragged over a Missouri state flag and U.S. flag to flank the chair. And we cleared a lot of extraneous clutter from behind the chair that would denigrate our background. How peculiar that for the first time in my dealings with presidents I don't recall seeing any Secret Service attachments in the room. They had to be somewhere, but I didn't see them. It is as if they had taken a break. If President Bush ever thought it was "lonely at the top," this was one of those days of executive isolation.

Presidential Press Secretary Marlin Fitzwater paced the hall outside the interview room with a really silly-looking crushed hat on his follicularly challenged dome. And secretary of state and campaign manager, Jim Baker, not known to accept any candy from strangers, was wrapped in what appeared to be a CIA-issued trench coat. A sour-faced Baker had marked out his own private pacing path. Woe be unto anyone who stepped into Baker's invisible lines of demarcation. The temperature was way too cold for me to try to strike up pleasantries with Baker. I wanted to remind him that it was he who had given final approval for me to do that exclusive interview with President Reagan. But I took a pass. His thoughts were very obviously far, far away from an interview in St. Louis.

"Okay, let's get this interview going," the president ordered, as he clapped his hands to underscore the fact that tempus did, indeed, fugit.

"We're ready, Mr. President," I assured. "Roll it!" (Count to ten slowly to let the tape get up to speed as you use the dead time to pretend to look over your notes.)

"Welcome to St. Louis, Mr. President, and thank you for the opportunity to have a few words with you," I opened with a standard courtesy of words in a style that my grandmother would want me to waste in formal greeting.

I could tell by the mood displayed on the president's face that I had better not piddle around. On this one, I would get right to the point:

"Mr. President, just yesterday you openly referred to your opponents, Bill Clinton and Al Gore, as (quoting you verbatim here) . . . as 'bozos.' In a kinder, gentler, day in your life, might you regret that characterization?"

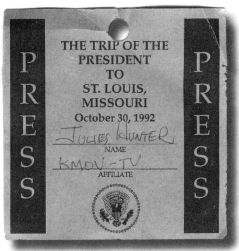

The president was, without a doubt, agitated. "Look, look . . . you guys . . . you guys always hang on to stuff like that. These political campaigns are tough; they're war. And the gloves come off. . . ."

The pager on my belt went off. Fortunately, it was on "vibrate." With a subtle sweeping motion I pushed the button to turn the damn thing off. I was aware that any motion under my coat could be misconstrued by a Secret Service agent somewhere in the environs, and I could have been blown away suspected of trying to pull an assassination attempt.

But the goddamn pager started vibrating again, and in my retrospective recollection of the moment, the buzzing vibration was like the phone ringing and dancing off the hook in an old movie cartoon. I pressed the button off again. I didn't hear exactly what the president was saying in his harangue because in my mind I was cursing whichever silly assignment editor back in the newsroom was bothering me when I was in the middle of a one-on-one interview with the president of the United States.

Sheer stupidity regularly finds incubation and birth in TV newsrooms across this great nation every day. There is some phenomenon that reigns supreme in a TV newsroom that causes anatomical and cerebral synaptic madness. Once when I was conducting a live interview on the news set, my pager went off, and it wasn't on vibrate. It played one of those silly little tunes that might cause a great, classic composer to roll over in his grave. That on-air page was from none other than the assignment editor. Despite all those monitors in the newsroom showing my face live, and despite the fact that I was the regular daily anchor of the six o'clock newscast, I was being paged. Paged while I was on the air! The idiot!

Just about the time I was trying to dismantle or disengage my damn pager, Marlin Fitzwater, the likeable and loyal Bush press flack, darted into the room. "Excuse me," he said, directed toward my general direction. He leaned over and whispered something into the sitting president's ear. President George Herbert Walker Bush's face grew ashen and displayed surprise/frustration/anger all in successively quick order. He was obviously rocked by whatever it was that was whispered into his ear.

"Oh, no," Mr. Bush moaned. "Oh, no. Why? Why now? Why would they do this now? No . . ." Anguish took over. For all intents and purposes, my interview was over.

After a few bobbled questions, and a few unrelated attempts at answering, the President Bush apologized, "Gentlemen, I'm going to have to cut this short. Thank you." Usually, there is an officer from the Navy Signal Corps to put on and take off a president's microphone. But this time, the Bush entourage was almost down to nobody, and Mr. Bush took off his own microphone. He abruptly disappeared from the room. And once again I saw the sparsest Secret Service contingent guarding a president I had seen to that date or have seen since.

I couldn't wait to get to a land line.

"Newsroom," somebody answered cordially.

"This is Hunter," I roared. "Which one of you idiots was paging me right in the middle of my interview with the president?" Yes, there was foam and fire coming from my mouth. "Give me the desk!"

The assignment editor began: "Julius. Julius. Why didn't you answer your pager?"

"Why didn't I answer my pager, you idiot? I didn't answer,

dammit, because I was trying to have a decent conversation with the president. The president of the United States, dammit!"

The assignment editor had obviously taken a course in anger management. He lowered his voice in direct inverse proportion to my raising the decibel level of my voice. "Julius, we were trying to give you information on what is going to be the biggest story of the day. Caspar Weinberger, Bush's defense secretary, has been indicted. Again!"

"Again?" I mumbled in shock.

"Yes, again," the assignment editor responded. "This time he's been nailed for lying to Congress about Iran-Contra. Why didn't you answer the page?" asked the assignment editor, whose voice rose to the maximum volume allowed for a person of his rank to speak to a senior anchor. Then the news director came on the line and joined in the inquisition, and I soon realized what a mistake I had made by ignoring my pager.

I apologized and admitted that this was my error—my BIG error, and I returned to the station and to my little office muttering curses directed at the only person I could blame . . . me.

There were a couple of silver linings to the speckled cloud of stupidity that hung over my head for a while. For one thing, while watching President Bush on *Larry King Live* the same night of my interview earlier that day, Larry asked Mr. Bush if he might one day regret calling his two Democrat opponents "bozos." The president had gotten not only some discouraging poll results that day, but he had also learned that his good friend and onetime Defense Secretary Cap Weinberger was back in trouble, and back in the bad news column.

To Larry King's questions about Bush's use of the term "bozos," the president snapped back: "You're the third journalist who's asked me that question today!" *Hooray!* I thought. There are at least two more colleagues like me around the country who are asking that question. I would have "high-fived" myself if I were not still smarting from the Weinberger goof.

But even that matter got ameliorated in short order. President Bush removed the lump of coal from Weinberger's holiday stocking on Christmas Eve and replaced it with a full pardon.

GERALD FORD

The morning of September 12, 1975, was a particularly exciting day around the Channel 4 newsroom. We were expecting none other than the most powerful man in the western world at the time—maybe in the entire world. President Gerald Ford was dropping in at the station to be my exclusive guest for a taping of my half-hour *Newsmakers* program. When word made it around town, I learned for the first time of my then five-year career that "hell hath no fury like the competition scorned."

President Ford was coming to town to speak at the National Baptist Convention at Kiel Auditorium, the municipal center in the heart of downtown St. Louis. When we learned he was coming, we approached a friend of a friend of ours in the White House communications office and made a simple but unprecedented request, which received a simple and unprecedented response. The president would be happy to come by. Stringent details would have to be worked out first, though.

One of the plusses in our offer to play host was that we told the White House just how close our studios were to Kiel Auditorium. We were just down the street. We, of course, did not let on that my old station, Channel 5, was actually on the same street and actually closer to Kiel than we were. We quickly accepted the invitation, and we began pulling out all the stops to prepare for the distinguished drop-by. In the strictest of secrecy and stealth, a very small group of Channel 4 staffers began corresponding by phone and letter with the White House office. No e-mail yet. We needed to get all the specifications attendant to the visit of a president. And there were quite a few prerequisites we had to satisfy for the honor.

No problem. If the White House had insisted that we do the exclusive interview underwater, we would have quickly investigated getting me outfitted with a deep-sea diving suit. To the best of anybody's knowledge, no sitting president had ever come to a television station for an interview. News stations, so far back as we could research, always had to send a reporter and crew to a visiting president's hotel, or to some other secure spot.

The most important of the White House pre-conditions had to do, of course, with security. Right after the agreement was made, a contingent of local and White House Secret Service agents descended on Gateway Tower at 1 Memorial Drive, the twenty-story high rise that housed KMOX-TV on its entire ground floor. On the day of the first examination, agents scoured the entire building from its underground parking levels to its easily accessible patio rooftop. That unusual space could be reached from the KMOX Radio studios. The tippy-top rooftop was not so easily accessible. One had to pass through a narrow crawl-up space after exiting the elevator on the top floor. I had only squeezed through this eye of the needle on a couple of occasions to get a sweeping panoramic view of the city for "beauty shots." The trip was not my favorite exercise, and I was much thinner in those days. I remember going to the building's top heights once to provide a vista for a piece on earthquakes. I don't know why I didn't just give the cameraman instructions and remain in the comfort of the newsroom. I learned the hard way that it was impossible to squeeze through the space without getting dirty and grimy, so I always appreciated the station giving me notice a day in advance that I would be rooftop so I would not wear any of my designer suits to work on that day.

Apparently, our building checked out on the first pass from the Secret Service, but there were these added security measures to which we had to comply:

The building opened by 5:00 a.m. for the beginning of the floor-to-floor sweep by the bomb-sniffing dogs and human inspectors.

No window shades were to be drawn closed on any of the floors in the entire building. They all had to be hiked up to expose the whole window.

Newsroom employees were issued color-coded lapel pins to indicate to which floors and even to which spaces staffers could travel before the president arrives and while he was in the building.

All lockers were ripped away from the walls in the technicians' locker room and both the men's and women's dressing rooms. The tops were also taken off the commodes.

And there were even more precautions taken to tighten security. The corner mailboxes and newspaper stands disappeared. The sewers on all streets surrounding the building were sealed. Later, we learned that sharpshooters were assigned to the rooftops of our building and the building across the street. Since the station is only a spit from the Mississippi River, all boat and barge traffic on the river in our vicinity, upriver and downriver—would be stopped. All bridge traffic across the Mississippi River would be halted one hour before the president arrived. A Secret Service unit was assigned to the area in the shadow of the Arch and our building on the east side of the river in Illinois. And there were at least two police helicopters monitoring the skies over and around Gateway Towers. No TV or radio station news helicopters would be allowed to fly anywhere near downtown St. Louis when the president was in town. The no-fly zone applied to fixed wing aircraft, too.

In addition to the Secret Service contingent, I knew that the president's safety was also being guarded by the local FBI, St. Louis City Police, St. Louis County Police, East St. Louis Police, the U.S. Marshal's office, National Park Service rangers, police detachments from neighboring municipalities, and lord knows what other law enforcement offices and officers. Maybe it is best that we don't know the full details of the security detachments when a president is in town, because when law-abiding citizens learn the details, so do the bad guys and gals.

I began thinking what this appearance on my *Newsmakers* program would cost taxpayers. Then I realized that the cost of a presidential visit was a story that would best be covered after the president had come and gone. Wouldn't want to offend any of the president's communications staffers. I especially would not have wanted an enterprising journalist from a competing station to do a story on the cost of the president's visit to my station's digs out of spite. We've certainly seen stories on how much it costs to fuel Air Force One when the president makes political trips; we've learned what a presidential candidate can shell out for a haircut or manicure; we've found out what a presidential hunting trip costs. So I would not care to have anybody calculate the cost to America for that September visit to Channel 4. We do have better access to once-classified information about a president's travel costs. Air Force Secretary Michael Wynne reportedly told a group of dense industry folks in 2007 that for that year alone it cost $6 billion for aviation fuel to operate Air Force One. Let's see . . . that would come out to roughly $68,000 an hour, wouldn't it? And you thought you were paying a lot at the pump.

The news business does not run primarily on fuel of any kind, but it does run on information. And the ethyl of information is the "leak." It is virtually impossible to keep anything inside a station a secret. And it is almost impossible to keep the competition from getting classified intel. So it was that news about my coup that was beginning to leak like a sieve around town. The competing stations began the first of many rounds of bitching and bellyaching about Channel 4's apparent covert relationship with the White House. Honestly fellas, in order to get our exclusive one-on-ones with the chief executives, we reverted to a basic step. We asked. Ask and it shall be given if you are able to look down the line at a president's travel plans and put in a detailed request. And here's another little secret for posterity. When making a request for a presidential interview, be sure to bullet-point what the president will get out of the deal. Is he slipping with any demographic group—the artistic community, white women over fifty, Hispanics with college degrees, gays? I'm sure too many "asks" from news operations don't include points like:

Our station has the largest late-night viewership.

We have the largest number of college-educated viewers.

Our station has the strongest bi-state signal in town and can reach 150 miles into Illinois without cable.

Our station does frequent polls with the largest daily newspaper in town, and our most recent poll says you have a 73 percent (or 27 percent) approval rating in the metro area. You'll be in a friendly community; (or you can help build up your slumping numbers) in an interview with the #1 ranked newscast in town.

Your sales pitch can go on:

We will play segments of the interview on all our newscasts at noon, five, six, and ten, AND we will air the half-hour interview in its uncut entirety in prime time at 7:00 p.m. and then repeat a segment of the interview on our early morning newscast the next day. That would be the equivalent of about forty-five minutes of free air time.

We'll put together and pay the entire cost of the president holding an hour-long studio town hall meeting with no commercial breaks.

Yum. Any or all of the points should sound like a tasty treat for a White House communications office. I won't confess all the things I've done to get a one-on-one with an incumbent president. But I will tell you that one of our scores followed a bottle of Dom Perignon Champagne sent to a key White House scheduler. (Not Bill Clinton's schedule-keeper, Nancy Hernreich.)

When the news was full blown among the competing stations and the print media, the station brass and I hit upon a plan to really rub our score in the face of our competitor TV news operations. In fact, we decided to be unusually and wickedly magnanimous. We would invite a reporter from each of the daily newspapers, the *Post-Dispatch* and *Globe-Democrat*, and a reporter from our then sister station, KMOX Radio, to participate in the questioning on my *Newsmakers* program. That move would quell some of the howling protests we would get from the press and from broadcast; it would indemnify the White House from any accusations of showing favoritism (my least measurable concern); our promotions department would be delighted that the interview would get sure coverage from the newspapers and radio station; and most joyously and smugly from my standpoint, we'd be able to rub the exclusivity in the faces of our TV news competitors.

The *Post-Dispatch* chose its chief Washington correspondent, the veteran Richard Dudman; the *Globe-Democrat* picked my friend Jack Flach, its political editor; and longtime broadcaster and director of KMOX's special events, Bob Hardy, was the radio station's representative. This was a monumental and historic gathering. To our knowledge, there had never been any other joint interview of its equal in St. Louis history. Each journalistic wing was previously too jealous and guarding of any "exclusive" interview to share with its competitors of any branch of the news business.

I was concerned, quite honestly, that these senior journalists might try to take over *my* program. And I was more than a little suspicious that maybe the reason that my bosses came up with this generous spotlight sharing was that they were afraid that I would not be able to carry such a big project on my young and relativity inexperienced shoulders. I had, after all, been a newsman for only five years. And I had been at Channel 4 for only a year at the time of the Gerald Ford interview.

Collectively at the station, we all began to fear that the president's people might cancel the appearance after a startling event captured the headlines a very short time before his scheduled visit to St. Louis and Channel 4. We had known and kept secret for at least a month that we had a Ford exclusive in the bag for September 12. But after we secured that date, there had been an assassination attempt on President Ford's life. A Charles Manson cult disciple, Squeaky Fromme, had pointed a loaded .45 at the president on September 5—just a week before our big date with Mr. Ford. Fortunately, the president was not hurt, and we were assured that the president's visit with us was still on. I am sure that the planners of the National Baptist Convention event at Kiel Auditorium were also saying prayers for the president's continued good health and prayers of thanksgiving that he would be speaking to them after his interview with us. The president was also going to officiate at a White House conference on domestic and economic issues while in St. Louis.

President Ford and his press secretary, former NBC war correspondent and White House correspondent Ron Nessen, arrived right on time with their retinue. As the president and I approached each other, I think I was relieved and a little intimidated at the same time. I was a bit surprised at President Ford's height—just a hair taller than my own height of six foot one. I liked the fact that he had a good, strong, business-like handshake as I introduced myself. Immediately after I let his hand go or he let mine go, I introduced him to my confreres. The president recognized the Dudman name, and Dick lit up with the recognition. The president immediately patted himself down looking for his pipe. It was not there, and he concluded with Ron's help that he had left it, and his tobacco, on Air Force One. It was during this self-pat down that I noticed something that would become the basis for my first question on videotape to the president. Stand by for that. Back to the missing pipe: I will swear to you that the presidential pipe made the trip from the airport in about five minutes flat. I now believe it was flown down by helicopter or sped down the closed and nearby Interstate 70 at a hundred miles an hour with sirens screaming and red lights flashing. It is good to be the king.

After Mr. Ford had taken a few puffs and we made light conversation about the show's format, there were several other prerequisites that I've not told you about regarding the interview of this president. The White House communications office had decreed that the president's chair had to be on a raised platform just a few inches higher than the other chairs on the set. We had been made to understand that the president would not be using any of our station's clip-on microphones. A specialist from the Navy Signal Corps arrived and affixed the president's mike to his necktie, right above the bottom of the V-line made by the presi-

President Ford on my Newsmakers *program with (from left to right) Richard Dudman,* Post-Dispatch; *Jack Flach,* Globe-Democrat; *and Bob Hardy, KMOX.*

dent's vest. Ah, the meat of my first question came up in my mind again.

Nobody other than that corpsman and the Secret Service was allowed to touch the president, with the exception of his close personal staff, of course.

Then came the final of the executive orders. We had been told not to pour any water for the president, and he would have his own drinking glass. A Navy steward would step up soon with a case of canned and bottled drinks, and a glass for the president. But, oops! While the mike clipping ceremony was going on, the president of the United States reached over and grabbed my glass of water, from which I had already taken a sip, and took a big gulp. I saw the Navy steward and a couple of Secret Service agents turn momentarily pale. But they didn't say anything, and the steward, after quiet orders from the Boss, went through his ritual of selecting a little bottle of water and pouring it as ceremoniously into the presidential glass as if he were pouring a vintage Champagne.

A final check of the our microphones, the station audio man in the control room checked the host's and the reporters' mikes after the signal corpsman had scooted into the control to personally check the president's audio. Everything was copasetic, and we were underway.

An actual transcript of the questions I asked the president follows. Questions from the other reporters can be found in the archives of the Gerald Ford Library. Here we go, and remember my attention to the president's vest I had observed when standing very close to him. There was definitely a bulletproof vest under his tailored vest.

Julius: *Welcome to* Newsmakers. *I am Julius Hunter. My guest today is the most consistent and most recognized newsmaker in the world. President Gerald Ford is in St. Louis to attend a White House Conference on Domestic and Economic Affairs. The conference is billed as a town meeting, a chance for the president and the members of his administration to exchange views with the citizens of St. Louis.*

Joining me in the questioning of Mr. Ford today are Richard Dudman, chief Washington correspondent of the St. Louis Post-Dispatch; *Jack Flach, political editor of the* St. Louis Globe-Democrat; *and Bob Hardy, director of special events for KMOX Radio.*

Mr. President, welcome to St. Louis, and thank you for making this your first stop. . . .

Our first question concerns a matter of major concern to the vast majority of Americans; that is, your personal safety. It is a frightening fact that a president of the United States would have to wear a bulletproof vest, and we wonder whether this is going to become standard hardware, standard issue from the White House for future American presidents and yourself? We also wonder whether or not you feel that in the interest of national security, world security, you should modify your campaign style?

Ford: *Julius, let me say at the outset I don't think I should discuss whether I wear or don't wear—or whether I do something or don't do something that involves the security.*

The Secret Service makes recommendations. I feel an obligation to follow their recommendations. But to identify, Julius, what I am doing or why I am doing it, involving security, I think makes security that much more difficult.

As to my desire to meet people when I come to either St. Louis or in New Hampshire, where I was yesterday, I feel it is important for the American people to have an opportunity to see firsthand, close-up, their president.

In any job, you know, there is a risk of some kind. I feel that you have to balance or weigh the risks as to my own personal security against what is a very important aspect of our political life in America.

It is helpful for me to meet with the people, shake hands with them, get their questions, and it is just as important for them to have me say hello or to answer their questions.

So, as I put the alternatives or the contending arguments on the scales, it seems to me that what is good for the country over-balances anything else.

Julius: *We can see that your vest today, that we can see, matches your suit and is quite attractive.*

Ford: *Thank you. . . .*

Julius: *Mr. President, you seem to be doing more than just*

AT YOUR SERVICE, MR. PRESIDENT

The majority of the Navy stewards, cooks, housekeepers, and other domestics I've seen and been served by (on the presidential yacht, *Sequoia*, and with Ed Rollins in the White House mess) and who comprise the majority of the White House staff are Filipino. They are also generally the ones who carry the president's potables. The preponderance of staff from the Philippines occurred after President McKinley issued General Order Number 40. That executive mandate opened the door specifically to five hundred Filipino recruits to work specifically in the U.S. Navy Insular Force. The Filipino population in the U.S. Navy has now grown to nearly twenty thousand—more officers than in the Philippine Navy.

And if you are ever asked, you should know that the Navy stewards who carry the little case of beverages from which presidents are poured, tote around Pepsi and its bottled water, Aquafina; Coke and its bottled water, Dasani. That might be because Coke and Pepsi have always provided the White House with free beverages. Mountain Valley Water is also carried for presidents who prefer it. This water, bottled near Hot Springs, has been poured in the White House con-sistently since President Eisenhower's doctors prescribed the sodium-free water after Ike's 1955 heart attack.

meeting the American people, though. You are actually campaign-
ing at a breakneck speed, with the election still fourteen months
away. You seem to be campaigning as if it is going to happen next
week. Why are you doing that? Are you afraid of Ronald Reagan
as a possible rival? I'd like to ask you, also, if you think this is a
wise use of your time when there are so many problems of gov-
ernment bearing on you?

Ford: *I will answer the last question first. I work a minimum of*
twelve hours a day, and usually it is fourteen, and the odd times
that I take out to come to St. Louis, to New Hampshire, do not
in any way whatsoever interfere with the conducting of White
House business by me as president.

I have an excellent staff. They prepare the options for me to
make decisions. I have ample time to read and to study. So, when
I come to St. Louis, or Kansas City, where I am going, or New
Hampshire yesterday, it in no way whatsoever interferes with the
responsibilities I have, which are the highest, of being president
of the United States.

Now, I don't consider coming to St. Louis a campaign effort. I
didn't go to New Hampshire yesterday for myself. I went there
for the purpose of trying to elect a Republican candidate for the
United States Senate.

Governor Reagan had been there the night before. That was not
for me, but for him or for our party's candidate. So, any personal
campaigning has been minimal. The aim and objective of com-
ing here is to appear on this program, to attend a White House
conference, to help the Republican Party in Missouri and Kansas
City. I don't consider it a personal campaign effort. . . .

Julius: *Mr. President, if Israel is expelled from the United Nations,*
would the United States withdraw, and can you foresee any circum-
stances that might prompt the U.S. to withdraw from the U.N.?

Ford: *I don't expect the United Nations to kick Israel out, and*
of course, the United States would vigorously protest and vote
against any such effort on the part of any nation or nations. We
believe that the prospects for that happening have subsided con-
siderably, particularly since the agreement between Egypt on the
one hand and Israel on the other.

If we can continue to have momentum in the Middle East—
which I think will continue—the prospects of Arab nations and
other nonaligned nations trying to kick Israel out becomes less
and less.

In other words, the position of Israel in the United Nations becomes stronger as we keep momentum going for a solution, a long-term solution, to the problems in the Middle East.

To answer your last question, I foresee no circumstances where the United States would leave the United Nations. I think it would be a mistake. It is good for us to be a part of that forum, to have an influence . . .

Julius: *You know we have had problems there in the past.*

Ford: *We have problems in other forums as well. I have always found the best way to win a game is to play it, not to sit on the sidelines. And the United States ought to be in the game in the United Nations to protect our interests. It is a lot better inside than sitting out doing nothing.*

Julius: *Would it be in the interests of the United States to try to arrive at a formula sometime so that North and South Vietnam could enter the United Nations? They were vetoed this time because of the connection with Korea. But isn't it true that the United States continues to have a great interest in that part of the world, and isn't there a danger that relations with North and South Vietnam can get into a deep freeze the way China and Cuba did for so many years, to nobody's advantage?*

Ford: *We believe in the universality of the United Nations. We feel that it is in the interest of the world as a whole to have all nations that want to become a part of the United Nations be members, but the effort of North and South Vietnam to get in was predicated on their coming in alone. We felt if North and South Vietnam were to be a part of the United Nations, South Korea, that has had its application in to be a member for a good many years, also ought to be included. You can't be selective on who or what nation should be a part of the United Nations.*

I presume, based on our overall interest in matters involving Southeast Asia, that it is conceivable under certain circumstances that our relations with North and South Vietnam will improve, but a lot has to happen.

For example, North Vietnam continues to refuse to give us information concerning the MIA's, and they try to bribe us by saying, "We will give you information about MIA's if you will let us in the United Nations."

Well, North Vietnam agreed in January of 1973 to give us information, to give us access to North Vietnam to find the MIA's, and they have not lived up to it. So, how can we trust them? They have got a lot of things to do before we are going to be very receptive to their participation.

With the half-hour program over, our news staff and I were surprised as the president to learn that he would be sticking

President Ford is stalled in the Channel 4 newsroom while a report of a sniper is investigated at his next stop, as White House Press Secretary Ron Nessen looks on.

around our newsroom for almost an hour. We weren't told at the time but learned just before the president left us that somebody at Mr. Ford's next stop had thought they had spotted a rifleman in the rafters at Kiel Auditorium. While that reported sighting was being thoroughly checked out, News Director Fred Burrows and I were stuck trying to make small talk with the president. Fred told him how we had recently dumped film and had gone to all videotape electronic news gathering (ENG). The president seemed to be at a level slightly below "bored." But he was a good sport about the stalling exercise. He actually went around to the desks of every working staffer and pressed flesh. One staff person working behind the assignment desk was looking down and eating a Hostess Twinkie when the president stood right over him. The rattled staffer looked up, nearly choked as he packed in the Twinkie, jumped up, and mumbled a mouthful-of-Twinkie greeting.

When the all-clear was given at Kiel, a president who had spent more time in the newsroom than some of the employees who work on the other floors in the building departed in peace to address the waiting Baptists.

JIMMY CARTER

The newsroom at KMOV received word that President Jimmy Carter was going to be in our neck of the woods—or more appropriately, our neck of the water—on Thursday, August 23, 1979. He would be sailing casually into St. Louis aboard the historic paddle wheeler, *Delta Queen*, to culminate his historic cruise down the Mississippi River begun in Minneapolis. The year 1979 was not Mr. Carter's best year. Among his headaches: inflation at 13.3 percent and the prime rate at 15.75 percent. Also, Soviet forces invaded Afghanistan, Vietnam took over Cambodia, China invaded Vietnam, the Shah of Iran was deposed, opening the door for fifty-two Americans to be taken hostage in the U.S. Embassy in Tehran by militants. In addition, a $1.5 billion Chrysler bailout was approved, the Three-Mile Island nuclear accident happened, and nine hundred Jim Jones cult members drank his Kool-Aid. Wanna get away? Carter did. And the word went out from the White House: The president did not want to be disturbed. No media was allowed aboard the *Queen* for the entire trip. But Dennis Riggs, a cunning and clever Channel 4 reporter, managed to slip onboard and actually talked one of our Secret Service buddies into allowing Dennis to use an official telephone to give a live report. Aircraft are not allowed to fly directly over a vessel carrying a president, but we put our news helicopter up just to the edge of what could be technically called "over" the boat. At one point, the copter pilot radioed that he was just about out of fuel from hovering, and he reported that the engine was overheating.

After Dennis's exclusive report, all of us at the station were shocked to disbelief when during the commercial break that followed his report he asked, off-camera, if I wanted to speak with the president. You bet I did! But Dennis, are you pulling my leg?

Then I heard:

"Hello, Julius?" a semi-familiar voice asked at Dennis's end of the phone. "Hello, Julius (more like *Joool-yus*) Can you hear me? This is Jimmy Carter . . ."

I started to say, "Dennis, that's not a bad impersonation of President Carter's voice." But thankfully, I held my tongue and

made an instant assessment.

"Mr. President?" I stammered, with a good deal of apprehension and obvious hesitancy in my voice.

"Yes, Julius. Can you hear me?"

"Uh, yes . . . Mr. President. Uh . . . I can hear you just fine. Could you hold on just a second please while we make a tiny adjustment here?"

"Yes, I can. I'll hold on," the more than cooperative president of the United States volunteered.

I put my hand over the receiver and yelled to anybody within earshot, including the production crew in the control room. "Kill everything in the next section. I've got the president on the phone!!!"

Those were the days when we broadcast the news right smack dab in the middle of the bustling, noisy newsroom. Channel 4 was first in the world to do that. The mumbles and hand gestures I got were corporately like: "Yeah, yeah, yeah. Right . . . And I got the man in the moon in my refrigerator . . ."

"Ten seconds!" the stage manager shouted. "Five!"

On cue, I shocked everybody in the newsroom, control room, at home, and certainly at our competing stations with these actual words as I, with about fifteen seconds of warning, launched into an exclusive one-on-one chat from shore to ship with President Jimmy Carter aboard the *Delta Queen*:

Julius: *Okay, we are on the phone here, believe it or not, with the president of the United States, Jimmy Carter. Right now. He's on the telephone. Mr. President, how are you this evening?*

Carter: *We're fine. We just passed Louisiana, Missouri, and we're getting ready to go through the railroad bridge heading toward Lock 24, I think it is.*

Julius: *I understand Dennis says you have not had much sleep.*

Carter: *Oh, we've had enough sleep. It's been a great trip.*

Julius: *Well, we have a helicopter that's flying above the* Delta Queen *right now. I don't know whether you can hear it or see it. Can you?*

Carter: *Yes, we see it. He's been around a long time. We're going right through the railroad bridge now.*

Julius: *Right, we can see that.*

Carter: *Oh, can you? Well that's great.*

Julius: *Well, sir, could you give a wave to Jetcopter 4?*

And he did.

During the interview of approximately twelve minutes, the president told me he had learned a lot from his weeklong cruise down the Mississippi. Among other things, he said that he found that Americans were far less concerned about petty issues like those inside the Beltway seemed to be. And he said: "I hate to see the trip end, but if it has to end somewhere it could not possibly end in a more beautiful place and a more exciting place than under the tremendous Arch in St. Louis."

After a few more softball questions that one would ask any tourist, the historic first-of-its-kind interview was over.

Okay, Okay. So it wasn't exactly a Peabody or Pulitzer Prize–winning interview. I had very little notice to prepare any tough zingers, and I have often wondered whether I would have pulled them out of my quiver even if I had been fully armed with slings and arrows. After all, the moment and the setting were peaceful and tranquil. We had broken all kinds of rules of national security to get the interview. The president was gracious enough to talk to us at a time when he could have told us to jump in the lake, or river. And we had set a precedent with a shore-to-ship-via-air live interview for what was certainly a first for a local station.

I closed out the interview and pitched to the next commercial break with words that many of my viewers, the newsroom team, and I will never forget. I said: "So, there you have it, a chat with President Jimmy Carter live aboard the *Delta Queen*, with our own Dennis Riggs, the only reporter to get aboard the cruise. We'll be back with . . . with . . . God knows what, after this."

I want to be sure to mention that our Chief Engineer Wilbur Allmeyer, the helicopter pilot, and the photographer deserved medals for their intrepid valor during this unprecedented exclusive interview. We marveled for years about how our overheated whirlybird—with its thimble full of fuel left—made it through an interview that those of us on the ground made appear smooth and easy. Those brave men aboard Jetcopter 4 were lucky to avoid an unhappy ending to a triumphant story.

Early the next morning, the *Delta Queen* steamed toward its final port: St. Louis. A crowd estimated at fifteen thousand came out to greet the president. He spoke to the throng about how he and Rosalyn and First Daughter Chelsea had enjoyed being in this part of the country for a week. And he spoke of the energy crisis and asked St. Louisans to practice conservation.

And what of our intrepid hero, Dennis Riggs, who had made our exclusive happen? Well, he was not aboard the *Queen* when she chugged into port in the shadow of the Gateway Arch the morning after his historic report and ours. Sadly, the howls of protest from the local and national news corps were so loud and raucous, our friends in the Secret Service were forced to make Dennis and our Channel 4 crew walk the plank. They were kicked off the boat at the very next lock and dam through which the *Queen* passed. But the deed was done. We were the only news operation in the world to conduct a one-on-one interview with President Carter while he was aboard a historic paddle wheeler and cruising down the river on a Thursday afternoon. He would soon find himself up the creek without a paddle, however, as the 1980 presidential elections results rolled in.

BILL CLINTON

William Jefferson Clinton's kingdom and reign as the nation's "First Black President"* is still intact, but there can be no question about the fact that his crown has been tarnished a bit. And the damage was done mostly by Bill himself. He may have shot himself in the foot more than once on the 2008 presidential campaign trail on behalf of his wife, Hillary.

Bill kept claiming that the Obama camp was playing the race card. But every time he made the charge, the Obama handlers accused the former president of slipping the race card out of his sleeve. Bill Clinton's most egregious error was probably the time following Obama's January 2008 primary victory in South Carolina. Barack's win, to paraphrase Bill, was no big deal because even Jesse Jackson had racked up a victory in South Carolina back in 1988. And Bill was so fierce and vocal in defense of his wife on every front that a firestorm of criticism was directed back at him. Many of his detractors were heavy hitters, like the highest ranking African American congressman, James E. Clyburn of South Carolina. Clyburn issued the now-famous quote: "Chill a bit, Bill." And there were brickbats hurled by some former Clinton allies like Jesse Jackson, Al Sharpton, and Richmond, Virginia, Mayor Doug Wilder. The former governor of his state, Wilder said he doubted whether Bill Clinton would ever be able to fully atone for what Wilder called attacks on Obama. Al Sharpton acknowledged that he, Sharpton, was one of America's most outspoken people, and Clinton should know when it is time to shut up. "That time has come," the Reverend Al advised Bill Clinton. Jesse Jackson was a little more leavened in his criticism and asked both Barack and Hillary to take the campaign "to a higher ground."

There was even evidence that Hillary, herself, had told her rambunctious spouse to simmer down. When she reported that she had come under sniper fire when landing in Bosnia one

---

* President Clinton was given that title by Nobel Prize–winning American author Toni Morrison to recognize the trials and tribulations over which he had triumphed.

time, Bill came to his wife's support when others doubted the veracity of the Hillary account. Bill messed up his wife's defense so badly that the missus told him to butt out. And according to a CNN report, Bill got a full reprimand from Hill, who told him in one incident: "Let me handle it." According to the CNN report, the nation's former commander-in-chief replied simply: "Yes, ma'am."

Short of the impeachment dust-up, things were going pretty well for the forty-second president of these United States when I spoke with him one-on-one in Milwaukee on April 18, 1994. White House press offices had gotten so much flack from my competition in St. Louis over my past exclusive interviews with Presidents Ford, Carter, Reagan, and Bush I that those press offices had started nixing any exclusive interviews given to a reporter in his hometown. But if one has friends in high places and a little cleverness, one can get around the prohibition on presidential interviews given to local reporters.

My friend of almost thirty years who snagged the exclusive interview with Clinton for me couldn't have been much more highly placed in the Clinton White House. I had met Nancy Hernreich when she was a student at Webster College (now Webster University) in the summer of 1966 before she was a Hernreich. I was a program assistant in a summer program for poor, but talented, high school students, Upward Bound. Nancy was a standout on campus way back then in brains, energy, and beauty. And she had the sexiest Southern accent that sounded like she kept it fresh by drinking honey daily out of Dixie cups.

Nancy went on to become the scheduler, or what some in-siders have called the "gatekeeper," for Bill Clinton when he occupied the Arkansas governor's mansion. I had kept in touch with her and a lot of her buddies from the Webster campus over the years, particularly when they returned to St. Louis often for class reunions and other Webster alumni functions. We would always get together for dinner and/or drinks over the years. In 1994, Nancy held a post in the White House that was very simi-lar to the position she held for Clinton in Arkansas. Her Clin-ton Administration business card was almost filled up with her official job title: deputy assistant to the president and director of oval office operations. You may remember seeing an oval office secretary, poor Betty Curry, darting in and out of office doors to avoid the press of the press. She unmercifully got put on the hot seat during the impeachment investigations and hearings. Well,

Nancy, accustomed to keeping a much, much lower profile, was Betty's boss.

In my lobbying Nancy to fix me up with her boss, she reminded me of the new practices of presidents avoiding local reporters in their backyards. But one day in early 1994, Nancy hit upon the idea that if I could slip up to Milwaukee on April 18, she could pad a little time into the schedule of the most powerful man in the western world to get me ten minutes or so alone with him. Wow, Nancy! You go girl!

I was to be in place at Milwaukee's Italian Community Center an hour before President Clinton spoke to a group of Italian-American business people at 11:50. And, shhhhh! Mum was to be the word so the White House would not get savaged by the competitor stations in St. Louis, as my exclusives had provoked them to howl and bellow in protest several times before.

I had heard from many network reports that the president is no keeper of the clock. And for all intents and purposes, he probably never bothered to wear a watch during his public life. I'm saying that Bill Clinton was notoriously tardy. Sure enough, as I paced outside the little room at the community center, it began to occur to me that it was already well past 11:30. And no president. But nearer to 12:40 than not, a bustle and scurrying began as the traveling press corps and a contingent of Secret Service agents blew through a door from outside, and the crew and I snapped to readiness. But when the president came through the door in a bath of artificial light, his entrance had a strangely calming effect on me. The man wasn't racing or huffing or puffing or grooming or perspiring or anything. He looked as if he had arrived an hour early to talk to me and the Italian businesspersons. He appeared to be ready to lounge for a while before doing anything.

And then I saw that certain Clintonesque something that had perhaps bowled over a bevy of ladies in his lifetime. I'm a dude! I'm a man who stands solid in his sexuality. But when Billy Clinton put his face within ten inches of my mug, I felt transfixed. His piercing blue eyes locked contact with mine, and then the famous two-handed Clinton handshake where rather than pump my hand up and down in the traditional manly greeting, he just slowly, gently rolled my hand from side to side in his big, but soft, mitts.

The only time I have seen that kind of intense attention to my face and eyes and lips is when I was confronted up close by a person who was hard of hearing and basically using my whole face as a TelePrompTer. I bet he seldom if ever forgot a person's name. Okay, so I came close to swooning. His aides quickly told us that we had roughly ten minutes to chat and that would be all. I should look to their signaling just off camera to tell me when to wrap up and end the interview. They would give me a countdown till the end just like in the studio. Agreed.

And you know what? Clinton allowed me to go way over my allotted time. The more frantically his aides gave me a clearly visible finger windmill wrap-up, I'd pop a juicy question in and the president would turn to tell his nervous-Nelly assistants: "I want to answer that question." And that would send the aides into a synchronized checking of their watches, and a synchronized communal shrug.

One of the questions I popped in to stall for more time with the president was a hot issue of that particular day. Should federal authorities have the right to conduct unannounced raids on federally subsidized public housing units in search of drugs?

Finally, I had gotten sufficient footage, and, in a great deal of sympathy for the frustrated presidential aides, and sensing that some of the Italian business leaders were probably *non troppo felice*—not too happy, if my Italian serves me right—I concluded the interview.

Practicing the proper protocol for the situation in which one is in the room with a president or other high-ranking notable, my photographer turned off the lights but left the camera rolling. One never knows what can evolve after the lights go down low. The practice had yielded a big bonus when I had my one-on-one with President Reagan.

I thanked the president. He thanked me. I then told him that I had gotten the interview with him through Nancy.

"Oh, you know Nancy?" he asked with genuine surprise. And I told him from whence I had known her and for how long. "Well, I'll be," he said with incredulity. "You know Nancy."

And then he made me an offer I could not refuse:

"Would you like to send her a note?" he asked.

"Why, yes. I'd love to," I said.

And then I ripped a piece of paper out of my steno pad and went to a nearby table and wrote:

> *Dear Nancy:*
> *The President and I had a great time today.*
> *Where were you?*
> *J. Hunter*

Mr. Clinton took a quick look at the note, chortled that famous hoarse Clinton chuckle, folded my note, and put it in his shirt pocket. Could I be audaciously asking my nation's commander-in-chief, and perhaps the most influential man on the planet, to act as a courier for me? Yes!!!

And then I showed my further fearless temerity by whispering to him: "You know, Mr. President, I'm about the only news anchor at my station who likes you. So don't embarrass me."

He hoarsely chortled again and gave me a clap on the shoulder. We shook hands, exchanged thanks again, and another presidential scoop was in the can. My shooter and I raced to the local CBS station where we quickly edited and fed segments of the interview back to KMOV for my live wraparounds from a studio at the station.

I was shocked that the very next day I got a call from Nancy in the oval office to thank me for my note and let me know she had gotten it. I thanked her, and we took a few minutes to catch up on news about our families and her old pals from Webster.

Little did I know—but Nancy surely did—that all hell was going to break loose in the White House and beyond after President Clinton *did* embarrass me, his family, his loyal staff, and the office of president. On January 17, 1998, the story blew up all over the world that President Bill Clinton had had a two-year sexually charged dalliance with a White House intern who was twenty-one years old when the fling started. And that was just two years after the president had laughed at my admonishing him not to embarrass me. Monica had cajoled and pestered Betty Curry into allowing her access to the president as the young intern began the ruse of delivering pizza and other things to the oval office after-hours and on weekends.

Nancy took a real drubbing on the story. The last time I saw her in St. Louis as the earthshaking story was unfolding, she looked drawn and battle-weary. By my count, she testified six times before the grand jury investigating the Lewinski case. She was nothing like the gorgeous thing that used to turn heads on the Webster campus. She confided in me over drinks that she could not take the strain anymore. I told her at the time that some of my bosses from the Belo home office in Dallas had been in town and had strongly hinted that I should take down the photo of Bill and me hanging prominently on the wall of a downtown restaurant.

I stood defiant—mostly on principle—and let the word go forth that if there was any attempt to force me to take the photo down, it would become a national story on every major broadcast and print medium. Something about my First Amendment Rights . . . and those of the restaurant owner. Nothing more came of the issue.

Nancy returned to the White House and told her boss about my obstinacy and fidelity. In a letter dated October 8, 1998, I received a letter on White House stationery. Here's what it said with its handwritten signature:

Dear Julius:

Nancy passed along the message about the photo of the two of us. Thank you for the show of support and friendship -- it means more to me than you'll know.

Sincerely,

Bill Clinton

Say what you will about the guy's morals, but we all have to agree that he is, at least, a real character. And, he is one heckuva charmer.

NOT SO FAST, MR. PRESIDENT!

"The No Child Left Behind Act is like a Russian novel. It's long, it's complicated, and in the end everyone dies."

—Scott Howard

Former school superintendent, Perry, Ohio

After teaching in the St. Louis Public School System, and after having spent nearly thirty-five years of my post-teaching job visiting and speaking with kids and teachers at hundreds of St. Louis metro schools, I was turned on by one school like no other. It was 1999, I was still on television, and a visit to the Laclede Elementary School was one stop on my busy itinerary of school visits for that year. The school is in a run-down, all-black, northside neighborhood with a plethora of boarded-up houses, highly visible gang-related activities, and what would appear at quick glance like hopelessness at every turn. But when I stepped inside Laclede, which was left mercifully untouched by the politics and messiness of the controversial desegregation program, I found an oasis from all that was ugly and troubling on the mean streets outside.

At the time of my first visit, the school was being run by Joyce Roberts, a tough, energetic, and innovative principal who was much loved by her nearly three hundred kids and their parents. She had been preceded at the school by a principal of equally impressive administrative skills, Lonzola Buford. Joyce and Lonzola were succeeded by yet another remarkable principal, Yolanda Moss. I feel blessed to have worked with both Joyce and Yolanda.

Law and order were the order of the day inside the school surrounded by crime and decay; cleanliness was so apparently next to godliness; the teachers all seemed to have been tailor-made for producing excellence; and the students from preschool through fifth grade seemed turned on by the very idea of going to school and by life in general. Their 96 percent daily attendance rate bore that out. One other factor that made Laclede stand out was the amazingly active attention by parents who all lived within a short walking distance of the school.

The men of Sigma Pi Phi worked with the author to provide rich experiences for Laclede School kids since 1999.

I wanted more involvement in this stunning success story in the heart of blight. So, I created a program that put thirty-one of my Sigma Pi Phi fraternity brothers inside the school to act as shining role models. My bros and I not only worked with the kids in the school, but each of us was also committed to bringing a group of his assigned kids to work with him to watch him on his job. That took Laclede students inside such places as a 747 jetliner for the first, and perhaps only, time; inside a federal courtroom to watch a trial presided over by a judge brother; we took the kids to audit college classrooms; and a prominent pediatrician brother took his group to his clinic. One of our guys even wrote a play for his class that included a part for every youngster in his pack. To help students capture images of their field trips, my brother/partner, Dr. Henry Givens, president of Harris-Stowe State University, and I purchased a dozen Polaroid cameras for the kids. And these are just a few of the experiences our Laclede students saw as enrichment from a fraternity made up of successful African American men. After one field trip to Harris-Stowe, a fourth grader in my hearing said to

Henry: "Dr. Givens, I like this college thing. I wanna come here. Will you still be alive, or will you be dead by then?"

A friend of mine, whose company had a year-end surplus of three-ringed notebooks for each of several years, donated more than a hundred notebooks at a time, and I supplied the filler paper to help the kids keep school diaries . . . and memories. When I was at SLU, I was given a private foundation grant for several years to take hundreds of kids by motor coach each semester for a day trip to a SLU wilderness property upstate. I always made sure that one teacher in particular and her class were included. Mrs. Byrd's class at Laclede was automatically placed at the top of the list of schools for five years running. I was impressed with how she excelled in making the escape from the concrete jungle to Pike County a uniquely rewarding learning experience for her classes.

And as "Book Buddies," the frat helped set up an outdoor reading room with plants and patio furniture on a safe low rooftop space at the school. Education is *al fresco*!

When an interim school board, in an attempt to balance a doomed budget, called for the closing of 16 schools and the slashing of 1,400 jobs, I got to go up against Al Sharpton. Reverend Al blew into town on Sunday, September 7, 2003, to call for a first day of school boycott to protest the school board's planned cuts. To counter, at the request of the school board, I recorded some radio tracks to be aired before school started calling for the kids to get their butts to school on the all-important first day. (Not exactly in those terms, of course.) Then I went into my piggy bank and purchased ten new bicycles, a passel of back packs, and other school supplies as raffle prizes for only those Laclede kids who defied the Sharpton call for a first day stay-away. It appeared the news that we spread through the neighborhood about the prizes helped bolster first-day attendance.

On a couple of occasions, Joyce Roberts hit me up to underwrite the cost of outdoor carnivals to celebrate the close of the school year. My pleasure.

But as successful as that mentoring program and my personal efforts at helping out at Laclede became, I realized that it was the Laclede principals, teachers, students, and the parents who had been doing the heavy lifting. In the year I got hooked up with Laclede Elementary, a third of the fourth graders met Missouri state standards in math; four years later the proficiency level soared to 66 percent. Reading levels that were at an abysmal

7 percent for Laclede's third graders in 1999 zoomed up to a remarkable 82 percent of the kids reading at or above the state minimum requirement by 2003.

So, you can imagine the surprise felt by many of us laboring in the vineyard when we got the word that President George W. Bush himself would be popping by the school on January 5, 2004. The occasion would be a photo op at the school to insinuate that the laudable achievement at Laclede was due to his No Child Left Behind program. In reality, the report card on Bush's NCLB push may not get a passing grade in many of the nation's school districts. The controversial program, on the other hand, gets generally high marks for raising the country's awareness that we'd better spend more time improving the quality of education in America. And soon!

I was one of the guests invited to sit in the audience on the presidential visit to the Blue Ribbon School. Since I was very familiar with the building's layout, I managed to sneak myself into the converted gym for the program before it got underway. Principal Moss was only too happy to vouch for my credentials at the Secret Service checkpoints. And I picked a front row center seat long before the audience was let in. I even snagged a seat next to me for my good friend, David Steward, the head guy at World Wide Technologies.

When the program began that day, Mr. Bush told a big audience: "One of the things you find in a successful school is a strong-willed, smart, capable principal. And that's obviously the case here." Yolanda and Joyce, both seated on the stage, could not help but beam. The president went on to say: "This school has defied expectation by raising the bar and believing that every child can learn."

Right on, Mr. President. But not so fast! Your No Child Left Behind program wasn't signed into law until January 8, 2002. And here you are making your appearance at Laclede Elementary School with paeans of profound presidential praise on January 5, 2004. Mr. Bush's appearance was almost two years to the day after Public Law 107-110 went into effect. Even under the best of teaching conditions and supportive programs, two years would not a school success story make. The seeds for the flowering of the Laclede School had been planted in rocky soil almost fifteen years before the president appeared at the state fair judges' table.

President Bush is informed about longtime support given to Laclede School, while David Steward, CEO of World Wide Technologies, looks on.

So in the photo you see here, I am informing the president of that fact. And I took the rarely given opportunity to trumpet the greatness of all the human elements—with little government money—that went into Laclede's commendable achievements. I even quickly got a word in about the work of my frat. To this the president said, "Is that right . . . that right? If I had known about that in advance I coulda had you on stage." No, Mr. President, you had the right people on stage: principals, teachers, parents, and students.

And then in the fleeting seconds left of what was a pretty long handshake, I half-jokingly commented to Mr. Bush about a very recent appointment of his: "Mr. President, you must not have checked out my old friend, Alphonso Jackson, before you just nominated him to be HUD Secretary." The president threw his head back and laughed his trademark laugh and said: "Secretary Jackson. I like the sound of that. Secretary Jackson. He's a good man, Al." And the president was off and away.

Jackson was unanimously okayed for the HUD post by the Senate on March 31, 2004, just a couple of months after the president and I had talked about him at Laclede School. When I was VP for community relations at Saint Louis U., Secretary Jackson's office called and asked if I could set up a photo op with Secretary Jackson talking to some students. But his representative told me that the students would not be allowed to ask their HUD Secretary any questions during the photo shoot. My answer to the request was a resounding, "No!"

I knew Al well during his time in St. Louis. We had tossed back more than a few cocktails over the years with friends at favorite watering holes like Culpepper's and Balaban's. He had worked as a CPA at a silk-stocking accounting firm, top guy at the St. Louis Housing Authority, and was named the city's public safety director in 1977. While he held the latter job, I engaged him in a one-on-one on-camera joust in which I asked him how safe the old Arena with its wooden roof was for hockey games, in particular. He said it was perfectly safe. And then I nailed him with proof that although the Arena was built to seat 12,000, more than 20,000 hockey fans were being crammed inside the "Old Barn" on game nights. More than his own public safety department should have allowed. I accused a grinning Jackson of turning a blind eye to what could be a fire catastrophe. I had had several area fire chiefs tell me on camera that the place was a firetrap. A tornado severely damaged the Arena roof in 1959. Fortunately, there were no people inside. Al promised, on camera, to check out my charge. Ultimately, nothing was done and the place remained overbooked.

At the time this book went to press, my old pal, Al, had been forced to leave his Housing and Urban Development post on April 18, 2008. He was being investigated by the FBI, a federal grand jury, the justice department, and the office of HUD's inspector general. Among the charges: Al applied a loyalty-to-the-president oath before contractors would be awarded large government deals; he's been accused of punishing contractors that wouldn't play ball with him; he faces charges of giving plum contracts to his best buddies; hiring old cronies and inflating their salaries; and he is suspected of doing business with companies with checkered records.

Jackson is innocent until proven guilty, of course. And while I wish my old friend good luck with justice, I guess it's not a good idea to pick a person for high office just on the basis of how his/her name sounds with the title "Secretary" stuck in front of it.

Doug Wilder

As I watched Doug Wilder on interview after interview on Tuesday, February 12, 2008, I had not seen such a twinkle and such pride in his eyes since I first met him in person and talked with him on April 27, 1991. In 1991, I interviewed Doug Wilder when he was Virginia's governor. He is now the mayor of Richmond, Virginia. He had become the first African American to call the Governor's Mansion in the Commonwealth of Virginia home, serving from 1990 to 1994.

The old Wilder's smile in 2008 accompanied the twinkle that had been part of his aura in the old days as he talked about the possibility—the inevitability—that maverick presidential candidate Barack Obama could take his commonwealth in the Virginia Primary.

Back in 1991, rumors swirled and test balloon after test balloon had been floated regarding the prospects of Governor Wilder entering the presidential race the following year. He confided in me that I was among the first journalists with whom he had hinted at his plans to become the nation's chief executive. On that Saturday night in April 1991, Governor Wilder spoke to an audience of more than 1,200 at a United Negro College Fund banquet in St. Louis. His theme was the importance of education to a sound society. As emcee of that event, I had the pleasure and honor before and after the event to talk privately for a few minutes with this distinguished grandson of slaves.

It was as if the governor was using me as a big piece of litmus paper to determine whether he should run for the nation's highest office. Wilder wanted to know what I thought his biggest obstacles would be besides the obvious—his race. I told him what he already knew, which was that money would be a key factor. He admitted that raising big money might be a formidable problem, although he shared with me that he had raised and spent a record $7 million on his gubernatorial campaign. That tidy sum would be peanuts in a presidential race. I also asked him if he had a competent staff to guide the campaign. He said that was something he was working on.

I asked him how soon he might make an announcement on whether the wind was blowing in the right direction. He projected that he would probably make the announcement in just about four months after our conversation. I thought that was a little too soon, although I'd never worked in a presidential campaign before. I'd covered many campaigns, but only as an outsider.

I thought the least I could do for a guy who shared my slave ancestry would be to help the governor test the waters in St. Louis. So I began to tease him from the podium with my emcee banter as he sat next to me on the dais that night in the Adam's Mark Hotel ballroom. *Post-Dispatch* Regional Political Correspondent Mark Schlinkmann wrote in an April 28 article:

"Although Wilder didn't mention a bid for the presidency in his speech, master of ceremonies Julius Hunter did, in tongue-in-cheek fashion. Hunter, an anchorman for KMOV, said Wilder was testing the waters and that as far as many of those in the audience were concerned, 'you will be able to walk on those waters' in such a bid."

The banquet attendees got my drift and cheered and applauded their support of the not-too-subtle plugs I was giving the governor. Shirley Chisholm, Jessie Jackson, and Al Sharpton, of course, had made runs for the presidency. But their efforts were almost symbolic. We could have no idea that a Barack Obama would be standing on the threshold of 1600 Pennsylvania Avenue seventeen years after the banquet at which Wilder spoke in St. Louis.

After the banquet, the governor gave me a clap on the shoulder and pretended, with tongue firmly in cheek, to scold me for blabbing the "secret" he had shared with me before the evening's program began. I was very moved by Governor Wilder's speech that night, even though he had advised parents not to allow their kids too much television and too much Nintendo. In fact, for a very brief moment, I thought I might like to join this heroic pioneer in his presidential aspirations. I thought at the moment I might be a very good media and/or communications consultant. I had, after all, enjoyed more than twenty years on the air at two TV stations

and several radio stations in St. Louis by the time I met Governor Wilder. Maybe, I thought, it was time to move on to something a bit more adventurous and risky than a job that was already adventurous and risky.

The governor and I exchanged numbers, and he told me that one of his daughters would be taking a key role in his run and he or she would phone me soon. I thought this was the "Let's do lunch" kiss off, but to my surprise, within a couple of weeks, the governor phoned me and we talked about the possibility of my coming to Richmond for a visit to discuss joining him in the run for the White House.

Just as he had indicated to me on the night I met him and in the subsequent phone call, Governor Wilder made his formal announcement on the South Portico of the State Capitol Building in Richmond on September 13, 1991. "I have decided to run for president of the United States in 1992," he declared in a strong voice. And he asked family, Virginians, and the people of the United States for "patience, support, and prayer."

But the *Wilder for President Campaign* was over almost before it started. He dropped out of the race officially on January 9, 1992. Just as I was weighing the options of quitting my TV job and moving to Richmond. How sad. His pipe dream and mine were dashed at the same time. Reporter B. Drummond Ayres, Jr., observed that Wilder was "unable to come up with a message or an organization that promised success in 1992." Others said Wilder's mistake and demise was caused by his playing the race card. Still others claimed that my new friend Governor Wilder just could not raise enough money. In fact, turns out that Bill Clinton's fundraisers helped cover Wilder's considerable debts incurred in the four-month campaign. In fact, Bill Clinton teamed up with Senator Chuck Robb to throw buffets and other fundraisers to help retire Governor Wilder's campaign debt. Isn't it ironic that Barack Obama offered the same debt-retirement offer to Hillary Clinton?

And, ironically, some sixteen years after Bill Clinton came to Wilder's financial rescue, on February 12, 2008, Wilder, no doubt stung the Clinton Campaign by proudly announcing that he was backing Barack Obama against Hillary Clinton. There was apparently quite a lot of bad blood that flowed somehow between Wilder and Bill Clinton. Their relationship came to a head the night of February 9, 2008, when my friend Doug Wilder announced that he was really pissed off with my friend Bill Clinton. Just before voters in New Hampshire had cast their primary votes, the former president actually referred to Obama's campaign as "a fairy tale." Wilder shot back: "Barack Obama is not a fairy tale. He is real." And Wilder's criticism of Bill Clinton and support of Obama had come as the former was campaigning right in Wilder's Richmond backyard and in three other cities in the commonwealth.

Wilder said he and black voters everywhere were outright offended by Bill Clinton's assertion that Obama's big victory in South Carolina was just because Obama is black and South Carolina has such a large black voter base.

Wilder let it be known: "It's not just me who feels that way; any number of people feel that. A time comes and a time goes. The president has had his time."

But Bill Clinton, often jokingly referred to as "the first black president" for all the troubles he had, would not fire back at the man who at one time had wanted to be the bona fide first black president. A Clinton spokesman would only say that the Clintons "have tremendous respect for Governor Wilder. He has been a trailblazer who made it possible for both Senators Clinton and Obama to run for president."

Without a doubt Wilder, for one shining moment, saw himself as the man who had a more than fair shot at realizing the dream of holding a higher office than any other black person in the nation's history—until that skinny senator from Illinois came along.

I wish I had known about the Wilder/Clinton rift when I had an exclusive interview with President Clinton on April 18, 1994. The acrimony certainly must have been brewing for years. I could have asked Clinton about that. But I also wish that I would have tried to see if there is something more about Wilder's turning his back on the Clintons than the governor's courtly Virginian manners would allow him to say publicly.

The author gives unsolicited advice to Barack Obama, as supporter Barbara Wright looks on.

Barack Obama was certainly a fascinating figure in my long list of interviews with luminaries. I had the privilege and pleasure to talk for a few minutes with the senator after he addressed a cheering audience of more than 20,000 in St. Louis on Saturday night, February 2, 2008. That was just one week to the day after Governor Wilder had blasted President Clinton and accused him of playing the race card. My friends in the St. Louis Police Department (of which I am a commissioner), and my friends in the Secret Service, brought the senator to me backstage following a rousing speech. Although he had to be absolutely exhausted, the senator was amenable to having his picture taken with me, during which we were able to have a little conversation. He seemed genuinely pleased that I found his post–South Carolina speech electrifying. I suggested to him that I always chuckled when he did the "whispering Republican" bit when a Republican—real or fictional—would come up to him and whisper that he/she was going to cross over and vote for Obama. And Obama claims he would thank the potential supporter in a whisper and then ask: "Why are we whispering?" The presidential candidate flashed that big smile when he learned that I knew the "whispering Republican" story by heart.

Seizing on the opportunity to be a campaign coach like I was not able to ultimately be for Governor Wilder, I suggested to Obama that he should modify a section of his stump speech. It was the part in which he tried to put to rest for good the rumors that he is secretly a Muslim. He often said in his standard speech: "I've been praising my Jesus every Sunday for my whole life." I suggested to him (and the Hunter instructional index finger can be clearly seen in one photo during this valuable campaign tip) that he take the word "Sunday" out of that statement lest he sound like a "once-a-week" Christian. He thanked me for that advice. And, you know, I heard him talk about his religious fervor several more times, but he had, indeed, removed the "Sunday" part of that little affirmation of faith.

As my time with him was up far too short, I told Senator Obama that I had had my picture taken with six presidents. Without missing a beat, he declared: "I'll be the seventh!" And then he turned to my photographer and flashed a big, pearly smile as he shook my hand. As he walked away, I imagined him as the reincarnation of Doug Wilder.

GOOFS, GAFFES, AND
DAN QUAYLE

"Yea, verily, I say unto you:
Let he or she who is without
gaffes cast the first malaprop."
—The Prophet Julius

Far be it from me to cast any stones about on-air, publicly heard goofs and gaffes.

After all, while on the air one time I recited a brief and irretrievable eulogy for a popular local priest who had made Catholic charities his life's work. After giving details of his life in appropriate sepulchral tones, I tagged the story with, "He and his tireless work will be greatly missed. Father Bill Smith. Dead at 78 . . . degrees."

No way to get that horrific error back in the tube. The situation would certainly have magnified if I had said anything like: "Uh, please scratch the 'degrees' part of that last sentence, friends." Nor would it have helped if I had said, "Of course, I meant the dear priest passed on at 78 *years* of age, and not 78 *degrees*." No, no, no. Just leave it alone and hang your head low for a couple of extra beats before moving on to the next story. Vince Lena, the newscast's control room director, did not help my embarrassment heal quickly. He activated my earpiece, and I could hear rolls of control room laughter. Vinnie choked back laughter himself as he said in my ear, "Hell, I guess he WOULD be dead if his body temp dropped to 78 degrees!" Ha-ha. Thanks for the support, control room.

I had on at least a couple of occasions slipped up and said "Kansas Shitty" by accident. Show me the anchor who hasn't said something of the sort. And I don't know whether this was a Freudian slip or not, but I once read some copy on the air that referred to St. Louis's governing body as the "Silly Board of Aldermen." Make that "City Board of Aldermen, folks."

The most celebrated and oft-repeated screw up in my on-air life came on the night of January 2, 1981. It was on the late newscast after co-anchor Steve Schiff, weatherguy Ollie Raymand, and I had come back from our regular Friday night dinner at a nearby Chinese restaurant. The three of us just loved to comple-ment the tasty Szechuan treats with our favorite wine for such oc-casions: *Wang Fu.* And I wish I could swear on a stack of

menus to you that three bottles between newscasts was our limit. But I'd be lying. We were always able to go back to the station and deliver sobering news, if necessary. But it might be a good thing that our microphones did not double as breathalyzers.

On that historic Friday night in January nearly thirty years ago, we had almost wrapped up the newscast when the stage manager, Jerry Rock, handed me an urgent bulletin the wire machine had just ding-dinged to our attention. I read it cold:

This just in . . . the serial killer British authorities have dubbed the Yorkshire Terrier *. . . uh . . . Yorkshire* Ripper *has just been arrested in northern England.*

When it occurred to me what I had just said, I immediately swung around to get a lifeline from Steve. But no help there. Steve had swung around in his swivel chair and was doubled over in paroxysms of audible laughter. Ollie was slapping his desk with both hands and guffawed uncontrollably. Even the stage manager who had ripped and handed me the bulletin had turned his back on me and was obviously shaking with laughter.

I looked at the tape of the incident several times later, and there was a look of utter panic and a bit of confusion on my face as to what I had said and why it was so damn funny to everybody.

Then from the control room into my earpiece came Vince, the director's, voice—accompanied by raucous control room laugh-ter. "Okay, girls," he said. "We can't go on. We're gonna shut it down. Say goodnight." And that's exactly what I did.

"And that's the news. Thank you for joining us. Have a good weekend!"

The closing traveling shot showed a lone, confused anchor completely abandoned in rough water by all his crewmates.

And then . . . the RED PHONE rang under the anchor desk. The call could come either from the station general manager; our more direct boss, the news director; or from the reincarnation of Mahatma Gandhi. Steve and I most often ruled out a communication from the latter gentleman, so it would be station GM Al Cohen or News Director Fred Burrows. Freddie was a talented, stable, chain-smoking newsroom boss who had risen from the ranks of office gofer. He prefaced his screamed comments with his usual preface during excitement:

"Holy geez! Holy geez! Did I just hear Hunter say something about British authorities arresting a goddamn Yorkshire Terrier! A goddamn Yorkshire Terrier? Holy geez!"

I tried to prevent an executive coronary by trying to calm down my boss and friend. My co-anchor partner was still wiping tears from his eyes as he stifled his laughter. Thanks, Pal.

"Fred, Old Buddy," I began. "I'm sorry, but what I said could have been a helluva lot worse . . ."

"How in the frickin' world . . . how in the goddamn world could it have been any goddamn worse?" Fred screamed as I could just imagine him clutching his racing heart as he sat in his TV room at home . . .

"Freddie," I reasoned. "'I COULD have said: 'The man British authorities have identified as the Yorkshire Pudding.'"

Freddie hung up on me. Understandably. My slipup was the buzz of the town for days and weeks thereafter. In fact, I still run into people who remember that dog-day night. About three quarters of the phone calls that poured in to the newsroom the night of the gaffe were obviously animal lovers and thought the mistake was adorable. Still others wanted the whole story repeated. A few old prunes thought the goof was unprofessional and not at all funny.

I didn't get into any serious trouble with the station management or with the viewers, and a lighthearted column by a newspaper critic carried this headline a few days later:

HUNTER NOT IN DOGHOUSE OVER TERRIER REMARK

Since I hold sincere respect for how things can come out wrong when stated publicly, I was eager to meet the one-time king of publicly declared goof-ups, Vice President Dan Quayle.

James Danforth Quayle had distinguished himself by far more weird sentences than his infamous misspelling of *potato*. Or is it *potatoe*? But among Quayle's other silly-putty sayings were:

> *"We don't want to go back to tomorrow, we want to go forward."*
> *"We're going to have the best educated Americans in the world."*
> *"If we don't succeed, we run the risk of failure."*

And, perhaps, the granddaddy of all the Quayle eggs was his interpretation of the United Negro College Fund slogan: "A mind is a terrible thing to waste." Quayle's take on that one:

> *"It's a terrible thing to lose your mind."*

The veep was in town in late 1992 toward the end of his stint as the nation's No. 2 executive officer to hold a media roundtable. The event was slated for the Adam's Mark Hotel just across the street from the station. The Secret Service had packed all of the working media outside the ballroom where the confab would be held. As I waited with my crew amongst my competition and colleagues, one of the hotel waiters sought me out and whispered quietly in my ear: "Hey, Julius, you ain't gonna like where they got you put in there . . ."

I must confess that it took me a second to try to decipher the meaning of this confidential message from a waiter who most certainly must have appreciated the fact that I am a heavy tipper.

My waiter friend continued over the din of the gathering media troops. "What I'm sayin' is that they got you waaaay on the other end of that table from the vice president. And they got Channel 5 and some other channels much closer to him than you."

I reached into my pocket and pulled out a ten spot and slipped it into the server's hand. "Is there anything we can do about that?" I asked.

"Sure," he said. "Come with me. But we got to hurry." The media herd would be allowed to get in and find their positions in about ten minutes, I was sure.

My guide slipped me around through the kitchen into the back entrance of the darkened ballroom. There was a huge table set up. There were tent cards at all of the seats, and the waiter was right about the seating arrangements. My card was so far away from the vice president's place that I would have had to mail my questions in.

I made quick work of the old switcheroo, a trick of legerdemain, even in the dark. I'd done stuff like this before. Within just minutes, the place cards of my main competitors, Channels 2 and 5, had been banished to distant positions around the round table. And guess who would be seated to the immediate left of Mr. Quayle? Now to slip out of the room the way we had come in. I thanked my waiter friend and took the back way to join the media throng. I was in no hurry to get back. My seat of honor was already secured, as all the photos taken that day will show.

Quayle had nothing to say of particular interest to anybody during the roundtable discussion. My colleagues and I all looked bored to tears—especially my fiercest competitors, who were seated so far away from the non-action.

Until more interesting news assignments came along after Quayle's visit, I'm sure all my colleagues and I could really buy into an enigmatic, but hope-filled Quayle declaration.

"The future will be better tomorrow."

THE PAPAL CHASE

Monday, rainy Monday. The weather couldn't have been
lousier. It was dark, dreary, and raining buckets. A heavy fog
made visibility limited. You could hardly see your hand in front
of your face, but there was no real incentive that day at Logan
International to stick a hand out from under your umbrella or
raincoat to act as a visibility gauge. The awful weather in Boston
on this particular Monday in some ways attested to the irrefutable omnipotence of the Almighty Weathermaker. Catholics
and the ecumenically minded throughout America had hoped
for a more hospitable welcome for a very special guest. But,
alas, this was the kind of day that the faithful would deftly re-
move from God's power and dump in the lap of *Mother Nature*.
One can point a critical finger at the good *Mother* in matters
such as bad weather, but never, never at *The Man Upstairs*. Yes,
Virginia, there *are* fair weather Christians. And none, devout
Roman Catholics in particular, would be a bit reluctant to refer
to October 1, 1979, in the words of the Psalmist David: "This
is the day the Lord has made! Let us rejoice and be glad in it!"
Not in Boston, anyway.

This was not an event the planning committee, the host committee, the prelates of the Catholic Church, the Chamber of
Commerce, nor any other high-powered political official could
call off or postpone. There would be no rain checks for this
event—not even a rain delay of the ceremonies. Too much was
already in motion, a reality that became crystal clear through
the thick fog that billowed in from Boston Harbor to cover the
Logan tarmac. First Lady Rosalyn Carter, the nation's princes of
the Church, and the phalanxes of the national and international
media began a soggy snap into position as two-way radios crackled a ten-minute warning. Faster than real time can sometimes
seem, we got the five-minute alert to get ready. Scores of camera
lenses were wiped dry. Light meter readings were checked as if
checking light levels would do any good. Test flashes of scores
of cameras sparkled in the fog. The central sound system was
checked with the familiar "Testing. Testing. 1-2-3-4. Testing."

Then, two-by-two the procession of bishops and cardinals

began with pomp and circumstance. They moved in slow motion, with hands folded in front of them, in reverential solemnity. They drifted past the grandstand on which I was standing shoulder to shoulder with print and broadcast news teams from all over the world. I counted myself lucky to have jockeyed to a second-row position as the red-tinged cortege of sixty-two cardinals and bishops floated by silently on a foggy cloud. In my mind I could hear a Gregorian chant accompanying the sacred sartorial stroll. Had I planned the event, I might have even used brass band-fare as an accompaniment to set a regal tone. But in actuality, there was no music of any kind. In fact, there was an aura of silence as if in great expectation. The silence prevailed until one of the princes of the Church, St. Louis's Cardinal John Carberry, broke rank and broke the stillness. While still in step with his brethren, Carberry turned toward the press grandstand, unfolded his hands, and pierced the silence as he waved a greeting with his right hand up to his pal. "Jooooolius . . ." he shouted up to me quite audibly. And that caused a ripple of laughter to roll through the assembled media reps as the prelates moved forward. I waved back, but was a little too pleasantly embarrassed to give the cardinal a shout back to this orthodox prelate's unorthodox cordiality.

Only a few more minutes passed before the most riveting, magical, mystical sight I have ever personally witnessed began to unfold. The nose of what appeared to be the biggest aircraft I had ever seen rolled in front of us through the thick fog. In actuality, this was just a regular Boeing 747. Yet, there was nothing regular about this Aer Lingus mammoth. It bore the name of the fifth-century evangelist, St. Patrick, with a big shamrock. I learned before I traveled to Boston that this aircraft had been specially outfitted to transport a special passenger. The globally popular frequent flyer, Pope John Paul II, had boarded the plane at dawn in Ireland for the six-hour flight on what would be his first visit to America as a successor to St. Peter. The papal plane, no matter the airline, was dubbed *Shepherd I* whenever and wherever it flew the Pope. The press plane on which I flew on this Papal Chase was called *Shepherd II*, and I learned there was even a *Shepherd III*. I supposed that *III* was the carrier of the world's smaller news outlets, or even some big ones that had registered late. All of us assembled at Logan that day witnessed the first visit by a Pontiff to the United States since Pope Paul VI addressed the United Nations in 1965. There was so much excitement and fervor in the air that day that we could never have figured that this would be the first of nine visits by the world traveler, Pope John Paul II.

When the door of the behemoth carrier opened, there he was. The sight had to make even the hardest of hearts skip a bit of a beat, and the throats present that had never before felt a lump must certainly have experienced a new kind of laryngeal clot. From our vantage point in the media roost, as the Pontiff stood in that plane's doorway and waved, he looked to be no taller than an inch arrayed in radiant white. As John Paul II descended the staircase, every person whose hands were not being deployed to operate some piece of equipment to record the event broke into wild applause. It was a standing ovation from those of us already standing. There were cheers and whistles of the type and magnitude usually allotted only to rock stars. And I was keenly aware that some of the droplets on the faces all around me—and streaming down my face—were not just rain. Wow! I'm a pretty tough dude, and I'd never felt that kind of electrical feeling before, and I must admit I've never sensed that chilling, goose-bumpy feeling since.

The rain did not let up for the Pope's much-anticipated ceremonial kiss of the rain-slicked ground. The roar of the applause and the bristling of camera lights hit their highest peak when the Pope knelt to kiss the Boston tarmac. One of his aides said the earth kiss is symbolic of the Pontiff's effort to bring the Church to the people. There is something impressive to see the leader of the world's 1 billion Roman Catholics, including the 65 million in America, humbling himself to his host nation. It was a practice John Paul II continued for sixteen years after this day in Boston. He wanted to continue the kissing of terra firma after his replacement surgery in 1994. So, John Paul II continued the practice through the kissing of a soil sample brought to him, often by children, in a little box, tray, or basket in countries he visited. Pope Benedict XVI has discontinued the practice.

After being officially greeted by Boston's Cardinal Humberto Medeiros, the Pope was warmly greeted by the princes and the secular assemblage of the official welcoming party. Then we were off and running! Six cities in seven days. After traveling from the airport through the streets of Boston, my crew and I made it to a Mass in a downpour on Boston Common. There was a thirty-seven-minute homily and distribution of the Eucharist to 160 congregants representing a beautiful bouquet of racial, ethnic, age and gender diversity. We stayed on the periphery of this mammoth throng so we did not get locked in. We headed to our hotel, letting CBS fill in the coverage gaps that were necessary for us to move around in cities whose layouts we did not know.

Imagine, if you will, the *Shepherd II* takeoffs and landings for the remainder of the whirlwind: Up bright and early the next morning for New York and a United Nations visit after eighteen hours in Boston. The major event in Gotham was an evening Mass at Yankee Stadium with an estimated eighty thousand in attendance. I remember Cardinal Terrance Cooke had to keep pulling down the wind-furled short papal cape. Another massive Mass at Shea Stadium was our next big event. Then, on to a Philadelphia Mass at Benjamin Franklin Parkway. Next to Des Moines just outside the city limits for a Mass at the six-hundred-acre Living History. We went on next to Chicago for a magnificent Mass at Grant Park. To wrap up the catch-your-breath-if-you-can juggernaut, the Pope dropped in on Washington, D.C. Somehow the Pope, who was still skiing and hiking in those days, looked absolutely healthy, well-rested, and invigorated. Here was one of the world's most powerful leaders obviously impressed by the turnout at each of the stops we made with him. We members of the media looked like we had been "rode hard, and hung up wet!" Literally wet from all the rain that bathed us on the busy journey.

I remember phoning my dear friends, Michael and Phyllis Ward, as soon as I arrived in D.C. I demanded that they put me up for the night whether they had plans or not. I told them I needed to stay in a home for the night, even if they weren't going to be there. They were gracious hosts. They even drove me to the National Cathedral that night for a live report back to St. Louis. (I wore one of Michael's neckties for that report after phoning Mike's mother back in St. Louis to be sure she watched. She had fretted that her son was not in regular church attendance, and I consoled her with the news that I could at least get his tie to make an appearance in church.)

There is a simple explanation of how the Pope could look so much fresher than the media that had traveled with him for a week.

Here is just a taste of the media schedule for those of us who flew on *Shepherd II.*

Arrive in Boston. Retrieve a ton of equipment and luggage from baggage carousel. Get to the cordoned-off media section on the airport tarmac grandstand.

Record a couple of video stand-ups to establish your presence at Logan Airport. Do some anticipatory stuff like: "Pope John Paul is in Boston right now. As you can see he is being greeted by . . ." (Even though he has not actually arrived yet.)

Quickly pack up equipment and catch a cab to Boston Common to cover essence of your presence in stand-ups at giant Mass. DO NOT GET ENTANGLED IN THE CROWD. Also cut and transmit some promotional shorts ("This is Julius Hunter in Boston traveling with Pope John Paul . . .") (Leave major video coverage to CBS network.)

Get to hotel. Unpack only the barest of essentials! Write script for live phone report to station for six o'clock news over video supplied by network. Incorporate your stand-up reports video-taped just before you had to flee Mass. Pretend in your phone report that you know what is going on at the Mass using data fed to you by the station from wire services. Call room service. Gobble food. Shower. Get into dry clothes. Write script for late news wrap-around. Phone it in to station writer-editor. Fit three thirty-second promos within the brief satellite window you are allotted to be used in Channel 4's early evening programming. Get cleaned up—at least above the waist—and stand ready for live appearance on ten o'clock newscast. Use footage from earlier stand-ups at airport and Boston Common Mass cut-in. Exchange comments live with anchor in St. Louis studio. Pre-arrange questions so there are no embarrassments about things you don't know. (Note: The satellite signal from the New York hotel was so intermittent and shaky that Channel 4's senior technical engineer, Wilbur Allmeyer, had to literally hold two wires together to get me on the air.) Pack up gear and take it to the in-spection room at the hotel. All baggage and gear carried aboard Shepherd II *(long before 9/11) had to be placed in a security room for inspection at each hotel four hours before morning departure. Since morning departure time was usually between five and six in the morning, you don't want to get up at 2:00 a.m. So, you take your luggage and your gear to the security room before catching three or four hours of sleep—max—each night on the tour. Before you hit the hay, try the futile attempt to get Room Service to bring you anything to eat. Inevitably, you'll end up eating something from the hallway vending machine for supper.*

Remember, you have to be up at least an hour before the media buses leave the hotel for the airport. If the bus leaves at 5:00 for the airport, count on getting up at least by 4:00. Probably earlier. Remember: "Time, tide and the papal bus to the airport wait for no man!"

Take the bus to the airport. Board Shepherd II *about an hour before* Shepherd I *takes off for the next city. (I was excited about being assigned a* Shepherd II *seat across the aisle from Don Novello, the zany TV and movie comedian who played the fictitious Father Guido Sarducci. He was covering the trip for* Rolling Stone Magazine. *He was a hoot on the entire trip. Just two years after I met him, he returned to the Vatican in his "priestly" garb where he was arrested by the Swiss Guard for "impersonating a priest." He later said he was going to Utah to see if he would be arrested for trying to impersonate a member of the Osmond Family.) You and your crew need to be set up with the rest of the traveling media to video the arrival of the Pope and his aircraft.*

Repeat the routine of the previous day for five more days.

Get the idea? Remember that you can never get to bed on the tour until the Pope has retired for the night, and the very robust, barrel-chested John Paul II of 1979 would sometimes not turn in from public view until after your late newscast. And you would have to wake up as early as the Pope, who rose around 4:00 a.m. each day.

I remember a live report I did outside the cardinal's residence in Chicago on our late newscast of the tour on October 5. Our report showed John Paul II giving the clamorous assembly a blessing from the balcony. I said something like: "Well, as you can see, the Pope has given the crowd below him a benediction of sorts and gone inside the cardinal's residence. And, as you can hear, the crowd is still chanting his name. And . . . wait a minute, wait a minute . . . He's coming out again! Wait a minute! He's on the balcony again. Unbelievable! Let's listen. . . ." The popular Pope raised his hands to silence the crowd. His obedient flock quieted instantly. And then, he belted out in a robust baritone the well-known "Alleluiah . . . Alleluiah . . . Alleluiah . . . Alleluiah . . ." The melody wafted down from his deep voice through the nighttime congregation until all were singing and swaying. And that was yet another magic moment in which this reporter just shut up and let the natural sound carry. At the conclusion of the song, the Pontiff gave another benedictory blessing, and I signed off for the night, returning control to the St. Louis studio. I'm sure we ran over our allotted time that night. But who would dare question the decision?

I had the opportunity on two more occasions to report on a papal visit. The second tour of duty covered the Pope in mid-September 1987. On this visit, I covered the Pope in Miami; Columbia, South Carolina; New Orleans; San Antonio; Phoenix; and Los Angeles, before turning over the trip to a co-anchor for the Pope's visits to Monterey, San Francisco, and Detroit.

I then had the privilege and honor of covering the historic visit of the now-frail Pope John Paul II's overnight visit to St. Louis on January 26, 1999. Let me just give you the highlights from the second and third visits.

On Trip 2, the station must have come to realize how much one of these papal whirlwinds could cost. In September 1987, in Miami, for the first and only time in my entire career, I was put up in the same hotel room with my photographer. It was his first time, too. Neither of us was amused at the double-bunking. We were told it was an "accidental booking error." At the hotel's front desk, Tom Martin and I didn't even look like we were engaged! Also in Miami, we were forced by a penurious field producer to rent a car from a company I had never heard of before. There was either a turtle or snail as part of the rental company's logo. As we were creeping across town trying to run parallel with a papal parade down Biscayne Boulevard, a tire on the cheap clunker blew. We didn't make one scheduled papal event of the evening, and my slow burn could have fired all the barbecues in Miami that night.

When aboard *Shepherd II* from Miami to Columbia, South Carolina, I borrowed a cell phone from a reporter from another city. His station had ventured to equip him with the then new commodity. I thought it would be cool, novel, and historic for me to phone in the first live report on our late newscast from thirty thousand feet up. I made a connection and reached an executive producer whose judgment was often questioned by newsroom staffers. After establishing contact with the station and the EP on the borrowed phone, I was shocked and then enraged that the young newsroom executive opted not to use my live report from the clouds because "it was not studio quality." Had I been a Catholic, I would have had to find a priest for confession when we reached our next stop. To the surprise and even amusement of some of my travel mates seated around me, I managed to string together a barrage of profanities I had retained from my days running around with my big brother, Van, in the old neighborhood. There can be a certain poetry to profanity if the nouns, verbs, adverbs, adjectives, and prepositions are all in proper expletive positioning. And, to think, I had just been with the Pope! And would be again.

As with the reporters on the first *Shepherd II*, the media corps developed a real camaraderie as we traded stories, played cards, and borrowed equipment. After the third city on each of the first two trips, the reporters and crew began to shout out the pre-takeoff safety spiel quite loudly with the flight attendant— word for word. Like a Greek chorus? No. More like a "Geek" Chorus. And upon the instructions on how to fasten the seatbelts, a ripple of more than one hundred clicks snapped almost simultaneously with the clicks on each belt sounded several times. It sounded each time like a field of mechanical crickets.

One reporter who boarded the press bus at the New Orleans airport fashioned himself a miter out of newspaper and sat in the last seat of our darkened Greyhound-type bus and kept an overhead light on as our bus roared through the night. As thousands of the faithful lined the announced route, the reporter/imposter gave the papal wave as the devout crossed themselves thinking for at least a brief moment our fellow reporter was the Pope himself, blessing them from in the illuminated back seat of the bus.

When we arrived in Phoenix, the journey from the press bus to the immense field where the Mass was to be held was, so far as I can remember, the longest trek I had ever taken to get to a story. And the fields were mighty muddy. Even though he was covered by a canopy, I will never understand how the Pope—under those heavy papal garments—could hold up under the extreme heat outside Phoenix. The notion that the dry Phoenix heat is more bearable than St. Louis's humidity can be described as one would describe the bovine animal clumps that were left on our shoes after the long trek to Mass and back to our bus.

The Pope's sensitivity towards the TWA pilots and flight attendants who served him devoutly on both trips became widely known and spread throughout each entourage. . . . In fact, one of the neatest stories attesting to Pope John Paul II's caring nature is that of St. Louisan Fran DiGregario, a young TWA flight attendant. The year 1987 was a particularly trying year for the financially ailing TWA Airlines and its staff. Flight attendants were on strike that year over a number of issues, and their union had actually contacted the Vatican beseeching the Pope not to fly TWA. (The Pope is perhaps the only world-renowned luminary in modern times that has people "beseech" him. Most other dignitaries are just "asked" things.)

Fran and some other conscientious pilots and flight attendants elected to take the service trip of a lifetime, attending the head of the Catholic Church. This band of the willing preferred to be called *crossovers* rather than *scabs*, as staffers loyal to the union called them.

The FAA and TWA officials blew into Miami two days before the 1987 papal trip began to give special training to the TWA staff that had been handpicked to serve the Pontiff. The crews were given strict orders on protocol. None of them was to address the Pope directly unless he spoke to them first. The Pope is never to be touched.

Interestingly enough, the TWA crewpersons were instructed by their bosses to take as many tasteful candid pictures from discreet positions as they wanted, so they could share them with each other and their loved ones later.

Shepherd I was a 727. I was on *Shepherd II*, and Fran worked on *Shepherd III*, one of two L-1011s filled with us raucous news papal paparazzi. But she told me she had frequent conversations with her colleagues who were privileged to fly with the Big Guy. She clued me in on some tidbits that were not commonly known and rarely if ever reported in the media. For example, she told me that the Pope ate very little inflight food, but he enjoyed a lot of fruit.

One of the most innovative moments of my Papal Chase was on the second trip when a special phone hookup was set up on *Shepherd I* so the Pope could give a sermon to congregants on the ground on the flight from Phoenix to Los Angeles. I could only think during that homily that if special hookups had been arranged from coast to coast, the Pontiff could have, from a pulpit closer to Heaven, addressed millions more Americans than turned out to see him in person. I also wondered if the Pope's airborne broadcast was of "studio quality."

Few if any of the TWA crew had cell phones in those days, so Fran told me that at the end of each day the crew couldn't wait to get to their hotel rooms to share the day's events with their families back home. Fran, a single mom at the time of the historic papal trip, told me her sons, four-year-old Nicholas and eight-year-old Michael, just wanted to know if they would be seeing their mother on television each night. "My dad, Vince, was overcome with awe, pride, and joy," Fran told me. "He just couldn't believe that a simple letter carrier's daughter was traveling with the Pope." Vince beamed with particular pride upon learning that his darling Francine was one of six flight attendants from St. Louis chosen from a national pool of 5,700 to serve on the three papal planes. And her mother, Vickie? "Well, she was also a very proud parent before, during, and long after that incredible week in my life. And like most moms, my mom, a stay-at-home mother of seven, had my safety on the trip and my safe return as her primary concern."

Fran's day on September 17 in Monterrey was a day burned into her memory for life. Although this was the end of the second trip, and although he would be on the ground in Monterrey for no more than a few hours, the Pope took time out of his incredibly busy schedule to meet personally with each of the six TWA pilots and twenty-two flight attendants. Each staff member received about two minutes of the Pontiff's time on the tarmac. The pretty young product of St. Louis's Italian Hill neighborhood's personal encounter with Pope John Paul II, as she described it to me, was eerily like Jesus's encounter with the woman at the well as told in the fourth chapter of John in the New Testament.

"There seemed to be an indescribable aura around him," Fran told me. "It was like all sound was shut off, but there could almost have been angels singing in the silence. I was slightly aware that Archbishop Rigali was the Pope's escort and moved him along after a certain time as he talked privately with us crew members, but I can only be sure that the archbishop was there by the photos I have that shows he was surely there. But I was, believe me, totally unaware of anything else around us. His eyes never left mine for a second. They were just . . . just riveting, like you wouldn't believe. Hypnotizing. You just knew it was all about you at this moment. My heart pounded. The look in his eyes encouraged me to open up to him. I told him that I had challenges and a bit of turmoil in my life at the time. I told him that my marriage had just ended, and I was trying to raise two young boys as a single mother. I felt like I was hardly pure and holy enough to be in his presence."

She went on: "And then I asked him if he would pray for me. What happened next changed my whole life . . . forever. We had been instructed in our orientation not to touch the Pope or to even reach out to try to shake

TWA Flight Attendant Fran DiGregario from St. Louis got a personal audience with Pope John Paul II.

his hand. But when I asked him to pray for me, he took my hands in his and said some words softly that I will never forget. Looking right into my eyes with his incredibly soul-piercing eyes, he said to me: 'I will pray for you . . . if you will pray for me.' With tears I could not hold back, I promised I would pray for him. And I left him confident that he would pray for me. I was really transformed at that once-in-a-lifetime minute or two in my life. I've felt specially blessed ever since."

A Pope does not speak directly to the media, so I could be envious of the special experience that Fran had—IF envy is not a sin. ("Thou shalt not covet thy interviewee's private audience with the Pope?") But at the end of the first papal visit in Washington, D.C., the Pope waded quite unexpectedly into the crowd of us weary reporters who were about to pass out from the rigors of the week. And he shook hands. Although I must confess (there's that Catholic influence again) that I did not get to shake his hand, I did get a really, really, really close-up unflattering photo of His Holiness that I'm including in this book. The usually mellow Don Novello actually got to shake the Pope's hand and snap a really close-up photo. With exultation, he shouted a line that got echoed on subsequent souvenir buttons and bumper stickers: "I got a peek at the Pope!"

My experience with all things Catholic made me the natural to serve as Channel 4's field anchor on John Paul II's ninth and last trip to America. There had been fear for years among the most faithful of the more than half-million Catholics in St. Louis that the Pope would never set the descendent *shoes of the Fisherman* in the Gateway City. How could that be? As a bishop, Justin Rigali had been a trusted, loyal, and respected aide and interpreter to the Pope for many years in the Vatican. The idle gossip in St. Louis was that the Pope was displeased with Rigali and had assigned him to St. Louis as punishment. Others buzzed with no foundation that the Pope hadn't visited St. Louis because the St. Louis Archdiocese had not been sending enough money to the Vatican. Still others said that scandalous behavior by St. Louis priests and those in the neighboring Belleville Diocese was too hot for the Pope to be near.

Well, all those riffs were silenced when the Vatican announced that John Paul II would, indeed, visit the city of his still humble servant, Archbishop Rigali. The dates, January 26 and 27, 1999, were circled on calendars all over town, throughout the region, the nation, and around the world. But with all the excitement, the media, in particular, did some things that helped drastically diminish the typical magnitude of a papal visit. The media predicted how difficult it would be to get around town when John Paul was in town. Also, there were dour forecasts on how cold, snowy, and generally ugly the weather was going to be when the Pontiff flew in.

Just two weeks before the Big Visit, St. Louisans were slipping and sliding on the traditional ice sheets the streets of St. Louis are accustomed to seeing in a typical January. It would be cold enough to keep anybody from lingering outdoors for too long a period passing from home to auto, let alone standing along a motorcade route. January temperatures in St. Louis are typically in the low to upper thirties. And there was, indeed, a fair amount of snow still on the ground in the weeks before the Pope arrived.

But something that can be considered by some as nothing short of a miracle happened with regard to the local weather just before *Shepherd I* touched down at Lambert. And the weather anomaly is being attributed by many to the order of nuns formally known as the Sister-Servants of the Holy Spirit of Perpetual Adoration. These nuns are cloistered in the Mount Grace Convent in North St. Louis and are unusual in that their habits are a pinkish color. That is why they are popularly and lovingly known as the "Pink Sisters." By tradition, the Sisters keep a twenty-four-hour prayer vigil at Mount Grace. They call their act of contrition a state of perpetual adoration—hence their formal name.

So many St. Louisans feel the prayers offered up by the Pink Sisters have an effective channel to the Almighty that the nuns receive more than a hundred calls a day for prayer. They, too, feel that their prayers are heard. Many months before John Paul II touched down at Lambert International, the Sisters began praying fervently for heavenly weather for the Pope's visit. And guess what? Inexplicably to even some statisticians at the National Weather Service, on the day the Pope arrived, it was a sunny 54 degrees. On the day he left for Rome after his thirty-one-hour visit, it was a balmy 68 degrees. The mercury had risen, along with the hopes and prayers of many true believers.

Also, the papal visit did not clog traffic at all. Many believe that normally conservative St. Louis motorists had taken a variety of steps to avoid being tied up in bumper-to-bumper traffic. And thus, the streets appeared to be deserted in many parts of town on the day the Pope was in St. Louis. It was almost spooky. The thin line of spectators along the motorcade route from the archbishop's residence in the Central West End near where I live to the domed stadium and back was so sparse that the papal motorcade whizzed by the spectator line to and fro simply because there were—relatively speaking—not many people for the Pontiff to give his feeble greeting. Those who turned out to get a peek at the Pope told broadcast and print reporters that they were both surprised to see so many people eschew the motorcade streets, and disappointed at the speed at which the Pope zipped by them.

Archbishop (now Cardinal) Rigali was host to Pope John Paul II on the 1999 papal visit to St. Louis.

And then the rumor mill began churning again. The undercurrent this time was that the turnout was so disappointing to the Pope that he personally ordered the speedy trips down the city's main stretch. And there was, in some of those dark corners of unsubstantiated gossip where rumors grow like poison mushrooms, a story that there was such papal disappointment at the turnout that Archbishop Rigali was embarrassed and would now certainly never be named a cardinal.

Sorry I never got to ask my friend, now Cardinal Justin Rigali, about those assertions before he was elevated and took up his post in Philadelphia.

Another fact I want to record for posterity about the Pope's brief but historic visit to St. Louis was the unusual anchor team that conveyed Channel 4's wall-to-wall coverage of those thirty-one hours when the Pope was in town. Would you believe that the Catholic priest who worked in the booth sites with me as my color commentator at every venue the Pope visited was a married man at the time of the visit? Seriously. And Father Greg Lockwood and his wife, Karen, were the parents of five children ranging in age from eight to eighteen. In fact, Father Greg's eldest child, Christie, was Channel 4's youth reporter for the Catholic events directed at the Church's young people during the papal visit. She did a fantastic job.

I think I had better explain this all to you. Father Lockwood was a Lutheran pastor for nearly two years after his ordination into that sect in 1984. But he applied to St. Louis Archbishop John May for admission into the Catholic priesthood in late 1985. The archbishop accepted the application and forwarded the request to Rome. Lockwood, a Vietnam vet, told me: "I was basically put into a three-year evaluation period after my request to change over. I was sent to be examined by several leading Catholic theologians. They found very few challenges to what I had learned about Christian faith from Concordia Seminary in Fort Wayne, Indiana. I also had to attend a certain number of seminars during the three years. And I was required to master the contents of nine books—mandatory reading—on such subjects as moral theology and canon law."

So in 1988, Greg Lockwood, a husband and father, became Greg Lockwood, a priest and Father. Under a special rule established by the Vatican's Sacred Congregation of the Doctrine of Faith, the so-called "Pastoral Provision Decision" opened the doors to Anglican, Episcopal, and Lutheran pastors whose theological tenets and order of worship were the closest of all Protestant groups to those held by the Vatican. Some say the special dispensation was to help offset the 12 percent annual loss of Catholic priests. And with about one hundred crossovers, there are many priests outside the Eastern Catholic Church who are legitimately married in the eyes of the Roman Catholic Church.

These crossover priests must undergo three years of "reorientation," and their side-door entrance to the church must be sponsored by their bishop. Archbishop John May sponsored the ordination of Greg Lockwood into the Catholic priesthood. Some viewers who identified themselves as devout Catholics wrote and phoned me in protest after our coverage. They implied that they clearly saw the gate through which the former Lutheran entered the church as not even a side door. They told me that Father Greg had entered by an illegitimate back door.

When Father Lockwood and I first met to discuss our broadcast strategies and styles a few weeks before the Pope's arrival, I knew he would be my kind of guy on at least three counts. First of all, when we had dinner at a downtown restaurant, he joined me in ordering a Manhattan on the rocks. And, here we were, two former members of the Lutheran Church, Missouri Synod doing the play-by-play and color on a Pope's visit to St. Louis. Plus, I was glad to learn that my new cohort had a good sense of humor. In many ways, I think our backgrounds were very helpful to our audience's understanding of Catholic liturgy and teachings. We were able to describe everything on the screen in terms that Protestants, Jews, Muslims, Taoists, Buddhists, atheists, and agnostics could clearly understand.

After a number of negative communications from a few vocal viewers, I became particularly cognizant of the fact that many non-Catholics were offended by my use of such terms as "the Holy Father." They would remind me in letters, phone calls, and on the street that the Pope was not their father . . . or Father. These plaintiffs were the same people who quite rightfully objected to TV stations who, by habit or convenience, show only worship services at the Old and New Cathedrals on Christmas Day, New Year's Eve, Thanksgiving, and Lent. I could assure them then and now that the Catholic services were covered only because the cathedrals were geographically close to all the TV stations and newspapers in town, and the Catholic renditions of Christian high holiday events were and are more colorful.

Devout Channel 4 viewers who followed the point-to-point coverage that Father Lockwood and I gave the 1999 papal visit to St. Louis were soon keenly aware of my contentious streak. I was very blatant on-air about the omnipresence of local and regional politicians fawning and grinning and kneeling and blanketing the Pontiff's attention. The poor guy was often so smothered by politicians and officials that I wondered how he could even breathe—especially with his failing health.

By late into the Pope's one full-day St. Louis visit, viewers heard me grouse aloud and on-air such sentiments as:

"Well, there they are again. That gaggle of politicians and bigwigs hogging the Pope's frail attention. Look at how they're bending and bobbing around . . . genuflecting and bowing with, quite frankly, folks, what we'd have to call charitably 'well-meaning over-exuberance.'"

"Wow! There's Hizzoner, the mayor, kissing the Pope's ring . . . again. I think that's at least his third time doing that on this brief visit. And I'll bet His Holiness had not counted on meeting the Missouri state auditor so many times in so many places in such a short period of time."

The most spectacularly idiotic imposition on the Pope's valuable time was instigated by then Vice President Al Gore & Company. At the official airport hangar send-off of John Paul II, he tried quite furtively to get to dozens of children who had been waiting patiently for hours to entertain the Pope with their singing. They had boarded buses much earlier in the day at a suburban shopping mall. The kids, from several parishes, had practiced singing "This Little Light of Mine" and were as excited as many of these totally selfish official adults about getting to see the Pope close-up. He seemed quite aware of their presence in a cordoned-off area at the very end of the big hangar. But every time he crept, in his bent and gnarled state, in the direction of the little children, he got waylaid by the likes of the U.S. vice president.

As he almost got mere feet away from the eagerly waiting youngsters—just like a wrestler in a tag team match trying to tag his partner on the ring apron for relief—the Pope was dragged away from his target. Shamelessly, somebody had set up a blue curtain background with two chairs set for a photo op with Gore. I was furious! I muttered:

"Well, it looks like the Pope has been Shanghaied for a photo op with the vice president. Let's see if we can listen in . . ."

Gore: "Your Holiness, welcome to America and to St. Louis. I bring you greetings from the president."

Pope: (Something totally unintelligible. I had hoped he would have mumbled something like: "Let's get this nonsense over, Mr. Vice President so that I can get to those children over there.")

Gore: "I understand this is not your first visit to St. Louis. You were here many years earlier."

Pope: (Something else unintelligible. But I had hoped it would be something mumbled like: "Do you know, you idiot, in how many cities in the world I've been since I was last in this cow town? How in the region of Satan do you think I would remember being in this town so many years ago?")

And I SWEAR to you, this was the vice president's last question to an infirm, exhausted, elderly gentleman:

Gore: "Has St. Louis changed much since you were here the last time?"

I didn't even give the Pope a chance to mumble anything in response to this utterly ridiculous photo-op question.

"Cut! Cut! Let's get out of this right now!" I shouted over the airwaves. "Enough of this nonsense. The vice president is quite obviously taking advantage of his office to detain and interrogate the head of the Catholic Church with absolutely silly questions."

And then, on camera, I said: "Ladies and gentleman, I hope you will be watchful with me of how many of these politicians will try to use photos they've taken with the Pope in their newsletters and campaign materials. Let's just not let them do it! Now, let's get back to the Pope, about to depart St. Louis after a little under thirty-one hours here. He's headed toward those children. Let's hope . . . let's pray that he gets there. . . . Oh, no, he's just been diverted off to the left there, and it looks like he will NOT get to hear from those dear, dear kids. What a shame. Jesus says in the Bible, 'Suffer the little children to come unto me . . .' Well, it looks like today here in St. Louis with the Pope, it's 'Let the little children suffer.'"

It is by this time, my friends, that I had violated every tenet of good journalism. I was spewing editorial comments without labeling them as such. But frankly, I didn't give a damn!

I'd take discipline or a firing before I would have remained silent on what my viewers, Father Greg, and I had witnessed live and in living color. Father Greg's comments echoed mine.

I then continued my commentary and recap of the highlights of the Pope's brief stopover as the stooped, ailing Pontiff faded out of our picture and eventually to the specially outfitted TWA Boeing 767 waiting to take him on the nine-hour nonstop trip back to Rome.

When I got back to the station that night, my voice mailbox was jammed. There were more than thirty messages, and I went through each one. The calls were overwhelmingly in favor of my observations. One woman who phoned said she had watched me for years but was furious. She ranted that she was never aware before that night how much I "hated politicians." She huffed that she would never watch me again. And she gave her name and community at the end of her recorded message. I used the phone book and a cross-reference book to find that angry caller, and I phoned her. She was absolutely stunned into silence when I identified myself. There was a pregnant pause that warranted the birth of a response. The caller then mustered enough courage to repeat her accusations directly to me. When I explained to her just how long those poor kids had waited and from how far they had come to sing for the Pope, the caller bowed to new understanding. She said she was unaware of the length of time the kids had waited. She apologized, and we ended up in a friendly conversation that included exchanging stories about our children and parenting. I made a new friend that night. She would call occasionally thereafter to comment, often favorably, on our news coverage.

The most touching phone call I received in the newsroom relative to the coverage of the papal day trip came on the first night of the Pope's St. Louis visit. A dear lady identified herself as one of the Sisters of St. Francis of the Martyr St. George. That is a mouthful of a title I had the soft-voiced caller repeat slowly a couple of times as I jotted it down. She further clued me in that her order is the one that takes care of the archbishop and his official residence. She wanted me to know that the entire staff at the residence where the Pope was overnighting watched me exclusively for coverage of the Pontiff's visit. She wanted to compliment me and find out what time our papal coverage would begin the next day.

I should have asked the dear Sister a key question: "Did the Pope watch Channel 4 while he was in town?" But if he did, I would never want the station's promotions department to know that fact. I had gotten that department and myself in a heap of trouble during my exclusive interview with President Carter when he was aboard the *Delta Queen*. From the anchor desk, I had asked the most powerful man in the western world to wave to "Jetcopter 4" hovering overhead. And he did. Following that audacious request, the station's promotions department ran an almost immediate promo with that footage. The outrage and uproar coming from the competitor stations in town forced the end of what must have been the shortest running pat-on-one's-own-back commercial in television news history. And remember the watchword I broadcast as the Pope was departing St. Louis about how disgusted we should be if photos politicians took with the Pope popped up in their campaign materials?

A PAPAL PALATE

For breakfast, John Paul II liked what the Sisters called "just an American breakfast." For lunch, the Pope ate lightly: bread, soup, and peach tea. On the one night he was in St. Louis, His Holiness dined on scrumptious delicacies with an Italian essence: tortellini in brood (broth) and gemelli, a pasta topped with basil sauce (the Sisters called it "Pasta di Papa," the Pope's pasta). The Pontiff was also served a small sampling of filet mignon, grilled lamb chops, veal, and salads. My source told me that the modest Sisters were undertandably "privileged and honored to serve him."

POPES, PRELATES, AND PRIESTS

In covering news of religion over the span of my thirty-three-year news career, I agree with a comprehensive report that does not put my former profession in a great light. Although the cut of my jib contains very little conservative fabric, I'd have to agree with the recent findings of the conservative watchdog group, Media Research Center, regarding the coverage given religious subjects by the media. After studying every religion news story on ABC, CBS, and NBC news in the twelve months from March 1, 2003, through February 29, 2004, MRC confirmed some things I saw clearly from the inside of the survey:

1. Religion coverage has more than doubled from ten years ago. And look at the number of times that *Newsweek* or *Time* magazine has featured a cover with a religious subject.

2. News about the Catholic Church received the most coverage among all faiths. That story count was boosted by the ongoing stories of alleged child sex abuse by priests and the globe-trotting of Pope John Paul II. News of Islam still trickled from 9/11 and from continuing news out of Iraq and that region. The MRC analyzed data that says the tone of network TV coverage of religious stories was hostile to orthodox faiths and supportive of minority religions like Scientology and progressive fads like *The Da Vinci Code.* Big news broke the last Sunday in June 2008 revealing movie magnate Will Smith's membership in the Church of Scientology.

3. The yearlong MRC study found that "the media's Rolodex of religion experts was dominated by those hostile to religious orthodoxy." In other words, media programs put religious scholars and theologians on the air whose theories and opinions often slammed conservative thinking.

4. MRC analysts also found that religious issues were most often covered through the secular eyes of the reporters bringing us those stories. The report also cites that Scripture and theological issues are often ignored. I'm proud to say this is one accusation of which I bear no guilt.

My credentials for credible ecumenical TV commentary? I was baptized into the Missouri Synod Lutheran Church at age six; belonged to a Catholic Cub Scout troop; hung outside a rocking Pentecostal church when I was a kid to hear the music and the sermons and testifying; played the organ for a Baptist church's vacation Bible school for several summers; dated a Baptist girl from high school to college who lived next door to a big, active A.M.E. church; married a Presbyterian woman and joined her church; recently hosted a big luncheon party to have a mezuzah ceremoniously installed at my front door; and recently learned through DNA testing that my ancestry is from the Nigerian Hausa tribe, which has been Muslim for more than nine hundred years. I can honestly swear (or affirm) that I've made serious study of all the religious sects and their dogma that touched my life. Now, can I get some props for ecumenism before I take you along on some of my TV stories on religion? Most of these stories covered Catholicism, since I became, in essence, the Catholic Bureau reporter for two stations over more than thirty years.

Confession time. Once again, I am NOT a real Roman Catholic, but I've played one many times on TV. In fact, devoted viewers of Channels 4 and 5 in St. Louis might swear—if their religion doesn't frown on swearing—that Mass would be a regular part of my life. But I confessed to you early on in the book that I was baptized into the Missouri Synod Lutheran Church as a young kid. While it might be taking you as long as this point in the book to absorb or believe that fact, please note that I am a current Presbyterian by way of the Lutheran Church, but I have covered almost all the major Catholic stories of our time.

Since I took my vows as a novice reporter in 1970, I have broadcast news on TV and radio regarding:

- The two historic 1978 trips to Rome with St. Louis's Cardinal John Carberry to bury two Popes within an incredible two months;
- The then robust and energetic Pope John Paul II's whirlwind tour of America in October 1979—six cities in seven days;
- The Vatican-mandated retirement of Cardinal John Carberry in 1979 when he turned seventy-five and all its implications;

- The Pope's second swing through the United States in 1987—nine cities in a remarkable eleven days;

- The appointment and installation of John May as archbishop of St. Louis in 1980;

- The Pope's appointment of Bishop (now Cardinal) Justin Rigali to succeed Archbishop May;

- The frail and greatly slowed Pope's historic visit to St. Louis in 1999;

- Regular reports on the ever-unfolding international story of child sexual abuse by priests—particularly in a neighboring Illinois diocese;

- And the spectacularly scandalous accounts of how a TV news story about a priest that never made the airwaves nearly destroyed a major market television station and all in it. Told here for the first time ever.

With that sort of career immersion, small wonder that viewers either tagged me as a devout Roman Catholic at most, or at least, the station's Catholic Bureau reporter. Some might have even accused me of being an agent of the devil run amok.

My baptism by travel in the Catholic arena was bolstered on August 7, 1978, with a midnight phone call from Channel 4 News Director Fred Burrows. Pope Paul VI had passed away on August 6, 1978.

"Pack your bags, son. You're headed to Rome tomorrow afternoon. The Pope just died, and you'll be meeting Cardinal Carberry out at Lambert (Airport) at noon. Your crew and a field producer will meet you there. Okay? Noon tomorrow. Rome. Cardinal Carberry. Pope died."

"How long will I be there?" I asked, still in a state of sleepiness. I still somehow had the presence of mind to try to figure out how much clothing I would need.

"Don't have a clue," Fred leveled with me. "We'd like to hang around until a new Pope is elected, but we don't have any idea, of course, how long that will take." That meant pack lightly with basic clothes that can be easily and quickly laundered, dry-cleaned, or if worn too long, jettisoned and burned.

Upon landing at Leonardo da Vinci Airport, we began to hear buzzings that Italian customs officials might make it difficult to bring expensive news camera equipment into their country. We heard from a flight attendant that customs might try to have us leave a deposit of half the value of our equipment, which we may or may not get back. Couldn't take that chance! So I tried a little street-smart dealings and took a real chance of being arrested for attempted bribery. I had gotten a stash of cash in those pre-ATM days from my bank the morning of our flight, just before zipping in and out of the newsroom. I went to the station to snatch up some wire copy nearly thirty-years before text-messaging and cell phones became standard operating tools for traveling reporters.

The bribe at customs worked like a charm. I rolled and then deftly palmed five crisp ten-dollar bills into a functionary's hand, and he waved my crew and I and all our equipment through as he slipped our fifty bucks into his pocket. It was legerdemain that would have defied the watchful eye of any security cameras. From my international travels—in Mediterranean countries, in particular—I learned there is a rather common term for the gratuity I had just illegally passed on. It's called *baksheesh*. A competitor from another local station apparently took on righteous indignation about posting a bond for his equipment, and I understand that he was held at the airport for hours after arrival. Ah, the power of the dollar bill—before it was devalued in 2008 to being of lesser worth than even the Canadian dollar.

Pope Paul VI's last will and testament had ordered a simple funeral, but that would be hard to un-orchestrate given the global love and reverence afforded the papacy. Our delegation from St. Louis, with Cardinal Carberry and the other local journalists, was swallowed up in the thousands of the faithful and the paparazzi who flooded Rome to see Paul VI off. I was able to describe the enormity of the event for my Channel 4 viewers back home thanks to wire service accounts I devoured at the CBS bureau office. My newsroom back home also fed more graphic news from St. Louis than I could glean packed like a sardine so close to Sardinia. Italian police estimated that my crew and I were in the

The author reports from St. Peter's Square in Rome, 1978.

middle of twice the mass of people that had attended the obsequies for Pope John XXIII fifteen years earlier.

My crew and I were pleasantly surprised that we were put up in the grand old (1906) Excelsior Hotel (now the Westin Excelsior) on the *Via Veneto*. Its 287 guest rooms and 32 luxury suites were an indicator to me that CBS *pater familias* William S. Paley and his network were not at all leery about sparing any lire on this trip. The Excelsior has snagged a berth on the prestigious Condé Nast Travelers "Gold List," and is a favorite lodge for the world's rich and famous. In fact, there were two world-renowned celebrities living down the hall from my room for the first papal funeral Mass of 1978: Imelda Marcos and Senator Ted Kennedy. I couldn't figure out if the menacing looking bearers of Uzis outside the Marcos suite down the hall, and the Secret Service detachment outside Kennedy's rooms, made me feel more or less secure. What, for example, would have been my fate had I sprinted down the hallway with reckless abandon to retrieve something I had forgotten in my room?

CBS, in the days when money flowed much more freely, provided its senior anchors from each of its five O & Os (owned and operated stations) with a chauffeur behind the wheel of a big, black Mercedes sedan. This convenience was provided for the anchors on both 1978 assignments in Rome. On the first trip, some of my counterparts from New York, Chicago, Philadelphia, and Los Angeles clamored for an English-speaking driver. I was intent on finding a driver who spoke little or no English so I could make my first visit to Rome a Berlitz experience.

On each 1978 trip to Rome, our handsomely uniformed Italian drivers worked the same very long hours as we did. They were expected to be in place outside the hotel at least a half hour before departure time each day—often around seven in the morning. And for the week we were there each time, the chauffeurs were released somewhere around midnight. I worried secretly about how our drivers were eating when working a sixteen- or seventeen-hour day. So, whenever my crew and I grabbed a quick bite at highly irregular times during the day, I always invited our drivers to dine with my entourage and me. Initially, the drivers each time were nervous and reluctant to be elevated from the status of humble liverymen to dining at the same table with the clients they drove. But I thought each time that Bill Paley—the son of Russian immigrants—really wouldn't mind. Or necessarily need to know. And my sainted Grandma Hattie, who was 102 years old that year back in St. Louis, would be pleased to know that the Southern hospitality she learned in Mississippi was still being practiced by her grandson in a foreign land six thousand miles from Honey Island, Mississippi.

My beloved grandmother was able to see my reports on the first assignment to Rome, but sadly she passed away while I was away on the second sweep. Knowing what a rigorous schedule the week of reporting was, my family was considerate enough to wait until I returned home before giving me the sad news of her death.

Just thirty-three days after Pope John Paul I's coronation, he died of a heart attack on September 28, 1978. Rather than give you a day-to-day, minute-by-minute account of both 1978 trips to Rome with Cardinal Carberry, I'll give you some vivid eyewitness accounts that will take you there.

The totally shocking and unexpected death of the "Smiling Pope" caught the Vatican, the City of Rome, devout Catholics worldwide, and journalists all over the world totally off guard. There was a real scramble to recover all of us and take our places again for the high drama and action for which Paul VI's death now seemed like a rehearsal.

During the official cortege of international diplomats for the first papal funeral of 1978, with the U.S. group led by First Lady Rosalyn Carter, I engineered a move that would certainly have gotten me killed in these terror-filled times three decades later. My driver had jockeyed my crew and I onto a side street perpendicular to the funeral motorcade. We could then be among the first cars to swing into line behind the last limo in the cortege of big shots. My crew and I were shocked to note that there was suddenly a gap in the motorcade's line of procession. Not a gaping gap, but a break nonetheless.

"Avanti! Avanti! Go! Go!" I ordered our driver. My heart began pounding vigorously as I shouted and motioned and pointed frantically with my right hand in a motion that could be universally interpreted as "Hit it!" My newly learned Italian had almost caused our slightly confused driver to swallow his cigarette as he turned right and swung the big Mercedes right behind the last black limo. When we had tried to make ourselves look like every other big, black limo in the line, I couldn't believe it, but we made it right up to the Vatican gate! That's where we found out that we had swung in line right behind—hold your breath!—King Juan Carlos of Spain and his Queen Sofia. Thank goodness it took the royal couple a few clicks to fully alight from their limo coach. As the Swiss Guardsmen moved to help the royal couple alight from their limo, I was given a brief time to try to figure out what my uncredentialed crew and I could say that would get us through the well-guarded Vatican Gates. Darn! The only thing we were missing were the little diplomatic flags mounted on either side of the hood. I was not at all surprised when the handsome Swiss Guardsmen deemed us unworthy to proceed any farther. And they quickly, firmly, and almost mechanically turned us around and got us away from the gates and off the premises. But we did get video of our brief participation in the official motorcade and of our quick ejection from the official motorcade!

I was impressed on both assignments to Rome by the dozen or so priests in black cassocks posted outside the massive doors of St. Peter's Basilica. Their duty was tough. I called them the "Proper Attire Police (PAP)." Using very sweeping Italian hand and arm motions, they determined with a bold manual flick which pilgrims, tourists, and sightseers were properly clad to enter the most sacred and largest cathedral in the world. No shorts of any kind for women or men. No bare shoulders for women or men. That takes out halter tops and muscle shirts. Women could buy a little doily

to cover their heads for
a dime or quarter. The
PAP probably preferred
that women wore a black
mantilla, the customary
black scarf to cover hair
and head. I wonder how
many were turned away
each day.

We almost made it! Swiss Guard eject us as we tried to get through the Vatican gate.

On the first day of
the first trip to Rome, I
found some grief-stricken
and awe-stricken St. Lou-
isans in Vatican Square,
which was packed tightly
with pilgrims and tourists
from all over the world. After doing some interviews, I entered
the Basilica and ventured through the lower level of the beyond-
mammoth cathedral to find a men's restroom. My role as a
dromedary for this day was over. On the journey through a place
I had no idea that St. Peter's has a footprint of 161,182.2 square
feet, I ran smack dab into a couple from the St. Louis suburb of
Ladue. They called out my name after I blew by them. They were
as surprised to see me as I was to learn they were homeys. They
told me they just happened to be in Rome at the time of Pope
Paul VI's funeral, and even though they were Jewish, they told
me they could not pass up a once-in-a-lifetime opportunity to see
an historic event of this magnitude unfold. Finding the restroom
and returning to my work in the Square was one of the longest
walking trips I took while in Rome on both 1978 visits combined.

On the night of Pope Paul VI's funeral Mass—August 11,
1978—there was a spectacular, though ironically scheduled, light
show in the heavens. While gazing skyward on the walk back to
our hotel, there in perfect view was a spectacular Perseid meteor
shower. The cloudless skies over Rome that night provided the
perfect darkened screen for the shower. I wondered how many pilgrims in town for the funeral would swear that the two events—the
papal funeral and the heavenly shower—were connected. Celestial
displays have been a major part of Christian and pagan lore for
centuries. The skyorama appeared again for two more nights.

On our trips to Rome we often passed makeshift street memo-
rials made up of candles and piles of flowers on the *Via Caetani.*

The site was set up just three months before we first arrived in Rome to honor the memory of murdered former Prime Minister Aldo Moro. *Caetani* is the street in the center of the city where Moro's bullet-riddled body was found in a parked car on May 9, 1978. The Red Brigades, a militant communist group, had kidnapped Moro on March 16 and demanded that some of their imprisoned members be released in exchange. The Italian government refused to negotiate, but oddly enough, Pope Paul VI whose funeral we were attending, had offered a "large ransom" for Moro's freedom. The Pope even offered to exchange himself for his dear friend, Moro. And the Pontiff, just months before his own death, had officiated at Moro's funeral Mass. It was on this occasion that the Pope shocked mourners at the Mass and surely all over the world by openly blaming God for "not answering our prayers for the safe deliverance of Aldo Moro." Continuing this shocker, the ailing Pope, with a physically and emotionally broken heart, suggested in his funeral homily—just three months before his own fatal heart attack that brought us to Rome—that God had allowed the Devil to enter the picture in Moro's case.

When News Director Fred Burrows awakened me just eight weeks after my return from my first crack at international, transcontinental news coverage from Rome, I seriously accused him of being "in the jar," or losing a grip on his senses.

Fred: "Jules, you're heading for Rome tomorrow at noon."

Jules: "What for?"

Fred: "The Pope just died."

Jules: "Fred, where are you?"

Fred: "Home . . ."

Jules: You been drinkin,' Freddy?"

Fred: "Nope . . .

Jules: "But you just said the Pope just died. The Pope already died—weeks ago . . . ."

Fred: "I know, but the NEW guy just croaked."

Jules: "The NEW guy? The YOUNG guy? The one that looks like Peter Sellers?"

Fred: "That's the one. See you at Lambert at noon tomorrow to meet up with Cardinal Carberry."

When we got to Rome the second time, it didn't take long to see that the vendors had wasted no time in printing up new T-shirts emblazoned with the image of the second dearly departed Pope. The ink on the buttons, postcards, banners, and flags was hardly dry when we got to Rome.

CBS was a bit more penurious on the second trip to cover the sudden death of John Paul I. Far across town from the Old World elegance of the Excelsior Hotel in the heart of Rome, my crew and I got to experience the New World inelegance of a Holiday Inn outside Rome. And you better believe that neither Imelda, Ted, nor even Miss Lillian was staying at the Inn. Miss Lillian was President Carter's mother and the head of the official U.S. delegation for this second papal funeral. You'll remember that First Lady Rosalyn Carter had been chosen by the president to lead the first delegation to Rome just weeks before.

One night on the second trip, my crew and I got lost from contact with then Father, now Monsignor, Joe O'Brien. As director of the St. Louis Archdiocese media relations office, the affable, cherub-faced priest had an obligation to serve all the stations represented from St. Louis, but I always felt Joe preferred hanging around with me and my crew. We were more fun and tried to make the work at least look simple and easy. Joe, too, was ensconced at the Holiday Inn. When we lost him in Vatican Square one night, I imagined he had gone back to the hotel to turn in early. But no; after midnight when we got back to our inn we passed by the bar, and there inside was Joe, dressed in a black suit and Roman collar. What gave sharp contrast to Joe's attire was the fact that he was sitting with a table full of Saudis in their full garb, from *ghutra* to *thob*. The international group was enjoying some wine and some laughs. Joe later confirmed something I had suspected: He didn't speak a word of Arabic; they spoke no English. Ah, the ecumenical universality created by the juice of fermented grapes! And are Muslims supposed to drink alcohol? We know that *vino* is okay for priests, right? Too bad Joe couldn't foresee way back then that gasoline would cost four dollars a gallon or more. Maybe he could have talked his new friends into lowering their prices per barrel.

I would like to dispel once and for all the notion any aspiring TV news journalists may harbor that such assignments as the two I had in 1978 should be coveted as glamorous, glitzy, or glorious. When reporting from Rome with such stringent scheduling demands, a reporter becomes three kinds of animal: a workhorse, a pack mule, and a dromedary. I need not explain in detail how a reporter on assignment must be the latter of the three listed here

A Dutch Roll

My field producer, Jim Thebeau, and I could not have expected any more adventure than we had experienced while covering the funeral of John Paul I. We had been ridden hard and hung up wet during that fast-paced, sleepless, mind-pressing week of giving viewers back home the essence of a papal funeral. I think we succeeded in giving viewers a vivid picture of the mourning, the pageantry, and the funeral rites associated with the death of a Vicar of Rome. But we were in for more thrills after we boarded our TWA Boeing 727 at Leonardo da Vinci Airport for the flight to New York.

Just as we hit our cruising altitude of 33,000 feet over the ocean and off the coast of Ireland, something really weird began to happen. Our aircraft began to uncontrollably, uncomfortably, and slowly roll from side to side. An unorthodox experience for even the most seasoned flyers as we were. When I think of the words *wing tips*, I want to be thinking only about shoes. Not what we were seeing as we looked at the wings tipping to a degree I had never seen before. And we had the distinct feeling that the plane's tail was doing a slow wag.

Just from an audible standpoint in the cabin, Jim and I got the distinct impression that there was a rush on barf bags. Passengers became a prodigious pack of pukers—to put it crudely. "Don't look at the horizon," I yelled to Jim as if I had found a cure. In fact, I shut my eyes tight. And I prepared to meet my Maker up there in the clouds with thoughts of "Nearer My God, To Thee" in the back of my head.

I dug my nails into Jim's arm and began an unsolicited confession: "Jim, I'm sorry if I was mean to you back there. I didn't intend to yell at you some of those times. I just felt under the gun . . . I . . . I hope you can forgive me." ("Hell," I thought. "Might as well try to settle up a few scores if we were, indeed, to be literally over and out soon." Too bad all the commemorative rosaries I had purchased at the Vatican for my devout Catholic friends back home were all packed in my luggage. I would have been a quick study with a rosary—even as a former Lutheran.)

Finally—mercifully—thank Godfully—our pilot came on the air. I had studied "pilotspeak" before, so I was prepared to interpret what he had to say, in layman's terms. The parenthetical, italicized blurbs, as we continued to roll, wag, and upchuck are mine:

"Ladies and gentlemen, this is your captain speaking."

(Who the hell else would be addressing us at a panic-stricken time

like this, Amelia Earhart?)

"We guess you're wondering what's going on up here."

(*No, pal. Through the mounting buckets of barf, we're wondering what the hell is going on BACK HERE!!!!*)

"We have sustained some mechanical difficulties."

(*We're toast!*)

"And we will be returning to the coast."

(*'Cause we've run out of our supply of barf bags.*)

"We'll be going into Heathrow in London,"

(*Heathrow?? That wasn't in our original tour package.*)

"where we have been cleared for immediate landing."

(*EMERGENCY landing!*)

"Bear with us as we turn the aircraft around, and we'll try to make our return to the coast as comfortable for you as we possible can."

(*Too late.*)

And sure enough, we finally were able to make a big, wide left turn in what seemed like almost an hour as the pilot dumped fuel. With the plane still in a nauseating roll from side to side, we finally arrived over Heathrow. Nice to see the white trucks and apparatus below with their lights flashing. They had come out, quite obviously to give us a royal welcome. No imminent danger, I tried to convince myself. Hah! And the landing was an experience to challenge the heart, nerves, and the vestibular fenestra. It wasn't pretty. But it was a happy landing after all. When we zigzagged to a big thud of a landing, the passengers, Jim and I among them, erupted in thunderous cheers, whistles, hoots of joy, and applause.

As we deplaned, my big newshound ears had picked up cockpit chatter among the flight crew about a tail rudder problem. But I learned later that the phenomenon we had experienced actually has a name. It's known to aviators and aeronautical engineers as a *Dutch roll*. (I'll bet if you check out this term on Wikipedia, you'll get sick just looking at the video!) It is caused when an aircraft's airspeed decreases as the altitude increases. The roll/wag is exacerbated by a tail rudder malfunction. The Dutch roll takes its name from either the movement used by Dutch speed skaters or from the original design of Dutch ships with their very rounded bottoms for lower draft. And to think, had a flight attendant offered us a Dutch roll and coffee as we winged our way home from Rome, I might have taken her up on it.

after telling you about my trek through the labyrinths beneath St. Peter's. So far as glamour, it is only found as a reporter peers across a plaza entering a Roman Catholic Church landmark to do some stand-ups. And glitz? You might be able to recognize a speck of glitz through bleary eyes as you whizzed back and forth between numerous "shoot" locations for interviews and color. Or you just might recognize glitz on your frequent trips to the editing station set up by the network. It was there if you noticed it on your buzz across town to the RAI studio (the Italian public broadcasting network, *Radiotelevisione Italiana*) to beam your reports back to your home town. Or is glitz what you feel in your gutz when you try to hit the limited and strictly monitored satellite "windows" purchased by the network for its five stations? And what about glory? My coverage was good each time in 1978, but I didn't win a Pulitzer or a Peabody. The real glory for me is that my mother, my grandma, and my Aunts Willetta and Gertrude could take pride in my reporting live from overseas. That was glory enough for me. That and the fact that I was paid well.

The most demanding part of foreign or extended assignments is the lack of much needed sleep. The reporter must hit the ground running after an arduous travel schedule, and there is generally no time for a rest stop or siesta before you are called on to stand and deliver. You can forget anything even resembling three square meals a day. Remember Pac Man? Whenever you are dispatched to a distant country, drastic changes in diet can be counted on to challenge the gastrointestinal system. You can count on an occasional local culinary treat, but you can count on Lomotil to treat you effectively. And when in Rome . . . you must do as the Romans do, particularly when it comes to dining. Don't expect to find a *good* Italian eatery—with the exceptions of the local versions of McDonald's or KFC—that are ready, willing, or able to serve you a palate-pleasing evening meal before 9:00 or 10 p.m. You can forget finding any semblance of the "Early Bird Special" at a decent Roman restaurant.

After working a ten-, twelve-, or fourteen-hour day and getting back to your hotel around midnight, and trying to get anything you can from an often nonexistent Room Service, get ready to phone in a live report for your station's noon newscast at 5:00 a.m. Rome time. For the "voice-over" reports, it's a good thing my audience back home could not see my attire—or lack thereof—as I tried to wax ecclesiastical clad only in my skivvies. If satellite time is purchasable, a reporter must be prepared to abruptly stop racing around collecting stories and be in place for a live report at 10:00 a.m. Rome time, which would be just in time for the early evening newscast for your local viewers. Then the reporter must gear up to shut down again at 3:00 p.m. in Rome for the 10:00 p.m. newscast back home.

On assignments like the back-to-back papal funerals, my stress levels could be at least theoretically relieved if I tried to assure myself that Rome was not built in a day. But trying to convince a news director and your producers back home of Rome's original construction time is generally less achievable.

Full disclosure presses me to confess that, in the super tight schedule we had on assignment in Rome the first time around, on our last day we played hooky and had our driver take us down to the south beach of Italy where we discovered the ancient Roman suburb of Ostia Antica. Some two thousand years ago, Ostia was a happening, booming seaport town that was the center of commercial trade for the Romans for eight hundred years. The ruins in Ostia are spectacular in their many ways. The remains give us a snapshot or videocam look at what life was like in the town's heyday. I wished that we had had more time to study the incredible floorings and walkways of well-preserved black and white mosaics detailing life at Ostia's peak. I could have done a little feature piece on the town, but I was afraid it would get swept onto the cutting room floor with all the Big Story news from Rome that had to be edited. It was a real treat to end a jam-packed, frantic week of no rest or sleep to be able to experience Ostia. The remnants of ornately laid out public baths, luxury homes, commercial outlet malls, and once-lavish watering holes provided a welcome change of mental scenery. We had a delicious, unhurried lunch at a little family-style diner. Our driver was once again reluctant to sit at the table with us, but he finally joined us. We walked on the beach and dipped our toes in the Mediterranean for a short time, before racing back to our hotel to pack up and head to the airport. There was absolutely no time for a return to Ostia on our second journey to Rome.

CARDINAL JOHN CARBERRY

I know that the word *avuncular* means "like an uncle," but I don't know a good synonym for "grandfatherly," which is how I felt about my relationship with Cardinal John Carberry. He and I developed a closer relationship than he might have had with any other Lutheran. In fact, I had been a lunch guest at the cardinal's home, and he had lunched at my house on a couple of occasions. I loved hearing his stories of growing up in Brooklyn, and if I listened carefully, I could pick up on the Brooklinese burnished with an Irish brogue.

I'm not quite sure I know how he and I became such good friends. I think he found it interesting that I knew so much about his Church, having come from a rebel spin-off sect. He was always slightly taken aback by my fluency in Church Latin. He was very interested in my stories about the development of the Central West End where he lived. And he begged for more stories about the nineteenth-century magnate who built the mansion on Lindell that is now the cardinal/archbishop's official residence.

His Eminence was intrigued that his house—such a respectable place for repose, relaxation, recreation, and the boarding of the high Catholic clergy—had been built by a beer baron. That's right. Barley, malt, and hops were figuratively the material of which the monumental stone residence on Lindell was built. William F. Nolker was the builder's name. When he was not welcomed into the exclusive residential enclaves of the silk-stocking crowd on Westmoreland and Portland Places, Washington Terrace, and Kingsbury Place, he decided to show them. Beer brewers were not accepted in the city's elite echelons in the late nineteenth century. It was far more acceptable to have made one's fortune in dry goods, banking, railroads, or even in dried fruit. To prove his comparable wealth and station, Nolker snatched up a prominent piece of property on Lindell very near the exclusive private places and built his statement of stone, marble, and mortar. And to really stand out, Nolker purchased not one, but two big lots on the southwest corner of Lindell and Taylor. His massive stone declaration of his wealth and the impressive carriage house in the rear and to the south was completed in 1894.

Cardinal Carberry loved those stories! I thought it was particularly interesting that almost nobody knew that when Pope John

Paul II did an overnight at then Archbishop Rigali's mansion in 1999, His Holiness was sleeping in a castle built with beer money. Catholic prelates, including Cardinal Carberry, have lived in the Nolker Mansion since Archbishop John Glennon moved into what became an official residence in 1924.

I think I was drawn to Cardinal Carberry by his soft-spoken gentleness and kindness toward me. While a journalist can pretty much target an adversarial interviewee right off the bat, I never wanted to put this gentle man of God on the grill. Here was a man—a prince of the Church—who seemed totally at peace in his world and in complete enrapture with "The Blessed Virgin, Mary." He was, indeed, a true Marianist, and I was sometimes amused at how any subject broached with him could be brought back around to the Blessed Virgin. You could talk to him about the weather, politics in limited degree, faith, daisies in May, the price of tea in China—anything. And the words "Blessed Virgin" would somehow come into his conversation.

After our handful of lunches enjoyed together, our dessert was for him to unpack his old violin from its weathered case. And then I'd seat myself at his or my piano and the improbable duo would play a few duet ditties. Some Irish folk tunes, and some Gay Nineties pieces, in particular. But the cardinal's all-time favorite song for our listening pleasure only was "Edelweiss." One of our renditions of this song was pulled from the station archives and aired by Channel 4 on the day Carberry died, June 17, 1998.

While I respected and enjoyed his company, I fully realized that the cardinal's flock was not at all unanimously enthralled and enamored with his guidance as shepherd. There were some women religious in the local Church who knew that only the Vatican could initiate change, but they were clamoring and petitioning Cardinal Carberry for more recognition. There were priests who thought their cardinal did not listen raptly to their petitions and protests. There were those in the local Church who wanted a softer stand on abortion. And there were still others who did not think that Carberry was in tune with Vatican II, Pope John XXIII's call to open up the Church and let a little air and light in, without damaging the fundamentals on which the Church of Peter was built.

Oddly enough, in the late 1960s just before I entered the broadcast world, I hung out with a little band of young Catholic rebels who were doing what was considered very radical. They

The author chats with Cardinal Carberry at Villa Stritch outside Rome, 1978.

Several things come to mind here: My friend, Cardinal Carberry, did not sanction these sepulchral Masses, but on any Sunday these days, you can find upwards of one thousand young people singing and praying the same songs and prayers at the College Church—in English. My little group initiated this liturgy forty years ago. And this was really spooky to me: This was the second time in my life I had slipped into a Catholic Church without authorization with monumental results to follow.

Despite the rebellion he faced and resisted, Cardinal Carberry and I maintained a close relation until he passed away in the summer of 1998.

How can I forget my first journey to Rome with him in 1978 to cover the death of Pope Paul VI? Travel-weary on the first night of my first foreign assignment, I overslept in my Excelsior Hotel room next morning until my phone rang. The voice on the other end asked frantically, "Jooool-yus. Where are you? We're at a reception at the house of the U.S. ambassador to Italy, and all the other news people are here. You should get here quickly." It was my friend and shepherd, Cardinal Carberry, with an unsolicited, but greatly appreciated wake-up call.

Then there was the time on that same first visit to Rome when I was interviewing Cardinal Carberry while standing on a balcony at the bucolic and picturesque Villa Stritch. That's where many of the U.S. cardinals stay when in Rome. We stood high above a valley of rolling green hills, with Rome in the distant background. Right in the middle of the interview on this gorgeous, breezy day, the wind lifted the cardinal's little red berretta from his head, and just like in an animated Disney movie, the red beanie wafted gently over the green hills and down into the valley below. I signaled my producer to fetch the independently airborne red cap, and when it was returned in a few minutes, I hit on an inevitable decision. We would have to double-fold some sticky, gray duet tape, press it into His Eminence's skullcap, and then press it back on his head to insure stability. I wondered to myself how much of the thin tuft of white hair would remain in the cap once it was removed. I apologized profusely and reverentially for this jury-rigged solution to us getting the interview done and into town for editing. Cardinal Carberry placed one hand on mine for a moment and said quietly: "Jooolyus. Don't worry. This is one time I don't have much to lose."

ARCHBISHOP JOHN MAY

A warm and friendly relationship with Archbishop May was almost instantaneous. Although some in his flock of more than half a million Catholics perceived this particular shepherd as cool, aloof, and humorless, I found him amiable and possessing a sense of humor that was far too subtle for many to understand.

Just before dawn on January 24, 1980, I found myself hustling to get to the Channel 4 newsroom to lay in wait. We were almost certain that the Vatican would, on this day, announce the name of the prelate who would succeed Cardinal John Carberry as archbishop of St. Louis. We had several false alarms in days past, but a highly placed source in the Church had told us to stand ready to spring into action on this particular morning. We had absolutely no idea where we would be going—north, south, east, west, or central. If the distance was too great to fly in a small leased plane, we were ready to hop aboard a major airliner to get out of Dodge in a hurry.

We were a motley, unlikely team on the morning watch that

day. Fred Burrows, the affable, chain-smoking news director who had risen to the top from his entry-level job in the Channel 4 newsroom as an office boy right out of high school; Father (now Monsignor) Joe O'Brien, the jolly, pudgy, cherub-faced director of the archdiocesan media office; three crewmen; and yours truly.

We paced as we glued our eyes and ears on the wire machines for a while in the newsroom with all the police and fire radios crackling out a cacophony in the background that meant absolutely nothing to our ultimate destination on this day. Wait. Pace. Check the wires. Finally, the tip line phone rang. It was our source. We all packed around Freddie. We were heading to Mobile, Alabama. The Vatican had just designated Bishop John May of the Diocese of Mobile as the new archbishop of St. Louis. Wait a minute. Who was May? We had never heard of him. There was a short list of possible successors to Cardinal Carberry, but this guy was not on anybody's list.

Freddie scribbled down the name of the new Catholic leader and the city to which we would be flying. That was all the information he could give at the time to the assignment editor— name and city. Can you believe we headed to Mobile without even an address? The plan was that the assignment editor would reach Bishop May and let him know we were on the way to wherever it was that he was. It probably occurred to all of us after we were airborne: How did we even know that May was still in Mobile? He could have been in Rome. He could have been lounging and waiting for the Vatican's call on a beach in Cancun. He could have been attending a bishop's conference in Omaha. He could have been enroute to St. Louis. This, my friends, was flying by the seat of the pants, literally! But we were hell-bent, or at least heaven-bent, on getting the scoop in Mobile, even if we had to interview the new archbishop's secretary.

We raced in two station cars to Parks Airport across the Mississippi in Illinois. Our rumpled young pilot, obviously asleep an hour earlier, arrived about ten minutes after we did. Quite frankly, he looked a little too discombobulated for my immediate comfort. You know, in retrospect, I don't think I ever got the pilot's name.

Getting airborne was a real struggle for the overloaded plane. Having flown plenty of times in twin engines before, it seemed to me that the tail end of the craft lagged low on the ascent for far too long to make me comfortable. After all, we were seven fully grown men and a ton of equipment. When we achieved an altitude at which my heart rate and lump in my throat could declare that we were actually "aloft," I felt I should lead the group in a prayer of thanksgiving even though Joe O'Brien was our flight clergyman. I made the sign of the cross, but not in any sort of mockery. I was moved to make this gesture. There we were: A young pilot who looked like he could have used at least four more hours of sleep; the news director sitting in the co-pilot's seat having never piloted a plane in his life; a Catholic priest whose perceived relationship with the Almighty afforded me no extra security on this flight; a young reporter who had always hated flying—especially after a jetliner he was on just two years earlier had experienced "mechanical difficulties" over the Atlantic off the coast of Ireland causing the TWA aircraft to make an emergency landing at Heathrow in London. The three crewmen were packed in the back so inextricably among the equipment that they might as well have been equipment.

Nothing was done for my confidence when Mr. Pilot turned to Mr. News Director and asked audibly over the noise of the Beech craft's twin engines, "Which airport are we going into at Mobile?" Oh . . . my . . . God! Literally. With no blasphemy intended. Pilot Guy didn't know where we were landing in Mobile? Isn't filing a flight plan standard operating procedure? I gave Joe O'Brien, sitting next to me a nudge. He shrugged and produced a nervous smile. I could tell that both Joe and Fred were dying for a cigarette. Maybe two or three smokes. At one time! The pilot told us he would radio Mobile when we got closer and take a landing suggestion. A suggestion? "Waiter, check please."

After a few minutes in the air, I forced myself to look out my window. I don't know at what altitude we were flying, but it was lower than I had ever flown. I asked nervously, "Uh . . . what river is that below?"

"I'm not sure," answered our pilot. Oh, brother. I voted silently in my heart to go back to Parks.

Then more comforting words from the man in whose hands was the safety of seven men and the stability and happiness of seven families: "Sorry guys, I won't be able to turn around and talk to you during our flight. The automatic pilot is out."

"Okay," I thought to myself looking at my white knuckles. (Yes, that's possible!) "Who hired this guy, and how can I arrange to strangle the 'hirer' when we got back home? *If* we got back home."

After what seemed like a flight to Australia, as he had promised, our "pilot" made some contact with Mobile. At least I *think* it was Mobile.

Thank God. We landed safely at some airport or another. I think it was an airport. Fred instructed the pilot to keep the engines running. Was that because we were going to do a hit and run with May? Or was it because Fred was afraid our pilot would not be able to get the engines started up again if they were shut down?

We phoned for two taxis from a little shed, and thank goodness (I'll save *God* for more serious oaths) our two cabbies knew the location of the bishop's office. When we arrived at the Chancery at 400 Government Drive, Fred and I hopped out first and burst into the office where we learned that our assignment editor had, indeed, succeeded in reaching the new archbishop to advise him of our impending arrival, ready or not! Thank God and goodness Archbishop-Designate May was in, and he would see us. A tall, darkly handsome man with mesmerizing eyes greeted us cordially, and we extended our congratulations—Fred as a devout Catholic; me as a Lutheran reasonable facsimile of a Catholic.

In order to allow us to do a drive-by interview and get back in the air and on the air, I suggested that we do the interview outside. That way we would not have to set up lights and such. And I could use a single "stick" mike rather than take the time to get the interviewer and interviewee miked up individually.

Almost inaudibly, the soft-spoken new archbishop of St. Louis offered us the confines of the lush Spanish Plaza, the park just across the street from the Chancery. St. Louis's new shepherd was a man I divined right away who would never run out of a burning building. He would walk out of potential peril, I was quite positive, with a certain ecclesiastical ease. The tripod was already set up by the time we got under the stately oaks of the park and found a bench.

With absolutely no time for the usual awkward warm-up chit-chat, I launched right into the interview that would get us back on the road and in the air.

"Your Excellency (Just the night before I had reconfirmed that that was the proper way to address an archbishop), on behalf of your new flock in St. Louis and Channel 4's viewers and staff, may I be among the first to officially welcome you to St. Louis."

"Thank you, Mr. Hunter," Archbishop May responded in his super-soft voice. His eyes were incredibly soul-piercing.

"Perhaps I will need pardon for this question, sir: You are not Cardinal Carberry's choice for a successor. And Lord knows there will be virtually nobody in the Catholic community in St. Louis who has ever heard of you. How does it feel to be the 'dark horse' archbishop?"

Without missing a beat, without batting an eyelash, without a moment's hesitation, May shot back: "YOU'VE got a nerve referring to someone as a 'dark' horse . . ."

And then, a smile appeared to almost slip through his churchly demeanor.

Fred, Joe, the crew, and I broke into uproarious laughter. The archbishop even allowed a well-controlled laugh. I yelled, "Cut!" When we had exhausted our amusement, we started rolling again. I rephrased the question that was still important. May's measured response to that key question of how he had suddenly appeared at the top of the Pope's list and the dozen or more questions that followed let me know he was a man who had anticipated and prayed over whatever could be thrown at him. I'm sure he would deal with me like he would the most inquisitive or unruly of his new flock of hundreds of thousands back in St. Louis.

In retrospect regarding the "dark horse" comment, few prelates anywhere have worked as energetically as Archbishop May did in St. Louis to improve harmony between the races.

We extended a warm farewell to each other and promised to meet again in St. Louis. Our troupe packed into the two waiting cabs and raced back to whatever airport it was at which we had landed.

The flight back was just as harrowing as the flight into Mobile for my little heart. From the tarmac shack, Fred had called ahead to the newsroom to speculate that we would be back for a live stand-up at Parks Airport for the five o'clock newscast. If we were not able to get any video on the air, I would simply paraphrase in my stand-up what May had just told me. Probably not the "dark horse" bit, though. And then I would remain at the airport to get ready for the six o'clock newscast with video of May that was microwaved to and edited on the other side of the river.

After my report at five, I sat triumphant in the warmth of the plane until . . . until "Curses, foiled again!" My former mentor and now fierce competitor at Channel 5, Chris Condon, had beaten me on the air with an actual sound bite from May himself. The old silver fox, Condon, had gotten to Mobile shortly after our departure, but instead of flying back to St. Louis, Chris had gone straight from Mobile to a sister station in nearby New Orleans. A bite from May was quickly edited and put on the air with Chris doing a report live from his sister station's New Orleans studio.

We was robbed . . .

POSTSCRIPT:

Archbishop May soon earned new respect for his humility and his total immersion in the Catholic and ecumenical community. When the archbishop was offered a limousine to pick him up to bring him to St. Louis, the prince of the church declined. He found a priest friend in Mobile who had a pickup truck. May reportedly threw all his stuff in the truck and drove to St. Louis. When he got to town, he also chose not to live in the "big house," the mansion that had been the official residence for the leader of the Catholic flock in St. Louis for almost seventy years at that time. May chose, instead, to live in the large carriage house out back.

And no chauffeur-driven limo for Archbishop May. He asked for and got a used two-door olive green Chevy. He put a lot of miles on that car as he showed up all over town at parish events. When his predecessor, Cardinal Carberry, became too debilitated to use his 1980 Chevy Impala, May reluctantly inherited that car. It lasted until May was broadsided by a driver who ran a red light near the Chancery. May was not seriously hurt, but the Impala was totaled.

The accident allowed May the opportunity to employ the mode of transportation he preferred more often: His bicycle. He could be seen regularly cycling through Forest Park and all over town every day of the week.

My friend, Archbishop May, resigned his post shortly after being diagnosed with brain cancer. He passed away on March 24, 1994. I covered his funeral Mass with the same respect for him as I developed on one sunny day in Mobile fourteen years earlier.

ARCHBISHOP JUSTIN RIGALI

Thursday, January 27, 1994. Kennedy International Airport in New York. It not only seemed strange that I was starting my workday in NYC, but what I saw ahead of me also seemed too strange to be true. There in a bustling concourse stood St. Louis's newly named archbishop-designate (A-D), Justin Rigali. All alone. No retinue. No attendants. No aides. No acolytes. No anybody. How could the man who would lead more than a half-million Catholics be all alone with no escorts? I circled Rigali cautiously, asking my photographer to fade for a bit. Yes, this guy looked like the photo I was holding. He looked mildly lost; a bit like a child who had given his parents the slip for the first time. There was a certain aura of wonderment about this hub of human hustle. Maybe he was thinking about the fact that spending so much of his life cloistered in the Vatican, he was, for better or worse, heading for a city that in the early nineteenth century had been called the "Rome of the West." Perhaps he was musing about the fact that he was to become the shepherd of the flock that had built, in 1834, the first Catholic cathedral west of the Mississippi.

"Your . . . your Eminence," I semi-stammered.

"Yes?" he turned and responded rather tentatively.

"My name is Julius Hunter. Welcome to St. Louis . . . well, when you get there . . . welcome to St. Louis. I'm here today with my photographer over there to accompany you to St. Louis. And I hope to get a little video and sound with you along the way."

After quickly interpreting what I was saying, Rigali responded with, "Oh, no. I don't plan to do any interviews till I get to St. Louis, thank you." His response was as final as if he had said, "Go. The Mass is over." When he had turned and started to walk away, I said to myself: "The heck you aren't going to be doing an interview before we get to St. Louis. Your Eminence, do I have a surprise for you!"

Then I looked across the airport to see Roche Madden of a competitor station, Channel 2, get the same rebuff. That was good. No scoop there. But you just wait, archbishop. And you just wait Roche (pronounced "Rocky"). I didn't mean to appear too coche (pronounced "cocky"), but I did have a few tricks up my sleeve.

Yes, I did have more than a surprise for the dear A-D. Through a friend of mine at TWA, in a scheme that would never fly today, I found out ahead of time that Rigali's seat was in first class. And I was able to get myself booked to sit in the seat right next to him.

When boarding began, even though I had a first-class ticket I waited for almost all the passengers to board before I casually sauntered to my seat. I feigned surprise at how undeservedly blessed I was to be sitting right next to such a blessed man of God. To be perfectly honest with you, Rigali was less than welcoming. In retrospect, what should I have expected from a man who might have preferred to use his "nearer my God, to Thee time" for prayerful meditation? And now I was invading his precious time and space.

In the minutes before takeoff, I began to think of some questions I could ask. And it was during this time I gloated in knowing that Roche and Channel 2 were back in coach.

I bit my tongue to keep from talking to Rigali right away. Didn't want to scare the poor guy to death. Other than a little nod of recognition, I didn't say even one word to acknowledge his presence until we were airborne. He might have been wondering why I was glued to his left elbow when there were so many empty seats in first class.

When a respectable amount of time had elapsed, I signaled my photographer seated across the aisle with the secret T.O.T.C.B.D.T.O.T.L. signal. Sorry, that's not a pronounceable acronym, but it means "Turn On The Camera But Don't Turn On The Lights." I used that tact quite often in the news biz, especially when in the room with a top newsmaker. The lightless technique once worked perfectly with President Ronald Reagan. In that situation, Mr. Reagan had spilled the beans to me about the upcoming, but unannounced, departure of his chief economic advisor, St. Louisan Murray Weidenbaum. The president and his aides, with the official interview over and the lights turned off, had assumed the two cameras were shut down. We got a real scoop because they weren't.

Very cautiously, I asked A-D Rigali a few innocuous opening, throwaway questions. His answers might have been good for cutaways, or "B" roll. "Is this your first time in St. Louis? How long were you at the Vatican? Did you get to see any television? Where are you from originally?" (Nothing to do with "original" sin.)

When I had talked enough to a man who didn't want to be talked to, I gave my shooter the secret T.C.O.N. wink—Turn Camera Off Now. I had gotten some juicy little comments.

And speaking of juice, the flight attendant asked if we wanted anything to drink. He had a cranberry juice; I whispered into the flight attendant's ear that I would like a screwdriver. But I didn't want the A-D to know that I drank booze, and I certainly wouldn't want to confuse him by my ordering what sounded like a carpenter's tool.

After a short time in the air, and after two screwdrivers, the pilot clicked on—the same pilot that records all the messages from the cockpit you've ever heard—"Ladies and gentlemen, we see some rather choppy weather ahead. For your safety, we think we should put down in Indianapolis for a while until some of this rough stuff passes over us. So, I'll ask you to fasten your seatbelts so the flight attendants can collect anything you might have on your trays. Please put your trays away, and then I'll ask the flight attendants to take their seats for our landing in Indianapolis."

This announcement didn't sound too good to me. But I felt I was as close to one of God's top guys as I could get, and surely the Almighty wouldn't take out the archbishop-designate of St. Louis before he began the work of the Kingdom.

I would not care to make the kind of landing we experienced again, but Rigali seemed to have enough calm to allay the jingle-jangle of my nerves.

So, there we were—in a torrential rainstorm on the tarmac in Indianapolis. A perfect time and studio for an expanded interview.

He was mine, and I had specifically asked the flight attendant not to let Roche up into first class because I told her ("liar, liar, plane's on fire") that he tended to get a little loud and unruly during his interviews. Just another of the dirty tricks typical in competitive broadcast journalism.

I persuaded the A-D that since we would be sitting idly for a while, a little interview would be "painless." He agreed, and I began to ask questions of more substance: How might his leadership differ from that of Archbishop May's? What would he consider to be "Job 1?" How would he address the prominence of "Cafeteria Catholics?" How does the Pro-Life movement in St. Louis compare to cities of similar size?

And then a wrap and a rest. I advised Rigali that if he was not able to see the tape we shot, he could, no doubt, get one of his parishioners to get him a VCR of the interview. "VCR?" the A-D asked. And then I remembered how long he had been cloistered in the Vatican. He had served the Roman Curia in the Vatican for twenty years.

Four hours is a very long time. Anywhere. That's the amount of time we spent in the downpour on the Indianapolis tarmac. But the delay drove home an important tenet of theology. All of us stranded passengers now had a better idea of the notion of "eternity."

When the flight attendant apologized that there was no food on the flight, I turned to the A-D and let out the all-time corniest and perhaps the most offensive remark to a clergyman, especially of Rigali's rank. I'm sorry, but I actually said in response to the announcement that there was no food aboard: "Your Eminence, if we could scurry up a few fish and a few loaves of bread, is there anything you could do to help us?"

What if a tree fell in the forest and nobody was there? What if an outrageous proposition was posited on a rain-stranded jetliner and there was nobody sitting next to you who reacted to it?

One of the most incredible things happened, though, during what soon began to feel like an interminable storm. To save on fuel and to aerate the cabin, the flight attendants left the emergency exit door wide open. Suffering restless leg syndrome even before it was ever diagnosed for TV commercials, I got up and walked toward the open hatch to get some fresh air. While it rained literal sheets, up rolled a baggage handler on a cart to put something on the plane or take something off. I wasn't sure. But when I poked my head through the opening, he said, "Hey, I know you. You're Julius Hunter." I was astonished until the good fellow explained to me that he had once worked at the TWA hub in St. Louis and had watched me on TV for years and years. That ought to be worth something, I thought. I yelled out to him: "My friend, looks like we're going to be stuck here for a while. Would you mind giving me a ride to the terminal for a minute?"

"In this stuff?" he asked incredulously.

"Yeah, you could help me get a report on the air. I'll make it worth your while." I had pulled a fifty-dollar bill from my money clip and displayed it surreptitiously. Money talks.

"Well, can you get in?"

My new friend hydraulically raised the truck's platform, and I managed to get completely soaked jumping onto the cart, but his truck had a little top on it. When I told him I just wanted to make a collect phone call, he offered me the baggage handlers' little office. I rang up the noon show live and was able to give our viewers an explanation of why the A-D and I were likely to arrive very late in St. Louis. So far as I know, my report was the first and only definitive report St. Louis got on the cause of the delay. My friend, the baggage handler—fifty dollars richer— drove me back to our stalled plane through the driving rain.

I was too wet to sit right next to Rigali, and I explained that fact to him to elicit his appreciation. It was not at all difficult to find another seat after the amused flight attendants gave me some towels to help me dry off, and a blanket to stay warm a bit. Thank goodness I had left my jacket behind when I went out into the rain.

Upon arriving in St. Louis, it was time for the final little trick of this gambit in the ongoing news channel wars. Since Rigali and I were in the first two seats, I knew that we would likely be the first to get off the plane to greet those who had waited out the rain delay at Lambert. I had my photographer race out ahead of us and catch the grand walk-off. As we came down the ramp, I pressed so closely behind Rigali that on every television station's news that night—including Channel 4's—I looked to the entire world like I was Rigali's top aide. I can't imagine how pissed off all my competitors in broadcast and print must have been, especially my colleague, Roche Madden. He had gotten some material but certainly couldn't have gotten as much from the junket as I had, given my seat, and my adventure through the rain.

Many months later, Archbishop Rigali was at the station to tape a half-hour program for playback later. Monsignor Joe O'Brien, then head of the archdiocese's media office, brought the archbishop into my little office for a courtesy hello. Rigali looked at my "Wall of Fame" with all the presidents and celebrities I had interviewed—including a beaming photo of Cardinal Carberry. "These are all my friends," I told him.

"What? Am I not your friend?" he asked to my great surprise, posing the kind of question that Jesus often put to the Apostles and disciples.

An autographed color photo of the archbishop himself arrived in my office the very next day.

Some observers called the new friendship into question when I asked Rigali some tough questions on-air just before he departed St. Louis to become Philadelphia's cardinal. Here's how part of that live interview about the sexual abuse scandal went:

Hunter: *Your Eminence, you say that you will kick priests out of the ministry when there are substantiated cases of sexual abuse of a child. What is your definition of "substantiated?" Does the priest have to admit that he is guilty of abusing the child?*

Rigali: *No. Substantiated basically means what is proved. What is proved; what is moral proof. In other words, if there is a victim and a priest, obviously you listen to both. It's not that you discard either one, and you have tremendous sympathy. And this has to be seen in the individual cases.*

Hunter: *What about prosecution when a case goes to court? Is the Church willing to open up and say this is the information— no matter how damaging to the priest—we have about the case in question?*

Rigali: *Well, we are not hiding anything. We don't know anything about this. This is the first thing. We're not talking about any specific case that I've heard about. The Church is not a prosecutor. It never has been in two thousand years. The people that come to the Church, the victims that come to the Church, they come and they're free to go anyplace else they want. And that is very, very clear. If they come to the Church, then they come only to the Church. But these crimes have to stop. They are sins; they are crimes. They have effect in, they have effect in law. And it's not just a question of saying we don't take this seriously, and you can go out and be forgiven.*

Almost two years after that interview, the Catholic Archdiocese of St. Louis agreed to pay more than $2 million to settle eighteen civil cases of child sexual abuse by priests. This is in addition to more than $1.6 million to a local family whose son was abused by a priest. And a *St. Louis Post-Dispatch* article dated July 8, 2008, quotes a lawyer for the St. Louis Catholic Archdiocese as saying it had paid $8.2 million to settle 103 sexual abuse claims.

The St. Louis Sexual Abuse Scandal

St. Louis's problems with priests abusing the youngest in their flock was minimal by the standard set in some other cities. A Boston priest was accused of sexually violating as many as 130 children. But even if there was only one damaged child in St. Louis, that would be one child too many. Pope Benedict XVI can be credited with making the strongest papal statement yet on the Church's egregious crisis:

"It is a great suffering for the church in the United States and for the church in general and for me personally that this could happen. As I read the histories of those victims it is difficult for me to understand how it was possible that priests betrayed in this way. Their mission was to give healing, to give the love of God to the children. We are deeply ashamed and we will do what is possible that this cannot happen in the future."

—Pope Benedict VI

on first air flight to the United States

April 15, 2008

The accounting of my involvement in reporting stories about the Catholic Church and its popes, prelates, priests, and parishioners would not be complete unless I took you inside one of the biggest scandals and firestorms to ever explode in a local community and its major market television station.

I've decided that the impact of the story will not at all be dampened if I assign only job titles and positions to some of the characters in the story rather than use specific names. I do not want you to get hung up on the names; I do not want to open up any sores that have just about healed; and quite frankly, I will be able to see my grandchildren more often if I am not tied up in court and in lawsuits for the rest of my life.

Here's the powerful and absolutely true story in a nutshell:

Although I was sworn by my professional standards to keep my personal opinions to myself, I must confess that I had watched with dismay and alarm as I reported one story after another about child sexual abuse by Catholic priests near home, across the nation, and around the world. There are no firm figures on how many cases there have been in just the last couple of decades.

It is an irrefutable, unabashed fact that TV news operations look for the titillating, the sensational—even the outrageous—to attract viewers in large numbers, especially during the so-called "sweeps" periods. That's when viewership is tabulated and commercial rates are, thereafter, set. One of the topics that kept popping up during these ratings periods was the subject of child sexual abuse by Catholic priests. And it wasn't as if this was fodder that just appeared out of thin air. In St. Louis's neighboring Diocese of Belleville in Illinois, more than a dozen priests and at least one deacon were stripped of their priestly credentials and kicked out of the Church for sexual misconduct. Nationally, the John Jay Report, commissioned by the U.S. Conference of Catholic Bishops in 2002 and released in 2004, estimated that as many as 4 percent of the Catholic clergy had been involved in child sexual abuse between 1950 and 2002. And a forty-year study by psychotherapist and former priest, Richard Sipe, put the number of priest abusers at 6 percent. The Catholic League might reluctantly prefer the 2 percent estimate put out by Penn State University religious studies professor, Phillip Jenkins. The league would have us believe that the number of Catholic clergymen involved in child sexual abuse is no greater than in any other institution—like education—or than in any other religious sect. And, verily I say unto you, we must remember the poster boy of abuse by a Protestant clergyman: that Baptist preacher in South Carolina sentenced to sixty years for molesting twenty-three children. The Episcopal Diocese of Colorado has shelled out as much as $1.2 million to the victim of a priest's sexual misconduct. And lo, Evangelical Lutherans, the Assemblies of God, Christian Scientists, American Baptists, and the United Church of Christ are among the sects taking no-nonsense, zero-tolerance stances against child abuse by clergy. But the Catholic Church still leads the pack in either the number of proven cases of child sex abuse by priests or as being the most open these days about reparation. The $660 million paid out by the Catholic Archdiocese of Los Angeles to five hundred victims bears witness to the gravity of the crisis in the Catholic Church.

With news of the scandal popping up all around us, you might understand how keenly the ears perked up on a bunch of old newshounds when an incredible story dropped right into our laps.

Here is an abbreviated, but true version of this sensational story, the newsroom management and key reporters decided on an effort to give expanded, balanced, and fair coverage to an allegation that, if true, was cause for serious alarm. With the help of the activist group Survivor's Network of those Abused by Priests (SNAP) and a new friend, David Clohessy, national director and spokesperson for SNAP, I was introduced to some remarkable people. They were the alleged victims of priests and they all had, according to their stories, hair-raising, gut-wrenching accounts to tell. I personally interviewed a slew of alleged victims. And since my putting any of their stories on the air meant a challenge to their credibility and mine, this meant that I would have to give each of them the grilling of their lives. I set out to be a disbeliever in their horror stories to force them to put up their best defenses. I would question, challenge, debate, double-check, examine, and cross examine every single word they told me about the abuse they claimed to have suffered at the hands of one of God's anointed. I would base the interrogations on my many years of sorting truth from fantasy; facts from fabrication.

I will declare here that I was impressed, moved, and even devastated by the stories of the overwhelming majority of the quiet complainants. No alleged victims sought publicity. And none of them seemed to have an ax to grind nor crucifix to bash. None of the people I talked to about alleged sexual abuse from a Catholic clergyman sought reparation from the Church.

A few emblematic cases in point: One handsome young man in his late thirties to early forties told me that he had been abused by a priest who had been well-accepted into the young man's family rituals. Sunday dinner. Over to watch TV. Family picnics. Table games. He told me that when he was ten or eleven, the priest got parental permission to take him on camping, fishing, hunting, and hiking trips. The man told me that his parents seemed almost more excited than he was about their son being allowed to travel with a real, live priest, Father X. It was away from home and far from the eyes of the reverent and adoring parents that the priest began foisting himself off on the confused boy, my interview told me quietly. I could discern, in the quiet of this taped interview, that the man had no apparent reason to lie. The alleged abuse began and happened regularly in a big sleeping bag in front of a campfire. Or sometimes, I was told, the sexual abuse by the trusted priest happened in camp lodges. He told me he was even inappropriately touched while he sat in the passenger seat as the priest drove to and from outings. And with every single incident, the boy, who is now a grown man and an externally solid citizen, told me that Father X would caution the boy that if he told his parents about the deviant dalliances, they surely wouldn't believe their son. According to my interviewee, Father X cautioned him that he should not want to hurt his parents. And besides, he said the priest would ask him, "Doesn't it feel good anyway?" The man told me that as a boy he was trapped for years in this sick scenario. He said that he is now scarred with regard to his fear of priests and his inability to get close to women.

Then there was an attractive woman in her late thirties who told me another particularly horrifying story. She told me that as a twelve-year-old girl she suffered severe depression. Her South St. Louis working-class parents recognized this malady but were certainly not going to send their daughter to a "shrink." Not in that close-knit conservative Catholic community. No way. They decided, instead, my soft-spoken interviewee told me, that they would make an appointment for her to see the new twenty-six-year-old parish priest. They did. She did.

Father M, as we'll call him, told the twelve year old that what she needed was "love." He suggested, the very composed woman told me, that the priestly treatment begin with just some simple hugs. She told me, looking me straight in the eye, that the caresses turned to kisses, and the passionate kisses turned to sexual intercourse. She gave me testimony that all this was followed by Father M coming over from the rectory next door to the church school regularly and taking her out of class, with the principal's blessing. He would then take the girl to the rectory office to "counsel" her. Those intimacies, she said, lasted for a few sessions until the priest and the then twelve-year-old girl started going to her nearby house where they would often climb into bed together. Her parents were always away at work. Sex became frequent, she says. Two or three times a week. This went on, the woman told me with tears welling in her eyes, for more than a year. One day, she told me, her mother came home early and unexpectedly from work. Oh, my God! She caught daughter and priest in bed together. She told me there were shrieks and screams from her mother till Father M beat a hasty retreat. Soon, daddy came home. The woman told me that both parents then jumped all over her, and began screaming obscenities at her. They accused her, she told me, of being a slut, and they blamed her for corrupting God's anointed. She told me in my on-camera interview that her mother and father didn't speak

A Personal Experience

I have often pooh-poohed the stories that surface about celebrities who, after twenty or thirty years, have an epiphany that allows them to remember sexual abuse from their childhood. Well, I must confess that I experienced a powerful flashback while writing the story of the priest/abuser for this book.

When I was seven years old, something really weird occurred at the little all-black Lutheran church in which I had been baptized. In 1950, when Holy Sacraments Lutheran Church had its first pastoral vacancy since its founding six years earlier, something very odd happened. After the congregation's first pastor moved on to another calling, from out of nowhere there appeared a minister who introduced himself to the congregation as our new shepherd. There was absolutely no formal introduction that any of the old-timers can remember from any official of the Lutheran Church, Missouri Synod.

The name of this near-apparition was the Reverend Antonio Gianvittorio. All I remember about his physical appearance was that he wore little wire-rim glasses; had a five o'clock shadow at all hours of the day and night; was roundly shaped like the number 8; and wore very colorful vestments including, oddly enough, a red cummerbund and sash like a Catholic bishop would wear. Pastor Gianvittorio sported several colorful stoles to match the liturgical seasons: violet or purple for Advent; white and gold for Christmas, Easter, and Pentecost; green for Epiphany; black for Lent and Holy Week; red for Passion Sunday and Good Friday. Gianvittorio was a peacock of clerical color. And I can't forget that this enigmatic little fellow was topped off by a little black berretta. He wore his black cassock and his little berretta all the time. The cap neatly covered the bald spot on his noggin.

The odd duck who appeared to us in a nightmare initiated enough practices to tip off some of the more astute adult church members that this was, without a doubt, a former Catholic priest in our unwitting midst. Pastor Gianvittorio introduced incense into the Sunday morning worship services; he chanted parts of the liturgy, Gregorian-style; AND he instituted the sacrament of Confession. My mother wouldn't tell even her best friend any of her personal business, so there would be no way she nor most others among her band of new converts would give this strange little Martian any more than a courtesy smile and the time of day!

Here's where the scary child abuse incidents touched my life: Reverend Gianvittorio started an after-school program for us little kiddies. For a very short time, we would race out of Cole Elementary School and head for the church, where we would find group games, table games, cookies, and lemonade or milk. Sometimes, to our kiddy delight, we would find homemade spaghetti. We would also find, as I and others look back, a leering, lecherous predator who kept insisting that there be some child sitting on his lap at all times. My mother, to this day, remembers that I would come home often early in the existence of this after-school program and tell her that I didn't want to go play at church anymore. That was, I told my mother, "'cause that pastor man always wants me to sit on his lap . . . and he touches my legs." (I was still in short pants a lot.) Thankfully, my mother heard and instantly read my level of discomfort, believed my accounts, and pulled my sister and me out of the after-school program. Some mamas and papas may not have been so sensitive and sensible. Thanks, Mom!

And get this clincher to the "Case of the Pernicious Predatory Past Priest/Pastor": Almost two years to the day he had appeared out of thin air, Pastor Gianvittorio vanished. We got no official notice from the Lutheran Church, Missouri Synod that our pastor was leaving. I learned in my teenage years that some of the elders of the church were on to his game of improper contact with kids and his general weirdness, and they had helped him make the decision to get out of Dodge. Quickly.

Long after he abandoned or fled our church, I learned some disturbing information about this strange little man provided me by SNAP and Concordia Historical Institute archivists. Gianvittorio had a checkered life. In 1935, our man was thrown in jail in Indiana for beating his wife of three months. Somehow—with this record— he entered the Catholic clergy as a priest and monk. With his criminal record, how in Heaven's name—literally—did he get into the Catholic priesthood? But the former wife beater abruptly left, or was kicked out of the Catholic clergy, and went freely or fled to Italy. In 1948, he was back in the States and somehow entered Concordia (Lutheran) Seminary in St. Louis. There, he was put on a fast-track, one-year "specialized study" program and was ordained a Lutheran minister in 1949. With his criminal record and his mysterious past, how in Hell did he get into the Lutheran Church? He was soon dispatched (or had a "call") to a Lutheran church in Fort Wayne, Indiana, where he served for a very, very short time as a social worker among mentally disturbed and underprivileged children. Horrors! But hold on. In the same year of his ordination and work with the unfortunate kids in Ft. Wayne, Gianvittorio was installed as the pastor of a Lutheran church in Drake, Missouri. The very next year, 1950, he showed up at our little congregation. He was there for only two years, and then the nomadic gnome was off next to Selma, Alabama. Incredibly, there he taught at what was then the Synod's Alabama Lutheran College. After just three years at the college, he was installed as pastor of a little church in Oak Hill, Alabama. He was "removed from the clergy roster" three years later. No official reason is posted for his removal.

What a shaky ministerial record. We will never know how many, if any, of the other kids my age at my church were not so lucky, literally in the hands of Pastor Antonio Gianvittorio. And I feel sorry for those mentally impaired, underprivileged, and, perhaps, voiceless youngsters in Ft. Wayne. To this unsettling episode in my life I can say in the spirit of the church: "Hallelujah! I was saved!" As a seven year old, I am sure I escaped true evil. Thanks again, Mom.

to her for many, many painful months after that.

The story goes on that on one night in absolute loneliness, hopelessness, and despair the girl went unannounced to the only person she thought would understand her pain and depression. She slipped out of her room to go to the rectory. There, the door was opened by a partially clad priest, and she discovered that the philandering Father M was with another woman. She was distraught and broken, she said. Shortly after the incident, she had to be admitted to a hospital with a nervous breakdown. And here's the capper: She told me that years later she was watching Oprah's show, and who was on as a guest promoting a new book? Father M. And his new wife! The new book spelled out why this lascivious predator had left the priesthood. As a consequence of this trauma to which she had been exposed in her pre-teen years, the woman I spoke with told me she has never been able to develop a trusting relationship with a man. Nor has she been able to experience any sexual fulfillment, she confessed.

Those two stories and several others were to be part of a larger and expanded series of reports we planned to air for at least one week, maybe two. During my investigation, I spoke on camera with two therapists whose specialties are treating sexually disturbed priests. Then I spoke on camera with a priest who runs a retreat where priests are sent for treatment for sex abuse, alcohol, drug abuse, and other ailments.

The consensus of these two respected therapists and the priest is that offenders, whose sexuality has been repressed, starting before they enter high school, tend to want to hook up with juveniles of the age at which they, the priests, had lost touch with sex. They also agreed that the seminary and the priesthood provide safe havens for young men whose homosexuality has already been determined and either repressed or practiced. One of the experts suggested that Catholic seminaries have to do a much better job of identifying potential predators, getting them out of training to be priests, and directing them to counseling to enable them to enter the secular world. Outside the clergy, they should be allowed by law to pursue private, consensual relationships if they chose. I found no expert to suggest that gay priests can be re-oriented—through counseling, through imprisonment, or through prayer.

To cap off my part of the big story for our planned multi-part presentation, I interviewed, one-on-one, a priest who had just gotten out of prison after serving ten years in prison for the sexual abuse of several high school boys. Most shocking to me is that when I asked him at the top of the interview how I should address him, he said that he was still "Father" So-in-So because he had not heard anything from the archdiocese to change his status. The Church later "laicized" and excommunicated the offender.

During my one-on-one interview, the recently freed priest explained to me how he had repeatedly worked his elaborate scheme to snag young boys. He said he would regularly comb the hallways of the high school that adjoined the rectory. He said that he would be on the lookout for any boys with discipline issues, poor schoolwork, or other personal problems. He preferred boys, he told me, from single-parent homes. He'd make casual acquaintance with them, he said; get the principal's permission to work with the kid; and then he would have the troubled youth come over to the rectory. Next, on a highly planned schedule, the ex-con priest told me, he would eventually give the young man some light house chores at the rectory to earn a little pocket money. He'd have the boy take out the trash and garbage, vacuum a few rooms, and dust some books on bookshelves. Next, as the predator's con unfolded, he'd offer the kid one beer, then another. Sometimes wine was on the after-work menu. Then this accomplished vulture would give the now tipsy lad as much as twenty-five dollars. The predator would then dismiss the prey with instructions to be back the following Saturday. This time, the work would be much more strenuous. He would have the boy move heavy furniture that was, unknown to the youngster, in a constant state of flux between floors of the rectory. The maneuvers were all carefully designed to wear out a boyish helper.

At the end of the rectory work session, the fatigued, unsuspecting victim would be offered a beer, wine, hard liquor, or all of the above while listening to soft, soothing, suggestive music. Then the predator priest would grimace in well-rehearsed mock pain and suggest that his back hurt from all the heavy lifting. Close on the heels of the back pain report, he would ask the youngster to put his drink down for a minute to give the priest a backrub—first with his shirt on, and then with it off. Then the cunning clergyman would offer to switch places and give his ward the same backrub deal. As the booze flowed, the back rub would deftly evolve into a frontal rub. Some of the youthful victims would be so wasted, the offender priest told me one-on-one, that with a little hand guidance, the minor could be coaxed into reciprocation. What a disgusting abrogation of the ancient Christian ritual of the laying on of hands to evoke the Holy Spirit.

The tipsy kid would then be presented with a new fifty-dollar bill and cautioned not to tattle to anyone. And that first intimate experience would hook the youngster for many more Saturdays and other encounters to come.

"How in the world did you learn this calculated procedure?" I asked the cunning con.

"It was done to me," he responded to me without skipping a beat.

"By a priest?" I asked, afraid of the answer.

"By my parish priest," this sad excuse for a priest confessed.

"Are you . . . cured . . . rehabbed after your time in prison?" I wanted to know in what was intended to be a leading, but not stupid question.

"No, I'm not," he answered promptly.

The sum and substance of all the preceding interviews and more would yield at least a weeklong series on child sexual abuse by priests in our midst, I thought.

In early spring 1993, two other on-air staffers started working on another key plank in the series. They had gotten in contact with a former St. Louis–area man who was now working as a prostitute in Kansas City. So his story goes, he was kicked out of his house at a young age and ended up in the care of three priests who took him in—and eventually took him. Eventually, he said the priest hosts began to sexually molest him. At this point in his life—we'll henceforth refer to him as MP—he said he wanted to get even with those who had abused him. And he told our reporters that he wanted to blow the whistle on all the sexual misconduct he alleged was going on at the time in the Belleville Catholic Diocese.

I'll move the story along expeditiously. The station management and investigative team approved the use of MP as an "embed" (a dangerous word formation here!). The term *embed* reached the apex of its usage to describe journalists who were allowed to travel in the units of Allied troops in the Iraq War. In late March 1993, the station paid MP's way to St. Louis; put him up in the Adam's Mark Hotel directly across the street from the station; and listened in on MP's initial phone call to a Belleville priest.

When MP rang up the priest, the latter seemed ecstatic to hear MP's voice and subsequent invitation to come from Belleville over the river to downtown St. Louis the following Friday night. *Good Friday* night. The conversation gave a clear indication that these two were no strangers. When MP asked the priest how quickly he could get to the hotel, the priest then emitted the sleaziest response that could ever come out of the mouth of God's anointed: "As soon as I knock off the Stations of the Cross, I could be there in about forty-five minutes!"

A Channel 4 camera was set up that could peer directly across the street into the kitchen window of the Adam's Mark suite the station had ordered for the encounter. Right on time, the priest showed up and gave MP a tender kiss of greeting on the lips. As determined in advance, MP sat down with the priest in clear view at the kitchen table, and in the wired room the two old friends made often adult-rated conversation. Among the indicting comments, the priest asked if the fee was "still $200"; he asked if that meant for the entire night; he asked MP to step closer so he could "feel what he would be getting."

By a predetermined plan, MP coaxed the priest to go down to the bar with him for a few drinks before they got down to the business of pleasure. The priest agreed, and this move allowed members of our investigative team to slip into the room and video the contents of the priest's valise: condoms, porn magazines, and porn videos.

A hidden camera videoed the two chums drinking at the bar for a while. Then the two took the elevator back upstairs to their room. More conversation of a salacious nature was recorded, and then, when the light went out in the suite, our camera and sound were completely shut down. On purpose. We had enough on tape to make a case; we didn't need, nor want any more of the stomach-turning episode.

A small committee made up of the principal photographer, news director, executive producer, the two reporters, a station lawyer, and I sat in the news director's office behind a closed and locked door to view and hear the revealing video. Our videotape started with MP's initial phone call to the priest in Belleville. When all the tape had played before the ad hoc jury, there was dead silence in the room. Someone finally volunteered, "We can't use this. We can't put this stuff on the air." The ensuing silence seconded that motion. I asked, almost rhetorically, if any well-edited bits of it could be incorporated into the pieces I had done. Could the slime with the Belleville priest be given a minor—even "voiceover"—play? Again silence, as my colleagues pondered the disgusting enormity of what we had seen on videotape.

It was a relatively short, nonverbal meeting. A unanimous decision was made rather quickly. The three highly offensive tapes were handed over to the station's lawyer. He was instructed, in no uncertain terms, to lock up the tapes in his office safe, and none of the contents were ever to reach the airwaves. That was not to say that a pirated copy or two might have been made— for posterity and protection.

Word got back to MP that the story got cut. His reaction was swift and scurrilous. Knowing that we had formally killed the project, he got on the phone and called the priest. He told the priest that he, the priest, had been on candid camera on Good Friday night. And here is the lesson one can learn about playing with garbage: MP, knowing full well that the feature would never air, told the priest that he, MP, could keep the piece off the air—for a fee!

Fastforward to an action that just might blow your mind. The station's lawyer got an unsettling phone call at home the following Sunday night. It was the priest's attorney! He threatened to sue the station and all therein for entrapment, extortion, and unnamed other legal transgressions if the segment were ever broadcast.

Then the wheels, the chassis, the hood, the trunk, the windows, the doors, and every other part fell off the bus that was marked "CHANNEL 4."

A friend of MP's phoned a reporter at the *Post-Dispatch* and told him all the sordid details. Well, maybe not ALL the sordid details, but enough to get a buzz going around town that Channel 4 was going to air a blockbuster piece that caught "a St. Louis–area priest in the act of sexual misconduct with a young boy."

And just like in the old parlor game of "telephone," the story that came out near the end of the buzz evolution bore little resemblance to the true story. What wafted around town like the plague was that KMOV-TV, Channel 4, had set up an innocent young priest by entrapping him with the lure of a bad old male prostitute, totally against the youthful priest's intentions and vows.

None of the ensuing fables zeroed in on the flagrant history of obscene behavior the dirty priest had in his secret portfolio. No rumor spewed that this priest was hardly a young man; he was fifty-nine years old at the time of the troubling tryst, and the illicit encounter we taped was presumably not his first. None of the whispers I heard nor protest letters I received accused the veteran priest—ordained a full thirty-three years earlier—of sacrilege, blasphemy, violating his vow of chastity, and of committing totally vulgar desecration of such holy rituals as the Stations of the Cross.

The preponderance of the hostile, nasty, threatening, excoriating, vilifying tons of letters and cards, and every one of the un-Christian, profane, obscene, taunting phone calls received in the newsroom for months thereafter were one-sided. The fury failed to ask key questions like "Who is this priest?" "Does he have a history of sexual perversion?" "Will this priest still be able to use his dirtied hands to baptize my granddaughter? Is he scheduled to officiate at my son's wedding?" No, all the criticism was directed at the station for a report that would never see the light of day after management, on second thought, ordained that the tape was dead on arrival in the news director's office.

Self-righteous and totally misinformed advertisers—particularly some big-time car dealers—banded together and pulled millions of dollars of commercials off Channel 4. Their boycott was fueled solely on hearsay.

My good and longtime friend, Interim Bishop Ed O'Donnell, was serving as administrator of the St. Louis Archdiocese at the time. Ed took the drastic and unprecedented step of sending a pastoral letter to every Catholic Church in St. Louis. In that missive, he announced that the archdiocese's thirty years of cooperative TV programming with Channel 4 was now officially over. He asked the city's half-million Catholics to stop watching Channel 4. Bishop James Keleher of the troubled Diocese of Belleville became an ally in the protest. Bishop O'Donnell promised to file a complaint with the FCC; file a civil lawsuit protesting any payment MP might have received; and express the archdiocese's disgust explicitly to Viacom, the then owners of Channel 4. All this thunder over a report that never aired; that never lived beyond a closed viewing room.

Bishop O'Donnell said further in an open letter to KMOV General Manager Allan Cohen that "I will not watch KMOV-TV programs until [some] resolution is achieved. If others feel the same way, they may wish to do the same. If so, their protest will not be effective unless the management of the station is informed of their actions." In other words, get those cards, calls, and letters flowing, flock and friends. Perhaps the interim bishop's pastoral letter should have included: "And you should know that all your protests are relative to a story Channel 4 chose of its own volition NOT to run."

Way to get that boycotting and letter-writing campaign going, Ed, my friend. It worked. In my twenty-eight years at Channel 4 and thirty-three years in the news business, I have never seen anything approaching the volume of mail or the number of screaming phone calls we got on this story that never aired. Thank goodness e-mail had not been invented yet! I had to wonder a few times to myself what power there would be if these self-righteous Christians applied all this anger and vitriol to all the other significant ailments that plague our society.

The overwhelming protest had some silly aspects to it as well. A good friend of mine was called by a friend of hers to ask my friend to tape segments of *The Young and the Restless* for her because her church no longer allowed her to watch Channel 4. And we learned that the businesses of some of the boycotting advertisers were starting to suffer, especially those car dealerships. The auto hawkers may have had to learn the hard way that not

only does pride go before a fall; so, too, can unfounded righ-
teousness go before a fall. Advertising is a symbiotic proposition.

Some of my more Bible-thumping on-air colleagues began
voicing and writing comments sympathetic to our new adversaries about the report that never aired. I remember suspecting
at the time that a team spirit was much needed at the station.
A devout Catholic sports director refused to show up for a big
Saturday promotional shoot. Other newsroom staffers gave aid
and comfort to our critics. And for some reason, I think "names
may have been taken" by the management of those who were
not exhibiting esprit de corps.

I gave quick response to every signed letter I received threatening my station, my job, my life, my family's life, or those
communications that predicted the end of the world was nigh
for all who worked at Channel 4. I created a form letter that was
personalized to each protester.

In my letter, I asked for calm to prevail; I asked that if the
viewer had ever trusted me over twenty years, that they please
trust me again; they were told that they could not possibly know
all the facts. And my letter intimated that they would not WANT
to know all the ugly facts about this story we had wisely nipped
in the bud. I asked for the dissident's Christian kindness in
exercising forgiveness. Then I asked them to pray with us that
Channel 4 had learned a valuable lesson—even about sins that
were planned but never executed. Audacious, eh? But, incredibly, I got a whole host of responses back to me thanking me for
taking time to address their unhappiness with the station. Some
of our angry viewers promised to come back, maybe even just for
programming like *The Young and the Restless*.

Punishment was still demanded by some angry viewers, and
by some who just heard something or other about the incident
fifth-hand. The contract of the principal reporter on the MP/
priest story was not renewed. The news director at the time
of the conflagration "resigned," acknowledging that his leave-
taking was directly related to the scandal. The city prosecutor
issued a rebuke of the station that I had to read on our three
evening newscasts. And I was forced to issue an official apol-
ogy on three evening newscasts. I had not been so embarrassed
since I was forced years earlier to report three times on the air
that the station's director of standards and practices had been
led away in handcuffs by federal agents. When his office was

raided by law officers, it was found that he was one of the biggest purveyors of child pornography in the Midwest.

While the fires of Hell still burned fiercely under Channel 4's butt, I learned that there was going to be a conference call in the GM's office during and right after my six o'clock newscast. I asked and got permission to come up to Al Cohen's office to at least listen in and chime in any of my thoughts on how Channel 4 could achieve resolution and absolution. Participating in that conference call, from what I could ascertain, was the station GM; the Viacom president, Pat Brady, in New York; the station attorney who had locked the questionable tapes in his safe; and two different crisis management counselors in New York. There might have been even more conferees on the line. One of them might have been in Philadelphia. From the time I picked up the phone, I could tell that the conversation participants were on a road to disaster—or at least to non-productivity. In one plan, they were going to wait for New York Cardinal John Joseph O'Connor to intercede with Bishop O'Donnell on behalf of Channel 4. Brady thought the cardinal was on a trip to Europe, and he knew that O'Connor went to Rome about once a month. When His Eminence returned to New York, Brady was sure he could get this prince of the Church to phone Bishop Ed O'Donnell. That would certainly revive the expression "waiting for a red cap to help us with our baggage!"

I thought this Brady Bill was the craziest idea imaginable on solving our crisis. To let the rancor go on much longer would only cause a nastier, deeper wound, I was sure. We had to move more quickly and decisively than waiting on the sheer possibility of what would have been *almost* Divine intercession. And we didn't know if a call on our behalf would have, at the time, been somewhere near the bottom of the cardinal's "to-do" list. He was having one helluva time with his own problems in Gotham. He was catching bolts of hellfire and damnation from the media and from some other corners of the community for his not-so-subtle involvement in local school politics; he was embroiled in an ongoing battle against what he dubbed "Catholic-bashing"; and the cardinal was catching flack regarding his temporary temporal hookup with Pat Robertson's anti-gay/lesbian Christian Coalition. His Eminence's homophobic stance was being made at the same time he was being accused of playing a shell game in his bailiwick with priests charged with child sexual abuse. In fact, just one week to the day before our crisis phone huddle in Allan Cohen's office, the *New York Times* reported that Cardinal O'Connor was publicly confessing a major *mea culpa*. The shepherd of the fourth largest Catholic diocese in the nation had admitted in a June 2 *Times* article that he may have gone too far in speaking up too often on secular matters. Precisely, he said:

> *Time after time I have to ask myself if the Church would be better off—certainly I would be better off—if when I came here I had just become a silent servant of the people.*

And to make it even more unlikely that Cardinal O'Connor would have jumped into the St. Louis mess with gladsome heart, the then seventy-three-year-old prelate had health problems. He had undergone surgery to relieve an enlarged prostate just a month before Pat Brady came up with the idea that his cardinal would have given a rodent's rump about a problem between a TV station in an archdiocesan galaxy far, far away from the planet Gotham.

Thank God—or Goodness, depending on your personal preference—we did not wait for Cardinal O'Connor to dismiss us and aver that his own cup overflowed at the time. In my opinion, the conference call was ignoring a key Latin phrase: *tempus fugit*. Tempus was fugiting like I had not seen it fugit before in a situation this critical. I excused myself to my seen and unseen phone confreres and hand-signaled to Allan Cohen that I had to make a quick call. I assured him I would be right back.

I took the elevator down a floor and went straight to my little office off the newsroom to consult my trusty PalmPilot. Yes, Virginia, there was an era predating Blackberry and all the other modern berries. I looked up the direct line to Bishop O'Donnell's chancery office and his private home number. I was fortunate to reach him on my first call. We greeted each other, not as adversaries, but as old friends. We then took turns lamenting the current tragic situation, and I accepted the gentle lecture he had to inevitably lay on me. I told him how sorry I was personally and told him that I thought a few troublemakers, out of sheer malice, and a few others, out of sheer ignorance, had helped carve the situation into something much uglier than it was in actuality. But, I told Ed, what we did at Channel 4 was ultimately inexcusable. He, of course, agreed.

"Ed," I asked plaintively. "If we could fly our top guy out—the head of Viacom in New York—and in here tomorrow morning, would you talk with him? I am positive he would be here in a flash. Would you please sit down and just talk to him to try to make peace?"

"Oh, I don't know about that, Julius. I don't think that can happen," O'Donnell opined. "I mean, this thing has really gotten to a bad point . . ."

"Well, but Ed, can't you just talk to our guy? Just talk? He'd drop everything in New York and get here to show you how . . . how penitent, how sorry . . . we are."

Pause.

"There are several people I would have to check with first before I could even give you the possibility of sitting down to talk in any detail," Ed leveled with me.

"Ed?" I interrupted and held out for this dramatic intercession.

"Yes?" Bishop O'Donnell asked with hesitation.

"What would Jesus do in this situation?" I asked.

Pause.

"Well, well, can I call you back . . . call you back in about an hour or so?"

"Ed, you can call me anytime you can. But let's make it with some good news," I said with obvious relief in my voice.

I then gave him several numbers at which I could be reached. I was jubilant. All the king's horses and all the king's men (and women) couldn't have hoped for this much action in this short a time. I had a good feeling in the same area of my gut where all the knots had been before Ed had promised me he would call me back.

I took the elevator back up to the GM's office and waited for an appropriate lull in the conversation to announce proudly that we just might be able to sit down with the bishop in the morning. There were no hoorays on the phone. My colleagues might have thought I was nuts, or the possibilities may have been just too tentative at that point. But, quite frankly, I don't have a great deal of faith in so-called crisis management folks. What did Mayor Daley say back in 1968? "The police are not here to create disorder. They are here to maintain it." That's how I personally view crisis management people.

"Pat," I addressed the head of Viacom whom I had met only a couple of times, "How early could you get here in the morning if I can set up a meeting between you and the bishop?"

Brady indicated that he certainly could get to St. Louis before noon. I told him to be prepared to take an early plane out, and I told him I'd get back with him in a couple of hours with more details on time and place if there would be a meeting. Nothing like giving orders to the Supreme Boss.

I can't remember being quite as nervous as I was after that bold half-promise to my boss of bosses and everybody else on that conference call. No supper for me. My fingernails would have to suffice.

After almost an hour, the phone buzzed at my office desk. It was—HALLELUJAH!—Ed O'Donnell.

"Look, Julius," he said cautiously. "I've talked to my people, and it's a reluctant, cautious 'go' on a meeting tomorrow morning. What time could your guy get in town tomorrow?"

I could hardly hold back my excitement. "I know the home office would jump through hoops to meet with you. Probably would fly in here tonight if that's what you asked. But just to be on the safe side, Ed, let's say noon. Where?"

"My office," he said. "On Clayton Road just west of Brentwood. But I want you to sit in on that meeting with us."

"Well, I don't know about that, but we'll make it noon in your office with Pat Brady. That's the president of Viacom. Pat Brady. Noon," I repeated to make sure Ed would know for sure the name of the man with whom he'd be meeting.

"See you then, Julius, buddy," said Ed. "And thank you."

"Jesus would be proud of you, Ed," I said with more sincerity than I say many things.

I raced back up to announce to the crisis management conference that they could go home or to dinner, and they could stop their running meters. Pat Brady was basically incredulous that he would be flying to St. Louis early the next morning to perhaps heal the separation 'twixt church and station.

Allan and I picked up Brady at the airport around nine the next morning. Allan looked drawn and still appeared to be shattered by the avalanche of hateful reaction he had received over the last couple of months. He appeared to me to have lost a lot of weight. He seemed grayer and was always rubbing his stomach, indicating that there were some gastrointestinal demons churning under his shirt. No matter how close one is with one's boss, one does not assume that one can tell his boss that he looks like crap. But, I'm proud to say, I had Allan's back through the firestorm and had almost earned the right to advise that he hide away in one of his favorite places—the south of France—for three or four months. On the way down to the station, I gave Brady the hurry-up offense/defense. I told Brady what kind of guy Ed O'Donnell was. Affable. Good laugh. Fair. Very bright. Articulate. Twinkling eyes. Former editor of the town's Catholic newspaper. In a tough interim job right now.

When we got back to Allan's office downtown, I sat down with Brady, a good Catholic, and told him that I had jotted down a lot of stuff the night before. Sounds crazy, but I suggested to Pat that he should speak to Ed Catholic-to-Catholic and along the outlines of the liturgy.

"You need to open with a good 'mea culpa,'" I advised. "Right off the bat, say that we're sorry. Truly, truly, really, really sorry. Then go into the 'confession.' We know what we did was wrong. *Mea maxima culpa.*" Then I advised Pat to do an "act of contrition." "Ask what we can do to make up for our sins. He won't order you to do penance of a certain number of Hail Mary's or Our Fathers," I advised. "But, quite frankly, I'd offer the Church some dough. Something to support a rehab program for abusive priests, or one of Ed's favorite Catholic charities. But I don't want to know any of those details," I said holding up one hand to fend off compromise. "That's between you big guys. If my fingernails are pulled out somewhere down the line, I can swear that I don't know about any money changing hands."

"Then," I suggested, "do a good *Agnus Dei* and ask that our sins be taken away so we can have some peace," I suggested, referring to the Catholic liturgy again. "And then you can pray, Pat, that he gives you the kind of absolution and benediction you came down here to get."

Pat listened intently and seemed to take my advice and counsel gladly.

Soon, it was time for us to head out to the bishop's residence on Clayton Road. On the drive out west, I attempted to give Pat even more coaching on the local Church and clue him in on some of the key issues in it and to it. When we greeted Ed, he was in a casual sweater instead of any of his ecclesiastical garb. Good sign. I think that helped set an instant tone of comfort and informality. One can't be stuffy and hard-nosed dressed that casually. After the formal introduction and handshakes all around, I begged off.

"I've decided I should not stay, Ed," I apologized. "I might be out of my league with you heavy hitters in this situation. It might be improper for me to stay even though I know you asked me to," I apologized. "Besides, I can imagine an O'Donnell and a Brady ought to be able to work things out." My friend, the bishop, seemed genuinely disappointed that I was going to get the hell out of there. I handed Pat my card with my home phone number on it and told him I could be back in fifteen minutes after a summons.

The two heavy hitters were together for well over an hour. When I picked Pat up, the two looked like they wanted to stay together longer. And these two new Irish buddies were actually talking about playing a round of golf next time Pat was in St. Louis!

When we got inside the confines of my car, Pat shook my hand and said, "I think we worked this thing out."

Needless to say, I was relieved. And so was Pat. And so was Allan when I phoned him on the way downtown and let him talk to Pat about our good news. And then came this memorable conversation on eastbound Highway 40:

Brady: "Man, Julius. This is really your town, isn't it? How'd you manage to get that meeting set up? And so fast?"

Hunter: "Well, I must say I'm blessed with a lot of good friends in good places in this old town," I acknowledged trying to feign modesty.

Brady: "I don't know how we can ever make this up to you . . ."

Hunter: "Oh, I'll have a few suggestions for you, my friend. I'll think of something," I said as I turned to him and shared a little chuckle with him.

And, yeah, verily in time, I must say that the GM, Brady, and Viacom found a way to show their appreciation for my diplomatic intercession, if you know what I mean.

On the evening of June 10, 1993, on the day that the historic O'Donnell/Brady Conference had taken place, Pat went on TV that night on three newscasts, five, six, and ten. Our PR guys helped craft Pat's apologia. He was carefully and intentionally billed as FRANCIS PATRICK BRADY in the name font under his mug. That was just in case any good Irish Catholics missed the fact that this New Yorker was one of them. Pat confessed in part:

It is clear that we made a number of judgment errors in the course of pursuing this investigation, [but] we identified errors in judgment and decided not to air the story. It is important to note that we did not air the story.

However, the fact that we did not air it does not absolve us from our responsibilities, and we deeply regret, and I apologize for, the errors in judgment. We value your trust and confidence, and we hope to work with you in restoring your trust in our relationship.

In absolute candor, the trust was hard to recover from some of our viewers, advertisers, and from some of our adversaries who had heard the story way down the line. There was an appreciable ratings slump for a while; some advertisers took a while to come back, and those who preferred to hate the sin rather than the true sinner may have abandoned us for good.

But I, for one, was just thrilled that the woman who had to get somebody else to tape *The Young and the Restless* for her could now watch her favorite program straight as it came down the line. And that soap directly precedes our five o'clock newscast.

CATHOLIC TREATMENT CENTER

While the priest who was at the center of the sting operation managed to temporarily use the legal issue of possible entrapment to his advantage, he was moved from his parish work in the Belleville, Illinois, area. His next address was a Catholic treatment center in rural Franklin County, Missouri, where priest sex offenders are counseled.

NONPARTISANSHIP:
MEL CARNAHAN

One of the most difficult decisions I have had to make in my news career was whether or not to accept an invitation from Missouri Governor Mel Carnahan. In November 1996, the governor sent me an invitation/request on his personal stationery asking me to serve as Master of Ceremonies at his second Inaugural Ball. Although it seems obvious that I would accept such a high honor, I had learned that partisan involvement in any form is improper and dangerous for a public figure that has an obligation, like I did, to at least appear nonpartisan.

After I got the invitation, I spent a couple of days pondering and getting counsel on the efficacy of acceptance. I phoned the governor's top aide, Chris Sifford, to ask whether there were too many political considerations to be made regarding a nonpartisan, or bipartisan, TV news anchor serving in such a capacity. Chris wrote back immediately on November 25, 1996, letting me know that:

Date: Nov. 25, 1996

*Missouri's Inaugural Ceremonies are strictly non-partisan.

*The entire Legislature, all statewide officers and all judges are invited and participate. That includes both majority and minority members of the General Assembly and the Missouri Supreme Court, six of which are Republicans.

*State Auditor Margaret Kelly also will be introduced and attending.

*Missouri's Congressional delegation, Republicans and Democrats, are invited to attend.

*All former governors are invited.

*The Inaugural is considered an "official" state function. The event is included in the State's Fiscal Year 1997 Budget.

Channel 4 General Manager Allan Cohen thought the letter from Sifford was sufficient enough to guarantee minimal flack from critics, and so I contacted Chris and formally accepted the invitation to emcee the event.

On December 23, 1996, the 1997 Inaugural Coordinator Tom Vansaghi sent me a letter confirming my participation. Vansaghi then turned me over to a lieutenant colonel in the State Highway Patrol who arranged for me to be picked up in St. Louis and driven to the state capitol in Jefferson City. I like that kind of service!

Before I got to Jefferson City, I had, as was my practice, inquired about the proper pronunciations of the more difficult surnames to be announced at the Inaugural Ball, and I practiced saying them aloud.

It would be important, I knew, to know whether Rep. James Froelker is a *FROHL-ker* or a *FRELL-ker.* Does Rep. Sam Leake pronounce his name like the cousin to the onion, or does he say his name like how you describe an old roof when it rains a lot? Do I dare give the French pronunciation to the surname of Rep. Bill Boucher as in *boo-SHAY?* Or is it some Missouri pronunciation like *Butcher?* And I needed to know if I should pronounce the name of State Senator Walt Mueller at the Inaugural Ball as *Muler, Miller,* or like FBI Robert Mueller pronounces his name: *Muller.* That kind of thing is important to an anchor's or an emcee's credibility.

Fast forward to the awful night of October 16, 2000. On that stormy evening, the sixty-six-year-old governor; his son, Roger ("Randy"); and Chris Sifford, the governor's aide who had written me to assure me of the nonpartisan nature of my inaugural assignment, were killed when their twin-engine Cessna went down in dense fog and a violent thunderstorm. Randy might have experienced the same fate as John F. Kennedy, Jr., when he experienced what flight experts call *spatial disorientation,* which is the inability of the pilot to see the horizon. The Kennedy Piper Saratoga went down in fog and darkness in a flight from New Jersey to Martha's Vineyard. The Carnahan plane crashed in fog and a torrential rain into a densely wooded area near Barnhart, Missouri. That's about thirty-five miles south of St. Louis. Given the bad weather, Carnahan took a big risk that stormy October night to make it to a campaign stop in New Madrid, Missouri, in his hotly contested race against incumbent John Ashcroft for the U.S. Senate.

The whole tragedy was an eerie deja vu experience for those of us in the Channel 4 newsroom who had covered and

The author was given a Missouri Highway Patrol escort at the Carnahan Ceremony in 1996.

reported on the campaign plane crash of Missouri Congressman Jerry Litton on August 3, 1976, in the same kind of deadly weather for flying. The flying that Carnahan and Litton were doing against the odds to get to the next campaign stop was a result of "campaign angst."

We in the newsroom began to be certain that there was something wrong that night when Governor Carnahan didn't show up in New Madrid on time. His was expected at New Madrid for an eight o'clock rally. The plane went down around 7:30. It was, after all, a true "dark and stormy night." Some of those in attendance at a campaign party in the Central West End of the city were rather surprised that the governor was leaving the party dead set on making it to his next stump stop in downstate Missouri. Our fears were heightened when we got several phone calls from campaign workers in New Madrid. Did we know if Carnahan's plane had left St. Louis on time? Did we hear whether or not he and his party had experienced any weather delays? Might the Carnahan party have been forced to make a landing somewhere between St. Louis and New Madrid? What were the weather conditions from our Channel 4 weather team? With each inquiry came an increase in the knots of the stomachs of us old hands who had covered tragedies of this type in large number.

Dare we go on the air with a sensationalistic headline like: "Here is a Channel 4 News Bulletin: A plane occupied by Missouri Governor Mel Carnahan and his party has failed to show up on time at a campaign stop in New Madrid, Missouri, after a fundraiser in the Central West End."

If you had been the person making the decision of coverage that night, would you have allowed your staff to put "two and two together and go on the air by 8:30 with a bulletin that was a bit more conclusive . . . and sensational?" Remember, you are in fierce competition with a couple of other stations. What's more important: speed in order to "break" the story; accuracy at all costs; a combination of at least two sources before announcing the worst?

Channel 4's news team exercised some commendable restraint that night. We reported in our earliest newsbreaks the fact that the governor's plane had taken off from St. Louis but had not showed up in New Madrid yet. I even editorialized in an ad libbed tag at the end of the brief newsbreak ". . . And we're hoping we can bring you the best of all news on this story in our next newsbreak. Stay with News 4." There was not a tinge of sensationalism in the story. No early facts had to be retracted. We confirmed every detail before we ran with it.

By the time we went on the air, we had confirmation from the highway patrol, sheriff's deputies in the area, and eyewitnesses.

Tom Hunter (no relation), who lived near the crash site, told one of our reporters: "I thought 'what a crazy person, in this kind of weather.' Next thing it sounded like it was in a eery steep dive . . . the engine was just screaming." Hunter said he then heard a loud explosion and the sky turned red. "That was it," Hunter said. "It was total silence. I told my wife to call 911."

If you were Channel 4's chief decision maker, would you put the interview with Tom Hunter on the air right away? Especially if you were almost certain it would be the first on the air in St. Louis? Would you have any concerns that the families of the passengers onboard the downed plane had been notified and wouldn't get their first information on the tragedy from television?

Would you get somebody—maybe campaign officials—from New Madrid on the phone to put live on the air to paint the scene in the place to which the governor was flying? Why? Why not?

I pose these questions to you to show you what tough decisions newsrooms must make—often on a minute's notice. It's not as easy as you may have thought, eh?

I was hesitant in my reporting of the story that night, and in subsequent days, to delete some of the gruesome facts news people learn. I avoided reporting: "The wreckage, in small pieces, was scattered over a wide distance, making it difficult to identify some of the body parts." Some of my colleagues at Channel 4 and at the other stations were not so sensitive about reporting the gruesome details. But I was older and steeped in more sensitivity than some of the younger reporters.

The political quandary I found myself in with the Carnahan inaugural invitation reminded me of a much bigger challenge I had to face eleven years earlier. In early January 1986, around lunchtime, I received a very interesting phone call at home. It was about two hours before I went in for a regular day in the Channel 4 newsroom. (Actually, there are NO "regular" days in a TV newsroom.) The call was from former Governor Kit Bond, the Republican from Missouri. He had served his two-term limit, and there was speculation as to what he would be doing with himself. He had handily handed over the keys to the Governor's Mansion to an up-and-comer, John Ashcroft. After the exchange of a few pleasantries, Bond asked me what I was doing for lunch on February 12, 1986. I quickly checked the calendar on my study desk and found that I was free.

"How would you like to have lunch with me?"

"Uh . . . yes," I responded, rather surprised by the invitation. "Any particular agenda? Is there anything I need to prepare for? Anybody else going to be with us?"

"Well, you'll be sitting next to President Reagan at lunch," the former governor informed me.

"I . . . I . . . beg your pardon. Did you say President Reagan?" I stammered.

He assured me that he was serious, and I became one of the first persons to learn that Bond had decided to announce his run for the U.S. Senate to fill the spot vacated by Senator Tom Eagleton. Bond continued that he was going to make a big announcement at a luncheon at Union Station. He wanted me to be the Master of Ceremonies.

I told him I was honored but that I would have to check with my news director and general manager. He said he didn't understand why I had to check, but I assured him I would phone him just as soon as I got to the newsroom and checked with my superiors and advisors.

Then, within a few minutes, I got a phone call from newly elected John Ashcroft. He was calling to urge me to emcee the big announcement event. I gave him the same answer and promised a prompt return call. The future U.S. attorney general also did not seem to understand why I would need to check on such a high honor as introducing the president.

Well, I quickly checked with my closest advisers and my

superiors. After only a few inquiries I could feel the opportunity slipping right through my hands. The consensus was that I should not emcee the event. I should not sit next to President Reagan. I could not introduce President Reagan. I was crushed, since I had conducted a knee-to-knee exclusive interview with the president three years earlier, and I was SURE the most powerful man in the western world would remember me! Hah!

I phoned the former Missouri governor and future U.S. senator back and I called the current Missouri governor back. These were two of the most difficult calls I've ever had to make. I gave them the news they considered to be a bad call on my part. Each was incredulous and each implied—in so many words—that I was nuts to refuse the offer. I thought, at least momentarily, that I might have been a little nuts. Both Bond and Ashcroft chided me for years for making what they considered a bad decision.

So, with a broken heart, come February 12, I accepted the assignment of covering the big announcement as just another reporter. And I've got to admit, it made me more than a little jealous and even internally angry to see that Bob Hardy of KMOX Radio had accepted the invitation I had spurned. There was Hardy sitting in my chair on the dais, right next to the president. Chatting away. Probably talking about some stuff I could have made more interesting to The Gipper. It was an even sharper insult to my pride to see Hardy in that chair for a reason that I've never told anybody about before.

In 1967, when I was working at KSLH, the public school radio station in St. Louis as a writer/producer/announcer, I had made some audition tapes. I had been told by quite a few friends, family, and colleagues at KSLH that I had the voice for radio. (Some of my buddies told me I had a good *face* for radio.) So, filled with a good deal of hope, I phoned the KMOX station switchboard and got the name of the person to whom I should apply. I was told that that kind of material should be sent directly to the news director. I packaged up and sent off those tapes to the mighty KMOX. I wanted to be a radio announcer, I said in my cover letter. I also sent some samples of my immaculate writing. I waited and waited and waited for a phone call at home or at the radio station. I checked the mail a couple times a day at home and at the radio station.

Almost a month after I sent in my carefully produced portfolio, I still had not heard anything from the radio station. So, with a very nervous hand I called and reached the news director directly. I was not put on hold for long. The news director came on with a cheery greeting. He had, indeed, received the material and thought it was good, he said. But then his tone took a drastic turn. This was a man I had never met, but I had heard that voice daily since I was a kid. In fact, KMOX Radio was the only station my mother and grandmother ever listened to morning, noon, and night. They woke up to KMOX, played it all day long, and literally went to sleep quite often with KMOX's late-night programming. When I was a little boy and came home for lunch, I could count on hearing Rex Davis and the news at noon. And I'd hear some part of the popular radio soaps of the day, *Our Gal Sunday* (1937–1959), and *The Romance of Helen Trent* (1933–1960).

After the telegraphed turn in his tone on this fateful day when I gathered up enough nerve to check my status as an announcer candidate, the news director said he had to level with me. He told me, quite frankly and stunningly, that the mighty pioneering KMOX Radio, with its 50,000 watts of power, was— in his own words—"not yet ready to hire a Negro announcer." He assured me that the decision was not his to make. He projected that the station's listeners would not accept a Negro at that time. What about my own family? I wondered.

That news director was Bob Hardy.

POSTSCRIPT:

As fate would have it, just three years after I had gotten the Big Rejection from KMOX Radio, I began working as a reporter for KSD-TV and KSD Radio. And after nearly five years working for the NBC broadcast affiliates in St. Louis, I was hired by KMOX-TV. The CBS-owned-and-operated TV station was just a couple of floors below KMOX Radio in the same building. Having become a recognizable figure and voice on KSD-TV and KSD Radio without any significant racist backlash, it wasn't long before I was asked to substitute not only for veteran Rex Davis, I was asked often to fill in for Bob Hardy when he was on holiday, vacation, or on sick leave. My mother, grandmother, and all the rest of my family knew how deflated I had become when KMOX refused to hire me in 1978. So it's an understatement to say that they experienced indescribable pride and joy in hearing me say on the station they never turned off: "Good morning, I'm Julius Hunter sitting in for Bob Hardy." ——

And Bob Hardy got to sit in for me on February 12, 1986.

HANS VONK

It's a real pity that most concertgoers on two continents did not get to know the real Hans Vonk. I consider myself fortunate for being in the minority.

When Maestro Vonk first came to Powell Symphony Hall in St. Louis in 1992 to wield his baton over the nation's second oldest symphony orchestra, the visit was as an accomplished conductor and music director. The flying Dutchman achieved such instant camaraderie with both orchestra and audience during that guest appearance that he emerged as a favorite to succeed the popular, talented, and animated Leonard Slatkin.

Vonk's credentials were impeccable. He made a name for himself with his very first gig, conductor of the Netherlands National Ballet. Hans always kept his feelings close to his black tie, but the ballet job was not his favorite. Nonetheless, his stint with the ballet changed his life forever. It was there where he met, fell in love with, and married a dynamic standout dancer from the ballet troupe—Jessie Folkerts. With Jessie's support, Hans accepted other prestigious pre-St. Louis appointments. Among them were the posts as music leader of the Residentie Orkest and the Netherlands Philharmonic Orchestra, as well as the distinguished positions of principal conductor of both the Dresden Staatskapelle and the Semper Oper in Dresden. Both of the latter positions presented serious problems for Vonk and helped mold a part of the personality he brought with him to St. Louis.

Unfortunately, at the height of his soaring career, when he conducted at La Scala in Milan, the tall, willowy maestro was stricken with the first wave of the rather mysterious disease that destroys muscles and nerves. It's called Guillain-Barre Syndrome. He then, with Jessie at his side, took a year off the podium for intense physical therapy along with doctor-ordered rest. In 1991, Hans was in enough recovery to accept the position of chief conductor of the WDR Symphony Orchestra in Cologne, Germany. Just three years after he made that first guest appearance in St. Louis and a year after it appeared he was well again, Vonk accepted the top post with the St. Louis Symphony

Maestro Hans Vonk at the piano under the baton of an amateur conductor.

Orchestra. He and Jessie moved to St. Louis in 1996.

In fact, the happy couple moved right down the street from me. Soon, my friend, Jennifer, a native of Holland, and I were introduced to Hans and Jessie, and the friendship was instantly cemented.

The relationship was solidified even more after Jennifer and I attended a Sunday matinee right after the Vonks arrived in St. Louis. There was an oddly dressed young couple that made a noticeable rustle in the very front row left. I remember the woman had very red hair, and the man was dressed in—horrors!—bib overalls. Then, during the intermission, the obnoxious couple somehow commandeered some front row seats abandoned during intermission and positioned themselves directly behind the maestro. They were having such an audibly interruptive repartee that Hans turned a couple of times and stared down at them with an unmistakable glare of what he and I later called "Dutch Disdain." Finally, when the couple's jabbering competed with a pianissimo passage, Hans Vonk, while still conducting, turned around to his left and pleaded— no, ordered—audibly, "Please!" Jen and I were completely embarrassed, as were music lovers throughout the hall.

Next day, after conferring with Jennifer to get some help in identifying a certain Dutch word, I wrote Hans a little personal note that said:

Sorry about the noise at Sunday's concert. I'm afraid that here, as in every hall in which you've conducted, you will find a few klootzakken.

That's a word that Jennifer had taught me. I will task you with finding somebody Dutch to translate it for you. But it is a two-syllable English word. The first syllable is a synonym for *donkey*. Hans loved the note!

I had had a great love of classical music since. As you read earlier, my big brother, Van, would sneak me into the big Catholic church in my old neighborhood. It was in the darkened sanctuary of St. Alphonsus Rock that Van and I directed our untrained, but fascinated, ears to the commanding strains of the magnificent organ. And, thus, I grew an ear for classical music. It was almost natural that I came to perform dozens of times with the St. Louis Symphony Orchestra, as a narrator. I just might hold the record for the number of times I appeared onstage at Powell Hall for children's concerts. I almost know the words to Benjamin Britten's "A Young Person's Guide to the Orchestra" and Sergei Prokofiev's "Peter and the Wolf" by heart. But I must admit towards my last appearances, my heart wasn't in it. I must take the credit or blame for rewriting parts of both pieces—with no one, not even purists, calling my hand. Hans delighted in my telling him that after what seemed like the 9,999th time of narrating each piece, I decided that I could no longer stand to characterize the double basses as "grumpy old grandfathers," especially when at least one female double bassist sat right behind me in the orchestra. So I changed the narrative to "grumpy old grandfathers and grandmothers." What did Britten care about gender when he wrote the piece in 1945? He probably never saw a single female double bassist. Roll over Benny!

And with regard to my revisionist swipe at "Peter and the Wolf," I decided all on my own that a modern day audience—especially if members of PETA were present—would not accept the hunters killing the wolf, as Prokofiev ordained in 1936. During a rehearsal for a road trip with the orchestra, I devised a more humane demise for the wolf! I completely broke the orchestra up when I belted out the final words of the piece: "And the hunters took the wolf to a nice condo in the suburbs." This improvisation emboldened me to use my very own ending at an event with the orchestra in a packed gymnasium in a small rural Missouri town. Hans giggled when I told the story of the wolf in the suburban condo.

Soon after the Vonks arrived in St. Louis, Jennifer, Jessie, and I were meeting Hans in his dressing room while he changed into his civvies after a concert. We would often have a glass of wine while the maestro civvied up. And after I realized that the maestro's wine glasses were "déclassé," I gifted him with some "classy" glasses so that we would not always have to scrounge around for clean vessels backstage. Often, we would go to Hans's favorite restaurant, King Louie's, where the amiable chef and owner, Matt McGuire, would offer our party creative and sumptuous off-menu cuisine. Laughter would abound, and Hans was not at all the stiff, formal, distant, aristocratic Dutchman the audiences and even some members of the orchestra might have perceived him to be.

Once, while we were having coffee at a Starbuck's in Clayton, Jessie asked in her pronounced German-Dutch accent that I explain a frightful sport she had heard about on television: dwarf throwing. Was it really a popular sport? For some perverted fun, I did not tell her that there was no sanctioned or even politically correct sport by that name. Humanist that she is, Jessie was most concerned when she asked, "But what do they throw them *against*? Something soft, I hope." That comment produced a cascade of giggles from our little group. That time and for many other times afterward. We were honestly not making fun of little people so much as we were Jessie's genuine concern about a sport she seemed to fear might someday become the national pastime.

Hans, Jessie, Jennifer, and I would often meet for Saturday lunch. They liked the nearby Bar Italia for a stroll to and from lunch. Food be damned, Hans loved the grappa, a brandy-like beverage made from the grape dregs of wine barrels, at the restaurant owned by our friend from Eritrea. I'm almost positive that a standard offering of grappa at Bar Italia features only one or two flavors. But the host-owner will, upon gaining familiarity with regular patrons, drag out more flavors of his homemade brew than one can shake a swizzle stick at. I think Hans might have liked to pour grappa over his Belgian pancakes.

When we needed a break from dining out, I would often phone my Dutch neighbors and ask them if they had eaten yet. If they hadn't, they would invariably walk the short distance to my house, bringing with them a bottle of something vintage along with healthy appetites. Those impromptu meals would always feature lively political, social, theological, and of course, symphony conversation with whatever dish I had concocted. I was, and am, a master of disguised leftovers when I'm not creating a gourmet offering. During our meals, I sometimes had to remind the three expatriates of Holland that I did not speak fluent Dutch.

One Saturday afternoon, after I had given Hans a T-shirt that bore a caricature of me drawn in conjunction with a little book I had written on family genealogy, I was as surprised as I've ever been. When I opened the front door, there was the internationally respected maestro, Hans Vonk, proudly wearing the stupid T-shirt bearing my contorted image and ready to head to a crowded restaurant. Here was a man—more often than not nattily attired in formal white tie and tails—sporting a T-shirt as proudly as if it were tailored for him.

Soon Hans and I addressed each other exclusively as "Neighbor." I never called him Hans; he never called me Julius. Except for a time or two when he was in my car or in my living room, I would audaciously flip on a homemade CD of some local orchestra or choral group I was conducting. On those occasions, he would invariably use my given name. "Julius! Julius! You're losing them!" he'd shout as if I were about to crash the car into the back of a bus.

Once, Hans and I popped into Vintage Vinyl on Delmar. He was looking for a CD and I was pursuing a piece of sheet music: "Carmina Burana." When I was in Ken Billups' A Capella Choir at Sumner High School, we had sung "Carmina Burana" with the St. Louis Symphony. I had heard it recently on KFUO and wanted to show a non-believing Hans that black high school students could sing the complicated piece written in ecclesiastical Latin, German, French, and no Ebonics! With the orchestra he now conducted! After we had made our respective purchases, the two of us arrived at the cashier about the same time behind a customer being served.

Without warning, and without rehearsal, Hans pointed at me and ad-libbed: "Pardon me, sir. I hate to bother you. But aren't you the black fellow I see on television news?"

Without missing a beat, I improvised: "Yes, yes, I am. And say, aren't you that guy from Denmark or someplace that conducts the big band down there on Grand? Nice to meet you," I said as

I extended my hand for a shake.

The look on the clerk's face, as he looked back and forth between us, was one of classic confusion. "Who's next?" is all he could muster in his befuddlement.

Hans and I did our best Alphonse and Gaston act as we made sweeping hand gestures to offer the other the chance to be checked out first.

Finally, I offered, "Why don't you go first, because you're from another country, right? Sweden?"

"Yes, Sweden," Hans agreed. "And you sir? You are from?"

"Down the street," I said. "Just down the street a bit."

We managed to hold ourselves together until we got into the street, where we exploded into sidesplitting laughter.

Why might the general audience at a Powell Hall concert never have perceived that kind of fun coming out of Hans Vonk? He confided to me that he hated to talk to an audience. "Julius," he would say unapologetically, "talking to an audience is so *un*-Dutch, so *un*-European." He would go on to say that the Dutch hardly share their thoughts and emotions with loved ones and each other, let alone with perfect strangers. I would hear these words again on the last day I saw Hans.

Hans's entire life in music had been spent at the helms of state-sponsored European orchestras. With money flowing in from the European states to support him and his orchestras, he would often tell me that that was the reason he was totally unaccustomed to schmoozing with sponsors and heavy-duty donors. "I don't know how to kiss their asses," he would say. When I was with him at receptions, luncheons, and dinners at the homes of the benevolent angels who kept the orchestra afloat, it was easy to see how uncomfortable he was. On a couple of occasions, he actually begged a host if I could accompany him under the guise of his being unfamiliar with the location of the host house. He would register real disappointment when he had to delay a dinner with our foursome to attend a reception for groups like the auto dealers who provided the orchestra's auto fleet. It is so "un-Dutch," isn't it? I would ask him to confirm. He joked with me about the orchestra having an "official doughnut."

Here's another reason why his interaction with the audience might have been strained: While he was principal conductor of the two orchestras in Dresden in 1985, the communist authorities watched him like hawks. He was under strict orders by those officials, whom he called "meddlers," to have absolutely no contact with orchestra members outside of rehearsals. It became clear to him after a short time in Dresden, he would tell me, that even conversations with members of his adoring audiences were highly discouraged. Hans even suspected that government spies operated as musicians in his orchestras. He referred to the five-year span he and Jessie spent in Dresden under a gag rule as "a very stressful period." He fled the Dresden posts to conduct in Cologne.

Although I have told you that King Louie's was Hans's all-time favorite dining hang-out, I learned that a close second thrill for the Vonks was walking and munching along the food stands at Soulard Market. His third choice favorite was Billy Sherman's Deli. The Vonks' favorite treat at Sherman's was the "mish-mash," a soup with a little bit of this and a little bit of that in it. Not only would they always have a big bowl of steaming hot mish-mash there, they would always take a double order to go.

One Sunday afternoon while we were driving out to the deli on Olive Street, I learned that hell hath no bilingual fury like a Hans Vonk storm! (Maybe the orchestra saw those flare-ups far more often than I did.)

Here is what ignited the fuse: Hans had a dream of putting together a five hundred–voice children's choir performing Beethoven's Ninth Symphony with the orchestra on the riverfront in the shadow of the Arch on the Fourth of July.

True to my philharmonic, but neurotic, way of getting things done yesterday, I began to try right away to find ways and means to patch together five hundred youthful voices. I phoned music directors in public, private, and parochial schools, churches, and youth groups all over the metro area with which I had some association at one time or another. After three or four days of soliciting, I phoned Hans with the happy news that I thought his dream could, yea verily, come true. We would, with more than a little effort, be able to get five hundred young voices for "The Ninth on the Fourth." That was the name I had dreamed up for the event, thanks to my days as a copywriter at the big ad agency in Chicago.

But then, a wet blanket was thrown on the grand plan to hold the massive music project under the Arch on Independence Day. I did not know of the debacle until Hans and Jessie climbed into the back seat of my car to go with Jennifer and me for Sunday lunch at Sherman's Deli.

Hans hardly said hello and didn't even attempt to pass pleasantries with his neighbor.

"Julius," he began through clinched teeth as if trying to contain his rage. "Do you know what THAT woman is trying to do to my concert under the Arch?" He didn't wait for me to hazard a guess. "SHE wants to take my July 4 concert and hold it in January! *Godverdomme!* (No translation needed.) Can you believe that? *Godverdomme! Hardstikke gek!* (THAT woman is crazy!)" he screamed. "She says if we can move the concert to January—to JANUARY—she can get YOUR president to attend. Bush! Bush! Bush on the Riverfront in the winter! The children will have to wrap up in blankets to keep them warm while they sing. The musicians would have to wear coats and hats and shawls and gloves. And the instruments would never perform well outside in cold weather! *Godverdomme!*"

"THAT woman" was a certain society dame who was scheduled to chair the big event.

"Julius. Do you have a phone in this car?"

I handed him the phone as quickly as his anger demanded, and he dialed "Directory Assistance" as quickly as his anger demanded.

"Operator, would you please give me the listing for (name withheld for privacy and propriety's sake)." "Thank you." The Lord's name was once more called upon in Dutch as the operator searched for the name and number of "THAT woman."

What would my enraged neighbor possibly say to the person he had blamed for what he perceived as making his dream concert *finito?* Get ready to learn some music terms if you don't already know them as I replay Hans's call on my car phone. He started out *piano,* the Italian music term for soft. And then he passed into a conversational *andante* (a walking pace with innocuous and fake greetings and small talk), then *poco a poco,* little by little, the flow of his words built. Then Hans's tenor got base. *Forte ma non troppo forte,* louder, but not too loudly. The audience was hearing a steady crescendo in his voice. It was getting louder and more *agitato* (I KNOW you got that one). Soon, the flow was *fortissimo con tempo rubato!* Loud with an irregular beat as the society woman might have tried to get a word in edgewise.

The mostly one-way conversation went on from Kingshighway and Highway 40 all the way to Sherman's, sixteen miles away. As we rolled onto the parking lot off Olive, Hans, ever the meticulous, metronomic *maestro di tempo,* master of time, ended the conversation right on cue with this conversation ender.

"Well, my dear lady, if you insist on having an outdoor concert in the dead of winter—outside—in January, for God's sake, just to get your president there—you will have your concert without me! Thank you and goodbye!" Click. He thrust the phone into my hand. *Finito!* Maestro, take a bow.

Jen, Jessie, and I gave a collective "Whew!" Without conferring, or even daring to exchange looks, I think we had all held our breath for sixteen miles.

As we exited, Hans looked to his audience for a grade on his performance. "Well, how did I do?"

I led a chorus of six hands applauding with shouts of "Bravo! Bravo! Bravo!" I didn't dare shout "Encore!" on that lot. He might have called the woman back again.

It is amazing how Hans's health began to deteriorate after memorable times like this. When he and Jessie arrived in town, while Jessie practiced her kayaking on a private lake, the maestro could be seen vigorously riding his bicycle all over Forest Park and the Central West End. He played tennis at least once a day. For all the time he spent in concert halls all over the world, Hans Vonk was an outdoorsman at heart. He told me one time that when he was a young boy he hated school. And on his way to and from school, when he would pass the neighborhood bicycle repairman, free as a bird working in the great out of doors, he dreamed of one day becoming . . . a bicycle repairman. Can you imagine?

I will never forget how hard he trained to throw a baseball when he was asked to throw out the first pitch at a Cardinals game. Leonard Slatkin was a rabid Redbird fan; Hans was not. No matter how hard he tried, baseball would forever be a UFO to him—an Unfamiliar Foreign Object. Too bad he couldn't kick a soccer ball at a goalie standing behind home plate.

Jennifer and I often sat with Jessie at Powell Hall as concert-going St. Louis watched Maestro Vonk shuffle onto the stage and painfully mount the podium as his body began to betray him. Jessie sobbed quietly. Often. Then she stopped going to some of his performances. Hans asked me over and over in private if I thought the orchestra would mind if he discontinued use of the baton. "I feel I can get more expression out of them these days if I just use my hands," he offered. Truth was, he was unable to hold on to a baton anymore because of rapidly deteriorating muscle and nerve loss.

Soon, the once vibrant and dashing Dutchman was conducting on the Powell Hall stage, in front of God and everybody, while sitting on a ratty old brown stool. Some concertgoers showed sympathy. Some displayed empathy. Others seemed less sympathetic and empathetic. These patrons clucked in sub rosa conversations about how the orchestra should get rid of the crippled conductor who had once impressed them.

In an attempt to lift his spirits and make his stool-sitting look more formal, I phoned a furniture maker I know and ordered up a custom-made stool for my dear friend and neighbor. I told the furniture maker that the stool had to look as formal, as shiny, and as black as the patina of the grand pianos that graced the Powell stage when a soloist performed center stage.

I phoned Hans and asked him for his height, and then I said I was going to send someone over to get an impression of his "butt cheeks," so slight indentations could be made in the seat on the stool. He thought that was wildly hilarious and laughed just as loudly as he had on the street outside Vintage Vinyl that Saturday afternoon of our comic improvisation. Through his labored laughter, I could hear that my neighbor was deathly ill.

Once the custom-made stool was ready, I had a little bronze plate inscribed and placed on the underside of the stool so that my message would remain just between us neighbors. It read simply: "To Hans . . . from your neighbor." It did me proud to see Hans sitting on a classic piece of furniture at the few concerts he was able to conduct thereafter.

It broke his heart when the orchestra management unceremoniously informed him that he would not be allowed to lead the orchestra at a much-anticipated Carnegie Hall concert appearance. He knew he was too sick to lead. But it would be, I'm sure, very "un-Dutch" to admit that he was slipping fast. A physically broken man now had a broken heart. Thank goodness his pride, at least on the surface, remained intact. He realized his career was over. If he had any hope for the return of a vigorous career, that hope was dramatically dashed, I'm sure, when he became stricken on the podium on a tragic night in February 2002. Neuromuscular lightning struck during a performance of Barber's "Medea' Meditation and Dance." The victim of a severe physical breakdown, the once-jaunty master of the baton could no longer turn the pages of the score that Samuel Barber had written. He feebly motioned for help and had to be helped down from a suddenly challenging height—from the podium all the way down to the floor. Hopeless . . . helpless . . . stranded . . . disabled, the perennially proud maestro shuffled painfully off stage. For a few minutes, the hall was appropriately, respectfully silent and motionless. The orchestra and audience were eyewitnesses to the end of a triumphal seven-year reign in St. Louis. The illustrious career of a master of music, whose meteoric career had taken him to heights infinitely more lofty than that held by most bicycle repairmen, was over. Although he struggled and languished at the podium for one more concert a month after his neuromuscular system shut down in front of the world—and Jessie—a dynamic run came to an all-too-early conclusion. Like a candle in the wind.

Jessie phoned shortly after that heartbreak to tell me that Hans had decided to formally resign his position at Powell Hall. And he had decided to take a pass on accepting a consultant position with the orchestra. She wanted to know if I would help him physically write his farewell message to his beloved orchestra. Of course I would. It would be a difficult task for me, but it was the least I could do for my "Neighbor."

Hans was intent on walking the half block to my house on that dark day in 2002. The sun was shining, but it was still a dark day on our street. I paced nervously when I learned that he was en route. Should I have walked down to walk back with him? No. He would have been too proud to allow that.

It took him forever to walk the half-block to my house. I sat on the piano bench in my living room and watched through the window as he grabbed the wrought-iron railing and struggled to mount the three concrete steps from the sidewalk to the walkway. Then, he labored across the length of my walkway toward my front door. There were four wooden steps for him to conquer to get onto the front porch. I couldn't resist the urge to help him with those four steps. To hell momentarily with his pride. I helped. Once inside my house, he asked if he could sit in the living room for a while before trying to ascend to my second-floor study. He gasped from fatigue. He declined my offer of a drink of water.

I excused myself on the pretext that I had to clear some things on my computer before we began to write his final words to his orchestra. There was really nothing pressing on my computer screen, but I wanted to allow Hans the privacy to collect his breath and his dignity without the presence of a witness. I sat for a few minutes at my desk and found tears in my eyes.

After at least five minutes, I bounded down the stairs and asked: "Ready, Neighbor?" He agreed to make the trek. "We need not be in any hurry," I assured him as I tried to make him know that I was willing to help him for as long as it took.

When we finally made it to my study, my good friend collapsed in a lump on a black leather chaise. My debilitated neighbor finally caught enough breath to begin our project. I suggested that the private farewell statement to his orchestra be brief and to the point. He nodded in agreement.

"Okay," I said in an attempt to lighten the tone of the occasion. "How about this as a start:"

"This is a very difficult decision . . ."

My Neighbor agreed this beginning was appropriate, but then it became a bit more difficult coming to a meeting of the minds on the ensuing sentences. I was at a distinct disadvantage because I knew only as much as Hans had wanted me to know about his relationship with his musicians. I know that several of them regularly joined him after night concerts at King Louie's. I had also divined that there were a few others in his orchestral flock who would love to see the shepherd head out to pasture. At one point I suggested to continue the speech:

"I would like to say from the bottom of my heart . . ."

"No, no, no," Hans interjected as he labored to raise an index finger. Forcing out the words slowly, he struggled, "No, Julius. No! We Dutch people . . . never talk about . . . anything regarding . . . our hearts. That . . . is . . . very . . ."

We both said in unison: "Un-Dutch."

"Now you are getting it, Julius. Now you are getting it," Hans assured me.

We finished the statement with much labor and difficulty. I typed the message in eighteen-point type. It was short and to the point. I read it back to him, and he nodded his approval.

After he delivered the message to the orchestra, I phoned him to see how it had gone. Jessie told me he was resting. We would talk later. And later Hans told me he thought his little message had gone well with the musicians he would be leaving soon, but he said he was not able to tell who was crying real tears and who was crying tears of joy that he would soon be gone. After all, Hans had taken a very strong stance against a senior orchestra member he considered incompetent going to the same Carnegie Hall concert that Hans was not allowed to conduct. The old-timer Hans would have left behind had mustered some support among his fellow musicians. Ironically, the orchestra member Hans did not want to make the trip ended up performing in New York. Hans did not.

Jessie, who by this point was having to hand-feed Hans, had agreed with him that he would go back to his native Amsterdam—to die. We spoke frequently until I was unable to discern what he was saying. And I began to realize that his pitiful condition would not allow him to hold the telephone. We were both noticeably shaken by the fact that we could no longer carry on the giggle sessions we had once enjoyed.

On March 10, 2004, I received a package in the mail from Amsterdam. I opened it anxiously. It was from Hans and Jessie. It was a fifty-six-page score of Mozart's "Sinfonie Es-Dur" on which Hans had, prior to the orchestral performance of the piece, made many handwritten directorial notes and scribbles in red.

That Mozart score shall always be one of my most treasured possessions.

It was sent shortly before Hans's drawn out death from ALS. The personal dedication on the inside cover of the Sinfonie score—almost surely by Jessie's hand—are these words:

For Julius. To our favourite Neighbor.
Love, Hans and Jessie.

One of Hans's greatest fears—even more than hospitals, physicians, nurses, needles, catheters, and medical machines that go beep in the night—was the dread that his body would be abandoned shortly after his death. He feared, almost more than death itself, that his body would be placed on one of those cold morgue slabs in a drawer. To comply with that fear expressed by her beloved husband and partner, Jessie kept Hans's remains in his bedroom in their Amsterdam house on the park for nearly a week. Even with his death, the two remained together until a proper memorial could be held. She told me that she would go in every day after his

"Neighbors," sculpted by Jessie Vonk.

passing and have a few words with what remained of her husband of thirty years. She said she was coping with the death better than she had anticipated. And she shared with me that she had started talking to God again after Hans's death. She touched my soul when she told me that many of her prayers to the Almighty began with: "Hi, Honey . . ." Strong woman.

Jessie, quite a gifted and talented sculptress now living in a house she built in Tasmania, gifted me with two large interlocking pieces of black angular rock that fit snugly together on a lighter colored platform. The unique sculpture she created maintains a prominent place in my backyard and takes on seasonal nuances. On one of her last visits to St. Louis, she seemed happy that the sculpture had taken on its autumn look. A few golden maple leaves naturally adorned it. In the next season, its black stone would be laced with white snow. The Widow Vonk made a slight and tender adjustment to the positioning of the two rough-hewn, almost intertwined pieces of the sculpture. She titled the piece simply: "Neighbors."

BERRY B. GOODE

It's hard to believe how many times and on how many occasions I have crossed paths with Charles Edward Anderson Berry, a.k.a. Chuck Berry.

Chuck has been one of my idols since I first danced and sang along with his earliest hits. At an early age, I came to realize with sheer amazement that I had grown up breathing the same air that Berry had breathed in the 'hood: The Ville. That little north St. Louis neighborhood produced many big newsmakers from its humble homes, churches, and sidewalks. including Metropolitan Opera stars Grace Bumbry and Robert McFerrin, and his "Don't Worry, Be Happy" son, Bobby McFerrin. And when I was singing "Up, Up and Away" with the *Fifth Dimension* in the late 1960s, I was proud to know that the three male singers, Billy Davis, Jr., Ron Townson, and LaMonte McLemore all grew up in St. Louis. (I figured out early in my career that if I had to adopt a name that would suggest a handsome, dashing stud, I might like to have the name *LaMonte McLemore!*)

I was one of the thousands of 1960s teens who thought rock and roll superstar Chuck Berry was the bomb. In fact, during the third of a century I spent delivering the news in St. Louis, I always balked and flat out refused to refer on-air to Elvis Presley as "The King," as my youthful writing staff often wanted me to do. I don't think even Elvis would have allowed himself to be referred to that way. After all, Beatle legend, John Lennon, had said of Chuck, "If you tried to give rock and roll another name, you might call it 'Chuck Berry.'" Those who would coronate Elvis "king," should hear what Rolling Stone Keith Richards, who had a brief but notorious tiff with Chuck, confessed about the rock genius from north St. Louis: "It's hard for me to induct Chuck Berry [into the Rock and Roll Hall of Fame] because I lifted every lick he ever played."

Listen to the music of the Beach Boys, The Who, and even tunes crooned by Bob Dylan, and you will hear some Chuck Berry seeping through.

We kids in the Ville began to realize a star had been born nearby after we began bopping at sock hops and house parties to the beat of "School Days," "Sweet Little Sixteen," "Rock and Roll Music," and the classic "Johnny B. Goode." My favorite was "Maybelline," which he recorded in 1955 when I was in the sixth grade. That ditty was originally called "Ida May," by the way. But that name is just not as funky as "Maybelline!"

"Maybelline" was what got Chuck Berry an exclusive, long-term contract with Chess Records of Chicago in 1955. It was during this period that Berry began to experiment with the limits and boundaries of the blues. In the old Ville neighborhood, mind you, near where I was born and hung out as a kid. What came out of Chuck's mouth and guitar was a kind of baffling "hillbilly" sound. The importance of that sound was that it got Berry audiences that were sometimes racially mixed. What a mind-bending challenge that had to be: how to satisfy his black audience, which was, at first, weirded out by the style, and how to hold onto the white audience, which expected "country." But Chuck methodically worked it out and cranked it out, holding onto both audiences and fusing them into one record-buying, Berry-hungry mélange. What do you get in the kitchen when you mix the theretofore immiscible ingredients of blues, country, mischief, duck, and a dash of salsa? Out of the oven emerges the uniquely delicious dish of *Spicy Chuck with Berry Sauce*.

I'm proud to boast that Chuck Berry and I got bitten by the same performance bug on the same stage of the same high school auditorium, even though we were about a dozen years apart. But the neighborhood, high school, and Libra connection (his birthday is October 18; mine October 13) were enough for me to feel a kinship with Berry. At his first high school outing, Chuck and his guitar belted out Jay McShann's "Confessin' the Blues" at a Sumner High School talent show. The student crowd might have been a little tentative about the style of the stuff they heard, but Berry's music had a tantalizingly danceable beat. They loved it! Eventually. I, on the other hand . . . in another decade . . . emceed and did stand-up comedy routines at four or five after-school talent shows at Sumner during my sophomore, junior, and senior years.

In fact, my senior class was bold enough to invite Chuck to come to the last talent show I emceed at Sumner. As senior class president, I was given, or took by fiat, the awesome assignment of making contact with Mr. Berry to issue the invitation. Through somebody who knew somebody who knew somebody else, I got his actual phone number, and after several attempts, I reached him. I must say that my hero of rock and roll was incredibly dry, laconic, and quiet on the telephone. I gave him the fawning speech I had rehearsed in my room at home and for days walking to and from classes.

I provided Mr. Berry with the time, date, and place for the talent show. Surprisingly, given his lack of apparent friendliness, he agreed to come to our little amateur production. My stomach was in knots from the day he gave me the quietly stated commitment until the day he actually showed up—right on time—at the Sumner High auditorium door. How did I spell relief for my knotted-up stomach? "B-e-r-r-y-S-h-o-w-s." But no guitar and no entourage. No back up band. No nothing. Mr. Berry was impeccably dressed from head to toe. I noticed that he appeared to be wearing rather heavy makeup. Maybe—just maybe, I thought—the cosmetics were laid on in anticipation of doing a little bit on the stage.

As a bunch of us producers of the show gathered around him in disbelief after he was spotted and the word put out, Mr. Berry informed the student greeting party and me pointedly that he would not perform anything. We gave each other quick glances of surprise, then disappointment. But, hey, we had The Man himself.

Berry was shown to a seat in the middle of the auditorium where he sat alone, displaying little more than faint smiles at some of the student performers' acts and lack of real talent. Not one *American Idol* candidate in the bunch. My stand-up jokes went pretty well, although I was afraid to look directly at our special guest in the audience for fear he would not share my brand of humor. And, believe me, my humor way back then was as corny as it is today.

At the end of the comedy routine, I thought I would challenge Mr. Berry's initial announcement that he would not perform under any circumstance. I went ahead and introduced him as our special guest, the man who had supplied the hottest dance music for our last sock hop—Mr. Chuck Berry. "Mr. Berry, come on up on the stage and say hello." The students cheered and clapped and hooted and gave the Sumner Bulldog Bark. But Mr. Berry stood up, waved with one sweep, and sat back down almost immediately. When the coaxing noise went on a little too long for him, the stone-faced super entertainer put an index finger in the air and waved it as if to say, "Shut it down. That's enough. I ain't comin' on stage, kids."

Right after the unsuccessful attempt to get him on stage, the lone star got up and slipped out during the next horrible talent act. We never saw him again, and I was never able to reach him again to thank him for coming back to his alma mater. Don't know whether he was pissed off or not.

That all happened in 1960. Little did I know at the time that this was not my last brush with the great Chuck Berry.

My next encounter with Chuck came eight years later. At the time I saw him next, I was living in Chicago and working as a copywriter at Foote, Cone & Belding,

The author poses in a mock whiskey ad while working as a copywriter at Foote, Cone & Belding, Chicago, 1968.

then the third largest ad agency in the world. I helped write copy for Dial Soap and Deodorant, PF Flyer tennis shoes, Kraft Italian Macaroni Dinners. I also worked with a team that included the very talented cartoonist, Don Peglar. If the name doesn't ring a bell, his work should. He's the artist who created all those clever ways to kill bugs in those hilarious Raid House & Garden Spray TV commercials—the ones where the cartoon insects scream, "*Raaaaaaaiddd!*" And then the back stem of the letter "d" moves up and becomes a canon that blows the bugs away in a colorful poof of cartoon smoke.

Although I had a Chicago address, I often came home to St. Louis for long weekends. I'd fly into St. Louis on a Friday evening and return to the Windy City on the first Delta Airlines flight early Monday morning, to get to my Michigan Avenue FCB office in ample time to start an ad agency workday. Nobody in the creative department at FCB punched a clock, so it didn't matter much if my flight got stacked up in a massive air traffic jam over Michigan waiting to land at O'Hare. If I had to slip into my office as late as 11 a.m., that allowed enough time to leave for a restaurant with my creative colleagues to beat the lunch rush before noon.

On one Monday morning at Lambert, whom would I espy waiting at the departure gate for Chicago but my old friend and fellow Sumner alum, Charles Edward Anderson Berry. He didn't recognize me, of course, but I certainly remember at least the back of him from the time he had scurried out that auditorium door to get away from bad high school talent.

Almost eight years older now—both of us—I pondered if I should approach the real King of Rock and Roll. Oh, well, why not?

Charles was once again dressed to the nines. Suit and tie. Crisp white shirt. Spit-polished black shoes. He was even wearing a Homburg-type chapeaux tilted a bit rakishly to the side. Once again, it looked like he wore makeup. This early hour in the morning? Maybe he even slept dressed this dapperly, in makeup even, I thought to myself.

"Mr. Berry. You won't remember me, but I met you back in 1960," I prattled. "At Sumner High School at a talent show. I was the one who called you to ask you to come. My name is Julius Hunter, and I'm now working at Foote, Cone & Belding up in Chicago as a copywriter—the first black writer they hired," I spilled out proudly, in what was probably way too much information.

"Yes," Chuck barely mumbled. It was more of a statement confirming all that I had spewed out than an acknowledgment that he had any recollection at all of a silly talent show eight years earlier.

"Heading up to Chicago?" I asked.

"Yes." That was all the Great One would volunteer.

"Well, I hope we get in on time," I offered, as if he or I gave a real damn.

"Yes," Mr. Berry whispered.

Okay, I thought to myself. This guy either a) is not a morning person, b) thinks I'm an intrusive groupie, c) has a hearing loss from playing in front of all those bands, or d) thinks I am an intrusive groupie. (I realize that "b" and "d" are the same possible reaction.)

I decided to leave him alone and make an ungraceful, awkward slither-away from the Chuck Berry wax mannequin.

Upon boarding, I was shocked that Mr. Berry was not flying first class. He was back in coach sitting across the aisle and not far from me. The seat next to him was vacant. Would I? Should I? Nope. I'm no dope. Besides, I had had that morning's minimal daily requirement of "Yeses" from Berry.

Chuck sat almost perfectly still, staring out at the clouds and perhaps creating another big hit in his mind at thirty thousand feet.

After a landing at O'Hare that was almost on time, we stood silently waiting for our bags at the whirring and dizzying baggage carousel. That's where the Silent One startled the hell out of me with, "Need a ride into town?"

I alertly and smartly replied, "Huh? I beg your pardon. Didn't hear you."

"Do you need a ride? A ride into town? I'm getting a rental car."

"Uh, yes. Yes. YES, thank you."

Chuck Berry, one of the hottest rock-and-roll artists on the planet, the duck-walking, guitar-twanging, Maybellinin' superstar, my homey was going to give me a ride from O'Hare to the Equitable Building across from the Wrigley Building on Michigan Avenue in Chicago. And I didn't have a camera!

His bag arrived first. Not a big one. His may have been a one-day or overnight stay. He waited. Still no conversation volunteered. Then my bag arrived. Whew! The silence of the wait for my bag was nerve-wracking.

"Okay, I think we go this way," he said as he looked up at the signage. Chuck was not an ambler. Not a moseyer. He proved his athleticism during his performances, especially with his famous "Duck Walk," the equivalent of Michael Jackson's "Moonwalk" for us sixties boppers and hoppers. Quite frankly, I had trouble keeping up with Chuck as we zoomed through O'Hare as if we were on a mission.

What kind of car would he be renting? I mused. Guess it wouldn't be some big, pink Cadillac with guitar tail fins and musical notes painted all over its body. Avis didn't stock a special car for the Great Chuck Berry. I learned later that Chuck had to fly back and forth between his homes in St. Louis and Chicago regularly when he worked with Chess Records from 1955 to 1966. He had left Chess after 1966 but had returned just two years after what was to be my very memorable ride into town with him.

No big Caddie. Just a mid-size Ford Something-or-other. Nice ride, but there was no seatbelt in that car. Seatbelts weren't all that popular and certainly not mandatory in 1968. But, man, I wish I had been strapped in during what would be the ride of a lifetime. And blindfolded. Chuck Berry is, without parallel, the wildest, fastest, most lane-changing racecar driver I had ever sat next to. I know that "white knuckles" are generally reserved for rough airplane flights and generally the province of Caucasians, but I gotta tell you, during the ride into town, my knuckles were completely drained of blood as I gripped the seat beneath me. Was there a Patron Saint of Terrified Passengers? If there was, I would have petitioned for all of his or her attention as I offered up fervent prayers during that unsettling ride. We were exceeding the local speed limit and entering the NASCAR realm.

Still no conversation from the Master Musician. I hoped his silence meant he was using his full concentration to weave and speed. And then, out of nowhere, a siren and a blue light speeding up to catch us. A one-word assessment of the situation from the Music Master: "Shit!" The "s" word was uttered just as softly and impassionately as all those "yeses" I had gotten in my initial Lambert conversation with Chuck.

Berry pulled over and brought the rent-a-car to a stop on the shoulder. Whew! My heart might now be allowed to slow down and leave my throat for a while.

One of Chicago's Finest approached the driver's side of our car with traffic whizzing by. Officer Unfriendly looked particularly menacing behind those intimidating cop shades. As he sauntered up, Chuck rolled down the window.

"Yes, sir, officer?" Chuck said in a deferential style I would guess that he hated to feign.

"Sir, do you know how fast you were going? You obviously don't. I got you at least twenty miles over the speed limit. Twenty miles more than the law allows you to drive out here." Officer Unfriendly looked down and past Berry to check me out. Glad he didn't check on my knuckle color. He might have mistaken me for a hostage!

"Well," said Berry. "I think you got me dead to right, Officer. I'm sorry. Really sorry."

"'Sorry' don't cut it," the officer mocked. "You drive like you were driving and you put everybody out here in jeopardy. You put yourself and this young man in jeopardy. You're putting *all* these drivers' lives in your hands driving that fast. And you even put me in danger out here trying to catch up with you. And, sir, I want to get home to have a nice dinner with my wife and children tonight. Let me see your driver's license and registration."

"My wallet and driver's license are inside my jacket pocket here, officer. I'm going to get it out now. . . ."

I later realized that Berry was posting a telegraph of his intended movement so a jumpy officer wouldn't shoot him thinking he was reaching for a weapon. It was obviously a cautionary note Berry had given police officers before.

"Go ahead," the cop allowed.

With his left hand, he made a smooth move to draw back the upper part of his jacket, while his right hand retrieved the wallet, Chuck began to slip out his driver's license. Much to my quiet surprise, Berry, with incredible legerdemain, slipped a folded fifty-dollar bill he conveniently kept behind the license card. With remarkable sleight of hand, Officer Unfriendly palmed the bill and, *presto*, it disappeared.

Suddenly, Officer Unfriendly became Officer Friendly as he checked out Chuck Berry's name.

"Charles Berry. Hmm. From St. Louis. What do you do for a living, Mr. Berry?"

"I'm a musician," Chuck responded.

"A musician, eh? Do you have a wife and kids?" Bending and looking at me, the traffic cop asked, "This your son? Your brother?"

"Yes," Berry responded laconically to cut off conversation with no need for further discussion as to whether I was his son or his brother. It was rather obvious that the policeman didn't really give a damn who I was. He already had pocketed what he really wanted.

"Well, Mr. Berry, I want you to be able to get home to the madam and the kids tonight safely. So slow down, will you, please?" The officer, now Chuck Berry's newest best friend, handed back the driver's license sans fifty bucks.

"You guys have a nice day. And slow down."

"Thank you, officer," Chuck said, as he seemed to force a quarter smile. He rolled up his window, and we were off again, much more slowly this time. Thank God.

"That was kinda scary," I said, breaking my silence for the first time since we were pulled over.

"Happens all the time," Chuck said. "That's how these guys supplement their income. Whenever I'm going to do any driving around Chicago, anywhere in Chicago, I first put a fifty-dollar bill right behind my driver's license."

"Wow!" I reacted. "How do you know they won't nab you for trying to bribe a law officer if you offer them money?"

"There's a little game there. Don't know whether you picked up on it. When an officer is open for you to grease his palm, he mentions something about his "family." That's the code word, *family*. He mentions wife and kids."

"Ah, I see," I said, having learned a lesson I kept at the ready for the rest of my time in Chicago. I used the palm-off once very successfully, but added a little twist to my larceny. In my experience, the bad cop, a "brother," approached my car after I was caught zipping too fast through my neighborhood in the north-side Belmont Harbor area of Chi Town. When the tall, tough-looking cop cautiously approached my side of the car, I slumped a bit over the steering wheel, enough to keep from appearing drunk or drugged up. I grimaced.

"You know you're not only speeding with your damn Missouri license plate, brother, you did a rolling stop through that stop sign back there like it wasn't even there. That kind of stuff can get your ass in a lot of trouble around here. Let me see your license and registration."

"Yes, sir. It's in my back pocket here."

"You ain't drunk or on drugs or nothing are you, Mister from Missouri? I'm hoping that nobody in my family is out here on the street with you driving like a fool."

Bingo! There was the magic word. "Family." Thanks, Chuck!

"No, sir. No, sir. Haven't had anything to drink. Don't do drugs. I'm just trying to get to my doctor's office to get a drug refill for my heart. Uh, here's my driver's license (with the fifty bucks I had started carrying around in my wallet properly affixed behind my license). I've got a heart problem and was trying to get to the hospital. Could you please . . . could you please, give me, like, an escort or something? To my doctor's office?"

"Are you shitting me, kid? I ain't got time for that kind of shit. Get the hell out of here and try not to speed taking your sorry ass to the damn doctor's office or the hospital or wherever your sorry ass is goin'."

There's no doubt that he had taken notice of, and custody of, the green bill under my driver's license.

Ah, the compassion, the love, the magic he displayed in making my hard-earned fifty-dollar bill disappear right before my eyes. Wonder if sleight of hand was a Chicago Police Academy course in the late 1960s.

"Thank you, officer," I said, as he returned my driver's license. I remember how cool, courteous, and compliant the Great Chuck Berry had been at the mercy of the law. How am I doing, Chuck? I put the card back in its slot and put the wallet back in my rear pocket. I drove slowly away, as the police officer, no doubt, continued the scowl while I had a slight grimace of pain plastered on my face. As I got out into my lane, the officer, who was now fifty dollars richer, yelled out after me: "And get rid of that damn Missouri license plate or I'll bust your ass if I ever catch you out around up in here again!"

Ah, the love.

With that sendoff, I headed to my "doctor's office," better known as Uno's Pizza. I'd have to do without a few drinks with the boys at the Pioneer Court Bar under our FCB offices to make up for the loss of fifty dollars, but this little charade was a creative extension of the lesson I had learned from none other than Chuck Berry that was well worth it.

I was now a fabulously free, non-impounded, non-bond-producing, and wiser offender. My mentor Chuck Berry's words still rang in my ear, no matter that they were uttered softly: "If you don't know the game, or if you refuse to cough up your dough, the officer will threaten to haul you to the nearest police station, tow your car, and make you post big-time bond. That turns out to be a lot more time-consuming and expensive than going ahead and playing their game. Fifty dollars is cheap for what you could go through if you don't play and pay."

Well, well. Not only was Chuck Berry a savvy survivalist, he was also capable of stringing more than one word together when he wasn't plucking the strings of his guitar. When we got to my office on Michigan Avenue, I thanked my new motoring mentor for the ride and the lesson. We shook hands and Chuck roared off, faster than he should have. Too bad none of my FCB buddies were coming into or leaving the Equitable Building when Chuck dropped me off. You better believe, though, that they got the full story at lunch and over cocktails that evening after work.

Now, don't go away quite yet on my encounters with Chuck. I ran into him several more times. Fast forward to 1987, if you will. I was by then a recognizable reporter and anchor at the CBS-TV affiliate in St. Louis, and Chuck was booked to be my guest on my half-hour *Newsmakers* program. He would certainly know who I was this time, not from the experience at Sumner

High way back in my fuzzy-cheeked days in 1960, not from the wild, hair-raising 1968 ride on the Chicago highway, but because by 1987 I had been delivering the news on-air for seventeen years. Surely, he had seen me on at least one of the Berry televisions in one of the Berry estates.

It took no time at all in the Channel 4 studio for me to realize that this was a totally different Chuck Berry than the person I'd met before. He was glib, loose, "up," and really funny. He was at the studio to promote his then-new autobiography. It was then that I noticed something else about Chuck that was later confirmed to me in some national periodicals. Just as there were no hangers-on with Chuck when he showed up at the Sumner auditorium, and just as Chuck was a loner in the Lambert and O'Hare airports, the Real King of Rock and Roll had no retinue, no groupie residue, no entourage on this evening he appeared at Channel 4 for the *Newsmakers* taping. He was by himself, and he greeted me with a mock courtly bow and: "Good evening, Sir Julius. Watch you all the time."

What a difference twenty-seven years can make. We hit it off instantly, and soon we were referring to each other by the nicknames we use to this very day: "Sir Julius" and "Sir Charles." I found his choice of greeting interesting, because I had learned during my research that Berry had cut his teeth at the local Cosmopolitan Club. There he was merely a member of "Sir John's Trio."

The *Newsmakers* program was hilarious. Here are the highlights:

I opened with a good straight line for him: "Chuck, tell me about your records."

"Phonograph or prison?" he shot back swiftly. That got chuckles from the studio cameramen. I was sure there would be chuckles from viewers at home, too.

Later in the taping session, I asked about the crime that put him in the pokey for the first time. He told me that in 1944, he and some buddies had decided to go across the state to Kansas City to seek their fortunes. But they had no money. So, according to Chuck, he and his friends tried to stick up a barbershop.

"But my hands were shaking so much, and the damn pistol was so old that it literally fell apart in my hand as I was pointing it at the barber," Chuck told me. He said that the barber quickly noted what was happening to the holdup weapon and he turned and reached in a drawer and pulled out his own pistol. "And the dude started firing at me and my buddies," Berry continued.

"Man, we got the hell out of there in a hurry. We weren't hit, but we got caught by the police just a short time later, and that is the first time I spent any time behind bars."

"How long were you in?" I asked.

"Ten years. Ten long years."

An aside here: The reader should not presume that Chuck got in trouble because he was from an indigent, broken family. He came from a respectable middle-class family in the Ville neighborhood, sometimes called the "Harlem of St. Louis." Chuck's mother was a no-nonsense school teacher who later became a principal, and his father was a contractor and deacon at the historic Antioch Baptist Church. Antioch was fertile ground for Chuck Berry's early interest in music. Antioch rocked! Hundreds of youngsters, myself included, rehearsed with Kenneth Brown Billups' Sumner A Capella Choir after school at Antioch. The Legend Singers, a semi-professional group founded by Billups, also practiced at Antioch. As a kid, I even attended Camp River Cliff, run by the YMCA, Antioch Baptist Church, and its dynamic preacher, the Rev. James Cook.

But I digress, again.

When I asked Chuck during the *Newsmakers* taping about another incident that put him in prison stripes, he deflected the story with blunt denial, and humor.

"Now, Chuck," I said. "Tell me about that incident in which you were busted for bringing that young girl—a minor—over the state line for immoral purposes, or whatever the formal charge was. Her name was Princess Something or Other, an Indian girl."

He made derogatory comments about the girl, calling her a name that rhymes with "itch." "I didn't hire her for indecent sex stuff. I hired her to be a hostess, a receptionist kind of. That was supposed to be her job. She was just supposed to greet people and hang up their coats at the club. But hanging up coats turned into that broad taking off her coat and everything else. I guess she wanted to make a little extra money, so she started doing some of the men customers for money."

"And Chuck, what was your biggest hit ever?"

"Well, I've been blessed with a lot of hits, Sir Julius," Berry answered. "In the summer of 1956 I got in the *Billboard* Top 100 with 'Roll Over, Beethoven.' And even with 'Johnny Be Goode" and 'Maybelline' and 'Rock and Roll Music' and 'Sweet Sixteen' and others. But believe it or not, Sir Julius, my biggest hit that made it to number one was my 1972 song, 'My Ding-a-Ling.' I don't think you're going to let me sing that one on this show."

"You are so right, sir. This is a family show, and I would imagine that if anybody wants to learn the text of that song, they can find it at their neighborhood library, don't you think?"

"Probably not," Chuck said with a laugh that got a chuckle from the production crew.

"But I've got to tell you this, Chuck. My family—my wife and two daughters—were vacationing up in Nova Scotia one summer recently, and we were taking a stroll along the beachfront. And as we were walking, we heard this raucous singing coming from what sounded like a whole crowd of people wailing away in a saloon with a white front. As we got closer to the caterwauling at the piano bar, we could clearly hear the piano player and the well-oiled bar singers belting out, you guessed it, 'My Ding-a-Ling.' Wild! We were careful not to let our daughters hear the lyrics of the song clearly, but Barb and I had heard the words before."

Berry laughed with pleasure and shook his head in an acknowledgment of just how popular he was everywhere. That bunch of howling piano bar singers weren't singing any Elvis songs that day in Nova Scotia. Not that I heard.

His attorneys would never let him talk to me about the incidents at his Wentzville farm and restaurant, in which he was accused of using video cameras to spy on women in the restrooms. I made several attempts to reach Berry to talk about that subject, but no such luck.

My most recent encounter with Chuck Berry was at the Variety Club Telethon, and it went this way as we greeted each other with exaggerated courtly bows:

"Greetings, Sir Julius."

"And equal greetings to you, Sir Charles. I trust you have been well?"

"Very well, Sir Julius. And you?"

"Well, indeed. I say, may I fetch you a libation?"

"Yes, and while you're at it, please fetch me a drink."

Yep, my vote for King of Rock and Roll would definitely go to Chuck Berry. But in addition to his often-imitated style and music, I have to admit that I am biased. My historical encounters with Chuck Berry are enough to put him at the top of my list of Rock and Roll talents. If you don't want to lay the Rock and Roll King's crown on Chuck Berry, I've got another homeboy I interviewed who would certainly be in line for the honor, albeit posthumously. I nominate one Izear Luster Turner, Jr., for the title. You may know him better as Ike Turner. I know about all his transgressions, including beating his wife and partner. The sultry beauty, Annie Mae Bullock, took some hard knocks at the hands of her onetime husband. The R&B chanteuse who became known as Tina Turner posed an episode in his life that Ike Turner told me brought deep regrets. He told me what anybody who had followed his troubled life would know well. He was not perfect, by any means. And he made no bones about the recurring, devastating problem he had with cocaine.

When I interviewed Ike in 1989, he seemed to me the most penitent person I had ever known. He hardly held his head up during our entire session together. He was fifty-eight years old when he sat across from me for the interview, but he looked much older.

When I asked him about the well-publicized accounts of his widely alleged spousal abuse, Ike only told me that what happened with Tina and him was nobody's business but theirs. What he gave me in the way of information about being a husband who terrorized Tina was no more than a so-called "Alford Plea." He admitted neither guilt nor innocence, but Ike told me he knew he had no other choice but to accept the eternal condemnation of former fans and people who had heard the stories third or fourth hand. I was not able to get much in the way of a coherent statement out of him about his domestic strife.

Some years after my interview with him, Ike was saying that he and Tina were never actually married.

When I asked him about his notorious drug abuses he told me, "Yeah, I done cocaine. Yeah. Man, we used to have big ole bowls of that stuff. And I learned it can really mess up your life. Your life and the lives of other people, too."

The words "big ole bowls" began to resonate around the Channel 4 newsroom in unabashed derision in the days and weeks and months that followed, as my newsroom colleagues mocked Ike's use of the words. Everything possible for a long time after my interview had an association with "big ole bowls." There were mentions of things like that "big ole bowl" of candy;

that "big ole bowl" of chili; that "big ole bowl" of cereal. Once, even, a newsroom staffer referred to "that 'big ole bowl' of scripts over there."

"Are you clean now?" I dared to ask the man who appeared to be a little boy with his head hung low. In fact, to give you an even more graphic description of Ike Turner's appearance during my interview with him, I'll use the old Southern metaphor again: "He looked low enough to crawl under a snake with a high hat on."

"Yeah, I'm clean. Been clean a long time. And I plan to stay clean a long time. That stuff made me do some bad things I didn't even know I was doing."

But Ike would have more bouts with cocaine abuse just a few years after I talked with him, even though I was impressed with his oath he volunteered to me. In fact, Turner was back in prison just after my interview with him. His incarceration kept him from attending the induction ceremony in 1991 that put him and Tina in the Rock and Roll Hall of Fame.

St. Louis Mayor Francis Slay was not impressed with Ike's reputation and proven violations of the narcotics laws. Thus, he refused to proclaim an "Ike Turner Day" in St. Louis. But Ike was given a star on the "Walk of Fame" in the Delmar Loop.

Post-Dispatch Pop Music Critic, Kevin C. Johnson, who interviewed Ike Turner after I did, wrote in a December 2007 column that "Turner said he initially didn't pay much attention to (Mayor) Slay's rejection of an 'Ike Turner Day,' but he was forced to after his website was flooded with comments."

Ike Turner's vanguard rock hit, "Rocket 88," is credited with laying the foundation for all the rock and roll to follow. This first big Ike Turner hit featured a funky, raunchy electric guitar that can be heard in Chuck Berry's vamps and the music of many other hot musicians who carried out the style launched by a troubled man who just couldn't get his life straightened out. I learned recently that when he was a young boy, Ike Turner witnessed his Baptist preacher father being beaten by a white Mississippi mob in an attack that led to his father's death. The tragedy happened in the state in which my great-great former slave granddaddy got the maternal side of my family started. That made me understand Ike Turner's pain to a degree, without excusing his criminal life. I think I could understand how this guy could get so screwed up.

WE'RE TALKIN' BASEBALL

I must admit, I don't know beans about sports. I grew up with baseball heroes like Bob Gibson, Curt Flood, Orlando Cepeda, and Stan "The Man" Musial, but I don't know batting averages or any other stats in any other professional sports. My interest in tennis was piqued only when Arthur Ashe breezed into my Sumner High School and captivated the attention of the girls in my circle. Somehow I missed basketball as an interest, even though in 1960 Wilt "The Stilt" Chamberlain brought all 7'1" of himself to one of my high school gym classes. He was at Sumner to promote the idea of keeping sports in perspective. He told us teens that we should never, never allow sports to distract us from staying in school and doing our best scholastically while we were there. That was, as I remember it, a year or so after the Philadelphia Warriors had drafted him; by then, I had already pledged never to let sports get in the way of anything in life.

I never got invested in hockey or golf, but I shelled out the big bucks to become a season-ticket holder when the Rams first came to town. I've written articles that tout St. Louis as having been the Jai Lai capital of the United States. And I wrote many a print article and produced many a TV piece about the 1904 Olympic Games. But that's the extent of my sports acumen.

So I should confess to the very fine sports anchors I sat next to for all those years—as if it weren't crystal clear to them—during their sportscasts I was doodling, scribbling poetry, composing music notes, writing an upcoming speech, or composing my grocery list. No disrespect. They were probably doing the same things when I was spewing news about a new development at City Hall or about a tractor-trailer overturn on Highway 40. Despite my sports deficiency, I was privileged to brush shoulders with some of the all-time greats of the sports world: Stan Musial, Curt Flood, Lou Brock, and Yogi Berra.

STAN THE MAN

"The reason I have a bad knee is that I hit too many triples and slid into third too many times during my career."
—Stan Musial

"The Man" made the above statement to the packed house at Busch Stadium on May 18, 2008, as he was helped away from the microphone during special ceremonies honoring him. Emcee Mike Shannon referred to Stan Musial that day as "the greatest living Cardinal." In addition to the mayoral proclamation naming the third Sunday in May as "Stan Musial Day" in St. Louis, a block of Eighth Street in Stadium Plaza was named "Stan Musial Drive."

I had the opportunity on a couple of occasions to sit and chat with the inimitable Stanley Francis ("Stash") Musial. If you're not a hardcore Cardinals fan, here's all you need to know about the remarkable Stan "the Man" Musial:

.331 career batting average

.417 on base percentage

.559 slugging percentage

3,630 hits

725 doubles

177 triples

475 homers

1,949 runs

1,951 runs batted in

played in 895 straight games before tearing a muscle and chipping a bone

elected to the Baseball Hall of Fame on the first ballot on January 21, 1969

And he hit five home runs in one day in a doubleheader against the Dodgers in 1954. That single-game homerun record was not broken until a guy from my old Cole School neighborhood, Nate Colbert, took the honors in 1972.

I had run into Stan many, many times in the press box at Busch Stadium when the Channel 4 anchor team could steal away to catch a few innings and a free meal between the six and ten o'clock newscasts. I didn't know him well, so imagine my surprise when I got a call in the newsroom one day in 1981.

"Hunter!" a staffer called out. "Stan Musial for you on line two!"

"Yeah, yeah, yeah," I thought, wondering, "Which of my smart-ass friends is this going to be?"

It was, indeed, the legendary "Stan the Man." I hoped he was

not able to sense my shock through the phone lines. He said in his halting, then rapid, then halting speech pattern that he had noticed on TV that I seemed to like history. He had seen, but could not name by title, the fifty-part series of one-minute bits about St. Louis history I researched, wrote, and produced that peppered the daily program lineup for a long time. The morsels in "Gateway Gazette" became extremely popular around town because they featured historical facts that few if any local history buffs knew. One of the pieces, on street names, told viewers that one of the city's main thoroughfares, Gravois, which St. Louisans anglicize in pronunciation, means "garbage dump" in French and was originally the road to the city dump.

Stan loved history. And he was calling me to ask if my wife and I would like to join him and his wife, Lil, to have lunch with his good friend, James Michener, and his wife, Mari. I could have dropped the phone as quickly as my jaw dropped. When I regained my composure, I accepted the invitation as if Stan phoned me to invite me to have lunch with internationally known authors a couple times a week. But I asked myself again and again, "How in the world would Stan have come to have Michener as a friend?" The answer was simply that Stan had friends in more corners of the world than there are corners of the world.

The variegation of those friendships would astound many. For example, Musial had a special friendship with President Jack Kennedy. Stan proudly wore a PT-109 pin that JFK had given him and Stan always prefaced JFK's name with "my buddy." Also, Stan, who was devastated by Kennedy's assassination, struck up a relationship with Lyndon Johnson, who gave Stan a special appointment as presidential physical fitness guru for the nation.

And I would learn later that Stan and Michener had more in common than you might think . . . if you just looked on the surface. They shared a fanatical interest in baseball, both had grown up within a fast pitch of each other in Pennsylvania, and they were each baseball standouts in high school. And I learned that each would have been satisfied with careers in basketball, their second love in sports. Michener might have seemed like an odd duck hanging out with Stan and Red Schoendienst down in Florida at the Cardinals spring training facility, but Stan told me that was not the case. "The Man" did not mention that he and Michener and the boys loved to bend the elbow a bit when they got together for years at Cardinals training camps in Florida. The great author loved bourbon, and Stan's libation of choice, of course, was the nectar that flowed from the Anheuser-Busch barrels.

The two buddies had even traveled together far, far away from Florida. Stan had journeyed to Poland with Michener when the highly productive author had gone to Stan's ancestral hometown of Mojstava while Michener was researching his book *Poland*. To this day, years after Michener's death in 1997, Stan serves on the board of the James Michener Society. Who would have thought that a lanky kid who ended his formal education at Donora High would ever hook up with a guy who wrote some thirty-one books?

On the day of the lunch, Barbara and I nervously arrived at— where else?—Stan Musial and Biggie's Restaurant on Oakland Avenue. That was the eatery Stan co-owned with Julius "Biggie" Garangani.

It was an interesting lunch to say the least. Michener, whose books Barb and I had read, was a literary giant. Barbara had borrowed her parents' copy of *Iberia* and was reading it because we were heading to Iberia—Spain and Portugal—in just a few weeks.

During our conversation over lunch, I had lots of questions for Michener, like how in the world one man can turn out books the size of *Centennial, The Covenant, Hawaii, Sayonara,* and at least a dozen other robust bestsellers. Michener, who did not at all seem well at the time, mumbled a few responses and then deferred to Mari, his third wife, each time one of my questions came up. He and Mari had been married for twenty-six years at the time we lunched; it took only a couple minutes to realize that she was the more articulate, and perhaps deeper, of the two. For example, I wanted to engage him in a conversation about the reign of Carlos Quinto—Charles the Fifth—and his influence on the evolution of Spain and Portugal. (This, by the way, was not my typical lunchtime conversation.) Michener immediately tossed my question to Mari. Then later, not to be a pseudo-academic, I asked him about some of the details about his awesome *Centennial*, which I had almost used for kindling midway through the first tedious chapter. But it turned out that I eventually couldn't put the weighty tome down.

Stan and Lil and Barbara and James were rather quiet as the two "talkers" in the sixsome jabbered on. I did take note of the fact that Michener was nuts for baseball and had once starred in the sport in high school. When I asked how he could churn out literally (or literarily) more than two dozen books the sheer size of his bestsellers, we learned from Mari, and through Michener mumbling in, that the prolific author often worked with as many as three secretaries and on as many as three different typewriters at a time. Michener, without Mari's statistics, would acknowledge only that he had help in writing his voluminous books. He also acknowledged having researchers but emphasized that he alone ran the show on the writing projects. One could easily get the idea that Mari was a principal figure in her husband's productivity. If he wore the literary pants in the family, Mari was the belt.

Barbara and I produced the copy of *Iberia* we had brought to ask for an autograph. And the Great One scribbled:

To Julius & Barbara Heater,

I hope you have a great visit to Spain.

James A. Michener
1981

We thanked Stan and Lil and James and Mari for a good lunch and stimulating conversation. Eight years passed before I would have another sit-down conversation with Stan. That happened on September 29, 1989—the day that the King of Beers, Gussie Busch, died.

My first interview on that day of multiple Busch eulogies was with KMOX Radio topper, Bob Hyland. Attesting to what a small world this is, Hyland's physician father, surgeon Robert F. Hyland, had treated Stan Musial during the 1947 baseball season when the senior Hyland was the team physician. Stan had suffered from an inflamed appendix *and* tonsillitis.

As it turned out, my second interview to get reflections on Gussie Busch's life that day would take place at the suburban Musial home. As we were leaving Bob Hyland's office for the Musial home, I found myself in distant thoughts about what a great guy Stan was. He was exactly the same good guy whether I ran into him at the ballpark or at a civic event, or during those wonderful sit-down sessions. I also remembered what Jackie Robinson had said about the All-Star Cardinal who wore No. 6 on his jersey. Robinson had said that while he was catching the nastiest worst hell of his life, with catcalls and objects being hurled onto the field in a very racist St. Louis at the time, Stan was one of only a couple of the Cardinals who stayed above it all. Robinson often noted that Stan never said a discouraging word to Jackie. Some thought that Musial was too much of a superstar to lower himself to racial mudslinging with players or fans who had much less talent of any sort to offer the world. Stan had taken to the field in high school with black baseball players at Donora, but I had always given Stan extra props for not joining the rampant mistreatment leveled at the black trailblazer on his first visits to the old Sportsman's Park in good old racist St. Louis.

When the crew and I reached the lovely Musial property, a white painted metal street barrier had to be removed before we could take the unmarked road to the house. Stan greeted us with an outstretched hand and his patented rapidly pitched triple-play "Whadyasay, whadyasay, whadaysay?" Lil, to whom Stan had been married by that time for nearly sixty years, had suffered a bad bout with arthritis and was wheelchair-bound. Pleasant, always gracious, she, too, extended us a warm welcome. So that we wouldn't have to set up lights and trudge in and out of the house, I decided that Stan and I could repair to the backyard for his thoughts on the death of his old boss and friend, Gussie Busch. "The Man" was happy to accommodate.

Stan said Gussie had been a tough businessman, but kind, bossman. He said that he liked the fact that the Old Man hated formality and liked being "just one of the boys a lot of times." He mentioned how kind and even solicitous Mr. Busch had been to him after the brewery purchased the Cardinals in 1953. After Stan's record-breaking performance just four years after the acquisition, the Old Man, Stan told me, rewarded him with a nice raise. In fact, the pay hike, Stan said, was much more than Stan had expected. Stan had never even had an agent before. Stan told me, with a very sad look in his eyes, that he would really miss his boss and his pal.

After a weak 1963 season of batting only .255, Stan said he had thought it was best for all concerned for him to give up the game, ten years after Anheuser-Busch took ownership of the team. Stan said he was happy that the Old Man let him hang around the old Sportsman's Park, by then named Busch Stadium. He was also happy to be around the team when the new Busch Stadium had its grand opening in 1966. The team's new home made Gussie proud, Stan said.

After the one-on-one interview, the crew went to the microwave truck to beam the recording back to the station downtown—using the technology Channel 4 had pioneered decades earlier. That allowed me time to continue a leisurely conversation with Stan. In retrospect, I should have taped our informal chat, too.

During the talk, I learned some things I had never known about Stan the Man. As we sat in lawn chairs on his well-manicured property, Stan told me that in high school he was as interested in basketball as he was in baseball. At one point he could have gone either way, because he was offered a basketball scholarship. Think of baseball—or the Redbirds—without Musial's historic participation.

Even more mind blowing to me was that Stan's baseball career—long before he mastered the art of playing outfield—might have been as a pitcher. He was a pretty good hurler in high school and in the minors. The road towards the pitcher's mound was barricaded when Stan badly banged up his pitching arm while playing outfield. If that hadn't happened, can you imagine Musial starting a game as a pitcher? Or relieving Gibson?

And on the subject of injuries, I asked Stan what he thought about all the players being out on the disabled list for extended periods. I could tell he wanted to be diplomatic here, because he declined giving me any responses about current players on the subject of injuries. No matter how cleverly I cloaked my questions, Stan showed an amazing talent and a sly smile while dodging my curve balls. But he didn't mind talking about the guys who played the game during his heyday.

"We were a tough bunch of guys back then," he said. "We played hurt a lot. We had a game to play, and when you hit the field you forgot a while about this or that hurting you. You get a bruise, you pour a little iodine on it and keep on playing. You get a sprain, either you or the team doctor would tape it up real tight and you'd head back out in the field. I used to think of all the fans that paid their hard earned money to come see me play. They didn't buy tickets to see me sitting on the bench."

Stan was too modest, or had forgotten the exact number, but later on I learned that he had played in 895 straight games! The long streak was ended by an injury that you just know had to be serious. I mean, here was a guy who took just five days off the field after his tonsils and appendix were yanked out in '47. That must be what "playing with pain" really means.

What about the big salaries being commanded these days by players? Stan, again, wouldn't condemn any current players or salaries, and he told me, with a little coaxing, that he never made much more than $100,000 in any one season. What's more, he said the team bought the first pair of shoes for players in his day, and they would have to buy any second pair they wanted. There was no players union in his prime, and owners tried to get away with paying players as little as possible.

In our post-interview conversation, Stan mentioned that Gussie had wanted to keep him around after he hung up his cleats. So when the year 1967 rolled around, two years before Stan breezed into the Hall of Fame, Busch anointed Stan as Cardinals general manager and gave him a nice office befitting the title. Stan twiddled his thumbs in the front office for less than a year till, he told me, he "couldn't stand being cooped up not knowing what I was doing in there." Stan quit that job, even though the Cards shortly thereafter won a World Series.

I've been privileged to run into Stan frequently at civic events, especially those with a patriotic flavor. We really laid on the red, white, and blue when we appeared together one night at a Queeny Park concert in July of 2001—Stan with his harmonica and I with a tribute I had written to America.

When one is in the presence of the great Stan Musial, one

could easily echo the inscription on the bronze statue of Stan that was carefully moved from the old Busch Stadium to the new Busch Stadium:

"Here stands baseball's perfect warrior. Here stands baseball's perfect knight."

CURT FLOOD

When Cincinnati traded Curt Flood to St. Louis in 1957, the brilliant young centerfielder struck up a relationship with the then-flamboyant and irrepressible Sergeant Fred Grimes of the St. Louis Police Department. The colorful sergeant and his partner, Oscar Farmer, kept more law and order in my old neighborhood than was maintained in the sum total of all TV series on the subject. Sergeant Grimes's daughter Sheila was the apple of my youthful eye at Sumner High, and we were in the same homeroom. In fact, Sheila was my first date in high school. She was also at the top of our class in math and science, giving balance to my bottom-dwelling status in some of those subjects, as my report cards show.

I prevailed on Sheila to give me tutorial assistance in math, and super-tough Sergeant Grimes, much to his dismay, would occasionally find me studying with his daughter. In fact, I remember the hell he raised one time when we were studying and the door to Sheila's room was closed during the tutorial session. I believe he threatened me with arrest and more that night. It is only through the intervention of Mama Grimes that I wasn't tossed out onto the street.

It was in the lovely Grimes home on Margaretta that I began to see Curt Flood hanging around. Some of the black baseball players like Ted Savage and Lou Brock have told me how difficult it was for black players to find places to socialize between home games during the 1950s and 1960s, in particular. No country clubs, no fine-dining restaurants, no admission to most of the town's movie theaters, and no hotel accommodations until federal law changed things in 1964. So Curt was among the black Redbirds who, between home games, could not check out a flick at the Loewe's State or Loewe's Mid-City or any of the other movie theaters on Grand Avenue. Nor could any of the brothers join the local country clubs to play a few hands of gin. They weren't even allowed to play the country club courses as guests of members. The Missouri Athletic Club was not open to hosting blacks for a quick dip in the pool or a crab dip in the dining room. How about a nice pasta dinner at any of the fine restaurants on The Hill? Fugetaboutit! Surely a black Cardinal baseball player could just lounge around in his hotel room. Well, not at the Chase, the Ambassador Kingsway, the Coronado, the Statler, or any major chain hotel. Whether they had two or three Golden Gloves in their luggage, a batting average of .300, or even if they played for the home team, black players, like nonplayers of the same color, were barred from these establishments.

My friend, former Cardinal outfielder Ted Savage (1965–1967), brought tears to my eyes at lunch one day when he told stories of how he and his black Cardinal teammates had to seek out black folks in a town on the road to put them up for a night or two or three—even long after Lyndon Johnson signed the Public Accommodations Act of 1964. And, Ted told me, often the funeral homes in a town were the most luxurious places available for players of color to lay their heads for a good night's sleep. Black players would actually bunk overnight there and in church basements when there was no lodging available in black homes during road series. And we're not talking ancient history.

When the Cardinals played in town, Lucille Grimes, Sheila's mom and police Sergeant Fred Grimes's wife, told me she could count on at least one of two things. She could be sure she would get a phone call from Curt Flood's parents in California saying they would be in town and would like to stay at the Grimes home, and there would also be a call from Curt Flood to tell Lucille that he would love to come by and put his feet under her kitchen or dining room table. That's how Curt Flood ended up so often at the comfortable and accommodating Grimes house. Mama Grimes always laid out some mighty fine grub. I was privileged to have lunch, or dinner, or a snack at the same table with Flood and the Grimeses on numerous occasions, while ostensibly studying with Sheila. Sometimes when the hash browns were being passed around, the adults hashed out some heavy-duty conversation. Talk about a "fly on the wallpaper." Had I been a sports reporter in those days, I would have had some juicy scoops. Flood thought he should be making a lot more than the $90,000 the Cardinals' front office was paying him at the time. And he was a grumbler, an unabashed bellyacher. But with some justification, I'm sure. Eventually, he thought, Gussie Busch and the management were trying to get rid of him. He was more than paranoid. He told the adults over a meal that there was a bulls-eye on his back because he was, in the words of the front office, "uppity, a trouble-maker, and a shit disturber."

It is understandably hard for us to fathom how much money $90,000 was back in those olden days. To offer perspective, I'll tell you that after getting our teaching degrees, Sheila and I began teaching full time in 1965 at $5,250 a year. And we thought we were in fat city. Those were the days when a loaf of bread cost nineteen cents a loaf. And my brand new '67 Chevy Impala set me back $6,100—stretched out in monthly payments for three years, of course. An economist friend of mine at Saint Louis University, Bonnie Wilson, computes that Curt's $90,000 salary in today's money would be about $507,332 and change, taking inflation into account. But I just read that Andruw Jones—whose centerfielding and batting average are somewhat comparable to Flood's—signed a two-year, no-trade deal that will put more than $36 million in his pocket. Curt Flood was a seven-time Gold Glove winner.

Curt Flood must be rolling over in his grave to learn what less than super-spectacular centerfielders are hauling in these days. The Dodgers are awarding Juan Pierre a five-year, $44 million deal; Gary Matthews, Jr., will take the Angels for a five-year, $50 million ride; and Torii Hunter, no relation, will dip into the Angels' coffers for a record five-year $90 million take. But, of course, a loaf of bread is no longer nineteen cents.

These multimillionaire boys of summer owe all they have in summer, fall, winter, and spring to little Curt Flood, the intrepid crusader. He boldly defied the rules of the day and refused to be traded to the city where he expected to encounter racially tinged epithets, catcalls, and threats on his life just like Jackie Robinson did. Certainly, he anticipated little "Brotherly Love" in Philly. Had I been old enough during the time we shared the Grimses' hospitality, I surely would have tossed back a few brewskies to commiserate with a guy many thought was philosophically and temperamentally in far left field.

Flood said eloquently on a number of occasions: "A well-paid slave is, nonetheless, a slave." And when he lost his Supreme Court case against baseball slavery, Flood dropped out of baseball. And ultimately he dropped—or was dropped—out of life. He even went into self-imposed exile in Spain while his landmark case was being tried before the Supreme Court. During my earliest days as a news anchor, in Flood's honor, I would violate the "no editorials" policy of my position. Whenever outrageous salary offers headlined the sports segment, I would invariably say on-air to my sports colleague, "You know, every player in major league baseball, and maybe even in the minors, should each send Curt Flood a hundred bucks as a tribute to their freedom." That would have made Flood an overnight millionaire many times over, and deservedly so. He can be called the father of free agency because of his refusal to be sold to another team.

Nonetheless, Flood's story ended sadly. Also sad was my last encounter with him. I was researching a "Where Are They Now?" series and asked viewers to send us the name of one-time newsmakers who had dropped out of the limelight. Curt Flood's name was high on the response list. But nobody I talked to or wrote to seemed to know where Curt was. A friend who knew him well said that Curt had become a virtual ghost, a fugitive, a runaway, a hermit. He had legal troubles and debts, I was told. And I heard from reliable sources that he had abandoned some domestic responsibilities. And a few friends who knew him suggested that Flood was hitting the bottle pretty good.

Around that time of my investigation, I was getting a haircut and mentioned to my barber that I was trying to locate the elusive, mysterious Curt Flood. A waiting customer in the barber shop overheard my inquiries and told me he thought Curt was living somewhere out in L.A. He wasn't listed, but sure enough, through some super-sleuthing that tested all I had learned about investigative reporting, I found him. I reached him on the phone.

Curt sounded depressed. I got him to recall some of the good old days, which happened just before the bad old days he complained about at the Grimeses. I tried to jog his memory of the skinny little boy that used to study with Sheila and occasionally eat with him and the grownups. He said he couldn't remember, and I reasoned, "Why should he?" When I told him about my "Where Are They Now?" project, he asked rather bitterly, "Who gives a shit where I am these days?" I assured him that there were tens of thousands of St. Louisans who would love to know that he was alive and well. He responded, "Well, I'm at least alive."

"So, are you not well?" I asked with genuine concern.

"I don't want to talk about it. We're not recording now, are we?"

I assured him we weren't. He asked what we wanted from him specifically. I told him I just wanted to fly out to L.A. and sit with him one-on-one and videotape some reminiscences with him about his twelve years in St. Louis. Just shoot the breeze. He then threw me a bit off guard when he asked what he would be paid for the interview. I told him that the station did not, would not pay for an interview of that sort.

Flood's response was: "You mean to say your cheap ass station is going to fly you out to California all expenses paid, and maybe put you up in a nice hotel someplace and pay for your meals and stuff, and they don't have something to pay me for my time?"

I was, quite frankly, a deer in the Floodlights at that point— stunned into a pause, not even a stammer—having flashbacks of those lively times around the Grimes kitchen table. Thankfully, after three or four beats or more, an embittered Curt Flood kick-started the conversation again.

"Well, where would you want to record this *free* interview, which I'm not much interested in doing?" he asked.

"We could, uh, uh shoot it at your house so you wouldn't even have to leave your house," I offered magnanimously . . . I thought.

"What?" Curt snapped. "You mean to say you wanna come trampling through my house . . . and use my electricity that I have to pay for . . . and your cheap ass station won't even pay me for my electricity?"

Deeply saddened and stunned by the lack of reciprocal cordial-ity, I counter-offered, "Well, is there a little park somewhere? We could do the interview on a park bench or even standing up. And not have to use any electricity."

"Tell you what, my friend," Flood said with a tone that did not make the word "friend" have its traditional drift, "Lemme talk it over with my wife. And why don't you call me back tomorrow or sometime."

"Alright, Mr. Flood. I'll call you back just about this same time tomorrow. Would that be okay?"

"Yeah. Bye." He hung up. I hung up second.

It would not surprise you to learn that I was not able to reach Curt Flood the next day, or the day after that, nor any day thereafter. I tried often. But it soon became crystal clear to me that I was never going to be able to reach Curt Flood again. Too bad.

Mr. Curtis Charles Flood, one of the greatest centerfielders in baseball history, passed away in 1997 of throat cancer about a year-and-a-half after our phone conversation. He died in virtual hiding, and in irreversible poverty. He struck out in life's big game while those he freed would make millions of dollars that he all but personally crammed into their bulging bank accounts. And sadly, some of baseball's millionaire players may not even know Curt Flood's name.

Lou Brock: Entering Baseball as a Punishment

There's not a single time that I've run into Baseball Hall of Famer Lou Brock that he hasn't hit some verbal line drives that caused me to run home to jot them down.

Did you know that this great base burglar (938 stolen lifetime) and ball banger (3,023 lifetime hits) got into baseball as the result of a punishment? Lou told me recently that when he was a boy of nine or ten down in northeast Louisiana, baseball meant nothing much to him. "I loved to pull pranks, and was a spitball artist in grade school. One time I fired a spitball at a girl in my class, but it hit the teacher by mistake," Lou told me. "Miss Sofonia Young didn't have much of a sense of humor about that. Ooh, was she hot!" Lou continued. "She made me study up and do a book report in front of the whole class as punishment. She'd handed me a *Life* or a *Look* magazine—I can't remember which—to get some information from an article about baseball."

"That's what turned my head and made me get interested in baseball," Lou remembers. "The article said that big league baseball players were earning ten dollars a day for meal money in those days. Ten dollars a day! Some of the grownups that I knew back then were making two dollars a day for hard labor. This baseball seemed like the big time to me! I wanted to make the big bucks playing a game."

"On our school softball team back in Collinston, Miss Young

made me play first base. Every time I'd drop the ball, Miss Young, who boarded with my family, would give me five licks with a leather strap for being clumsy. That's what made me a better player. I didn't drop a lot of balls knowing what I'd get if I did. That punishment helped my concentration a whole lot!"

I wanted to know how he got interested in running and stealing bases. It didn't take Brock a second to respond. "Up until the sixties," Lou told me, "players had to be good at everything in the game: hitting, throwing, fielding, and catching. Maury Wills wasn't particularly good at any of these things, so he concentrated on stealing bases. That fascinated me. The time of specialty skills entered the sport and began to dominate baseball. You could get by doing just one thing well."

Here's something I'll bet you didn't know unless you're a card-carrying member of the Lou Brock Fan Club: Lou got his training in mad-dash running from one of the most legendary, fleet-footed runners of all time—Jesse Owens. This superstar sprinter/dasher/jumper/relayer said, "Heil, no!" to Hitler and shattered any Nazi notions of Aryan athletic superiority at the 1936 Olympics in Berlin. "I worked for the Humble Oil Company up in Chicago off-season when I first joined the Cubs back in 1961, and Jesse ran a little club with a Tahitian theme in Chicago. My job was to deliver heating oil to places around town, including the club that Jesse Owens ran. That's when I struck up conversations with Mr. Owens and asked him to teach me some things about running. He told me and showed me on the Chicago University track and field that, while some folks mistakenly think running is all about your legs and feet, it's actually about getting the quickest start by leading off with your upper body—your shoulders." I'm sure you'll agree that Lou excelled like no other base-stealer you've ever seen. And now you know that Lou learned all he knows about base-burgling thanks in part to a gold-medal-winning tip from Jesse Owens.

Yogi Berra

I was both surprised and relieved when Saint Louis University President Larry Biondi summoned me to his office . . . this time. As his vice president for community relations, I also chaired the committee that chose the annual commencement speakers and honorary degrees recipients. The committee was ostensibly made up of representatives of the faculty, administration, and student body. After the first round of vetting candidates, the committee members and I realized that the Reverend Father President was, and would be, the final arbiter of that speaker choice. It was immediately apparent that Father Biondi did, and would, reserve the right to veto any of the committee's proposed speakers. I learned to console any of my committee colleagues who were dismayed that a committee choice did not rise to the fore with: "Hey, it's Biondi's candy store." And anybody who has worked for the outspoken and dynamic SLU president over his more than twenty-five years in that post knows how the door swings in that candy store.

So when he called me into his chamber in early April 2007, he announced that that year's speaker on May 19 would be "Yogi" Berra. Whew! That meant no more unnecessary committee meetings in my office. No more reading through reams and reams of resumes to find a slate of candidates that fit all the prerequisites of a Catholic Jesuit university commencement speaker—nobody with any identifiable political party affiliations; no speakers with any radical, unorthodox religious affiliation; and no speaker with pro-choice or pro-contraceptive philosophies. One year, the selection committee put the head of *Doctors Without Borders* at the top of the list of potential commencement speaker candidates. Then the committee began to realize that while this international organization of physicians had undertaken commendable healthcare services worldwide, the group also distributes condoms in Third World nations. Oops! Scratch!

So, the Biondi choice to address the Class of 2007 would be

the oft-quoted, legendary baseball hero. But I wanted to know right away from Biondi if he thought Yogi could hit a homerun with some 1,900 academically steeped graduates as they set out on a new chapter in their lives. Father Biondi acknowledged that trying to get Berra to appear to be a scholastic philosopher might be a large order; a daunting challenge. After all, we both recognized, Yogi is better known for malapropisms than brilliant oratory. Biondi's solution was that *I* should write Yogi's commencement speech. He thought that I could work famous Yogiisms into an informal address. Hmmm. Maybe instead of a soliloquy . . . I could write a colloquy. Hmmm.

I knew I would voluntarily be leaving my SLU post on the upcoming graduation date to move a step closer to retirement and write this book, so why not give the Yogi thing a shot! Would this be a strike out or a grand slam? I did want to leave in good graces. And besides—once again—I had learned during my five years at SLU that it is better to accept a Biondi order with: "Thy will be done," rather than, "Forgive me, Father, for I will fail!"

I got a hold of all the books and Internet pages I could find on the famous sayings of the St. Louis–born baseball legend. There were some real beauts in the bunch. After lots of fits and starts and a mound of shredded drafts, I came up with a script that would be way different than the typical, traditional commencement speeches you've heard over the years. I began to really believe that the Yogi Speech could be a hit. But if the Class of '07 rose as one body to give Yogi and me a resounding chorus of Bronx cheers, Yogi and I could probably scamper to the dugout together to safety.

On the day before the Saturday ceremony, Yogi and I, a rookie comedy team, rehearsed our act. I had never played the straight man in front of so many people. And I'll bet that Yogi had never given a "Godspeed graduates" speech patched together with his famous sayings.

Yogi and his beloved wife of nearly sixty years, Carmen, greeted me warmly when I arrived in the conference room at the Ritz-Carlton Hotel in Clayton for the morning rehearsal on Friday, May 18, 2007. I am sure I was much more nervous than Yogi. But, he made me feel more comfortable when he said he and Carmen had seen me on television through the years when they had come back to town. I certainly had seen a lot of Yogi over the years. I have, however, perhaps unwittingly, quoted his pronouncements throughout my public career.

We had sent the script to Yogi before he arrived in town, but I got the idea that this wasn't a piece of literature he had chosen to memorize in advance. We both bumbled through the script a couple of times. The Hall of Famer just could not get one of my best lines right. The exchange was supposed to go like this:

Hunter: *So, Yogi, how do you like that duck you work with?*
Berra: *With orange sauce.*

Try as he might, Yogi replied instead over and over, "With orange *juice.*"

My first corrections, I'm afraid, came off like scolding. He looked sadder and more frustrated with each attempt to make sauce out of that juice. The solution? We scratched the line. The 13,000 people at the ceremony never heard it.

I knew Yogi would score a home run immediately after I introduced him. When I announced to the audience that soon-to-be Doctor Yogi Berra had just celebrated his eighty-second birthday the week before this graduation ceremony, the fans in the stands burst into thunderous applause. When I announced his name, the assembly of thousands gave him a standing, rousing ovation. He must have felt like he was in a standing-room-only ballpark with a homer that cleared the bases. That relieved me of my gut fear that the young people in the graduating class might not have heard of Yogi Berra. They might have heard of the cartoon character whose name is a rip-off of Berra's name "Yogi Bear." And I had heard from a very reliable source that Yogi was not exactly fond of the cartoon characterization. The reception he received that day at the Scottrade Center proved me wrong on my initial trepidation.

Here's how the Berra & Hunter Comedy Show went:

INTRODUCTION OF THE COMMENCEMENT SPEAKER:

Hunter: *Members of the SLU Class of '07, it would be an understatement to note that those of you who leave here today with your new diplomas and degrees are going out into a troubled world.*

In fact, Volume 1 of the three-volume Encyclopedia of World Problems, now in its fourth printing, describes the alarming news that there are exactly 9,832 serious problems in the world

*you will enter outside these doors. 9,832 serious problems. One of
those nearly ten thousand world problems for some of us might be
that the Encyclopedia of World Problems costs $245 a copy! And
to be very parochial, another crisis for those of us in this auditorium is the coming havoc and mayhem that will be caused by the
reconstruction on Highway 40/64. That may make the number of
serious problems in the world number 9,833 by next month.*

*And to confirm that we've got some mammoth problems out
there, you can actually check with the Reuters news service's
"Alertnet" where you can find the list of the top ten world crises.
The Number One world crisis, as determined by Reuters, involves
the atrocities, past and ongoing, in the Congo.*

*Well, before you go marching off to the Congo or to any of the
other 9,831 global hotspots, let's take a time out for the rest of
this hour to lighten up a bit. And let me introduce you to your
guest speaker who will impart to you some invaluable, time-tested
wisdom this morning.*

He was mentioned just this week on The Daily Show *with Jon
Stewart. Your speaker should go down on your list of stellar,
quotable philosophers, right up there alongside Voltaire, Kant,
Aristotle, and Locke.*

*In fact, I'll bet you that you or someone you know has quoted
your guest speaker more times than you can count. And you
might not have even known it at the time. And let's face it, when's
the last time you quoted Voltaire . . . in casual conversation.*

*But your speaker for today is known more for his outstanding
accomplishments in the world of baseball than in his Aristotelian
pronouncements.*

*He began to put words in our mouths as he hung out in dugouts
and baseball fields all across the United States and Canada going
back forty years.*

*He was first signed to the New York Yankees farm team in 1942
for a whopping $500. That's $500 a year! When the Yankees
moved him up as a platoon catcher in 1946, he was known as a
wild, but hot hitter. In 1950, he struck out only twelve times in
597 times at bat!*

*He went on to become a fifteen-time All-Star, becoming the
American League's Most Valuable Player three times, in 1951,
'54, and '55.*

Your guest speaker played in fourteen World Series games and

snagged a bundle of records including most World Series games played by a catcher and most hits on a winning team.

What's more, your guest speaker for this special day hit the first pinch-hit homerun in World Series history back in 1947.

He became the New York Yankees skipper in 1964 and won the American League pennant that very year.

Then he went on to manage the "You Gotta Believe" Mets in 1972, and took the then-hapless Mets from last place in the final month of the season to win the National League Pennant.

That made "Old Deep Pockets," George Steinbrenner, hire your speaker back with the Yanks team in 1984.

It's no wonder that the man you will hear from next was elected into the National Baseball Hall of Fame in 1972.

And one of the things about which he is most proud is that he is a native St. Louisan—born in South St. Louis on the Hill, only a Roger Clemens pitch from where we sit today.

He is here today not to talk baseball but to impart to you some of the wisdom quoted by presidents, princes, and people like us everywhere.

Please give a warm Saint Louis University welcome to a love-

able guy who celebrated his eighty-second birthday just last
week. "The Berra of Truth and Wisdom," Mr. Lawrence Peter
Berra. You know him, and quote him often, as "Yogi" Berra . . .
Heeeeeeere's Yogiiiiiiiiii!

(Thunderous standing ovation. I move to the stage podium set
up on the left of Yogi's podium; Yogi moves to podium set up on
the right.)

DIALOGUE:

Hunter: *Mr. Berra, welcome home! And welcome to the Saint
Louis University Commencement of the Class of '07. We're so
glad you're here today because we've heard all the great things
you've said. . . .*

Berra: *Oh, boy. To be honest, Julius, I didn't really say everything I said.*

Hunter: *Well, Mr. Berra, how does it feel to be back in St.
Louis?*

Berra: *Feels like Déjà vu all over again.*

Hunter: *Since you've been back, have you been to the neighborhood bar on the Hill where you and all the old gang used to
hang out?*

Berra: *Nobody goes there anymore. It's too crowded.*

Hunter: *And now to the graduates who will begin to blaze
new trails today. What advice would you have for them when
they have to make a quick decision on which path in life to take?*

Berra: *Dear graduates, when you come to a fork in the road,
take it! In life the only poor decisions are the ones you don't follow through on. When you leave here today you will have more
choices than you ever thought possible, but when you have to
make a choice, make it because you believe in it. Then stick to
your guns.*

Hunter: *That is great advice: "When you come to a fork in the
road, take it." You know, the graduates have already learned
that this is not a perfect world, is it?*

Berra: *No. If the world was perfect, it wouldn't be. People always tell me that's a quote I said that doesn't make much sense,
but all of you understand what I'm saying, right? I know you*

got a good education at SLU, and I'm sure it's opened your eyes to the people in the world who need your help. But most important, your SLU education has prepared you to give that help.

True, the world isn't perfect, but you can make it closer to perfect than it is.

Hunter: *And what would you say to the graduates who will want to throw in the towel if they step up to the plate and strike out a few times?*

Berra: *I'd tell 'em it ain't over till it's over. I was a .285 career hitter. That means I succeeded in hitting the ball about 28 percent of the time. That made me a Hall of Famer! Think about it. Twenty-eight percent might not get you far at SLU, but when I was at the Yankees, I learned real fast not to worry about my failures. I did figure out how to learn from mistakes. That's real important in life.*

If I went back in the dugout and beat myself up, I would have been back down in the minors in no time.

There will be days when you wish you were back in class at SLU. Life gets tough, so be tougher. Stand up, take your lumps, and before long, you'll understand what it takes to be a winner.

Hunter: *Well, I'm sure there are some graduates out there who are still not sure where they want to end up in life. Got any advice?*

Berra: *Well, I say to that, be careful if you don't know where you're going in life, because you might not get there. Wherever you go, whatever you do, be the best you can be. Be the greatest. I always said. If I had been a plumber, I would have been a great plumber.*

Hunter: *You're certainly living testimony to what hard work can do for these graduates.*

Berra: *All they've got to remember is this: Success is 90 percent mental, and the other half is physical. No matter how you add it up, education is the key to success. I learned from the Hall of Famers I played with. You should try to keep learning for the rest of your life.*

You'll learn from great bosses, co-workers, family, and friends. Find out what they know, and never stop learning. And I hope you will always remember that the future ain't what it used to be. For example, a nickel ain't worth a dime anymore.

Hunter: *And should these graduates just jump right into life, or should they take a little time to check out the scene first?*

Berra: *Well, you can always observe a lot by watching.*

Hunter: *So true, so true. Anything you'd like to say in closing?*

Courtesy Saint Louis University

Berra: *I would like to thank Father Biondi and SLU for making this day necessary. It's like my old pal Joe Dimaggio used to say about opening day: You look forward to it like a birthday party when you were a kid. I say to you, Class of 2007, go out and live your life like every day is opening day. Thank you.*

Wow! Another standing "O." Yogi really hit it out of the park with his simple but straightforward advice to the graduates. The *Post-Dispatch* said of the presentation:

It wasn't so much a speech as a skit. Julius Hunter, the university's vice president for community relations, played the straight man, asking Berra questions to set up (Berra's) one-liners.

The *Post-Dispatch* quotes one graduate as saying, "He was funny, but it was kind of dry." According to the *Post-Dispatch* reporter, that student's grandmother quickly came to Yogi's defense, "I think he's precious." Another student, a twenty-nine-year-old med school grad from San Diego, is quoted as saying, "It's amazing somebody of his prestige, at his age, can still come in and motivate."

SOPHIA LOREN

"Although the Vatican opposes human cloning, an exception might be made in the case of Sophia Loren."
—Archbishop of Genoa, 2002

Amen, Brother Bishop! I can give personal testimony to how excited generations of men, in particular, might pray fervently that Sophia could somehow be selected as a candidate for genetic reproduction. My unequivocal vote for duplicating her face, form, and figure—at least once—comes after spending up-close, knee-to-glamorous-knee time with La Bella Loren. Looking directly into those sensuous almond-shaped eyes cinched my vote that she is arguably the sexiest, most naturally beautiful film star in the history of the silver screen. And I must admit that I was so transfixed in her presence that I could not determine if her eyes are green or brown. Through the fog of mesmerism, my vote is for green. But eyes can only be taken as one small part of the total breathtaking beauty of Sophia.

As I gazed hypnotized by the aura of her voluptuousness, I found it hard to believe how Sofia Villani Scicolone could have ever for even a minute been considered an ugly duckling and known as *stuzzicadente*. That's Italian for "toothpick"—her nickname when she was a skinny, but otherwise nondescript, young girl. Sofia was born of unmarried parents in a charity ward in Rome on September 20, 1934. I note the specific date on the odd chance that I will someday work up the nerve to send her a birthday card. When her father refused to marry her mother, Sophia and her sister, Maria, moved with their mama to the slums outside Naples. All who knew her in her youth were virtually shocked at how the age of fourteen seemed to be the magic year in which the toothpick burst forth—in all the right places— into a woman in full bloom.

Sophia resisted all urgings early in her film career to have her nose "fixed." That cad Marlon Brando first brought up the subject of Loren's nose after they shot a steamy love scene in the 1967 flick, *A Countess from Hong Kong*. The brutish and

Sophia Loren is mobbed by St. Louis media, October 2, 1980.

less-than-diplomatic Brando reportedly observed at a time that most men like me would be stunned by the sheer proximity to Sophia: *"Did you know you have hair in your nostrils?"*

Sophia did suffer a little shrapnel nick on her chin during World War II, but she apparently lost it as she blossomed into full beauty. She says she has publicly eschewed plastic surgery at every turn. She ascribes her beauty to spaghetti and an occasional bath in virgin olive oil. Pass the ciabatta bread, please.

Sophia stopped baring it all for nude scenes relatively early in her film career after offering a personal reason that would receive a chorus of "amens" from her fans, in particular: "When Sophia Loren is naked, that's a lot of naked."

On Thursday, October 2, 1980, the Channel 4 station management was livid over the fact that our news operation had missed the news conference at which Sophia Loren introduced her new Coty fragrance, *Sophia*, to St. Louis. We learned later that before she dropped into St. Louis on her promotional tour, Boston, New York, and Chicago smelled of *Sophia*. But now, the Channel 4 newsroom was watching the five o'clock newscasts on our competitor stations in utter embarrassment at the fact that we had somehow blown this news conference. "How? How?

How?" we asked ourselves as we wept, wailed, and gnashed our teeth. And this story on which we were scooped did not seem to be a little event. As we watched on the TV monitors showing the others stations' early newscasts, we could tell that Famous-Barr's ninth-floor downtown auditorium appeared to be packed with Sophia worshippers. There were some later estimates that as many as three thousand fans turned out that day to ogle, and we also learned later that about six hundred of her gushing adorers were fortunate enough to get Ms. Loren's autograph. She gracefully, graciously, and glamorously affixed her signature for a full forty minutes. And we—the proud and sometimes boastful Channel 4 news—were left apparently "nursing at the last mammary position" . . . if you know what I mean.

As the luscious Loren appeared on the five o'clock newscasts of all our competitors, Channel 4 staffers knew, without immediate validation, that at least one head would have to roll for this slipup. Would it be one of the assignment editors? The executive producer? Our entertainment reporter? While the trial of the guilty party was only at the arraignment stage, heads that had latent potential to roll later huddled in emergency session. There *must* be some way to get Sophia on at least our big ten o'clock newscast.

"Hunter, aren't you and Helen Weiss good friends?" the news director yelled halfway across the newsroom as I was editing and proofreading aloud my anchor scripts for the upcoming six o'clock newscast. Helen was Famous-Barr's mercurial director of special events and a friend and neighbor. She was an incomparably gifted publicist for the department store chain who was reminiscent of the legendary studio drumbeaters of the Golden Era of Hollywood. She threw the grandest galas, and she got her product sold to all available print and broadcast media whether to show off her company or its stars and products in the brightest of spotlights.

"Yeah," I answered. "Helen's set me up on a lot of big interviews." As I walked toward the agitated war council, I added that Helen's husband was the executive producer of the late news at Channel 5 (where I had worked as a reporter/anchor for almost five years). "She lives down the street from me." (I had learned a lot from Dick Weiss, whose signature ventings of anger in the newsroom included the hurling of a chair or typewriter across the room for argument punctuation employing far more bravado than Bobby Knight's tosses.)

"Well, goddammit, get her on the phone and get Sophia on our air for ten!" the enraged, embarrassed newsroom boss ordered. "And I don't need to know how you get it. Just get it!"

Helen was May Company's venerable flack in St. Louis for decades. When she turned in her keys in 2007, she had worked for the department store chain for more than forty years. She had served Famous-Barr and May Company as the host of such luminaries as Joan Fontaine, Polly Bergen, Pearl Bailey, Lana Turner, Julia Child, and Bill Blass when they were in town to promote a product or book over the years. The adorable and always entertaining Helen was proudly everybody's Jewish mother, aunt, sister, or cousin. I always teased Helen about the fact that she should give me special media attention because I am *mishpocheh*—Yiddish for "member of the family." I was sure that our bond was set when I once caught Helen smuggling a ham out of Straub's. She had given me many a tip-off of spectacular special events during my career as a reporter/anchor at two local stations, and I promised not to turn her in to her rabbi for the ham handing.

I dialed Helen up.

"Hello," Helen answered in a tone that sounded unusually busy.

"Helen, Sweetheart . . . Julius. I'm . . ."

"Where were you guys today?" She sounded agitated. Wounded. Miffed.

"You know you were the only station not here this morning? All of them were here but you. What's going on at that place? How could you miss Sophia Loren, for Pete's sake?"

I've studied Yiddish for years, and I studied the Latin liturgy, and if there was a way to say "mea culpa" in Yiddish, I would have sprung it on my old friend at this point just to remind her that I was, indeed, *mishpocheh*. Part of the family.

"We . . . we . . . just blew it," I stammered. "I don't know how we missed it. But we did. Is there any way we can hook up with Sophia this evening for our ten o'clock? Just five minutes? Two minutes? I'll owe you forever if you can work something out. Please. Please. Save my butt. I even promise not to mention the ham to your rabbi," I tried desperately to lower the intensity of the justifiable scold.

"You missed a big one." Helen went on so as to drag out a much-deserved spanking of my wrists. "*E-ver-y*-bod-y else was here." Her emphasis was so heavy that it almost hurt. I got the message.

"But can you help me out, cousin? It's going to be my neck— no, my ASS—if I don't get Sophia on camera. Is she going to be anywhere else tonight? When's she going home?"

"I don't know, I don't know," she mused aloud. "My boss (Stanley Goodman) is throwing a private dinner party for her tonight on the *Robert E. Lee,* but there's no press—absolutely no working press—allowed. Let me make a call or two and get back to you in a minute."

"Please, please, please, Helen. You gotta help me out. I'll take you to a good dinner at Tony's if you can help me," I whimpered.

"I'll get back to you, Babe." And (CLICK!) she was gone.

The news director was hanging over my shoulder when I gave my best performance of the year, and he should have been convinced that I had given it my best shot. All we could do was wait for Helen's callback.

A good anchor has to read his/her script aloud prior to on-air presentation so as to hear how the words will sound to the viewers. I began to mumble my scripts as if they were recitations with holy beads. I was almost totally unaware of what I was reading. I was just chanting the stories mostly to calm my nerves.

I waited. Mumbled. Waited. Mumbled. Proofreading stories of crime, war, financial uncertainties, politics, and other stuff that didn't seem that day to rise to the level of what I hoped would be my catch-up one-on-one with a certain Italian superstar.

Finally . . . finally . . . my line buzzed! I snapped up the phone while motioning frantically to the news director to get over to my desk.

"Helen . . . Sweetheart . . . Darling . . . ," I greeted Helen as if I could lay some special mojo on her answer to my request. "Are you going to be able to get my tuchis out of a sling on this one?"

"Well, you guys don't deserve it, but can you be at the *Robert E. Lee* at 6:30 sharp?" she asked.

"I can't be there at 6:30 sharp 'cause you now I have to anchor the six o'clock news. I'll say goodnight at 6:30; be in my car at 6:31; on the riverfront four minutes later. We'll speed. Yes, we can be there at 6:35 sharp. I'll have my crew ready to roll as soon as I step off the set," I swore.

Helen had stipulations. "And don't bring one of those big vans with Channel 4 smeared all over it. I told the other stations *that managed to get there this morning* (she emphasized for effect one more time) that they couldn't come tonight. It's a private event. No media! But if you're here right after you get off the news, I think I can swing something for you."

"Helen, I love you! If you weren't married to Dick I would marry you tonight!" I laid it on heavy with Dear Helen as I gave my boss the thumbs up.

He and I quickly huddled. We took an oath that we wouldn't tell a soul. Not even the crew that would shoot the story with me. We knew that if news leaked—and it often did—we would blow our second chance. The news director would, without detail, order the ten o'clock producer to leave a two-minute block open in the first segment of that night's ten o'clock newscast without further specificity. We would not take chances. And everybody at every station was aware that there was at least one mole; at least one disgruntled staff person; at least one mischief maker who would be on the phone to the opposition in a New York Minute (obviously faster than a "St. Louis Minute").

The six o'clock news came and went, but not without taking my nerves with it. Said I to my viewers: "And that's the news for now. Thanks for getting your news from us. See you again tomorrow at five, six, and ten." I am more than positive that I began rising out of my seat and taking off my mike at about the time I had reached the word *See*. I raced down the long hallway to the lobby and then into the waiting unmarked newswagon, where my crew was dawdling.

"Where we going?" Dick Deakin, the photographer and driver asked.

"*Robert E. Lee*. Riverfront," I responded super laconically. "And we gotta get there fast, man! Fast," I cautioned.

I've always loved cobblestones, but I realized at this moment that driving over them can add nanoseconds to one's travel time. To say nothing of what the effect the rudely cut cobblestones had on jangled nerves. Or vertebrae.

"So, who are we doing?" Dick demanded. "We need to know how much equipment to bring in."

"Bring in everything you got," I said without giving the three crewmen any more information that that—strange way of doing business with teammates. "I need the Hollywood lighting tonight."

As Dick; Ray Hofstetter, the sound man; and Al Amann, the

lighting guy, unloaded the heavy equipment necessary to videotape an interview in the yesteryear era of television, I blurted
out: "Sophia Loren. We're doing Sophia Loren!" What a choice
of words.

I raced inside the restaurant door where Helen, looking as
fashionably attired as always, was waiting. I hadn't been dream-
ing. This *was* going to happen. Helen and I exchanged an appropriate European clasp and pressing of the cheeks.

"You made it. She's not here just yet. How long is it going to
take those guys to set up?" Helen asked.

"Ten seconds," I lied. "Ten seconds."

The room in which I was to have the exclusive with Sophia
was tiny. Not much bigger than a big broom closet or cloak-
room. But, hey, the smaller the room, the closer I'll get to un-
paralleled, radiant beauty. As it turned out, barely an inch would
stand between my nervous knees and the glamorous gams of the
statuesque goddess. Does it sound like I'm fawning all over her?
Damn right!

It's amazing how much equipment had to be lugged around
in the good old days of television news to get an interview. The
so-called "minicam" was not all that "mini" in its earliest days. I
don't know how those guys hauled all that stuff around all day.
The sound man had to schlep around a suitcase full of wires and
cables and microphones from lapel clip-ons to tabletop mikes.
And he seldom knew in advance how many speakers he would
have to mike up. And the light man carried a couple of cases of
lights and cables and batteries in those days. The light guy—and
there were no female techs in either the International Brotherhood of Electrical Workers or the Stagehands Union—lucked
out quite often. If the reporter and the photographer could
convince the interviewee that a nice outdoor setting would look
flatteringly better than a dull, boring, traditional, standard office
setting, valuable time could be saved. And often when my crew
and I were in a hurry, or learned that the interviewee's office was
on the twenty-second floor, or when it was a nice day, or when
it was the end of a day, the interviewee and his or her PR flack
could hear the most convincing argument of all times from not
one but four eloquent advocates of the wonders of nature and
the outdoor interview.

But we would *never* attempt to interview the great Sophia
Loren in a grimy riverfront setting with the Muddy Mississippi

River in the background. Break out the movie-set lighting, boys! And if we were interviewing her outside on the cobblestone levee, I'd be sure that we would soon be swamped with paparazzi and competing stations, and the coveted interview would no longer be exclusive.

As I paced back and forth just outside the interview closet, where there was no room to pace, I thought about the questions I would ask her. I remember reading on the wires about the tax problems Sophia and her husband, Carlo Ponti, were having in Italy. I remembered it was a conflict over mere peanuts—ten thousand bucks—that she was accused of owing in back taxes. Heck, I would have loaned her ten grand that very night—after the interview—if that would keep Her Royal Highness out of the calaboose—or *prigione,* or whatever they call jail in Italy. I wouldn't dare fire a question at *her* about her tax hassles. She's too much of a lady, and I'm too much of a gentleman to embarrass such a distinguished guest in my hometown.

Years after our encounters with Sophia, I sat at King Louie's bar to check notes with one of my favorite feature writers for the *St. Louis Post-Dispatch*, John McGuire. Helen Weiss had, as she often did, allowed a newspaper reporter or two to get an exclusive interview with one of her star guests before the TV and radio guys and gals were allowed to get their stories. The newspapers were always at a disadvantage since they came out only one time a day; TV had as many as five deadlines per day to meet. John got his opportunity in the morning before Sophia was thrown to the broadcast folks on the day she was in town.

Seems I fared a lot better with Loren than John had. And he was well aware of the reason for that. He told me he had gone for a hard news story spun off a story about a perfume and a movie goddess. McGuire learned that asking Sophia about her tax problems could have dire consequences. McGuire had been given the honors with Sophia just minutes before her grand entrance to meet the mob at Famous-Barr. In fact, my old buddy had been afforded a much more intimate setting to chat with La Loren. Helen had set it up for John to talk with Sophia in her suite on the seventeenth floor of the downtown Marriott Pavilion Hotel.

John acknowledges, even unto this very day, that he committed a regrettable number of fatal errors in trying to get a unique angle on what could have been just another powder puff celebrity interview. Like mine would be. And he had lost the interview as Sophia flew the coop in a snit.

"Barkeep, bring John and me another brew," I said as I wanted John to continue his tale of woe. John admitted that he could have been a bit more tactful. After all, she wasn't the secretary general of the United Nations.

As we commiserated at that bar years later, John told me: "I was just trying to ask her why grown men react to her like boys from a Catholic school attending their first party with girls from the all-girls school across town. The giddy boys mess up each other's hair; do hand stands; make faces; giggle."

Sophia responded rather coolly: "You will have to ask those people why they react to me that way. I can't answer that question. It is not for me to answer."

John's interview went downhill after that. He followed with a question about Sophia's tax problems back in Italy. Before John knew it, the interview was over.

I could count my lucky stars that my encounter with Sophia later that same day came out a lot more cordially. I think there are some times when softballs, rather than no game at all, is the way to go.

Back to the night of my big date with Sophia. It was now about 6:50 and no sign of Sophia on the *Robert E. Lee.* I am sure I was close to burning a hole in my watch and through my wrist as I kept checking the time. And then . . .

"She's here!" Helen shouted to me as I had made it down the hall to the southernmost part of my pacing track. I swung around and headed to the door as the crew packed into our tiny room.

I didn't go outside. Too nervous? Maybe. I peered through the door window. Or do they call it a "porthole" on a fake riverboat? What followed was a scene right out of a movie. And right out of my dreams. A shiny black block-long limo rolled up on cobblestones to my villa hideaway outside Rome where Sophia and I had our little tryst every Wednesday night at this time. The champagne was chilled; the fireplace roaring; the vanilla-scented candles flickered; the servants sent away for the night. My heart raced with excitement and anticipation as I hoped her heart would.

Alfredo, her trusted chauffeur of more than twenty years, was paid handsomely to keep his eyes diverted, his ear plugged, and most importantly, his mouth shut. Alfredo sprang from his door.

He was handsomely attired in his Alberto Cillini–designed livery outfit; his black polished boots and cap set down to the top of his Giorgio Armani dark glasses. As I adjusted my cravat and smoking jacket I was careful not to come outside to greet my love, lest potentially lurking paparazzi get the "money shot" of Sophia and me together. It was rumored that Carlo Ponti was on to us, but he was so engaged in his own assignations that he had no real time for investigation of Sophia's and my ever-increasing stolen moments together.

Alfredo, whom I had at one time considered a possible double agent also working for Ponti, moved quickly around back of the limo to the door through which my true love would emerge. On first glance through my window, I could not see her through the darkly opaque limo glass, but after the limo door was slowly opened, the camera and my eyes focus down to the cobblestone. Just like in the movies. A black designer shoe with stiletto point heel came down quietly on the pavement followed by that leg. That leg. That long, sleek, well-turned seemingly endless leg. Its sheer length was a heart-stopping precursor of much more loveliness to follow. She emerged in ballet-like slow motion. And then a long graceful arm and delicate hand appeared next, summoning Alfredo's extended arm and hand. (I had long ago dismissed my suspicions that the handsome and debonair Alfredo and my Sophia were having a secret affair.)

"Oh, good," I thought. "She was wearing those big clunky eyeglasses that hide her beauty as part of her disguise."

As Alfredo rushed to open the door of my villa, Sophia discreetly did not call out my name before she brushed ever so gently past me to enter our love nest.

Okay, okay. Daydream over! Return to reality. I elected not to have one of the crewmen give me a sharp slap across the cheek while shouting: "Julius. Julius. Wake up. Get a hold of yourself, man!"

Helen, the veteran hostess and PR maven, took charge.

"Welcome, Sophia. I hope you have had a relaxing day. I'd like you to meet a good friend of mine, Julius Hunter. He's from Channel 4, and he and his crew had a little accident this morning on the way to see you and missed your news conference."

"Bona . . . bona serra, Signora . . . uh . . . Sophia," I stumbled in basic pre-Berlitz Italian. Remember, I had picked up quite a bit of basic Italian during those two trips to Rome just two years before this special night with my Sophia. My fumbled attempt at being suave and debonair featured a greeting that would have to be cobbled together to make any sense. She extended her black-gloved hand, and I took it gently. I did not want to give her a manly hand mashing. And so, yes, I bent to kiss her outstretched hand. Not a real pressing, firm kiss. She smiled her approval. And then she took her hand back. Just in case I had not had enough hand. And I determined instantly that I would never again wash my right hand.

I motioned toward the closet studio and pointed to the chair procured from the restaurant's bar that would be her simple throne during my interview. Couldn't they have found something a bit more appropriate? I thought. Jewels. Precious metals. Ermine? Guess not.

Ray Hoftetter, the sound technician, nervously and delicately clipped Sophia's microphone on her dress. I had seen Ray clip microphones on hundreds of other interviewees in the past. No other clip-on seemed to require so many adjustments.

And then Al Amann, the lighting tech, clicked on the harsh lighting necessary in those days to get a good mini-cam picture. This was hardly "Hollywood" lighting. This was more like "Gobi Desert" illumination. Sophia gasped audibly at the light shock and then shaded her larger-than-life eyes ever so briefly. Then she said in a soft but declarative voice: "Mama mia! Thosa lightsa are so brighta!" Without missing a beat, I responded: "They *are* bright, Miss Loren. Believe it or not, when I started out in this business ten years ago, I used to be YOUR color!"

She let out a melodic little titter. She got the joke. I was pleased. My crew had heard lines like this from me before, so their reaction was more of a groan than a chuckle.

"I'm rolling," Dick tipped me. And now the questions. Those viewers familiar with my reporting over thirty-three years know that I can fire nuclear-tipped questions with the best of them. I've engaged tough cookies like Senator Stuart Symington, Spiro T. Agnew; Bob Dole; Barry Goldwater; incumbent Presidents Ford, Carter, Reagan, the first Bush, and Clinton; Harriett Woods; Senator Ted Kennedy; Pat Buchanan; and Mike Wallace in toe-to-toe verbal contact. But I could not find a single poisoned dart or curare-tipped arrow for this gracious, gorgeous, charming, suave, soft-spoken, gorgeous, dreamy-eyed, innocent-looking, non-combatant (did I say gorgeous?) beauty.

As I looked into the old question quiver I could find nothing but Cupid's arrows and softball questions for Her Loveliness. If critics wanted to give me demerits for going easy on Sophia, then let them go right ahead. They would be writing from a position of green-eyed envy on my interview with the most famous of green eyes.

I didn't learn anything earth shattering. She was very cautious in her answers. Probably because of the fact that English is her second language, and she is often asked questions she finds too personal— like those asked by a certain friend of mine who works for the *Post-Dispatch*. My viewers and I learned or had it reconfirmed that her favorite actor *might* be frequent co-star and paisano Marcello Mastroianni; but, she told me she considered Cary Grant a dear friend. Her favorite pastime, I was informed, is watching football ("you call it soccer"), especially her favorite team, *Napoli.* Her favorite food is really spaghetti—that's not just a joke she makes. She told me she could eat small portions of pasta three times a day. Just watch the sauces, she said. And her happiest moment, she confided, *might* be her acceptance of the Academy Award nineteen years earlier for her role in *Two Women.* So you can see, this was far from an interrogation. Not one mention of her tax troubles, and I didn't know at the time of the interview about the purported whole body dips she takes in olive oil. No way could that be *extra virgin* olive oil, I was sure. Yes, I was more Larry King than Mike Wallace that night. But check out what being nice got me.

With the ten-minute interview concluded and the bright lights turned off, I thanked the leggy lovely leading lady for allowing us the opportunity to talk with her, and I watched as Ray gently and meticulously removed Sophia's microphone. Lucky devil.

A banquet room with several hundred VIP guests of the May Company and Famous-Barr eagerly awaited my Sophia's arrival as guest of honor. Helen Weiss—ever full of surprises—said to me as if I had missed a previously arranged cue: "Well, Julius, aren't you going to escort Miss Loren into the banquet room?"

Ever the suave, cool, calm, and collected gentleman reporter, I stuttered: "Uh, what? Uh . . . well, yes. Yes. I . . . uh . . . er . . . would be delighted! Miss Loren?" I offered her my right arm, which I later determined must have been developed in vitro specifically for this moment in my life.

And so we strode—as if we had done this together before— on a grand promenade toward the noisy dining room. A smiling waiter bowed courteously and then opened the door to the banquet room for us. There was, unfortunately, no fanfare to announce our arrival. But something magical and even weird happened next. The Dixieland band that was playing an up tempo ditty ground to a complete shutdown, and the Dixielanders appeared to lead the ripple of gaping mouths in the banquet room. And, in fact, the room got absolutely quiet with nobody's signal. As they used to say in my old neighborhood, "You could have heard a mouse wet on cotton." Make it ermine, in this case.

With Sophia beaming radiantly, and with me smiling nervously, I escorted Sophia to the table to which Helen directed us. I pulled back my "date's" chair and gingerly pushed it in as the hush continued over the room. All eyes were on us, no doubt about it.

I then moved around to offer my hand for her to place her hand on mine. I gave her a courteous light kiss on her right hand, and suddenly, the room erupted in thunderous applause and wild cheers and even whistling. Mine was chivalry at its most efficacious. I could have announced my candidacy for mayor in that room that night. And I would have won if ballots could have been counted on the spot.

As with the initial greeting kiss on Sophia's hand, the second was also more of a "buss" than a lip smack. No, it was not a slurp. But this was the second time in one night I had touched the hand of this pulchritudinous priestess. I gave Sophia a gentleman's bow as I thanked her again and backed away from the table as if I had been groomed to do that. "*Arrivederci,*" I offered, having learned that farewell from the song that wished arrivederci to Rome. She just smiled and nodded gently as you might expect a demure lady to do. What gorgeous teeth!

As I wheeled around, hoping that my heart would now settle down as I walked away, I heard a soft accented voice behind me calling out to me in a velvet tone:

"Uh, Giulio . . . Giulio . . ."

I turned around. It was Sophia. I imagined she was calling out my name to ask if she could be with me forever. I imagined that she was not ready to have our wonderful time together end so early. I imagined that she wanted to invite me to her hotel suite after the banquet for a nightcap.

Silly man.

"Yes?" I responded.

"Whata time isa thisa going to be on TV tonight?"

I could not believe my ears. This international film star, recognized in every corner of the civilized world, wanted to know what time the minute-and-a-half piece would air on my newscast.

"Uh," I answered, "it will be on tonight at ten."

"Thanka you," she said almost inaudibly with that alluring smile.

I must confess that I have never been so shaken up by an interview in all my life. I have put on my oxygen mask and interviewed people in extremely high places. Check out some of the other names I've interviewed in this book's index. I've reported via satellite in cities from Rome to Los Angeles. I have been in life-threatening situations during my tenure in television news—I had even climbed onto the tippy-top of the Arch when the strobe light was installed—but I have never been as discombobulated by an interviewee as I was with Sophia.

On the news that October night in 1980, I was nothing short of blithering. On *all* the stories I reported on. It was so noticeable that my often unbridled co-anchor, Steve Schiff, said—on the air—after I had presented a very short segment of my interview with Ms. Loren: "Jules, my man, you look a little rattled . . ."

"I apologize, pal," I admitted. "You've obviously not sat knee-to-knee with Sophia Loren before. We'll be back with a lot of less exciting stuff after this."

SUPERFAN

My grand finale with Sophia in the *Robert E. Lee* banquet room included one more reportable event that made history. It's a story about one of my print cousins, *Post-Dispatch* city editor and columnist, Harry Levins. Old Harry had written a September 19, 1996, column about his fascination with Sophia from the first time he had noticed her:

"Actually, our relationship began in the Paramount Theater in Rutland, Vermont, on a November afternoon in 1958," Harry told me. "I was in high school and Loren was in *Houseboat*. She reached off the screen and touched my soul, flicking away earlier schoolboy crushes on such lesser goddesses as Virginia Mayo and Rosemary Clooney.

Sophia was The Real Thing, and remains so."

When Harry got the assignment to meet Sophia and do a feature on her, he admits that the opportunity "changed my life."

Harry was at the banquet at which I escorted Sophia to her table and confirmed in his column that when somebody saw Sophia making her entrance (with me), "the reception's Dixieland band suddenly ran down into silence, as if somebody pulled a plug on a record player." (A good newspaper reporter would never acknowledge a TV reporter's presence as being anything near significant in a happening like this.) Harry dismisses his failure to recognize yours truly as Sophia's escort in a statement he gave to *Post-Dispatch* columnist Bill McClellan: "I didn't notice (Julius). She could have been with Winston Churchill, and I wouldn't have noticed." See? I'm *still* just a parenthetical entity to Levins in this Sophia story.

Harry's column on Sophia continued: "In truth, she radiated a force field. When we (Harry and Sophia) were introduced, she clasped my hand and said, 'Very pleased to meet you.' I replied, 'A-bah, a-bah, a-bah.'"

After dinner, when Sophia arose—obviously to rush back to her hotel room to watch her interview with me—that sly and cunning Harry Levins watched like a hawk as Sophia dabbed her lips with her cloth napkin and that napkin dropped beneath the table.

As Sophia left the table, Harry lost all couth, all decorum, all dignity, all dinner table manners he had learned as a child, all rules of etiquette, and this grown man literally dove under the table. In his words: "I crawled like an animal beneath her table to snatch that linen napkin." And what did Harry's colleague and buddy, John McGuire, think of the spectacle? Harry says: "I mortified John by rooting about. I didn't care. I had the napkin, with it voluptuous lipstick stain."

And Harry STILL has the napkin with Sophia's luscious full lipstick print still vivid nearly thirty years after he "liberated" it from under Sophia's banquet table. The sacred artifact is his own personal version of the Shroud of Turin. He will not say much about where he stores it. Safety deposit box? Shoebox under his bed? Buried in a coffee can under his rosebushes? Nor was he willing to discuss any line of possession succession—and whether McGuire and I hold a place in that line. But he did allow McGuire, Bill McClellan, and I to view it as we gathered for a toast to Sophia recently at P.J.'s Bar in Kirkwood. And he did let me have a photo for this book of him clutching the notorious napkin.

But that's it. I wasn't allowed to hold the napkin in my own hot little hands.

McClellan noted in a *Post-Dispatch* column about a reunion of us three old coots who are, in any order you want to list us, president, treasurer, and secretary of Sophia's St. Louis fan club. I've not been able to bring the proposal to the floor for a vote, but I propose calling our little club "Fans of Sensuous Sophia Loren Evermore." The acronym would describe Harry, John, and me perfectly: "FOSSLE." Bill observed in his column: "Loren celebrated her seventy-third birthday last month. Being guys, Levins, McGuire, and Hunter are still fifteen."

OPRAH

Okay, okay. I don't have a clue as to how much Oprah weighs today, nor can I say for sure how many diet plans she has been on since she started alerting us every time she decided to shed some pounds. In May of 2008, she was telling all her fans that she was going to embark on a twenty-one-day diet that would allow her to consume no animal products, caffeine, sugar, gluten, or alcohol. This particular weight loss program is taken from a book by Kathy Freston called *Quantum Wellness*. The book caused Oprah and, perhaps, hundreds of thousands of her fans world-wide, to take a quantum leap into lean.

At the conclusion of the twenty-one-day sojourn Oprah reported no specific weight loss but claimed she was "baptized in vegan land."

Long before the word *Oprah* was as much a household word as *air, water*, or *iPod*, I not only had the privilege of interviewing her, but I also took her out to dinner.

The TV diva was in St. Louis and at Channel 4 in 1987 to promote her show, which had just gone into national syndication with King World. Most viewers of this interview on our five o'clock newscast would not have been able to pick Oprah out of a lineup. She was just beginning her ascent to becoming the highest paid woman in showbiz with 9 million daily viewers and a fortune that *Forbes* magazine estimates at $1.5 billion.

Oprah was apparently not a dynamo back in the day, and she was not exactly an overnight success. My friend, Phyllis Ward, worked as a documentary producer at Baltimore's WJZ, the Westinghouse TV station at which Oprah co-hosted a morning show. Phyll remembers Oprah as a young woman who was not so self-assured and who was conscientious of her rotund figure. WJZ had tried to give Oprah a makeover. According to my friend, Oprah was sometimes down in the dumps about not being able to find any guys to date. A WJZ producer, Debbie DiMaio, who had become a friend of Oprah's at the Baltimore station, landed a job with WLS in Chicago. And soon thereafter, DiMaio suggested to Oprah that she apply for a vacated job as a co-host of *AM Chicago*.

Phyllis tells me that she was just one of many friends Oprah consulted about taking the chance on the big jump to Chicago. Phyllis says, in short, she told Oprah that "she would be crazy to stay in Baltimore." Oprah applied, and WLS station management decided to take a chance on the relative newcomer to TV co-hosting. Soon, Oprah was up against the popular Phil Donohue in his own hometown, and in some ratings periods she began to beat Phil. And the rest is spectacular history.

Following my interview, as Oprah was taking off her microphone, I whispered to her that I'd like to take her and her friends out to dinner at my restaurant, J. Hunter's, which was a few blocks west of the television station. To my surprise, she accepted the invitation. Oprah had to sit around the station and wait for me to finish the six o'clock newscast. An hour's wait. No problem.

I suppose the invitation did not appear to be lechery, and she was accompanied by a couple of members of her entourage. After the newscast, we walked down to the Creole/Cajun-themed restaurant, where Oprah was given free reign of the menu. I instructed my cook to prepare a sampler of some of the house specialties, since Oprah could not decide on a single entrée.

And for dessert? She concocted this off-the-menu caloric treat: our famous "Mississippi Mud Cake" topped with "quadruple" chocolate sauce, then French vanilla ice cream, and crowned with fresh blueberries. Yum-yum. Avoid the scale for a couple of days!

Our dinner, and dessert, was a short time before Oprah went on the celebrated liquid protein diet that carved off sixty-seven Winfrey pounds, which she had hated since she asked my friend Phyllis if she should dare try her luck in Chicago. The Queen of Daytime TV dragged a little red wagon full of sixty-seven pounds of disgusting animal fat onto the set of her TV show. It was her highest rated show to date, but Oprah expressed almost immediate remorse for the shtick. From her own lips: "I starved myself for four months, not a morsel of food to get into that pair of size 10 Calvin Klein jeans. Two hours after that show, I started eating to celebrate. Of course, within two days the jeans no longer fit." A year later, she had gained back seventeen of those sixty-seven pounds. Pass the Mississippi Mud Cake topped with the chocolate sauce, extra ice cream, and fresh blueberries, please.

Meanwhile, back at J. Hunter's . . . a comfortable time had elapsed since the "substantial" Oprah had the last bite of the special sampler laid out before her. We really didn't need to wash her dinner plates. They were clean as a whistle! I then invited Ms. Winfrey into my luxurious bar area for a cocktail. She chose some non-alcoholic beverage. As I looked around the rather crowded bar, there was nobody who seemed to be overwhelmed by the presence of the superstar-to-be. It also appeared to me that she was looking around in a little anticipation that some of the bar patrons would approach her. A few did, but none asked for an autograph. She had received an Oscar nomination for Best Supporting Actress in her role as Sofia in *The Color Purple*. But my bar patrons may have been seeing colors of a different shade that evening: like pink elephants; or seeing red that they had been chewed out by the boss that day; or being green with envy that the accountant over there that they had a crush on was drooling over another woman at the bar. But purple? Nope. I had to scurry back to the station to get ready for the ten o'clock newscast, so I excused myself, bid my guest and company adieu, and Oprah's tiny entourage made arrangements for her to get back to her hotel.

In retrospect, there are several monumental anomalies in the encounter I had with Oprah Winfrey.

1. Can you imagine the Oprah Winfrey of today WAITING AN HOUR for me to get off work to take her to dinner? Hell, I don't even think she would wait for her boyfriend, Stedman, or gal pal, Gayle, that long!

2. Can you imagine Oprah eating a dessert like the one she created at my restaurant anywhere in public these days? And if she did, can you see the tabloid headlines:

TV DIVA DITCHES DIET, DIVES DEEP IN DESSERT DISH

3. And finally, can you imagine Oprah sitting and dining in any restaurant or bar in the entire world without being mobbed?

This story has a postscript. About five weeks after my "date" with Oprah, my wife, Barbara, and our two daughters were doing some Christmas shopping in Chicago. At a department store, the three spotted, of all people, Oprah, who might have been shopping not far from her apartment or studio.

Jennifer and Julia—typical teenagers—begged their mother not to try to speak to Oprah. I can just hear them pleading: "Mom, mom. Don't say anything to her. Mom, don't embarrass us!"

Barb is cool. She has only been bowled over one time that I know of with all the celebrities she has met over the years. Once when Lou Rawls, our buddy Wayman Smith, and I were running around one evening, Lou said he desperately needed to have one of the beverages he touted publicly in words and song. So, I suggested we run into my nearby house to get a cold Bud for the parched Lou Rawls. In my home's large foyer with the high ceiling, Lou gutturally uttered but a few booming basso profundo words: "Nice pad you got here, Brother. How long you been living here?" Those words thundered through the house, causing a seismic effect rattling the dishes and windowpanes and rolling up the shades. Barbara came bounding down the winding staircase and sang, "I KNOW whose voice that is. Welcome, Lou." Her prescience was rewarded with a big hug and a "Hello, Dahlin'" from Lou.

But, Oprah Winfrey? I would have bet a Bud that she would not have been fazed at all. Jen and Julia told me they clinched their teeth and braced themselves as Barbara walked up to the TV star and said, "Hi, Ms. Winfrey. My name is Barbara Hunter. My husband, Julius Hunter, interviewed you on his newscast when you were in St. Louis a few weeks ago. And then, I believe, he took you to his restaurant for dinner."

The girls swear that Ms. Winfrey looked totally perturbed and snorted, "Yes. Thank you!" And then, the wary witnesses say, Oprah moved quickly away from the offending conversationalist to another aisle in the store. Hers was not even a response that was a sequitur to Barbara's introductory greeting.

"Aw, Mom. Mommmmm. We told you not to say anything to her, Mommmmm," our daughters spilled out in overlaying sentences of sheer teen embarrassment. The ends of the two-syllable word *Mommmmm* were turned up with all of the frustration two teens can muster.

To this day, my family and I surprise and send each other into grins, giggles, and sometimes even into hysterics by punctuating a sentence uttered by one of us with a snappy and cold response from the other, "Yes. Thank you!" Like at the supper table. "Would you like some more mashed potatoes?" "Yes. Thank you!" "Is this your coat or mine?" "Yes. Thank you!"

"Shall I turn off this TV? You're dozing." "Yes. Thank you!"

MEDIA PERSON
OF THE YEAR

I was duly honored when the Press Club of Metropolitan St. Louis named me Media Person of the Year in 1993. The award, as the Press Club describes it, "recognizes distinguished men and women from St. Louis media whose exemplary performance establishes standards of professional conduct." Some heavy-hitters had preceded me as honorees, including Joe Pulitzer, Jr., the great public relations genius; Al Fleishman; KMOX Radio Czar Robert Hyland, and sportswriters extraordinaire Bob Broeg and Bob Burnes.

One who is gracious and humble does not look a gift award in the mouth, but I was initially concerned about the location the awarders had picked: The American Theater, a venue reopened after having been shuttered for a number of years. My friends and family who turned out to hear me get savaged were going to be paying one hundred dollars a plate for the privilege. To my knowledge, there was no regular food service in the venerable old theater.

Because I am an imperfect perfectionist, I was concerned about the inability of some of my family and friends to pay the hefty price tag. So, I sniffed out those close to me who needed me to pay for their tickets. Confidentially, the number got to be rather large. That meant that I was paying for people to come out to honor me as if they were shelling out their own dough to celebrate my honor.

I then learned about something that heightened my anxieties regarding the big event. I found out that some of my old friends in the Stagehands Union were planning to picket the theater because the Press Club planners had flat out refused to pay for two guys to man spotlights for the event. I was, at first word, totally incredulous that my old stagehand friends would be so unkind as to sabotage my big night. After all, the Stagehands Union Local 6 was ubiquitous in my public career. In my earliest days, there were at least two stagehands with me every time I covered a story. The Stagehands Union had the authority to set up the lights and run the sound equipment on news stories for years and years. The two stagehand positions, plus a photographer, constituted the old TV news crew. I traveled with these guys, ate with the guys, drank with these guys, caught cat naps with these guys on overnight stakeouts, joked with these guys, got pissed off with these guys, looked after the welfare of these guys, and was often protected by these guys— every workday of the year. And now, their union was going to picket my big night?

And members of the Stagehands Union were also the labor force that set up and maintained the great stage at the Muny Opera, and did the set-ups and take-downs on the stage where the world-renowned St. Louis Symphony Orchestra made beautiful music at Powell Hall. The stagehands even worked the American Theater in its heyday. Legend has it that the stage-hands held the exclusive rights in any of their jurisdictions to repair a woman's broken heel, which I would imagine happened more often in the nineteenth century than in the twentieth.

And this really disturbed me about the planned protest: I learned that the head of the local Stagehands Union was a kid who had come into the ranks as a near-teen and had been slipped into the union as somebody's brother, brother-in-law, cousin, uncle, neighbor, or best buddy. That is how the Stagehands Union maintained its remarkable homogeneity—a word I would dare not use around some of my best buddies in the union for fear a misunderstanding of the meaning of the word might incite violence.

Anyway, this young kid that I once mentored as he toted around his case of microphones or lights initially didn't know his pass from a pole in the ground. When he and his wife gave birth to their first kid, I autographed a copy of one of my children's alphabet books for the newborn. When I learned that his wife, quite sadly, had a debilitating illness, I ALWAYS asked about her health out of genuine concern. So, I knew all this stuff about picketing the American Theater on my big night had to be some kind of misunderstanding. I rang up Gene, now the head

Julius Hunter

March 4, 1993

stagehand, to get to the straight skinny of the story from the once-skinny kid.

"So, Gene," I asked in my phone call. "How's the family? How's your wife?"

"Oh, she has her good days and bad days," he offered. "How you been doin'?"

"Let me ask you how your kid is doing first."

"He's growing like a weed. He's seventeen years old now."

"You gotta be kiddin' me," I said. "Glad to know everybody's okay."

"And you?" young Gene asked.

"I'm not so good, to be very honest with you, Gino."

"What's wrong?"

"Gene, buddy, pal, I just heard a nasty rumor that your guys are going to picket the American Theater on March 4—my Media Person of the Year Award night. Tell me that can't be true, Gene."

"Well," Gene said with a little hesitancy that might have been interpreted as a little embarrassment, "We tried to tell those Press Club people that they would need to hire two of our guys to run the spotlights. And . . . well, well . . . they not only said they would not put two guys on the thing . . . they wouldn't even talk to us anymore."

"So, you're going to picket? Picket my event? Embarrass me like that?"

"Jules, we gotta do it. I mean we're losing jurisdiction all over the place. Our guys gotta eat, too, you know."

"Okay, okay. How much money are we talking about here, Gene?"

I had expected some exorbitant amount of money.

"We're talking about just fifty dollars a man, that's all."

"That's all?" I asked incredulously. "One hundred dollars for the entire night?"

"Yep, that's all," Gene said. "A hundred bucks."

"Where can I send you a check?" I offered in sheer relief.

Gene gave me an address, and I went right away and mailed him a check to pay for two spotlightists for the entire night. Each time they blinded the roasters and me during the evening, I thought of the bright lights as a warm glow of labor peace and tranquility.

The oddest thing happened on the night before and on the actual day of the banquet/roast. Friends started phoning me—I counted seven different people—to tell me they were not going to be able to attend the roast. One dear friend phoned me within an hour of my leaving home for the American to say she just couldn't spare the one hundred dollars for the event. Is that what Emily Post would have us do when we need to decline a formal invitation? Phone a friend within an hour of an event in his honor to tell him that we will not be there? I was actually depressed about the last-minute no-show notices as I went out the door to go downtown for the event. Wouldn't it have been kinder to send me a note a week before? Or send me a note of regrets two days before the program to tell me that they are sorry that they were not able to make it (for unspecified reasons). I wish the friend who said she couldn't afford the one hundred bucks had told me a few days before the event. I probably would have added her to the roll; added her to the dole.

There were also a few out-of-town family members and friends that I wanted to attend, so I wired them money for plane tickets. And I thought I should buy at least a table of ten so the Press Club folks wouldn't think I'm a cheapskate. Cha-Ching! That was fifteen hundred dollars for the table alone.

I didn't want the place to be empty on my big night. I knew I had pissed off at least one person for every one I charmed over the years. I tried to do a calculation in my head and decided that I would beef up the number of invitees—at my own expense, of course. So, several weeks before the roast I got the Press Club to give me a big stack of the formal invitations to mail out. I would pay for postage. Cha-Ching! Add postcard postage to the price of the honor.

I thought I would have a limo pick up my good friend, and one of the roasters, Ed Rollins, at the airport. Once when he was working in the Reagan White House, Ed had sent a Secret Service car and driver to pick me up at the airport when I arrived in D.C. No kidding. Can you imagine what a scandal that might create today? Sending a limo for him on the night of my roast was the least I could do. And I would want the limo to drive my personal party of friends that night. Add the cost of the limo to my running tab.

And then I noted that my tuxedo was a little snug. So, what the heck! I had time to buy a new one and get it tailored. To be honest, my patent leather formal shoes looked a little ratty with the latest-up-to-the-datest tux. So I went out and bought new formal shoes. And a new formal shirt, too. And I also decided I could use a more prestigious pair of cuff links. I was out shopping already anyway. How much is my bill at this point? But who's counting?

That night, with no pickets out front, I was honored to have the great Bob Costas as the host. Bob wrote a complimentary blurb for this book at my request. I caught him just before he shut himself away to study up for his major anchor role with the '08 Olympics. Did I screw up when I asked Bob to emcee the roast? Although all the roasters at the head table had been given the word on wearing black tie, nobody, including the roastee had told Bob about formal dress for the stage party. He reminded the audience of that great line from yesteryear comedian George Goebel: "Ever feel like all the world is a tuxedo, and you're a pair of brown shoes?"

I think I had too many roasters. A lot of my old buddies. Frat brothers. Teachers. There were some good zingers. But maybe too many of them. While some of the cracks were funny, some cut rather close to the bone. My elderly mother, ill from the rarest meat she had eaten in her life, and not quite understanding of the good-natured humor inside the barbed remarks, had to be taken to the hospital the next day. Her doctor told me that her malady could have been the rare meat, but it was more than likely just frayed nerves over all those people saying all those nasty things about her only begotten son. I tried to explain to her after the event that they were just kidding. Or were they?

I remember that the three people who went with me in my limo and I were still hungry when we left the roast at the American. Our fifteen-hundred-dollar meal was just not enough—like the proverbial Chinese meal. So, I had the limo driver take us to one of the city's most posh after-hours dinery: White Castle. And since we were in a stretch limo I thought it was only appropriate that we go through the drive-through. We got a ton of belly-bombers to go. I picked up the tab for the late night snack, of course.

Next morning, I felt honored. I felt hung over. I felt relieved. And I felt broke.

What a night!

COLONEL SANDERS AND ME

Remember back in the day when guys wore their baseball caps with the bills turned to the front, when TV dinners were still eaten in front of TVs, and when "KFC" was still lovingly called by the long form, "Kentucky Fried Chicken?" Well, those were the days when KMOX-TV ruled the waves as the first television station in the nation to take the revolutionary step of scrapping its use of film. Videotape—and what became known as ENG, Electronic News Gathering—were the exciting, challenging, and innovative alternative. Without getting bogged down with the technical explanation of this innovation, let's suffice it to say that after shooting a story in the field news crews no longer had to race the 16-millimeter film to a lab, wait for the film to "go through the soup," run the film back to the station, and then edit the film for broadcast.

Live mini-cams were used to shoot a picture and send it back through a microwave dish on the top of the news vans to a relay antenna on strategic rooftops that bounced the picture back to the station in real time. This meant that as a reporter covered a major fire, a news conference, or an air show, the video was being seen back at the station by editors, who worked on the video while the event was still occurring. The station had the option of showing viewers the video "raw" and "live," or a reporter's piece could be fully edited and ready for air by the time he or she came in from the field.

Channel 4 was one of the five CBS "owned and operated" stations in those halcyon and totally anti-trust days when ownership was limited to just five TV stations or five radio stations. CBS owned and operated stations in New York, Philadelphia, Chicago, St. Louis, and Los Angeles. KMOX-TV, the smallest in the family, was considered the "baby" station and the test market for all the latest gadgetry, hardware, and formats. Under the able and creative leadership of station general manager and CBS vice president, Tom Battista, Channel 4 led the world in the implementation of ENG.

Those of us who were in at the beginning of ENG at KMOX-TV used to joke that if something new and revolutionary hit the market, CBS would buy it and try it out first at Channel 4. If it worked, our four sister stations would have it post-haste. If it flopped, the other four stations would never even hear of it. The fact that Channel 4 was CBS's test market meant that the other TV stations in St. Louis had to stay on their toes and stretch their budgets to the breaking point to stay competitive. Channels 2, 5, 11, and 30 were either affiliate stations of their networks or they were privately owned. Viewers in St. Louis were, without a doubt, the clear winners in this hot competition. They were seeing and hearing the freshest news of viewers in any city in the world—watching news *while* the news was happening.

While our station's ability to beam back live pictures was an important advancement for the world of broadcast communications, those of us who helped pioneer the mode had to wade through obstacles while challenging the intelligence of our viewing audiences on a daily basis.

In the earliest of days, we would cover anything live, just because we could. We used to joke that if a fly flew in front of one of our ENG crews while they were having lunch, they'd radio into the newsroom, and we would cover the "event" live. Because we could.

That's the way I felt about the assignment I was given shortly after I came over to Channel 4 from Channel 5. An assignment editor with whom I didn't share a close personal relationship slated me to go across the street one day to Stouffer's Riverfront Inn to interview, of all people, Colonel Harlan Sanders, the founder of the Kentucky Fried Chicken empire.

I was particularly bothered by the assignment for a number of reasons. First of all, I was in the midst of covering a story with much more substance. Secondly, I thought covering a fried chicken king just because he was right across the street was a poor use of our new microwave capabilities. And the third reason I was opposed to the assignment is that I was, even early on in my career, very guarded against demeaning my own image and the image of my race. I would, for example, never agree to be a judge in a watermelon-eating contest. And as an anchor, I never allowed a KKK logo to appear as the graphic behind my head.

So, in all due respect to the kindly old gentleman whose social philosophies I was not aware of, I thought that it was not good for my reportorial image to stand next to a Southern, white-suit-wearing, fried chicken magnate.

I challenged the assignment and told the assignment editor, in no uncertain terms, that he could take the assignment and stick it some place far away from the bright newsroom lights. So, on appeal, I stormed into the news director's office. At the time—and for a very brief time—that news executive was Herb Humphries, a Texas expatriate who made no bones about his racist upbringing. He attempted to cover this racism with joking and suggesting that racists were everywhere, and he was just one who didn't hide it and he wouldn't violate any obvious civil rights, he claimed.

The assignment editor must have phoned Herb ahead of my arrival to warn him that a storm was heading his way, because no sooner as I had darkened Herb's door (as he would have joked about the word "darkened"), he said without even looking up: "You're going to do it, Julius."

I didn't even argue. I just spun on my heels and started toward the newsroom door. Aware that my colleagues were following this reenactment of the Civil Rights Movement, I yelled on the way out, "Anybody got any ideas on what this black reporter can ask this finger lickin' plantation owner?"

Pat Emory, the station's star anchor and perennial *enfant terrible,* yelled across the newsroom, "Hey, Jules, ask him if he ever screwed a chicken!"

As I pushed through the exit door, I issued a universally known hand and finger gesture to Patrick that might have led him to believe that his suggestion was No. 1 in my estimation.

After I huffed across the street, I pondered just what, short of Pat's suggestion, I might ask the colonel. He was in town to talk to senior citizens about the importance of staying active and pursuing new goals even at an advanced age. Laudable cause. Could I make it work?

I was ushered out onto the hotel's rear patio area where, lo and behold, there he was—a guy I had only seen on commercials and on fried chicken tubs. It was really kind of weird and spooky approaching him and extending my hand for a shake without fries. The congenial old gent was comforting in his Southern charm, whether or not he cared viscerally that a black dude had been sent to interview him.

I must confess that the colonel looked markedly different up close than I had perceived him on TV and on those millions of commercial portraits. To be honest, and not intentionally demeaning, the white hair on his head and his beard was more yellowed than white. The perceived crispy white suit had some traces of extra crispy chicken and blotches of what I was sure was chewing tobacco or gravy stains on it. The suit reminded me of the color white paper turns if left out in the sun for seventy years. Yet his eyes smiled through very thick glasses.

News Director Herb Humphries, at left, and Anchor Pat Emory at KFWB Radio in L.A., 1968 (before either came to Channel 4).

An adoring clump of senior citizens looked on as I introduced myself and began my interview. It was they whom he was valiantly attempting to steer away from the Grim Reaper sitting in the Old Rocking Chair. For openers, I asked him how he had started his kingdom and learned that he had used a one hundred-dollar social security check to start the company when he was in his forties. That's an inspiration in itself for older Americans.

I noticed that after I asked him how often he ate his fried chicken, he was rather vague but courteous to the brand. Great answers on the first two questions, but I felt—especially in retrospect—that he fudged a bit on a full endorsement of the company, which was delivering to him his daily bread, and gravy and coleslaw and mashed potatoes as side dishes to the fried fowl. I later learned that the guy I interviewed under original protest was having one heck of an ongoing battle with Heublein, the company that had bought out the Kentucky Fried Chicken brand name in 1971 for $280 million. The colonel had sued Heublein about four years before I met him for cranking out a lot of products under his name that he had never even seen before. And in 1975, during the time I was interviewing him, Heublein was suing the fried chicken company namesake for claiming that a lack of Heublein quality control had created a gravy that tasted like "wallpaper paste." No wonder he was chicken about telling me how much of the company fried chicken he ate. Blasting Heublein during my interview might have cost the colonel a wing and a leg.

Oh, well, the interview ended with my asking: "Colonel, just between you and me—and I won't tell anybody, you can just whisper it to me if you want: What are the secret ingredients of your finger lickin' good recipe?"

The nice old guy just chuckled appropriately at my intentionally absurd question. And that was a good place to end the live interview with the gentleman that my sainted grandmother—who lived to be 102—swore was the spitting image of my great-great granddaddy. My great-great grandpop, ironically or not, was born a slave in *Kentucky* in 1825, sixty-five years earlier than Colonel Sanders was born in Kentucky. Hmmmmm.

I thanked the colonel and pitched back to Pat Emory in the studio. Pat did what caused terror in the heart of every reporter signing off live in the field:

Pat: *"Uh, Jules, before you get away . . ."*

Hunter: *"Yes, Pat?"* I responded with dread and an unsettling premonition.

Pat: *"Did you ask the colonel if he has any colorful and interesting chicken stories?"*

Hunter: *"He has thousands . . . too many to report here. Now back to you, Pat."*

With the interview over and a sense of relief that I had survived the "Pat Pat," I thanked the colonel and headed back to the newsroom. In transit, I couldn't help but mull over the doppelganger similarities between Colonel Harlan Sanders and my ancestor Ned Rounds. Hmmmmmm.

SHORT TAKES

A SHOW-STOPPING CHANNING PLUG

I loved the years in which Channel 4 allowed us anchors to interview guests live on the set in the newsroom. Remember, Channel 4 in St. Louis was the first TV news operation in the world to scrap the fancy designer sets and do the news *au naturelle* right in the newsroom. That was to give viewers the feeling that the news was hot—right from the source.

What viewers saw was, for some, too much to take in with the ambient newsroom sounds and busy-body background. Directly behind the news anchors who could be delivering a story about violence in Venezuela, a raging inferno in an old shoe factory, or Wall Street jitters, viewers could see staffers animatedly discussing story presentation; a paper airplane sailing from the sports guy to a reporter pounding out a story; to, in one case, the assignment editor being fired by a news director who had obviously watched umpires kick managers out of baseball games.

With this frenetic scenery in the background, viewers were treated to live interviews with Gregory Hines, Carol Channing, Gregory Peck, Julio Iglesias, Johnny Cochran, Oprah Winfrey, Regis Philbin, Dan Rather, Angie Dickinson, Milton Berle, and many, many more.

All were promoting something, selling something, or trying to slow their shuffle into that dark night called obscurity.

One of my most memorable interviews was the live on-set chat with Carol Channing. She was an adorable guest who exuded more bubbles and banter than many. I was most shocked seeing her up close and personal by the way her facial cosmetic makeup is painted on her face. Close up, Ms. Channing's makeup looks like that of a circus clown in a very distinctive red diamond with her nose at the center. But on the screen—TV and movie—the odd makeup just highlights her eyes and nose. I think the way she applies it makes her nose look more pixie-like. If you look closely, you can see the rather odd makeup pattern.

One of the highlights of my interview with her related to the fact that I owned a fine dining restaurant right down the street from

Ms. Channing's unusual makeup pattern is noticeable in a close-up.

the station. I had mentioned that fact to her in the warm-up. During the interview, after she told me about her appearance in *Hello, Dolly!* at the Muny Opera in St. Louis, she nearly knocked me off my anchor perch when I asked her: "So, Carol, where do you go from here?" Normally, when I ask a live guest that question, they say something like: "From here, I go to the Tivoli Theater in Gainesville where I'm opening tomorrow night." But Carol Channing's answer was: "Why, I'm going to J. Hunter's Restaurant down the street, of course! The food is fabulous there!" When I recovered from the unsolicited commercial from this international and beloved star of stage, screen, and radio, I began to dream how effective this plug could be to a struggling restaurant. What a charming lady and free spirit! (And what a touching personal moment in my life it was when I learned in Carol's autobiography that she has African American heritage.)

JULIO AND JULIO

Another memorable thrill was when I interviewed internationally known crooner Julio Iglesias in person on our five o'clock newscast. Iglesias is far better known in European and Latin countries than he is in the United States. In fact, by the time he sat with me for a one-on-one interview on our five o'clock newscast, this guy held the distinction of selling more record albums than any other singer in the word—ever. More than 100 million albums sold. He broke into the English market with one of my all-time favorite tunes, the 1984 duet with Willie Nelson, "To All the Girls I've Loved Before." And Julio had another big American hit when he sidled up to Dolly Parton for the harmony of "When You Tell Me That You Love Me" in 1994.

In my prep work for the interview, I noted that we are both "Julio" (Julius, in Spanish), and we were born in the same year, one month apart, with the better known of the two of us one month older than the other.

When we came out of the commercial break leading into the interview, I introduced my guest with: "Ladies and gentlemen, Julio and Julio!" It was a "bowl me over with a feather" moment with Iglesias, as it was with Carol Channing, when in the course of the interview I said: "Well, Julio, you've cut hit albums with Willie Nelson and Barbara Streisand. Who would you like to sing with on your next big album?" His response was instant: "How about you, Julio? We could call the album *The Two Julios*. Or just *Julio and Julio*," my guest offered. "I'll do it on one condition," I countered.

"What is that, Julio?" Iglesias asked.

"My name has to be the *first* Julio in the name," I said.

"Agreed!" said Iglesias. And there was laughter all around.

GREGORY HINES

As much as I hate to admit it, there are some interviews during my long career that I would like to call back for a do-over. One of them occurred in February of 1989. Famed actor/dancer/director Gregory Hines was my live guest on the five o'clock newscast via a satellite hookup.

Hines was on the circuit promoting his newly released movie, *Tap*. The movie, which grossed a modest $8 million, paid homage to the art of tap dancing. In the movie, Hines portrays an ex-con with a phenomenal tap dancing talent. He is greatly influenced by the spirit of his father, a legendary hoofer. The movie features supporting roles by some of the greatest tap dancers ever, including Sammy Davis, Jr., whom I had met several times at the Variety Club Telethons; and Harold Nicholas. The latter was, with his brother, Fayard, the acrobatic dancing sensation of nightclubs and movies during the 1930s and 1940s. Watching some of those old clips of the Nicholas Brothers can leave even the deadest soul with a dropped jaw.

The interview started out on a light, brother-to-brother level. I acknowledged that during my long TV news career I found myself slipping into the dialectical or regional patois of my guest or my audience. You heard that happen often on the 2008 presidential trail with ALL the candidates in both parties. Though she ran an amazing campaign, the most caricatured speech was given by Hillary before an all-black Baptist church congregation. Boy was that a bad mimicking!

You might have thought that Gregory and I grew up down the street from each other as we rapped comfortably on the air during the interview. And since it was a slow day, I begged a little extra time. I reveled with Hines in the art of tap from its earliest history. I had done my homework and engaged him in the little-known fact that tap dancing as we know it today is a mélange of African, English, Scottish, and Irish dancing. All these types met in the nation's cities and became refined during the 1920s, when tap went urban and dancers started nailing and screwing pieces of metal to the heels and toes of their shoe soles in order to make more noise. Then we talked about the challenges my guest and tappers his age experienced in trying to keep up with those incomparable old-timers during the movie *Tap*'s rehearsals and final cuts. And then something came out of my mouth that even surprised me. Just as the very pleasant star was in a full-smile state, I popped a question that caused his face to display utter shock followed by an unmistakable touch of anger.

My question? "So, Gregory . . . even with all the fun and hard work you and the guys had making this movie, did it bother you at all to realize that this movie might actually glorify the stereotype of the 'happy Negro;' the 'shiftless darkie' tap dancing through life with a watermelon under one arm and a plate of fried chicken under the other?" Bam! Hines seemed almost betrayed and ambushed by my abrupt switch off from the light and airy to the heavy and controversial. And Gregory's response to my barbed question made it abundantly clear that for all intents and purposes the interview was over. I will never forget the look of hurt on his face as I thanked him. And he just sat glaring out at me with disappointed eyes still reeling from the grenade I had tossed him. He seemed to be saying without saying a word: How could you hit me with a broadside like that? Especially since you're a "Brother?"

Would you have asked that question? Might I have put the question more tactfully if I just had to ask it? We'll never know, I guess. I have often analyzed the purported symbiotic relationship between those who are peddling news and those who are presenting news. Who's getting the best benefit out of the deal? Are we equally served? Perhaps I would be happy to position my interviewing style at the Larry King camp on the soft side than in Mike Wallace's blister chamber during the height of his career.

There is only one thing about which I can be sure, interviewing isn't as easy as it seems. And make no mistake about it; a well-conducted interview is a work of art.

JAMIE LEE CURTIS

As much as I enjoyed doing live interviews—the most notable being the famous exclusive interviews with Hubert Humphrey and with Jimmy Carter (both detailed in this book)—there is something utterly uncontrollable about them. Whenever the management or production crew had a hunch that a prospective interview was going to be poor—be it one-word answers, long-winded retorts, responses soaked in drugs or alcohol, or an oft-repeated stump speech—the interviewee would be relegated to placement on film or videotape. There is no control like "editing control." The editor has the power to chop off an interviewee in mid-harangue, mid-incongruent sentence, mid-snoozer, or mid-verbosity. Profanity can be bleeped out. Offensive religious doctrine can be neatly trimmed.

I vividly remember one incident, in particular, in which Channel 4's one-time entertainment editor, Dawn Meadows, was mighty glad she had chosen to tape her satellite interview. She was talking that day to one of my favorite actresses, Jamie Lee Curtis. I stood right next to Dawn as the interview was coming in live through the control room where real-time note-taking would allow Dawn to do a very quick edit. Sometimes an interviewer can discern that an interviewee is not exactly a willing participant. One begins to detect within a minute or two that the newsmaker—live or on videotape—is sitting before you strictly on the orders of an agent, a studio, or a publisher. The very facial expression, level of responsiveness, and substance of answers are key indicators that the celebrity would just as soon be skiing in Aspen. I could tell after a very short time into the interview that Dawn and Jamie Lee weren't connecting. These were two women you wouldn't want to invite to the same small dinner party. Near the end of the taped interview, Dawn stepped out on a limb that caused me to have an instant anxiety attack. And I was just a spectator. My colleague asked the daughter of Janet Leigh and Tony Curtis if she ever had regrets, remorse, or embarrassment about taking all her clothes off in so many of her movies. Jamie Lee's response to the armor-piercing question was a firm stab back at the questioner: "No!" The one-word response was followed by an unmistakable glare that would melt a nail. And that was all she wrote.

The laconic response threw Dawn for an apparent loop, and I felt Dawn's immediate regrets, remorse, and embarrassment.

The entertainment editor shut down the interview with a hasty: "Well, thank you, Jamie Lee Curtis."

Pointedly placing her middle finger directly in front of her face and giving that finger several pumps in a universally recognized gesture, Curtis responded: "Thank you, too, Dawn!"

Snip, snip.

Ironically, Ms. Curtis created quite a media buzz as she celebrated her fiftieth birthday in 2008. Dawn Meadows never could have guessed it, but Jamie Lee boldly posed gray-haired and *topless* for the cover of the May-June edition of *AARP* magazine. Said the popular star to anyone who would be shocked or disgusted about her top drop: *"I think I have finally found what I hope beauty is, or at least, beauty as it applies to me."* You go, girl!

SENATOR "KIT" BOND

I have enjoyed a great relationship with Missouri's Senator Christopher "Kit" Bond for nearly forty years now. The senator and I began to . . . uh . . . ahem . . . bond when I gave him his first TV interview. He was a candidate for Missouri governor in 1971, and I had started out as a TV news reporter just a year before his big run for the state house. In fact, to this day, even with all his accomplishments, I have never stopped razzing the good senator about the exceptionally cheap wine served at his first campaign reception for the gubernatorial post.

Our relationship was cemented when I was the only TV news anchor in town to get the natal announcement right after his son was born in 1981. While the competition was reporting that the new Bond was a girl named "Samantha," I broke the news that "contrary to what you might have heard on those *other* stations, the newborn Bond is a *boy*, SAMUEL!" And for many years thereafter, whenever the senator would appear as my guest on the news set, no matter how heavy, grave, or ponderous the subject of the interview, he and I always did our little signature shtick. Much to the consternation of the news director, the production director, and sometimes the station general manager, I always tagged the interview with the ad lib, "Senator, any recent pictures of Sam?" The control room always went crazy trying to get a camera in position to zoom in for the close-ups of the evolutionary growth and development of Sam Bond.

I'm proud—as is the senator certainly—that Sam, a Princeton grad like his Old Man, just returned home in 2007 from his second tour of duty in Iraq as a U.S. Marine first lieutenant. And part of that service time was spent in the hell hole called Fallujah. That's where five members of Sam's unit were killed by a roadside bomb.

Sam was careful to keep his connection to a U.S. senator quiet in his unit. He said he didn't want any special treatment. And sadly, the proud papa has had to keep his son's military position quiet because of security reasons. Sam would be a prime target for terrorist kidnappers.

But whenever and wherever I run into Senator Bond these days, I can pull him aside and ask that question I've been asking for more than a quarter century now: "Hey, senator, got any recent pictures of Sam?" And he always does—lately with Sam in his full, formal Marine Corps regalia.

As the senator marched and greeted in the 2008 VP Parade on the Fourth of July, I called down to him from my reviewing stand perch where I emceed the parade. And he was ready for my eternal question: "Hey, senator, got any pictures of Sam?"

Hubert Humphrey's Impromptu Visit

The 2008 Presidential Brouhaha, on both sides of the aisle, was packed with surprises, which reminded me of my biggest surprise during a major election year. It occurred during the 1972 Presidential Tilt, when Hubert Humphrey, the "Happy Warrior," thought he had figured out how to take down Dick Nixon. Humphrey, serving as the thirty-eighth vice president of the United States, had planned to improve upon the Johnson Administration's legacy by boosting the sagging economy and quelling growing civil rights unrest. The senator said eloquently, "You can't have civil order without civil justice." Right on, Brother. But ultimately, it was Humphrey's strong support of the war effort in Vietnam that sunk his boat.

Humphrey was barnstorming the country in 1972, shortly after he announced in Philadelphia on January 10 of that year that he wanted the nation's top job. One Saturday evening, Humphrey brought his stump to St. Louis. He came to town to drum up support at a labor group's national confab. The union's convention-eers were headquartered at the downtown Jefferson Hotel near KSD-TV, the station where I began my broadcast career. I was the weekend anchor on Channel 5, the NBC affiliate that year. I had gotten the anchor post by default after veteran newsman Dick Ford announced to station management that he wanted to spend more weekend time with his family.

I announced on the six o'clock news on that memorable Saturday night that the former vice president was leading in the polls at the time. And I told my audience that Humphrey was going to speak later that night to the labor group at the Jefferson. Don't know what got into me, but I blurted an ad lib inviting Humphrey to feel free to drop in for a chat on our ten o'clock newscast since he would be just a short block from the station. After the cordial and totally unscripted invitation, I went on to other news of the day.

I never gave the invitation any more thought as I went to din-ner and then came back to the station to get ready for the late newscast. Well, I'll be damned if right smack dab in the middle of that ten o'clock newscast, the heavy studio door swung open, and who to my surprise blew in? Why, Hubert Horatio Hum-phrey and his entourage! I was totally stunned as my peripheral vision took me beyond the camera and my occupied brain told me that, sure enough, it was the former vice president. I pulled myself together and made it appear that my introduction of our unexpected guest was a part of the script. Just before pitching to a commercial break I ad libbed something to the effect: "Com-ing up after this break, a visit with former Vice President Hubert Humphrey. He will join us live here on the set. So stay with us." During that break I waved Humphrey onto the news set. My goodness. There he was. After I introduced him, he actually said that famous Humphrey statement in that imitable staccato voice: "Julius, we're just as pleased as punch to be here tonight." The always exuberant Minnesotan went on to say that he had got-ten word that I had invited him to come over, "and by golly, we thought we'd take you up on your kind invitation."

We went right to some heavy stuff that allowed Humphrey to practice the stump speech we would be hearing right up to the Democratic Convention. I quizzed him about his stand on the Vietnam War (he thought it was necessary to spread democracy to that part of the world); where his base of support was (labor, African Americans, and Jewish voters—and he knew he had to do a better job of communicating with young people and anti-war activists and "heal the wounds of war"). I gave him a break to brag about the monumental Civil Rights Act of 1964, legislation that, without a doubt, made it possible for me to become Channel 5's first African American reporter/anchor just six years later.

The drop-in guest appearance on my newscast ultimately did not help Humphrey in his presidential bid. After a contentious, sometimes ugly, credentials battle at the Democratic National Convention in Miami Beach, my new friend, Hubert, withdrew his name from consideration. But it was too late for party unity. Even though Humphrey had run up an impressive string of primary victories, he got nudged out by George McGovern. I remember, being a news junkie, that the Democrats' big national convention was so screwed up, a dedicated group of Americans and I had to wait up till the wee hours of the morning to hear McGovern's acceptance speech. He didn't go onto the podium until about 2:00 a.m. St. Louis time! But the Happy Warrior went back to Minnesota, ran again for the Senate, and was re-elected in 1976.

Some pundits of the day contended that the fierce fighting on the DNC floor and in smoke-filled rooms left McGovern's campaign staff in such disarray that the result was his team's failure to thoroughly vet my friend Tom Eagleton's health history. We know how that McGovern choice worked out.

Chance Meetings

Although a vast majority of my interviews and encounters with internationally known celebrities were scheduled, I am absolutely amazed at how many luminaries I have met in chance meetings all over the world.

Once when my family and I were vacationing in Paris, we headed out immediately after we arrived to buy some sweaters because it would be "inseine" for anyone to walk along the Seine not warmly clad. We had walked no more than three blocks from our hotel when who should we espy? Why, Donald McHenry, the Carter Administration's U.N. delegate. McHenry was waiting at a bus stop and leisurely reading the morning paper. We both expressed shock at this chance encounter. The former ambassador, from East St. Louis, was in Paris to visit his daughter who was going to school there.

At Harvard, from which both of my daughters graduated, the

nearby Charles Hotel was a hotspot for bump-ins. We found ourselves sitting with ABC's Carole Simpson and her family at the Annual Clambake for new parents one year. Then one time when I was checking in at the Charles on a visit to my daughters, I found myself standing right behind actor Paul Newman and his wife, actress Joanne Woodward. First impressions? Gee, he's a lot shorter than I thought. (If you guess that he was 5'9", you'd be right.) And she was, in an off-the-shoulder flower sundress, the plainest-looking movie star I have encountered. I saw Newman in action when he fidgeted and patted himself down looking for something and exclaimed, "Damn, I left it in the car!" and bolted out of the lobby.

We stood in a very long line for my daughter Julia to register at Harvard right behind Richard Benjamin and Paula Prentiss waiting patiently with their son. I sat in the outdoor audience at Julia's graduation behind Hal Holbrook and Dixie Carter, who had a daughter in the same class.

And the most incredible encounter of all came in the Hunter family's favorite Cambridge restaurant, Henrietta's, in the Charles Hotel. I was visiting them one spring when we decided to go after brunch to a nearby theater's showing of the movie, *The Fugitive*.

As we were standing in the buffet line, we noticed that the fellow in front of us was trying to pile some things onto a plate held in his left hand but could not because of the big silver chafing dish lid he held in his right hand. What to do with the lid? I offered, "I'll help you with that, my friend." And he handed me the chafing dish top and thanked me. When he turned around to thank me, the girls and I did a family gasp. The man turned out to be Harvard grad, former roommate of Al Gore, and star of the re-release of *The Fugitive*, Tommy Lee Jones.

We told him where we were headed after brunch, and he told us he hoped we would like the flick.

Did I ask Jones to autograph my brunch napkin on this marvel of coincidences? Nope. That's one of the things about running into celebrities besides one's daughters begging you not to embarrass them. The really cool thing is to act like we did with Tommy Lee Jones standing a foot away from us. Gasp quietly and act as if the star is your next-door neighbor.

MAX ROBINSON

In August of 1988, just before the demise of my ill-fated restaurant, J. Hunter's, I had the pleasure and honor of sitting down for personal and candid conversations with one of the true heroes to black journalists everywhere. Max Robinson was in St. Louis to speak at the national convention of the National Association of Black Journalists (NABJ). My restaurant became a gathering place for the conventioneers after each day's formal sessions. My kitchen staff even modified our menu to serve up some soul food dishes some of my journalist guests had request- ed. For example, even though the items weren't on the standard menu, we managed to subtly serve up some fried chicken, col- lard greens, candied yams, smothered pork chops, and corn- bread to the few who knew the secret password and were willing to eat at a less-than-conspicuous table. I was commended for dishing up a tasty departure from banquet and hotel food.

In 1969, Max Robinson had distinguished himself by becom- ing the first African American TV news anchorman in Washing- ton, D.C. That was one year before I started my news career. Robinson went on to a network co-anchor position with Peter Jennings and Frank Reynolds for ABC's *World News Tonight,* the first African American to deliver the news on a national net- work. He served in that groundbreaking position from 1978 to 1983, but Max suffered bouts with some formidable demons— alcohol and depression. Plus, there were credible reports of a lack of self esteem behind the proud, bold, and sophisticated veneer the nation saw each weeknight.

Soon Robinson's behavior became erratic. He was some- times absent from work for days, and he reportedly began to be increasingly cranky and critical of the support staff at ABC in Chicago, from which Max reported.

Max's career began to spiral down pathetically, and he went into virtual seclusion in 1987. Some say out of shame. But he came out of hiding to attend and speak at the NABJ convention in St. Louis. I was thrilled to learn that he had come over to my restaurant while I was doing the ten o'clock news.

After I wrapped up the news on that hot summer evening, I raced over to the restaurant hoping to catch Max. The convention crowd was thinning out. Max was, indeed, there when I got back. He was looking extremely weak and sickly. I, of course, recognized him as one of my restaurant guests and one of my role models, and I was eager to speak with him. I assured the conventioneers who had brought Max to the restaurant that night that I would be happy to drive him back to the nearby Adam's Mark Hotel. Max seemed to dread going back to the hotel, and I would find out why later.

We sat and talked about the gate through which we had both broken ground in the TV news business. Of course, his trials and tribulations made my career path look like a flowerbed.

As with my career, Max had been the first African American on most of his jobs. He once said, "We firsts ought to get extra pay."

Max had been busted from his big ABC anchor job in 1983 after he failed, without explanation, to show up at the funeral of his co-anchor Frank Reynolds, where he was slated to sit next to former First Lady Nancy Reagan. That was the last straw for Roone Arledge and ABC. Max was booted. He was snapped up by WMAQ-TV in Chicago, but that gig didn't work out after Max's behavior became even more erratic. His accounts to me of the events that led to his career demise did not stack up with what was being printed in the tabloids and being rumored in the news biz. It was a sad, sad story, whichever account was true. The most devastating news he got was that, while being treated for pneumonia, the pioneering black TV news anchor was diagnosed with AIDS.

We all knew of Max's condition in 1988, but the fact was only whispered . . . out of respect. After the clock struck midnight and my guest seemed to be getting very weary, I set out to get him back to his hotel. Getting around was now a very difficult task for Max. I had to take his arm as he shuffled and ambled to get to the elevator in the lobby to go down to my car. We had to pause several times along the way for him to catch his breath.

When we arrived in the circular drive of the hotel and the doorman opened the passenger door, Max extended his hand to me and said plaintively, "My brother, I understand you're a big man in this town. Can you do something for me, please? Can you get them to turn up the heat in my room? It's so cold. I'm freezing to death."

I assured him I would make a call right away. And from my car phone I called the hotel's front desk right away and reported the problem in Mr. Robinson's room to the desk clerk. I was promised that the temperature in his room would be adjusted immediately.

Max Robinson died of complications from AIDS at Howard University Hospital about four months after I had the privilege of speaking with this legend one-on-one.

UNCLE MILTIE
IN THE JOHN

Idaho Senator Larry Craig proved that interaction with another man in a public restroom can lead to scandal and outrage. The veteran Republican was busted in June of 2007 when he was accused by an undercover cop in the next stall of being a bit too neighborly with his foot and hand. Not to take up the senator's defense, but I know from personal experience that some guys are just too innocently friendly in a men's room before, during, and immediately after they have done that which led them to the restroom in the first place. I have avoided hundreds of attempted handshakes and conversations in restrooms all over the country from glad-handers who just weren't thinking.

Some of my most awkward men's dressing room moments occurred across the hall from the Channel 4 studios in 1987. And the person who caused the most unsettling bit of angst for me was none other than Milton Berle.

When Berle came to Channel 4 to promote his new book, *B.S. I Love You: Sixty Funny Years With the Famous and the Infamous,* my guess was that about a fourth of the newsroom staff was excited to see him. Three-fourths of our staff may not have even been alive when Berle ruled the television airwaves as the undisputed king from 1948 to 1955. I figure I was five years old when "Mr. Television" took the throne.

Berle beat out fellow comics, Morey Amsterdam, Jack Carter, and Henny Youngman to become the permanent single host of Texaco's first TV comedy show in 1948. Berle did not tickle my family's funny bones until 1953 when my mother somehow joined about 2 million other Americans and managed to buy our first TV. Our set also had the distinction of being the first TV on the 3800 block of Windsor Place. (Don't let the regal-sounding name of our street fool you. It was a very poor neighborhood.) I remember the set as if the deliveryman had brought it into our house just yesterday. It was a big, boxy Motorola that sat on a table almost too rickety to support it.

I was ten years old at the time but comedy-conscious enough to wait eagerly every week with millions of other American television viewers for Tuesday night to roll around. The magic time was 8:00

p.m. Mr. Television's faithful flock didn't want to miss a zany second of the show that opened with four guys dressed in Texaco uniforms singing the opening song—cornball lyrics and archaic service principles by today's standards, but a snappy jingle for the times. Following the predictable opening by the nattily uniformed service station attendants that disappeared along with Berle's ratings, the Tuesday night audience never had a clue on how the inimitable funnyman would make his grand entrance. But it was always a hilarious, even outrageously big surprise. Berle never entered to titters. He entered our living rooms accompanied by a chorus of coast-to-coast belly laughs.

America set its schedule and lifestyle by Berle's laugh-a-minute show. No church choir rehearsals would dare be set on a Tuesday night; restaurants all over the country set up their menus and service so that early evening diners could be fed, paid up, and out by eight; and little league play was scheduled so that mom, dad, kids, coaches, and umpires could be home in time to tune in at 8:00 p.m. Too bad all the kids who worked in the newsroom missed all that national excitement.

So you can imagine how stage struck I was when I learned that I would be interviewing my comedic childhood idol, Uncle Miltie. I actually suffered P.I.P. (Panic in Preparation). Wow! I would be sitting next to and playing straight man to Milton Berle, one of the funniest comics in history!

What I had not anticipated was the surprise I got on the appointed day of the interview. I was applying a little cosmetic blemish and beard line control at the mirror in the men's dressing room. All of a sudden, the door burst open and in walked "Mr. Television" himself. I didn't get to speak first.

"What the hell do they expect you and me to do out there? A remake of the *Defiant Ones*?" Berle asked as if he had been rehearsing that line for days. (The *Defiant Ones* for all you kids reading this, was a 1958 movie starring Tony Curtis and Sidney Poitier as prison chain gang members shackled together after their escape and forced to work together to get free of their chains in defiance of their racial differences.)

Berle continued in a barrage of questions. "What is this thing we're doing? Is it live or tape? How much time we got? Are we doing it in that loud newsroom or is there a quiet set? What city is this anyway? Have we ever worked together before? Oh, Christ, they got me working with an amateur. A deaf and dumb black guy. Ever do comedy, kid? Bet you won't remember your lines. Just don't step on mine. . . ."

"Wow," I thought. "Is this guy wound up or what?"

I tried to bring the encounter back into the realm of common courtesy. After all, we hadn't even been properly introduced.

"I know who YOU are, sir, but my name is Julius Hunter, and I'll be interviewing you on the set," I said. "And our set is the newsroom."

"What are you gonna ask me?" Berle pounced. "What are we gonna talk about? I hardly know you!"

"I don't know yet," I offered. "We'll just ad lib it . . . wing it."

"Pal, what do you know about ad-libbing? Have we ever ad-libbed before? Ad-libbing is not ad-libbing you know. It's kinda rehearsed improvisation, you know."

"I think *I* can handle it," I bluffed, as if I were really confident.

"Well, just be sure you give me some set up lines so I can come back with some zingers . . ."

"Gotcha," I said, as if I had fully understood the rudiments of comedy in that quickie lesson.

Berle changed the subject as he took off his white shirt and let his suspenders slip over his shoulders and hang at his sides. The white shirt looked like a vaudevillian had to stuff it in a suitcase to get out of town in a hurry. Under the wrinkled shirt the top half of a pair of long underwear appeared. And there was a tuft of hair peeking over the top of the undershirt. Not a pretty sight.

"You work for that ****sucker, Hyland?" he wanted to know.

"No," I answered. "He heads up the radio part of this operation, KMOX Radio, and I work for KMOX-TV. He's actually something like the regional vice president for CBS. But he doesn't have anything to do with the TV side."

"Well, you're lucky," Berle seethed between clinched teeth. "That mother****** is the scum of the earth. Know what he did to me, that s.o.b.?"

Berle didn't wait for an answer. He pulled two little tins with a circumference of the old half dollar from his pants pocket. When he opened them with trembling arthritic hands I could see that one tin contained white grease paint, the other red. Surely he wasn't going to put that white stuff on his face. But he did. In very little amounts. With his pinky finger. He applied and smoothed in white grease paint to the smile lines, corners of his mouth, his chin, and the inlets of his forehead. White grease paint. He probably bought it by the caseload fifty years ago, but it seemed to work for him. He then continued his rant while he used his pinky finger to line his thin lips with the red grease paint ever so delicately. And then he took just a tiny smidge of the red stuff and rubbed it into his cheeks as a sort of rouge.

Gee, we were almost touching shoulders during all this. I consciously edged a tiny bit to my right.

"When Jack Carney died, in 1984, I think, he was doing this Saturday Morning Comedy Hour." Berle went on. "Using clips—stealing clips—from all the classic days of radio comedy. Show was heard all over the country since KMOX is about the only 50,000 watter around. Well, when Jack kicked off—and he was a very talented man, ya know. Knew his comedy like the back of his hand. Anyway, that mother****** Hyland gets in touch with my agent and wants me to take over the goddamn Saturday Morning Comedy Hour after Jack died. Tells my agent I would be a natural for it. Brags about his station being picked up all over the country and in Canada, promising my agent that I'd get a chance . . . ME get a chance . . . a ******* chance to pick up a following. *I* had a following when that jackoff was in kindergarten. He dangled a lot of money around and told me I could tape the intros and outros of the bits from wherever I was at the time. Well, after that ******* ******* hits the right number and the right deal, my agent called that lyin' con artist back. And you know, goddamnit, after we said we would do the friggin' show, we never could get back in touch with that connivin', weaselin' sonfabitch again. After we said we would do the deal, when my agent would call back, that ******* would always be in a meeting, or at Mass, or out of the country," Berle mimicked Hyland's secretaries. "I've never been so ****** over by anybody in my goddamn life. Not even by Texaco."

I would never have suspected that the Uncle Miltie I had idolized and even emulated in my early attempts at comedy in high school could have been capable of creating such multi-dimensional profanity in such creative profusion. I had never heard nouns, verbs, adjectives, pronouns, adverbs, suffixes, and prefixes turned and tossed in such a way before producing an X-rated product that if printed would have had to be inscribed on asbestos paper. Or toilet paper.

Berle had whipped himself up into a frenzy over the Hyland

matter, and I secretly hoped he wouldn't have a coronary—the Big One right then and there.

And speaking of "Big One," I gotta confess that there was something on my mind that made me a bit nervous standing next to a man about whom a certain grandiosity had made him as legendary as his comedic antics. When the word "endowment" came up around his buddies, they weren't talking about the funds that keep colleges and universities afloat. The jokes abounded—especially around and among Berle's Friar's Club cronies. I've heard Dean Martin, Sammy Davis, and even Johnny Carson make allusions that hit Uncle Miltie below the belt. Friar's Club legends have it that Berle had on occasion whipped out what one Friar referred to as "the anaconda" on several occasions without warning. Talk about a conversation piece, it is said.

The locker room humor is even tied to the fact that Berle had four different wives, the last of whom is reported to have made a plaster cast of the phenomenon.

At the Hollywood memorial service for Berle, comedian Freddie Roman intoned to the mourners gathered to pay their respects in less than reverent manner: "We are here today to honor Milton Berle, who passed away on March 27. On May 1 and 2, his penis will be buried." The so-called mourners reportedly broke into a rousing round of laughter and applause.

Unsettling thoughts for a guy like me who was standing almost shoulder to shoulder with a man who had just stripped off his shirt and was standing next to me with downed suspenders and perhaps only a pants button keeping him decent. And keeping me from passing out if the oft-prankish Berle had said to me: "Hey kid, take a look at this. Think this puts the kibosh on that myth about YOU guys, doesn't it?" I would have fainted dead away.

As I peered into the dressing room mirror, there standing beside me I could see an eighty-one year old who had seen a lot, heard a lot, and been a lot. And I became a little sad that my little three-and-a-half-minute interview was going to be so pitifully insignificant to the great, monumental, groundbreaking, earth-shattering, mountain-moving accomplishments of his career that had spread out three-quarters of a century. From Little Mendel Berlinger's stage debut at age five to those moments in the dressing room with me.

Despite the gruff, crude, cantankerousness of this giant of an entertainer, I had a quiet respect for him that was caused by what I had learned about him during my prep for the interview. I began to feel like I was standing next to the man who just might be entitled to the credit for getting me, an African American, on television. After all, I took my first television job in 1970 to become the first primetime black anchorman in St. Louis. And I might owe that distinction to—of all people—my dressing roommate, Milton Berle.

Back in 1950 when Milton Berle had taken the hill and claimed it as the master of TV comedy, he had been put to an awesome test of willpower and humanitarianism. Berle had booked a group of sensational, show-stopping black entertainers, the four Step Brothers, for his show without ever telling his sponsor, Texaco, or the sponsor's ad agency. Berle was king and considered even his sponsor as one of his subjects.

When Texaco learned about the plan to have the black dancers on the show, the oil company blew like a Texas gusher in true oil-wellian proclamation. Texaco declared, "There would be no black entertainers on the show that night . . . or ever!" Berle, no doubt, was well aware that he held four aces as the clock showed it was just ten minutes from striking "Showtime!" on that Tuesday night. In his autobiography, Berle said of the Step Brothers: "If they don't go on, I don't go on." Ten minutes till airtime.

Texaco executives bit the bullet and threw in the towel. The Step Brothers went on! And so did Berle. Many black entertainers were helped aboard the Berle Bandwagon after that, and the color line drawn in the sand was broken.

By now, I was ready to leave the dressing before Berle was. As I opened the door to head down to the newsroom, I said: "See you on the set . . ."

"Hey, hey, hey . . . wait," Berle shouted through the dressing-room door as I dashed down the long hallway to the studio. "What are you going to ask me?"

I yelled back: "Fun stuff. Just fun stuff."

As I walked down the block-long hallway, I thought about the fact that this legend I was about to interview was much, much more than he displayed on his exterior. Remember, the year I started out on television in St. Louis was 1970, and that was just a scant twenty years after "Berle's Last Stand" in his battle with racism.

Thank you, Uncle Miltie. I would have given you a big hug of gratitude in the dressing room. But then, there's that other story about you.

Index

KMOVIN' ON

For Julius—
Good Luck From One St. Louis Legend To Another!—
From The Post-Dispatch Weatherbird

Dan Martin 2002